PICTORIAL
PRICE GUIDE
TO AMERICAN ANTIQUES
and Objects Made for the American Market

1997-1998 EDITION

PICTORIAL PRICE GUIDE TO AMERICAN ANTIQUES
and Objects Made for the American Market

MORE THAN 5000 ILLUSTRATED AND PRICED OBJECTS

By

Dorothy Hammond

PENGUIN STUDIO

PENGUIN STUDIO
Published by the Penguin Group
Penguin Books USA Inc., 375 Hudson Street,
New York, New York, 10014, U.S.A.

Penguin Books Ltd, 27 Wrights Lane,
London W8 5TZ, England

Penguin Books Australia, Ltd, Ringwood,
Victoria, Australia

Penguin Books Canada Ltd, 2801 John Street,
Markham, Ontario, Canada L3R 1B4

Penguin Books (N.Z.) Ltd, 182-90 Wairau Road,
Auckland 10, New Zealand

Penguin Books Ltd, Registered Offices:
Harmondsworth, Middlesex, England

First published by Penguin Studio, an imprint of Penguin Books USA Inc.

First printing, January 1997
10 9 8 7 6 5 4 3 2 1

ISBN: 0-14-026031-5

CONTENTS

INTRODUCTION

The *1997-1998 Pictorial Price Guide to American Antiques and Objects Made for the American Market*, includes all new entries, prices and photographs. The format is designed to provide the collector and antiques dealer with an accurate market value of items sold at auction galleries from October 1995 through August 1996.

Entries are keyed to the auction house where an item was actually sold. A state abbreviation has been included for the readers' convenience–because of regional variations prices do vary in different parts of the country. Also the year and the month the item sold has been indicated. This method of pricing sets this publication apart from all other price guides on the market. And when the book becomes dated, it serves as an excellent reference guide for future generations.

Although most auction houses give detailed catalog descriptions of items sold, others do not, therefore, every effort has been made to include as much information as possible. When comparing similar pieces, the reader must take into consideration that fluctuations in the market during the year as well as the quality of an object, the region in which it sold, as well as demand determine the auction price.

Auction houses across the country have enjoyed brisk sales during the past year with a very healthy and diversified buyer response. Good early antiques in fine condition are so incredibly scarce that record prices continue to be realized in every field. As always, period furniture continues to demonstrate its strength in the market with many pieces exceeding expectations. Values of fine English furniture have set records during the past twelve months. In addition, values of furniture and decorative items produced during the Arts and Crafts movement continue to remain strong. Furniture manufactured during the 20s and well into the 50s continues to make the transition from tacky to trendy these days. Other fields of interest include walking sticks and canes which have set record prices across the country. Humble household items have remained popular, including enamelware, cookbooks, bottles, early kitchen appliances and Pyrex ware. Some of the most fascinating items of interest include early radios, Christmas items, juke boxes, slot machines and Disney items, all of which are in demand and command lofty prices when they come on the market.

Every effort has been made to record prices accurately and describe each item in the space allotted to our format. However, the writer cannot be responsible for any clerical or typographical errors that may occur. – Dorothy Hammond

ACKNOWLEDGMENTS

Many persons have generously helped in assembling the materials for this book. I am very grateful to the following auction galleries and their staff members for their help in making this edition a reality. Alderfer Auction Company, Hatfield, PA; Aston Auctioneers & Appraisers, Endwell, NY; Noel Barrett Auctions, Ltd., New Hope, PA; Early Auction Co., Milford, Ohio; Robert C. Eldred Co., Inc., East Dennis, MA; Ken Farmer Auctions, Radford, VA; Duane E. Gansz Auction, Lyons, NY; Garth's Auctions, Inc., Delaware, OH, Gene Harris Auction Center, Marshalltown, IA; Horst Auction Center, Ephrata, PA; James D. Julia, Inc., Fairfield, ME; Maritime Auctions, York, ME; Northeast Auctions, Hampton, NH; O'Gallerie, Inc., Portland, OR; Rafel Osona Auction, Nantucket, MA; Pook & Pook, Inc., Downington, PA; Skinner, Inc., Bolton & Boston, MA; and Woody Auction, Douglass, KS.

With exception of Duane E. Gansz Auction and Woody Auction, all of the above auction houses charge a buyer's premium, which is a surcharge on the hammer or finial bid price at auction.

ABBREVIATIONS USED IN THIS BOOK AND THEIR MEANINGS

Am. . . . . .American	gr. . . . . .green	pr. . . . . .pair
attrib. . . . . .attributed	GWTW . . . . . . .Gone With The Wind	prof. . . . . .professional
batt. .battery	H . . . . .high	Q.A. . . . . .Queen Anne
blk. . . . . .black	illus. . . . . .illustrated, illustration	reconst. . . . . .reconstructed
br. . . . . .brown	imp. . . . . .impressed	ref. . . . . .refinished, refinishing
c. . . . . .century	int. .interior	replm. . . . . .replacement
ca. . . . . .circa	irid. . . . . .iridescent	repr. . . . . .repair, repaired
compo. . . . . .composition	L . . . . .length, long	repro. . . . . .reproduction
© . . . . .copyright	litho . . . . .lithograph	rev. .reverse
const. . . . . .constructed, construction	lrg. . . . . .large	sgn. . . . . .signed
D . . . . .deep, diameter	lt. . . . . .light	sm. . . . . .small
dec. . . . . .decorated, decoration	mech. . . . . . .mechanical, mechanism	sq. . . . . .square
dk. . . . . .dark	mfg. . . . . .manufactured	T . . . . .tall
emb. . . . . .embossed	mkd. . . . . .marked	unmkd. . . . . .unmarked
Eng. . . . . .England	MOP . . . . .mother-of-pearl	unsgn. . . . . .unsigned
eng. . . . . .engraved	N. Eng. . . . . .New England	W . . . . .wide
escut . . . . .escutcheon	opal. . . . . .opalescent	wrt. . . . . .wrought
Euro. . . . . .European, Europe	oper. . . . . .operate	WMG . . . . .white milk glass
ext. .exterior	orig. . . . . .original	
Fr. . . . . .French, France	pat. .patent	
gal. . . . . .gallon	patt. . . . . .pattern	The common and accepted abbreviations are used for states.
Ger. . . . . .German, Germany	pc., pcs. . . . . .piece, pieces	

A-IL Nov. 1995   James D. Julia, Inc.

Left to Right, Top to Bottom
Sanitary Toilet Paper Dispenser, mfg. by Northern Paper Mills, replated. . . . .
. . . .$225.00

Four-Weigh Selective Mint Dispenser, ca. 1938, normal wear to the orig. brown Hammeroid finish, 18" H $150.00

Lil' Leaguer Football, mfg. by Oak Mfg. Co., ca. 1950's, 16¾" H . .$75.00

Mint Vendor, mfg. by the O.D. Jennings & Co., ca. 1932, paint loss over left tray, 18" H $175.00

Wooden Pulver, ...$325.00

Lot of Four Wall Speakers, $200.00

Nickels Coin-O-Matic Cashier, ca. 1930's, machine in bare aluminum finish, missing lock and painted model is missing the handle, 18" H $450.00

Snacks, 1936, slight rust around left coin entry, minor scratching in the orig. red and black paint finish, 20" H $100.00

A-IL Nov. 1995   James D. Julia, Inc.

Left to Right, Top to Bottom
Die Cut Tin Chewing Gum Display, dated 1916, good condition, 5½" W, 12" H. $750.00
Chiclet's Die Cut Tin Display, dated 1916, good condition, overall wear and white spotting to color, 9" W, 10½" H. $700.00
Beeman's Chewing Gum Die Cut Tin Display, dated 1916, some fading and chipping, 8" W, 10" H. $700.00
Die Cut Tin Adams Pepsin Gum Display, dated 1916, overall wear, some chipping and rubbing, 6½" W, 11½" H. . . . . .N/S
Gold Tip Gum Tin Display, fade to orig. stencil, some chipping, 3½" H, 13" W, 7½" L. $400.00
Adams Pepsin Tutti-Frutti Tin Store Display, general overall wear and some chipping, 6¾" H, 6" W, 5" L. $300.00
Star Pepsin Tin Display Box, good condition, 9½" H, 4½" W, 6" L. $450.00
Fan Tan gum Tin Tray, overall fading & slight wear, 13¼" W, 10½" L. .$800.00

A-IL Nov. 1995   James D. Julia, Inc.

Hires Mettlach Punch Bowl, repr. left handle, one hairline rim age crack, overall soiling, 18" H, 10" W, 13½" L. $35,000.00

A-IL Nov. 1995   James D. Julia, Inc.

Vigoral Dispenser and Advertising Cups, dispenser 10" D, 22" H, cups 3" D, 3½" H. $750.00

A-IL Nov. 1995   James D. Julia, Inc.

Left to right
Helmar Self Framed Tin Sign, hairline scratches primarily to bottom, 22" W, 28½" L. $1050.00
Brookfield Rye Self Framed Tin Sign, 23½" W, 33" L. $2100.00

A-IL Nov. 1995   James D. Julia, Inc.

Hoskins Self-Service Machine, ca. 1920's, machine in fair condition, 15" H $275.00
Northwestern Sellall Vendor, ca. 1925, replated, a couple of cracks in back of base plate, 13". $250.00
Columbus Model 46, ca. 1946, machine repainted, has orig. barrel locks, 14" H $175.00
Wilbur-Suchard Chocolate, ca. 1930, minor chipping and scratches along edges to the orig. paint, 15½" H $200.00
Premier Gum and Card Vendor, mfg. by the Oak Mfg. Co., Inc., 1956, very little plating left on mechanism, rest of machine in orig. paint with minor scratches, 13½" H $225.00
"Well, Here We Are", mfg. by the R.D. Simpson Co., ca. 1927, minor peeling to nickel finish on lid, 13" H $375.00
Venus Theater Machine, mfg. by the Advance Machine Co., ca. 1920's, repainted, 8¼". $200.00

A-IL Nov. 1995   James D. Julia, Inc.

Left to Right
Fontana Canned Peaches Embossed Tin Sign, inpainting, small holes, repr., minor dents, 11½" W, 15½" H. $2250.00
White Rock Tin Sign, light overall fade, scratches, 16½" W, 19½" L. $800.00
Crack-A-Jack Clothes Tin Flange Sign, 18"W, 13½ L. $1300.00

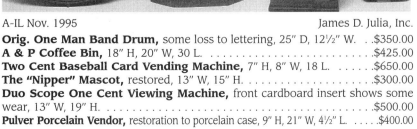

A-IL Nov. 1995   James D. Julia, Inc.

Orig. One Man Band Drum, some loss to lettering, 25" D, 12½" W. . .$350.00
A & P Coffee Bin, 18" H, 20" W, 30 L. $425.00
Two Cent Baseball Card Vending Machine, 7" H, 8" W, 18 L. $650.00
The "Nipper" Mascot, restored, 13" W, 15" H. $300.00
Duo Scope One Cent Viewing Machine, front cardboard insert shows some wear, 13" W, 19" H. $500.00
Pulver Porcelain Vendor, restoration to porcelain case, 9" H, 21" W, 4½" L. $400.00

A-IL Nov. 1995   James D. Julia, Inc.

Cent Jennings "Victoria" Golf Ball Vending Slot Machine, orig., unrestored, 24" H. $5500.00

A-IL Nov. 1995   James D. Julia, Inc.

Left to Right

412-Huyler's Chocalate/St. Nicholas Pepsin Gum, mfg. by the Automatic Vending Co., pat. 1899, coin entry and push button panels have been professionally redone, 30" H $15,000.00

576-Case Pepsin Gum, mfg. by the Case Chicle Gum Co., ca. 1906, repainted and in fair to good condition, orig. paint to gypsy in good to very good condition, 27" H .$5600.00

589-Smilin'Sam from Alabam-The Salted Peanut Man, ca. 1931,13" H $3500.00

214-Freeport Stick Gum Vendor, mfg. by Freeport Novelty Co., ca. 1899, hairline crack in front casting, overall paint loss to wood case, 16½" H $5500.00

A-IL Nov. 1995   James D. Julia, Inc.

Left to Right

Jennings in the Bag Machine, ca. 1934, repainted, missing bags, 26" H . $125.00

Blue Bird Peanut Machine, ca. 1915, repainted, chipping to bottom of globe, 16½" H $200.00

Asco Hot Nut Vendor, ca. 1946, orig. aluminum patina, 21" H $110.00

Choc-Liks Peanuts, ca. 1930, full length crack in glove, body repainted, the aluminum lid, mid section and flap have been buffed, 20½" H . . .$175.00

A-IL Nov. 1995   James D. Julia, Inc.

Left to Right

Brouse's Peerles Fruit Chewing Gum, ca. 1890's, wood repainted, some inpainting to coin entry and push button panels, 30½" H .$8000.00

Pepsin Gum/Chocalate/Peanuts, mfg. by Champion Vending Machine Co., pat. May 16, 1899, color loss to front of advertisement, 36" H $700.00

Wallace Chocalate, mfg. by Am. Automatic Vending Machine Co., ca. 1890's, cracks in wood base, 31½" H $3700.00

Dentyne/Chiclets/Chocolate, mfg. by Champion Co., ca. 1899, inpainting to three signs in front window, 32" H . . .$2500.00

A-IL Nov. 1995   James D. Julia, Inc.

Left to Right, Top to Bottom

Tab Gum Vendors, lot of two, Stewart & McGuire, ca. 1937

Six Column Tab Gum Vendor, mfg. by the Stoner Mfg. Corp., ca. 1940's. .$150.00

Lot of Two Machines, Topper half cabinet mfg. by the Victor Mfg. Corp., and a multi-vendor mfg. by CoastVending Inc. bulk vendor without a game motif, broken glove, rest of machine in good condition. . . .$75.00

Simmons Model A and Gumball Prototype, poor condition, reconditioned. $125.00

Mills Automatic, ca. 1936, 16" H $125.00

Hit The Target, ca. 1950, orig. paint w/ slight rust overall, 19" H . .$90.00

A-IL Nov. 1995   James D. Julia, Inc.

Left to Right

Ward's Figural Orange Crush Dispenser Base 8" D, 10" H. $400.00

Howel's Orange-Julep Syrup Dispenser, 9" D, 16" H. . . .$2250.00

Ward's Figural Orange Crush Dispenser Base, 8" D, 10" H. . .$600.00

A-IL Nov. 1995   James D. Julia, Inc.

Birchola Ceramic Syrup Dispenser, replm. pump w/ new cover cap and spigot, 9" D, 14" H. $1500.00

Hour Glass Hires Root Beer Dispenser W/ Orig. Pump, 7" D, 14" H. $750.00

A-IL Nov. 1995   James D. Julia, Inc.

Left to Right

Hires Celluloid Sign, some discoloration to lower right corner, light foxing and dirt spotting overall, 6½" W, 10" L. $1800.00

Hires Mettlach Root Beer Dispenser, some color enhancement, overall wear, cracks and chips, int. center pontil broken, 10½" D, 14" H. $2500.00

Moxie Die Cut Tin Horse Mobile Toy, minor creases, overall soiling, 8" H, 6½" W, 3" L. $1200.00

Hires Root Beer Mug, 4½" H, 5" W, 3" L. $400.00

Hires Root Beer Mug, 4½" H, 4½" W, 3" L. $450.00

A-IL Nov. 1995   James D. Julia, Inc.

Left to Right

Benedict Perfume Vendor Mach., ca. 1904, 26" H, missing some veneer on front. ....N/S

Mills Commercial Five Card Draw Mach., mfg. by the Mills Novelty Co., ca. 1904, some soiling to cards, 24" H with marquis. $6000

Lukat "The Lucky Cat" Lucky Number & Gumball Mach., manuf. by the Lu-Kat Novelty Co., ca. 1920's, missing tickets, prof. restored, 9" H $12,000.00

Regina Pepsin Vendor Style 18 Music Box, incorporating a 12 ¾" single-comb disc movement. $10,000.00

Fairest Wheel Cigar Trade Stimulator, private labeled the Albert Pick & Co. by Decatur Fairest Wheel Co. pat. May 7, 1895, missing glass in back of cash compartment, 22" H $800.00

Burger Slot Mach., manuf. by Paul E. Burger Mfg. Co., pat. June 21, 1904, professionally restored, 20½" H ....N/S

A-IL Nov. 1995   James D. Julia, Inc.

Left to Right, Row 1

4 in 1 Gum & Candy Mach., ca. 1935, slight oxidation to chromium finish, 17½" H $575.00

Gumball Mach., Model D, mfg. Ad-Lee Novelty Co., ca. 1920's, replm. back door, 16" H $350.00

Ace Gumball Mach., mfg. by Operators Vending Machine Supply Co., ca. 1930, some loss to orig. Ace decal, 16½" H

Columbus Model JMJ Gumball Mach., ca. 1950's, orig. paint w/ some inpainting to chips, 14½" H $900.00

Sellem Matches Cigar Mach., mfg. by Northwestern, ca. 1912, machine has been replated, 13½" H $500.00

Row 2

Twin Merchandiser Gum & Candy Mach., mfg. by the Stoner Corp., ca. 1941, left globe is not correct to this machine, ca. 1941, 13" H $300.00

Columbus Tri-More Model 38 Gum & Candy Mach., ca. 1939, has been repainted, 15" H $750.00

Natl. Pencil Machine, pat. May 30, 1911, mfg. by Elgin Pencil Vending Machine Company, ca. 1911, 17" H w/ marquis. $1,400.00

A-IL Nov. 1995   James D. Julia, Inc.

Zenith Fortune & Gum Mach., mfg. by Hance Mfg. Co., ca. 1915, orig. paint has some inpainting, some paint loss to front direction, 13½" H ...$3000.00

A-IL Nov. 1995   James D. Julia, Inc.

Caille Sunburst Gum Mach., mfg., by Caille Bros. Co., ca. 1909, top of lid and cash door recast and repainted, 20" H $7,000.00

A-IL Nov. 1995   James D. Julia, Inc.

Pegasus Porcelain Flying Horse, some porcelain finish missing in spots, crease in bottom of rear legs, 48" W, 36" H. $600.00

A-IL Nov. 1995   James D. Julia, Inc.

Regina Style 61 Musical Desk, restored cabinet & mechanism . . . .
. . . .$14,500.00

A-IL Nov. 1995   James D. Julia, Inc.

**Western Electric Cabinet Orches-
trion,** ca. 1920's, mfg. by Western
Electric Piano Company $12,500

A-IL Nov. 1995   James D. Julia, Inc.

**Regina Sublima Corona Style 31
Disc-Changing   Music   Box,**
. . . .$15,000.00

A-IL Nov. 1995   James D. Julia, Inc.

Left to Right

True Blue Gum Mach., mfg. by Automatic Sales Co., ca. 1906, fading and some
cracking to original True Blue decal on globe, 12½" H $1,500.00

Peaches and Cream Pepson Gum Mach., mfg. by Robertson Sales Co., ca.
1906, 12" H $3,750.00

Pulver Kola Pepsin Chewing Gum Mach., mfg. by Pulver Chemical Co., pat'd.
May 30, 1899, orig. paint on machine in fair to good condition, 24" H . . .$4,000.00

Perfection Peanut Vending Mach., mfg. by the Enterprise Vending Machine
Co., pat. February 11, 1902, crack in glass on trap door, paint loss to orig. paint
w/ some inpainting, good condition, 22" H $4,000.00

Advance Peanut Mach., pat. Oct. 23, 1900, repainted, stain drips on left side,
18" H $2,000.00

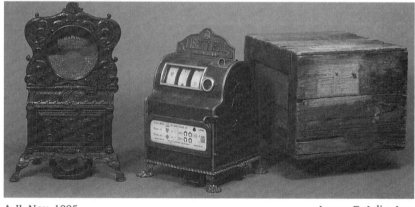

A-IL Nov. 1995   James D. Julia, Inc.

Left to Right

The Merchant Peanut Vending Mach., mfg. by Gabel Co., pat. Sept. 3, 1901,
23" H $95,000.00

Faye Liberty Bell Slot Mach., w/ orig. shipping crate, made in 1899, machine:
12½"x13"x20", orig. shipping crate: 21"x14"x16½". $130,000.00

Tivoli-Jr. Pinball Mach., ca.1933, 12½"x6½"x21½". $200.00

Derby Day Pinball Mach., mfg. by the Artists & Creators Guild Inc., ca. 1932, 16½"x8½"x32½". $240.00

Cigar Store Indian Mach., overall wear and chipping to wood and plaster, 72" H $350.00

One Cent Pinball Mach., mfg. by Genco, ca. 1932, play field in poor condition, 11½"x7½"x18¼". . .$100.00

Play-Boy Pinball Mach., mfg. by Gottlieb Mfg. Co., ca. 1932, play field in fair plus condition, 16"x9"x27". $400.00

Uncle Sam Mach., made in 1970, 76" H $400.00

Log Cabin Mach., mfg. by the Caille Bros. Co., ca. 1902, not working, good to very good condition, 14½"x10" x22". $2700.00

Baffle-Ball Pinball Mach., made by the Gottlieb Mfg. Co., Dec. 1931, play field is in good to very good condition, 16"x11"x27½". $550.00

Left to right
Regina 27" Coin-Operated "Dragon Front", ca. 1899-1902, mechanism restored. $22,500.00
Regina Sublima Corona Style 31 Disc-Changing Music Box, made in Rahway, N.J. by the Regina Music Box Co. $16,000.00

A-IL Nov. 1995   James D. Julia, Inc.

Hold-Over Pinball Mach., mfg. by the Stoner Mfg. Co., Nov. 1940, 23"x41"53" excluding legs. $75.00

A-IL Nov. 1995   James D. Julia, Inc.

Blue Bird Pinball Mach., mfg. by Bally Mfg. Co., Sept. 1936, 26"x50" x54". $700.00

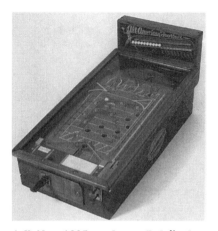

A-IL Nov. 1995   James D. Julia, Inc.

All Am. Football Pinball Mach., made by Peo Mfg. Co., June 1935, 20½" x18¼"x45" excluding legs. . . .$1100.00

A-IL Nov. 1995   James D. Julia, Inc.

Roly Poly Pinball Mach., mfg. by Genco corp., Jan. 1936, 20½" x 11" x 37½" excluding legs. $225.00

A-IL Nov. 1995   James D. Julia, Inc.

Big Six Pinball Mach., made by Keeny Mfg. Co., Oct. 1939, play field in good condition, 23"x64"x52". $250.00

A-IL Nov. 1995   James D. Julia, Inc.

Rapid Transit Pinball Mach., made by Chicago Coin Mfg. Co., Sept. 1935, 20½"x11½"x43" excluding legs.$300.00

A-IL Nov. 1995   James D. Julia, Inc.

Ballyhoo Pinball Mach., made by Bally Mfg. Co., Jan. 1932, play field in good condition, 16½"x9"x33". .$375.00

A-IL Nov. 1995   James D. Julia, Inc.

Bally Triumph Pinball Mach., made by the Bally Mfg. Co., introduced Mar. 1940, 23"x66"x45". $225.00

A-IL Nov. 1995   James D. Julia, Inc.

Favorite Pinball Mach., mfg. by Buckley Mfg. Co., Feb 1932, 16"x8"x33½". $275.00

A-IL Nov. 1995   James D. Julia, Inc.

Jacks Open Pinball Mach., made by Gottlieb & Co., Feb. 1977, 22"x69"x 52". $250.00

A-IL Nov. 1995   James D. Julia, Inc.

Eye of the Tiger Pinball Mach., made by D. Gottlieb & Co., June 1978, 22"x69"x52". $200.00

A-IL Nov. 1995   James D. Julia, Inc.

Cross Line Pinball Mach., made by Bally Mfg. Co., April 1937, 22"x 37"x56". $450.00

A-IL Nov. 1995   James D. Julia, Inc.

One-Two-Three Pinball Mach., made by Mills Novelty Co., Feb 1938, 25"x76"x46". $500.00

A-IL Nov. 1995   James D. Julia, Inc.

Humpty Dumpty Pinball Mach., made by D. Gottlieb & Co., Oct. 1947, back glass fair, 23"x68"x51". .$850.00

A-IL Nov. 1995   James D. Julia, Inc.

Peter Pan Pinball Mach., made by Williams Mfg. Co., March 1955, back glass in good condition, play field in fair to good condition, 26"x64"x 54". $400.00

A-IL Nov. 1995   James D. Julia, Inc.

Eclipse Pinball Mach., made by D. Gottlieb & Co., play field fair condition, 25"x71"x55". $350.00

A-IL Nov. 1995   James D. Julia, Inc.

Sinbad Pinball Mach., made by D. Gottlieb & Co., 1978, play field in good condition, 22"x70"x52". $225.00

A-IL Nov. 1995   James D. Julia, Inc.

Bumper Pinball Mach., Mfg. by Bally Mfg. Co., Dec. 1936, 23"x40"x 54" $250.00

A-IL Nov. 1995   James D. Julia, Inc.

Left to Right

Jennings Operator Bell Slot Mach., pat. Jan. 17, 1922, not working, 25" H $1,200.00

Caille Superior Jackpot Slot Mach., made by Caille Bros. Co., ca. 1928, cabinet restained, 22" H $1,050.00

Groetchen Columbia Slot Mach., escalating glass in rear broken, not working, 18" H $400.00

A-IL Nov. 1995   James D. Julia, Inc.
Mills 25¢ Slot, 17" W, 26" H. $1500.00

A-IL Nov. 1995   James D. Julia, Inc.

Left to Right
Mills Cherry Bell Slot Mach., mfg. by the Mills Novelty Co., ca. 1937, front repainted, case in fair to good condition, some crazing to glass, works good, 26" H $1,300.00
Jennings Standard Chief Slot Mach., ca. 1946, some pitting to front casting, not working, 27" H $1,400.00

A-IL Nov. 1995   James D. Julia, Inc.

Left to Right

Watling Baby Gold Award Ball Gum Vendor Slot Mach., ca. 1933, mfg. by Watling Mfg. Co., good overall condition, 21½" H $1,600.00

Jennings Club Chief Slot Mach., ca. 1949, good condition, 27" H $1,300.00

Watling Baby Ball Gum Vendor Slot Mach., mfg. by Watling Mfg. Co., ca. 1932, repainted in pink and yellow, good condition, 25" H $1,200.00

A-IL Nov. 1995   James D. Julia, Inc.

Left to Right, Row 1

Peerless Penny Drop Gum Mach., mfg. by Blue Bird Products Co., ca. 1926, replm. cash door, 20½" H $500.00
Columbus Model L. Gum Stick Mach., ca. 1910, repainted, 17" H   .$4,250.00
Soda Mint Gum Mach., mfg. by Standard Gum Machine Works, pat. 1907, front casting repainted in orange, yellow and black, orig. finish to case has paint loss, 17½" H $6,500.00
Roth's Pansy Gum Mach., ca. 1905, paint loss and light rusting to front casting, 20" H $1,100.00
Cardinal Gum Mach., ca. 1910, missing back door, porcelain restoration in area fo bird's beak, case repainted, 18" H $900.00
E-Z Drilled Gumball Mach., pat. Sept. 15, 1908, barrel locks not orig. to this machine, 16" H $650.00

Row 2

Bulls-Eye Ball Gum Vender Mach., mfg. by Exhibit Supply Co., 1931, 18" H $1,600.00
Master Target Practice Coin Prize Mach., mfg. by Norris Mfg. Co., ca. 1928, repainted, 18" H $700

A-IL Nov. 1995   James D. Julia, Inc.

Slot Machines, *Left to Right*

Jennings Silver Chief, mfg. by Jennings Mfg. Co., not working, top has been badly repainted, 27" H $1,050.00
Mills Mystery Golden, ca. 1933, missing back lock, fair to good condition, not working, 25" H $1,500.00
Jennings Operator Bell, with a Roberts Novelty Co. Jackport front, from Utica, N.Y., pat. Jan. 17, 1922, good condition, 24" H $950.00

A-IL Nov. 1995   James D. Julia, Inc.

Mills One Dollar Dell O Matic & 5 Cent Bell O Matic Alias Mills Open Front Slot Mach., ca. early 1960's, cases repainted, both not working, 24" and 23½" H respectively.   . . .$1,100.00

A-IL Nov. 1995   James D. Julia, Inc.

Left to Right

Quarter Scope Slot Mach., mfg. by Mills Novelty Co., ca. 1915, castings replated, 58" H $1,900.00
Rockola Five Jacks Slot Mach., wooden figure carved by Dick DeLong, ca. early 1930's, 66½" H $2,600.00

A-IL Nov. 1995   James D. Julia, Inc.

Slot Mach. Stands, pr. $300.00

A-IL Nov. 1995   James D. Julia, Inc.

Row 1
Vending Machines
NW Peanut Merchandiser Peanut Mach., ca. 1920's, replm. back door, some overall chipping and rust around edges with some inpainting, 17¾" H .$2,250.00
Petite Peanut Vendor Mach., mfg. by the Specialty Coin Machine Builders Co., ca. 1934, crack in globe, 10½" H $300.00
Goober Peanut Machine, private labeled for Goober Mfg. Co. by Advance Machine Co., ca. 1915, repainted, 18½" H $1350.00
Row 2
L.A. Wallace Gumball Mach., ca. 1930, 13½" H $700.00
Hance Peanut Vendor Mach., mfg. by Hance Mfg. Co., ca. 1915, pitting due to rust, repainted, fair condition, 18" H $900.00
Millard's Peanut Vendor Mach., ca. 1914, some chipping to lid area, 13" H $750.00

A-IL Nov. 1995   James D. Julia, Inc.
Row 1
Vending Machines
Zeno Chewing Gum Mach., mfg. by Zeno Manuf. Co., pat. May 5, 1908, some inpainting to all sides, 17" H $200.00
Wrigley's Gum Mach., mfg. by Hoff Vending Corp., ca. 1927, repainted, not working, 14½" H $325.00
Master No. 2 Gumball Mach., ca. 1925, some chipping and staining to base plate and lid, 16" H $350.00
Advance Gumball Mach., mfg. by Advance Machine Co., ca. 1915, chimney shaped globe is not correct for this machine, 17½" H $275.00
Row 2
Simpson Leebold Gumball Mach., mfg. by R.D. Simpson Co., pat. Jan. 1, 1923, marquis and decal are not correct to this machine, chromium finish shows wear and pitting, 13½" H . . . .
. . . .$250.00
Columbus Model 34 Gambler Gumball Mach., ca. 1936, 1 cent decal not correct to this machine, 15" H $275.00
Columbus Model 34 Gum Mach., ca. 1936, minor stain around bottom of body, lid has some fading & minor chipping, 14" H $300.00
Vendex Gumball Machine, ca. 1930's, repainted, 12" H $150.00

A-IL Nov. 1995   James D. Julia, Inc.
Left to right
Lucite Dice, 2" H. $125.00
Contemporary Mr. Peanut Figural Display, staining to body area, 18" W, 38" H. $600.00
Adams Blackjack Chewing Gum Sign, one small tear at bottom, 5½" W, 11¼" H inside frame. $600.00

A-IL Nov. 1995   James D. Julia, Inc.

Gum Wrappers, ...$1,500.00

Jan. 1996   Skinner, Inc.

Shaker
27-Utility Basket, lrg. round, some damage to handles, 10½" H, 23½" D $431.25
80-Field Basket, N.H., rectangular, ash, 10" H, 22¾" L, 16½" D . .$747.50
6-Basket, painted letters, 5¾" H, 17" L, 11½" D $460.00
89-Baskets, three; one rect., ash, 4½" H, one sq. bottom, round top, ash, some damage, 5¼" H, & one square, 7" H, 19½" D $57.50
49-Basket, swing handle w/ wooden bottom, ash, iron nails, 7½" H, 11" D . $316.25
40-Basket, square bottom, round top, blue-green stencil or painted design, 7½" H, 10½ D $172.50
22-Utility Basket, round, black ash, 8½" H, 12" D $2,645.00

A-MA June 1996   Skinner, Inc.

Row 1, Left to Right
Wood Splint Baskets, three, paint decor., East. Woodland Indians, 19th C., round basket w/ red & orange, 12" H, 14" D; round basket w/ blue, 13" H, 17½" D; sq. basket red & orange & stamped, 14" H, 21½" W, imperf. .N/S
Row 2, Left to Right
Splint Baskets, 2 of 7, NE Woodland Indians, 19th C., various forms w/ swabbed, plaited & curlicue decor., imperf., sizes 10"x11½" - 17" .$690.00
Splint Rectangular Baskets, two of five, Northeast Woodland Indians, 19th C., three w/ swabbed decor., four covered, one w/ handles, losses, sizes 16½" x 12" - 28" x 17" $230.00

A-KY Oct. 1995   Ken Farmer Auctions

A-MA Jan. 1996   Skinner, Inc.

Nantucket Lightship Baskets, nest of 4, 19th c., 4¾", 5½", 6¼", 8¼" D $4,025.00

A-MA June 1996   Skinner, Inc.

Nantucket Basket, S.P. Boyer, Nantucket, MA, stamped on base "Boyer," w/ hinged bail handle, minor losses, 12¼" Dia $1,150.00

A-MA Jan. 1996   Skinner, Inc.

Shaker Splint Basket, w/ handles 19th c., minor losses, 14¾"H, 19¼ D $1,495.00
Nantucket Lightship Basket, MA, paper label, 5¼" H, 7½" D . .$1,610.00
Oval Nantucket Basket, late 19th c., hinged bail handle, breaks, 11½" L $575.00

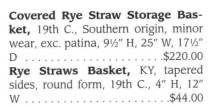

Covered Rye Straw Storage Basket, 19th C., Southern origin, minor wear, exc. patina, 9½" H, 25" W, 17½" D $220.00
Rye Straws Basket, KY, tapered sides, round form, 19th C., 4" H, 12" W $44.00

A-MA June 1996   Skinner, Inc.

Nantucket Lightship Oval Basket, labeled "Made on board ... shoal lightship Isaac Hamblen," splint loss to wrapped rim, 12½" L $1,610.00
Nantucket Work Basket, Nantucket Island, MA., 20th C., hinged cover w/ turned finial, some warping, 8" H, 9½" D $1,035.00
Nantucket Work Basket, Nantucket Island, MA., early 20th C., w/ pivoting cover, 4¼" H, 5¾" D $2,990.00
Nantucket Basket, Nantucket Island, MA., early 20th C., round w/ swing handle, 9" H, 6½" D $862.50
Lot of Nantucket related Sketches & Photos, late 19th / 20th C., ink & colored pencil drawing of Orange St., photos & postcards of the island, charcoal sketchbook "View Around Lynn", by E.J. Whitman, lot also incl. a sm. heart-shaped basket $460.00
Nantucket Basket, Nantucket Island, MA., 20th C., 12" H, 11½" D $1,150.00

A-PA Nov. 1995   Aston Auctioneers
                          & Appraisers

Row 1, Left to Right
Miniature Melon Buttocks Basket, w/ bentwood carrying handle $190.00
Hand-held Winnowing Basket, clam-shaped w/ leather thong . .$210.00
Miniature Algonquin Potato Basket, stamped, late 19th C. . .$240.00
Row 2, Left to Right Clockwise
Miniature Berry Basket, w/ wide splint handle $120.00
Miniature Splint Basket, w/ damage $50.00
Miniature Apple Basket, w/ bentwood carrying handles, raised bottom $410.00
Miniature Wall-Pocket Basket, ...$60.00

A-MA Apr. 1996 Tradewinds Auctions

Hearing Aid Gadget Cane, malacca shaft, French, ca. 1870. . . . .$5,200.00
Horn Horse w/ Silver Bridle, ebonized hardwood shaft, ca. 1880.
. . . .$700.00
Stained Hardwood Vintner's Cane, ca. 1880. . . . .$1,400
Narwhal Staff, made from a single thick piece of tusk, silver handle over-lay, ca 1850. . . . .$5,300.00
Wild Boar Crook Cane, cabochon garnet eyes, ca. 1870. . . . . . .$575.00
Carved Wood Erotic Lady, walnut handle, silver collar, hardwood shaft, ca. 1850. . . . .$3,000.00
Doctor's Otoscope Cane, ivory cap, silver instrument, single bark malacca shaft, ca. 1890. . . . .$4,500.00
Elephant Ivory Crook Cane w/ Cupid, ca. 1890. . . . .$2,100.00

A-MA Apr. 1996 Tradewinds Auctions

18th C Lovers, carved elephant ivory, ebonized hardwood shaft. .$4,200.00
Silver Plate on Brass Cheroot Cannon Cane, ca. 1850. . . . . .$1,250.00
Eagle & Ball Cane, walrus ivory w/ gold plated collar, ca. 1878. . .$525.00
Large Carved Ivory Elephant Cane, silver collar, single bark malacca shaft, ca. 1860. . . . .$3,400.00
Large Ivory Elephant on Barrel, ebonized hardwood shaft, ca 1890. . .
. . . .$3,400.00
Wood Wire-Haired Fox Terrier, dark cherry shaft, glass eyes. $700.00
Victorian Nautical Cane, carved whalebone ivory, ca. 1850. .$3,100.00
Gun Cane Curio, silver & ivory, metal shaft, ca. 1870. . . . .$3,100.00
Twisted Silver Topped Cane on Snakewood, ca. 1892. . . . .$800.00

A-MA Apr. 1996 Tradewinds Auctions
Silver Top Cane on thick malacca, ca. 1860. . . . .$100.00

A-MA Apr. 1996 Tradewinds Auctions
Large Carve Ivory Basket Weave Ball, ebony shaft, English, ca. 1860. .
. . . .$225.00

A-MA Apr. 1996 Tradewinds Auctions
Silver Cane w/ three faces, bamboo shaft w/ brass ferrule, ca. 1880. . . . .
. . . .$2,400.00

A-MA Apr. 1996 Tradewinds Auctions
Nickel-Silver Wolf Cane, glass eyes, shaft is worn malacca, good cond., Amer., ca. 1935 . . . .$275.00

A-MA Apr. 1996 Tradewinds Auctions
Elephant Ivory Whippet Cane, rose-wood shaft, Eng., ca. 1890 . . .$475.00

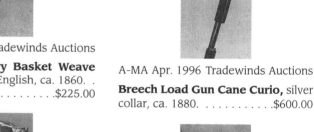

A-MA Apr. 1996 Tradewinds Auctions
Whale Ivory Hand on Twisted Rosewood Shaft, Amer., ca. 1850. .
. . . .$825.00

A-MA Apr. 1996 Tradewinds Auctions
Breech Load Gun Cane Curio, silver collar, ca. 1880. . . . .$600.00

A-MA Apr. 1996 Tradewinds Auctions
Horn Hoof on Whalebone Cane, white whalebone shaft, ca. 1860. . . .
. . . .$800.00

A-MA Apr. 1996 Tradewinds Auctions
Wood Bulldog Cane, malacca shaft.
. . . .$425.00

A-MA Apr. 1996 Tradewinds Auctions
Victorian Naughty Lady's Leg Cane, whale ivory leg & rhino horn boot, ca. 1860. . . . .$1,600.00

A-MA Apr. 1996 Tradewinds Auctions

French Watch Cane, silver handle w/ fine watch, works & in good cond., ca. 1885 . . . .$1,000.00

A-MA Apr. 1996 Tradewinds Auctions

Carved Staghorn Cane of Boston Terrier, rosewood shaft, Amer., ca. 1890. . . . .$400.00

A-MA Apr. 1996 Tradewinds Auctions

Lady's Sword Cane Curio, elephant ivory knob, bamboo shaft, ca. 1790. . . . .$375.00

A-MA Apr. 1996 Tradewinds Auctions

Ivory & Bamboo Sword Curio Cane, Continental, ca. 1850. .$425.00

A-MA Apr. 1996 Tradewinds Auctions

Staghorn Cane w/ Silver Mounts, malacca shaft, Amer., ca 1880. . . . .$200.00

A-MA Apr. 1996 Tradewinds Auctions

Horn Hoof Cane on Partridge Wood, Continental, ca. 1835 .$200.00

A-MA Apr. 1996 Tradewinds Auctions

Alligator Cane, brass tack eyes, bone teeth, hardwood shaft, Amer., ca. 1900 . . . .$225.00

A-MA Apr. 1996   Tradewinds Auctions

Carved Horn Bull Cane, glass eyes & silver plated collar, ebony shaft, ca. 1900 . . . .$150.00

A-MA Apr. 1996 Tradewinds Auctions

Silver Tiffany Cane, w/ gold over-laid insects, dark hardwood shaft decor. w/ acid etching, very good cond., ca. 1880 . . . .$3,100.00

A-MA Apr. 1996 Tradewinds Auctions

Ivory Eagle & Ball Cane, walrus ivory w/ glass eyes, gold plated collar, dated 1878 . . . .$525.00

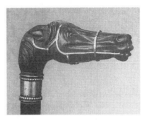

A-MA Apr. 1996 Tradewinds Auctions

Horn Horse w/ Silver Bridle, glass eyes & sterling silver collar, ca. 1880 . . . .$700.00

A-MA Apr. 1996 Tradewinds Auctions

Carved Ivory Elephant Cane, made of elephant ivory, solid silver collar, Amer., ca. 1860 . . . .$3,400.00

A-MA Apr. 1996 Tradewinds Auctions

Painted Wood Boxer Cane, carved from single piece of hardwood, ca. 1890 . . . .$275.00

A-MA Apr. 1996 Tradewinds Auctions

Carved Ivory Cane, elephant ivory handle, very good cond., German, ca. 1870 . . . .$1,700.00

ABC PLATES — Alphabet plates were made especially for children as teaching aids. They date from the late 1700s and were made of various material including porcelain, pottery, glass, pewter, tin and ironstone.

AMPHORA ART POTTERY was made at the Amphora Porcelain Works in the TeplitzTum area of Bohemia during the late 19th and early 20th centuries. Numerous potteries were located there.

ANNA POTTERY — The Anna Pottery was established in Anna, IL, in 1859 by Cornwall and Wallace Kirkpatrick, and closed in 1894. The company produced utilitarian wares, gift wares and pig-shaped bottles and jugs with special inscriptions, wich are the most collectible pieces.

BATTERSEA ENAMELS — The name "Battersea" is a general term for those metal objects decorated with enamels, such as pill, patch, and snuff boxes, doorknobs, and such. The process of fusing enamel onto metal—usually copper—began about 1750 in the Battersea District of London. Today the name has become a generic term for similar objects—mistakenly called "Battersea."

BELLEEK porcelain was first made at Fermanagh, Ireland, in 1857. Today this ware is still being made in buildings within walking distance of the original clay pits according to the skills and traditions of the original artisans. Irish Belleek is famous for its thinness and delicacy. Similar type wares were also produced in other European countries as well as the United States.

BENNINGTON POTTERY — The first pottery works in Bennington, Vermont, was established by Captain John Norton in 1793; and, for 101 years, it was owned and operated by succeeding generations of Nortons. Today the term "Bennington" is synonymous with the finest in American ceramics because the town was the home of several pottery operations during the last century—each producing under different labels. Today items produced at Bennington are now conveniently, if inaccurately, dubbed "Bennington." One of the popular types of pottery produced there is known as "Rockingham." The term denotes the rich, solid brown glazed pottery from which many household items were made. The ware was first produced by the Marquis of Rockingham in Swinton, England—hence the name.

BESWICK — An earthenware produced in Staffordshire, England, by John Beswick in 1936. The company is now a part of Royal Doulton Tableware, Ltd.

BISQUE — The term applies to pieces of porcelain or pottery which have been fired but left in an unglazed state.

BLOOR DERBY — "Derby" porcelain dates from about 1755 when William Duesbury began the production of porcelain at Derby. In 1769 he purchased the famous Chelsea Works and operated both factories. During the Chelsea-Derby period, some of the finest examples of English porcelains were made. Because of their fine quality, in 1773 King George III gave Duesbury the patent to mark his porcelain wares "Crown Derby." Duesbury died in 1796. In 1810 the factory was purchased by Robert Bloor, a senior clerk. Bloor revived the Imari styles which had been so popular. After his death in 1845, former workmen continued to produce fine porcelains using the traditional Derby patterns. The firm was reorganized in 1876 and in 1878 a new factory was built. In 1890 Queen Victoria appointed the company "Manufacturers to Her Majesty" with the right to be known as Royal Crown Derby.

BUFFALO POTTERY — The Buffalo Pottery of Buffalo, New York, was organized in 1901. The firm was an adjunct of the Larkin Soap Company, which was established to produce china and pottery premiums for that company. Of the many different types produced, the Buffalo Pottery is most famous for its "Deldare" line which was developed in 1905.

CANARY LUSTER earthenware dates to the early 1800s, and was produced by potters in the Staffordshire District of England. The body of this ware is a golden yellow and decorated with transfer printing, usually in black.

CANTON porcelain is a blue-and-white decorated ware produced near Canton, China, from the late 1700s through the last century. Its hand-decorated Chinese scenes have historical as well as mythological significance.

CAPO-di-MONTE, originally a softpaste porcelain, is Italian in origin. The first ware was made during the 1700s near Naples. Although numerous marks were used, the most familiar to us is the crown over the letter N. Mythological subjects, executed in either high or low relief and tinted in bright colors on a light ground, were a favorite decoration. The earlier wares had a peculiar grayish color as compared to the whiter bodies of later examples.

CARLSBAD porcelain was made by several factories in the area from the 1800s and exported to the United States. When Carlsbad became a part of Czechoslovakia after World War I, wares were frequently marked "Karlsbad." Items marked "Victoria" were made for Lazarus & Rosenfeldt, Importers.

CASTLEFORD earthenware was produced in England from the late 1700s until around 1820. Its molded decoration is similar to Prattware.

CELEDON — Chinese porcelain having a velvet-textured greenish-gray glaze. Japanese and other oriental factories also made celedon glazed wares.

CHELSEA — An early soft paste porcelain manufactured at Chelsea in London from around 1745 to 1769. Chelsea is considered to be one of the most famous of English porcelain factories.

CHELSEA KERAMIC ART WORKS — The firm was established in 1872, in Chelsea, MA, by members of the Robertson family. The firm used the mark CKAW. The company closed in 1889, but was reorganized in 1891, as the Chelsea Pottery U.S. In 1895, the factory became the Dedham Pottery of Dedham, MA, and closed in 1943.

CHINESE EXPORT PORCELAIN was made in quantity in China during the 1700s and early 1800s. The term identifies a variety of porcelain wares made for export to Europe and the United States. Since many thought the product to be of joint Chinese and English manufacture, it has also been known as "Oriental" or "Chinese Lowestoft."

As much as this ware was made to order for the American and European market, it was frequently adorned with seals of states or the coat of arms of individuals, in addition to eagles, sailing scenes, flowers, religious and mythological scenes.

CLARICE CLIFF POTTERY — Clarice Cliff (1899–1972) was a designer who worked at A.J. Wilkinson, Ltd.'s Royal Staffordshire Pottery at Burslem, England. Cliff's earthenwares were bright and colorful Art Deco designs which included squares, circles, bands, conical shapes and simple landscapes incorporated with the designs. Cliff used several different printed marks, each of which incorporated a facsimile of her signature—and generally the name of the pattern.

CLEWS POTTERY — (see also, Historical Staffordshire) was made by George Clews & Co., of Brownhill Pottery, Tunstall, England, from 1806–1861.

CLIFTON POTTERY — William Long founded the Clifton Pottery in Clifton, NJ, in 1905. Pottery was simply marked CLIFTON. Long worked until 1908, producing a line called Crystal Patina. The Cheasapeake Pottery Company made majolica marked Clifton Ware, which oftentimes confuses collectors.

COALPORT porcelain has been made by the Coalport Porcelain Works in England since 1795. The ware is still being produced at Stroke-on-Trent.

COORS POTTERY — Coors ware was made in Golden, CO, by the Coors Beverage Company from the turn of the century until the pottery was destroyed by fire in the 1930s.

COPELAND-SPODE — The firm was founded by Josiah Spode in 1770 in Staffordshire, England. From 1847, W.T. Copeland & Sons, Ltd., succeeded Spode, using the designation "Late Spode" to its wares. The firm is still in operation.

COPPER LUSTER — See Lusterwares.

CORDEY — Boleslaw Cybis was one of the founders of the Cordey China Company, Trenton, NJ. Production began in 1942. In 1969, the company was purchased by the Lightron Corporation, and operated as the Schiller Cordey Company. Around 1950, Cybis began producing fine porcelain figurines.

COWAN POTTERY — Guy Cowan produced art pottery in Rocky River, OH, from 1913 to 1931. He used a stylized mark with the word COWAN on most pieces. Also, Cowan mass-produced a line marked LAKEWARE.

CROWN DUCAL — English porcelain made by the A.G. Richardson & Co., Ltd. since 1916.

CUP PLATES were used where cups were handleless and saucers were deep. During the early 1800s, it was very fashionable to drink from a saucer. Thus, a variety of fancy small plates was produced for the cup to rest in. The lacy Sandwich examples are very collectible.

DAVENPORT pottery and porcelain were made at the Davenport Factory in Longport, Staffordshire, England, by Joan Davenport from 1793 until 1887 when the pottery closed. Most of the wares produced there—porcelains, creamwares, ironstone, earthenwares and other products—were marked.

DEDHAM (Chelsea Art Works) —The firm was founded in 1872 at Chelsea, Massachusetts, by James Robertson & Sons, and closed in 1889. In 1891 the pottery was reopened under the name of The Chelsea Pottery, U.S. The first and most popular blue underglaze decoration for the desirable "Cracqule Ware" was the rabbit motif—designed by Joseph L. Smith. In 1893 construction was started on the new pottery in Dedham, Massachusetts, and production began in 1895. The name of the pottery was then changed to "Dedham Pottery," to eliminate the confusion with the English Chelsea Ware. The famed crackleware finish became synonymous with the name. Because of its popularity, more than 50 patterns of tableware were made.

DELFT — Holland is famous for its fine examples of tin-glazed pottery dating from the 16th century. Although blue and white is the most popular color, other colors were also made. The majority of the ware found today is from the late Victorian period and when the name Holland appears with the Delft factory mark, this indicates that the item was made after 1891.

DORCHESTER POTTERY was established by George Henderson in Dorchester, a part of Boston, Massachusetts, in 1895. Production included stonewares, industrial wares, and, later, some decorated tablewares. The pottery is still in production.

DOULTON — The pottery was established in Lambeth in 1815 by John Doulton and John Watts. When Watts retired in 1845, the firm became known as Doulton & Company. In 1901 King Edward VII conferred a double honor on the company by presentation of the Royal Warrant, authorizing their chairman to use the word "Royal" in describing products. A variety of wares has been made over the years for the American market. The firm is still in production.

DRESDEN — The term identifies any china produced in the town of Dresden, Germany. The most famous factory in Dresden is the Meissen factory. During the 18th century,

English and Americans used the name "Dresden china" for wares produced at Meissen which has led to much confusion. The city of Dresden which was the capital of Saxony, was better known in 18th century Europe than Meissen, which was fifteen miles away. Therefore, Dresden became a generic term for all porcelains produced and decorated in the city of Dresden and surrounding districts including Meissen. By the mid-19th century, about thirty factories in the city of Dresden were producing and decorating porcelains in the style of Meissen. Therefore, do not make the mistake of thinking all pieces marked Dresden were made at the Meissen factory. Meissen pieces generally have crossed swords marks and are listed under Meissen.

FLOWING BLUE ironstone is a highly glazed dinnerware made at Staffordshire by a variety of potters. It became popular about 1825. Items were printed with patterns (Oriental) and the color flowed from the design over the white body so that the finished product appeared smeared. Although purple and brown colors were also made, the deep cobalt blue shades were the most popular. Later wares were less blurred, having more white ground.

FRANKOMA — The Frank Pottery was founded in 1933, by John Frank, Sapulpa, Ok. The company produced decorative wares from 1936–38. Early wares were made from a light cream-colored clay, but in 1956 changed to a red brick clay. This along with the glazes helps to determine the period of production.

FULPER — The Fulper mark was used by the American Pottery Company of Flemington, NJ. Fulper art pottery was produced from approximately 1910 to 1930.

GALLE — Emile Galle was a designer who made glass, pottery, furniture and other Art Nouveau items. He founded his factory in France in 1874. Ceramic peices were marked with the initials E.G. impressed, Em. Galle Faiencerie de Nancy, or a version of his signature.

GAUDY DUTCH is the most spectacular of the gaudy wares. It was made for the Pennsylvania Dutch market from about 1785 until the 1820s. This softpaste tableware is lightweight and frail in appearance. Its rich cobalt blue decoration was applied to the biscuit, glazed and fired—then other colors were applied over the first glaze—and the object was fired again. No luster is included in its decoration.

GAUDY IRONSTONE was made in Staffordshire from the early 1850s until around 1865. This ware is heavier than gaudy Welsh or gaudy Dutch, as its texture is a mixture of pottery and porcelain clay.

GAUDY WELSH, produced in England from about 1830, resembles gaudy Dutch in decoration, but the workmanship is not as fine and its texture is more comparable to that of spatterware. Luster is usually included with the decoration.

GOUDA POTTERY — Gouda and the

surrounding areas of Holland have been one of the principal Dutch pottery centers since the 17th century. The Zenith pottery and the Zuid–Hollandsche pottery, produced the brightly colored wares marked GOUDA from 1880 to about 1940. Many pieces of Gouda featured Art Nouveau or Art Deco designs.

GRUEBY — Grueby Faience Company, Boston, MA, was founded in 1897 by William H. Grueby. The company produced hand thrown art pottery in natural shapes, hand molded and hand tooled. A variety of colored glazes, singly or in Combinations were used, with green being the most prominent color. The company closed in 1908.

HAEGER — The Haeger Potteries, Inc., Dundee, IL, began making art wares in 1914. Their early pieces were marked with the name HAEGER written over the letter "H." Around 1938, the mark changed to ROYAL HAEGER.

HAMPSHIRE — In 1871 James S. Taft founded the Hampshire Pottery Company in Keene, NH. The company produced redware, stoneware, and majolica decorated wares in 1879. In 1883, the company introduced a line of colored glazed wares, including a Royal Worcester-type pink, blue, green, olive and reddish-brown. Pottery was marked with the printed mark or the impressed name HAMPSHIRE POTTERY or J.S.T. & CO., KEENE, N.H.

HARKER — The Harker Pottery Company of East Liverpool, OH, was founded in 1840. The company made a variety of different types of pottery including yellowware from native clays. Whiteware and Rockingham-type brown-glazed pottery were also produced in quantities.

HISTORICAL STAFFORDSHIRE — The term refers to a particular blue-on-white, transfer-printed earthenware produced in quantity during the early 1800s by many potters in the Staffordshire District. The central decoration was usually an American city scene or landscape, frequently showing some mode of transportation in the foreground. Other designs included portraits and patriotic emblems. Each potter had a characteristic border which is helpful to identify a particular ware, as many pieces are unmarked. Later transfer-printed wares were made in sepia, pink, green and black but the early cobalt blue examples are the most desirable.

HULL — In 1905, Addis E. Hull purchased the Acme Pottery Company in Crooksville, OH. In 1917, Hull began producing art pottery, stoneware and novelties including the Little Red Riding Hood line. Most pieces had a matte finish with shades of pink and blue or brown predominating. After a flood and fire in 1950, the factory was reopened in 1952 as the Hull Pottery Company. Pre-1950 vases are marked HULL USA or HULL ART USA. Post-1950 pieces are simply marked HULL in large script or block letters. Paper lables were also used.

HUMMEL — Hummel items are the original creations of Berta Hummel, born in 1909 in Germany. Hummel collectibles are made by W. Goebel Porzellanfabrik of Oeslau, Germany, now Rodenthal, West Germany. They were first made in 1934. All authentic Hummels bear both the signature, M.I. Hummel, and a Goebel trademark. However, various trademarks were used to identify the year of production.

IRONSTONE is a heavy, durable, utilitarian ware made from the slag of iron furnaces, ground and mixed with clay. Charles Mason of Lane Delft, Staffordshire, patented the formula in 1823. Much of the early ware was decorated in imitation of Imari, in addition to transfer-printed blue ware, flowing blues and browns. During the mid-19th centruy, the plain white enlivened only by embossed designs became fashionable. Literally hundreds of patterns were made for export.

JACKFIELD POTTERY is English in origin. It was first produced during the 17th century; however, most items available today date from the last century. It is a red-bodied pottery, often decorated with scrolls and flowers, in relief, then covered with a black glaze.

JASPERWARE — A very hard, unglazed porcelain with a colored ground, varying from blues and greens to lavender, red, yellow or black. White designs were generally applied in relief to these wares, and often times reflect a classical motif. Jasperware was first produced by Wedgwood's Etruria Works in 1775. Many other English potters produced jasperware, including Copeland, Spode and Adams.

JUGTOWN POTTERY — This North Carolina pottery has been made since the 18th century. In 1915 Jacques Busbee organized what was to become the Jugtown Pottery in 1921. Production was discontinued in 1958.

KING'S ROSE is a decorated creamware produced in the Staffordshire district of England during the 1820-1840 period. The rose decorations are usually in red, green, yellow and pink. This ware is often referred to as "Queen's Rose."

LEED'S POTTERY was established by Charles Green in 1758 at Leed, Yorkshire, England. Early wares are unmarked. From 1775 the impressed mark "Leeds Pottery" was used. After 1880 the name "Hartly, Green & Co." was added, and the impressed or incised letters "LP" were also used to identify the ware.

LIMOGES — The name identifies fine porcelain wares produced by many factories at Limoges, France, since the mid-1800s. A variety of different marks identify wares made there including Haviland china.

LIVERPOOL POTTERY — The term applies to wares produced by many potters located in Liverpool, England, from the early 1700s, for American trade. Their print-decorated pitchers—referred to as "jugs" in England—have been especially popular. These featured patriotic emblems, prominent men, ships, etc., and can be easily identified as nearly all are melon-shaped with a very pointed lip, strap handle and graceful curved body.

LONHUDA — In 1892, William Long, Alfred Day, and W.W. Hunter organized the Lonhuda Pottery Company of Steubenville, OH. The firm produced underglaze slip-decorated pottery until 1896, when production ceased. Although the company used a variety of marks, the earliest included the letters LPCO.

LOTUS WARE — This thin Belleek-like-porcelain was made by the Knowles, Taylor & Knowles Company of Easter Liverpool, OH, from 1890 to 1900.

LUSTERWARE — John Hancock of Hanley, England, invented this type of decoration on earthenwares during the early 1800s. The copper, bronze, ruby, gold, purple, yellow, pink and mottled pink luster finishes were made from gold painted on the glazed objects, then fired. The latter type is often referred to as "Sunderland Luster." Its pinkish tones vary in color and pattern. The silver lusters were made from platinum.

MAASTRICHT WARE — Petrus Regout founded the De Sphinx pottery in 1835 at Maastricht, Holland. The company specialized in transfer painted earthenwares.

MAJOLICA — The word MAJOLICA is a general term for any pottery glazed with an opaque tin enamel that conceals the color of the clay body. It has been produced by many countries for centuries. Majolica took its name from the Spanish island of Majorca, where figuline (a potter's clay) is found. This ware frequently depicted elements in nature: birds, flowers, leaves and fish. English manufacturers marked their wares and most can be identified through the English Registry mark, and/or the potter-designer's mark, while most continental pieces had an incised number. Although many American potteries produced majolica between 1850 and 1900, only a few chose to identify their wares. Among these were the firm of Griffen, Smith, and Hill; George Morely; Edwin Bennett; Cheaspeake Pottery Company; and the new Milford-Wannoppe Pottery Company.

MARBLEHEAD — This hand thrown pottery had its beginning in 1905 as a therapeutic program by Dr. J. Hall for the patients of a Marblehead, MA, sanitarium. Later, production was moved to another site and the factory continued under the management of A.E. Baggs until it closed in 1936. The most desirable pieces found today are decorated with conventionalized designs.

MATT-MORGAN — By 1883 Matt morgan, an English artist, was producing art pottery in Cincinnati, OH, that resembled Moorish wares. Incised designs and colors were applied to raised panels, then shiny or matte glazes were applied. The firm lasted only a few years.

McCOY POTTERY — The J.W. McCoy Pottery was established in 1899. Production of art pottery began after 1926 when the name was changed to Brush McCoy.

MEISSEN — The history of Meissen porcelain began in Germany in 1710, when Frederich August I established the Royal Saxon Porcelain Manufactory. The company was first directed by Johann Boettger, who developed the first truly white porcelain in Europe. The crossed swords mark of the Meissen factory was adopted in 1723.

METTLACH, Germany, located in the Zoar Basin, was the location of the famous Villeroy & Boch factories from 1836 until 1921 when the factory was destroyed by fire. Steins (dating from about 1842) and other stonewares with bas relief decorations were their specialty.

MINTON — Thomas Minton established his pottery in 1793 at Stroke-on-Trent, Hanley, England. During the early years, Minton concentrated on blue transfer painted earthenwares, plain bone china, and cream colored earthenware. During the first quarter of the 19th century, a large selection of figures and ornamental wares were produced in addition to their tableware lines. In 1968, Minton became a member of the Royal Doulton Tableware group, and retains its reputation for fine quality hand painted and gilted tablewares.

MOCHAWARE — This banded creamware was first produced in England during the late 1700s. The early ware was lightweight and thin, having colorful bands of bright colors decorating a body that is cream colored to very light brown. After 1840 the ware became heavier in body and the color was often quite light—almost white. Mochaware can easily be identified by its colorful banded decorations—on and between the bands—including feathery ferns, lacy trees, seaweeds, squiggly designs and lowly earthworms.

MOORCROFT — William Moorcroft established the Moorcroft Pottery, in Burslem, England in 1913. The majority of the art pottery wares were hand thrown. The company initially used an impressed mark, MOORCROFT, BURSLEM, with a signature mark, W.MOORCROFT, following. Walker, William's son, continued the business after his father's death in 1945, producing the same style wares. Contemporary pieces are marked simply MOORCROFT with export pieces also marked MADE IN ENGLAND.

NEWCOMB — William and Ellsworth Woodward founded Newcomb Pottery at Sophie Newcomb College, New Orleans, LA, in 1896. Students decorated the high quality art pottery pieces with a variety of designs that have a decidedly southern flavor. Production continued through the 1940s. Marks include the letters NC and often have the incised initials of the artist as well. Most pieces have a matte glaze.

NILOAK POTTERY with its prominent swirled, marbelized designs, is a 20th century pottery first produced at Benton, Arkansas, in 1911 by the Niloak Pottery Company. Production ceased in 1946.

NIPPON porcelain has been produced in quantity for the American market since the late 19th century. After 1891, when it became obligatory to include the country of origin on all imports, the Japanese trademark "Nippon" was used. Numerous other marks appear on this ware identifying the manufacturer, artist or importer. The hand-painted Nippon examples are extremely popular today and prices are on the rise.

NORSE POTTERY was founded in 1903 in Edgerton, WI. The company moved to Rockford, IL, in 1604, where they produced a black pottery which resembled early bronze items. The firm closed in 1913.

OHR POTTERY was produced by George E. Ohr in Biloxi, Mississippi, around 1883. Today Ohr is recognized as one of the leading potters in the American Art Pottery movement. Early work was often signed with an impressed stamp in block letters—G.E. OHR, BILOXI. Later pieces were often marked G.E. Ohr in flowing script. Ohr closed the pottery in 1906, storing more than 6,000 pieces as a legacy to his family. These pieces remained in storage until 1972.

OLD IVORY dinnerware was made in Silesia, Germany during the late 1800s. It derives its name from the background color of the china. Marked pieces usually have a pattern number on the base, and the word "Silesia" with a crown.

OTT & BREWER — The company operated the Etruria Pottery in Trenton, NJ, from 1863 to 1893. A variety of marks were used which incorporated the initials O & B.

OWENS — The Owens Pottery began production in Zanesville, OH, in 1891. The first art pottery was made after 1896, and pieces were usually marked with a form of the name OWENS. Production of art pottery was discontinued about 1907.

PAUL REVERE POTTERY — This pottery was made at several locations in and around Boston, MA, between 1906 and 1942. The company was operated as a settlement house program for girls. Many pieces were signed S.E.G. for Saturday Evening Girls. The young artists concentrated on children's dishes and tiles.

PETERS & REED Pottery Company of Zanesville, Ohio, was founded by John D. Peters and Adam Reed about the turn of the century. Their wares, although seldom marked, can be identified by the characteristic red or yellow clay body touched with green. This pottery was best known for its matte glaze pieces—especially one type, called Moss Aztec, combined a red earthenware body with a green glaze. The company changed hands in 1920 and was renamed the Zane Pottery Company. Examples marked "Zaneware" are oftentimes identical to earlier pieces.

PEWABIC — Mary Chase Perry Straton founded the Pewabic Pottery in 1903 in Detriot, MI. Many types of art pottery was produced here including pieces with matte green glaze and an iridescent crystaline glaze. Operations ceased after the death of Mary Stratton in 1961, but the company was reactivated by Michigan State University in 1968.

PISGAH FOREST POTTERY — The pottery was founded near Mt. Pisgah in North Carolina in 1914 by Walter B. Stephen. The pottery remains in operation.

QUIMPER — Tin-glazed, hand-painted pottery has been produced in Quimper, France, dating back to the 17th century. It is named for a French town where numerous potteries were located. The popular peasant design first appeared during the 1860s, and many variations exist. Florals and geometrics were equally as popular. The HR and HR QUIMPER marks are found on Henriot peices prior to 1922.

REDWARE is one of the most popular forms of country pottery. It has a soft, porous body and its color varies from reddish-brown tones to deep wine to light orange. It was produced in mostly utilitarian forms by potters in small factories, or by potters working on their farms, to fill their everyday needs. The most desirable examples are the slip-decorated pieces, or the rare and expensive "sgraffito" examples which have scratched or incised line decoration. Slip decoration was made by tracing the design on the redware shape with a clay having a creamy consistency in contrasting colors. When dried, the design was slightly raised above the surface.

RED WING ART POTTERY AND STONE-WARE — The name includes several potteries located in Red Wing, MN. David Hallem established his pottery in 1868, producing stoneware items with a red wing stamped under the glaze as its mark. The Minnesota Stoneware Co. began production in 1883. The North Star Stoneware company began production in 1892, and used a raised star and the words Red Wing as its mark. The two latter firms merged in 1892, producing stoneware until 1920, when the company introduced a pottery line. In 1936, the name was changed to Red Wing Potteries. The plant closed in 1967.

RIDGWAY — Throughout the 19th century the Ridgway family, through partnerships held positions of importance in Shelton and hanley, Staffordshire, England. Their wares have been made since 1808, and their transfer-design dinner sets are the most widely known product. Many pieces are unmarked, but later marks include the initials of the many partnerships.

RIVIERA — This dinnerware was made by the Homer Laughlin Company of Newell, WV, from 1938 to 1950.

ROCKINGHAM — See Bennington Pottery.

ROOKWOOD POTTERY — The Rookwood Pottery began production at Cincinnati, Ohio, in 1880 under the direction of Maria Longworth Nichols Storer, and operated until 1960. The name was derived from the family estate, "Rookwood," because of the "rook" or "crows" which inhabited the wooded areas. All pieces of this art pottery are marked, usually bearing the famous flame.

RORSTRAND FAIENCE — The firm was founded in 1726 near Stockholm, Sweden.

Items dating from the early 1900s and having an "art noveau" influence are very expensive and much in demand these days.

ROSE MEDALLION ware dates from the 18th century. It was decorated and exported from Canton, China, in quantity. The name generally applied to those pieces having medallions with figures of people alternating with panels of flowers, birds and butterflies. When all the medallions were filled with flowers, the ware was differentiated as Rose Canton.

ROSE TAPESTRY — See Royal Bayreuth.

ROSEVILLE POTTERY — The Roseville Pottery was organized in 1890 in Roseville, Ohio. The firm produced utilitarian stoneware in the plant formerly owned by the Owens Pottery of Roseville, also producers of stoneware, and the Linden Avenue Plant at Zanesville, Ohio, originally built by the Clark Stoneware Company. In 1900 an art line of pottery was created to compete with Owens and Weller lines. The new ware was named "Rozane," and it was produced at the Zanesville location. Following its success, other prestige lines were created. The Azurine line was introduced about 1902.

ROYAL BAYREUTH manufactory began in Tettau in 1794 at the first porcelain factory in Bavaria. Wares made there were on the same par with Meissen. Fire destroyed the original factory during the 1800s. Much of the wares available today were made at the new factory which began production in 1897. These include Rose Tapestry, Sunbonnet Baby novelties and the Devil and Card items. The Royal Bayreuth blue mark has the 1794 founding date incorporated with the mark.

ROYAL BONN — The tradename identifies a variety of porcelain items made during the 19th century by the Bonn China Manufactory, established in 1755 by Elmer August. Most of the ware found today is from the Victorian period.

ROYAL CROWN DERBY — The company was established in 1875 in Derby, England, and has no connection with the earlier Derby factories which operated in the late 18th and early 19th centuries. Derby porcelain produced from 1878 to 1890 carry the standard crown printed mark. From 1891 forward, the mark carries the "Royal Crown Derby" wording, and during the present century, "Made in England" and "English Bone China" were added to the mark. Today the ocmpany is a part of Royal Doulton Tableware, Ltd.

ROYAL DOULTON wares have been made from 1901, when King Edward VII conferred a double honor on the Doulton Pottery by the presentation of the Royal Warrant, authorizing their chairman to use the word "Royal" in describing products. A vadriety of wares has been produced for the American market. The firm is still in production.

ROYAL DUX was produced in Bohemia during the late 1800s. Large quantities of this decorative porcelain ware were exported to the United States. Royal Dux figurines are especially popular.

ROYAL RUDOLSTADT — This hard paste ware was first made in Rudolstadt, Thuringen, East Germany, by Ernt Bohne in 1854. A second factory was opened in 1882 by L. Straus & Sons, Ltd. The ware was never labeled "Royal Rudolstadt" originally, but the word "Royal" was added later as part of an import mark. This porcelain was imported by Lewis Straus and Sons of New York.

ROYAL WORCESTER — The Worcester factory was established in 1751 in England. This is a tastefully decorated porcelain noted for its creamy white lusterless surface. Serious collectors prefer items from the Dr. Wall (the activator of the concern) period of production which extended from the time the factory was established to 1785.

ROYCROFT POTTERY was made by the Roycrofter community of East Aurora, New York, during the late 19th and early 20th centuries. The firm was founded by Elbert Hubbard. Products produced included pottery, furniture, metalware, jewelry and leatherwork.

R.S. GERMANY porcelain with a variety of marks was produced at the Tillowitz, Germany, factory of Reinhold Schlegelmilch from about 1869 to 1956.

R.S. PRUSSIA porcelain was produced during the mid-1800s by Erdman Schlegelmilch in Suhl. His brother, Reinhold, founded a factory in 1869 in Tillowitz in lower Silesia. Both made fine qualtiy porcelain, using both satin and high gloss finishes with comparable decoration. Additionally, both brothers used the same R.S. mark in the same colors, the initials being in memory of their father, Rudolph Schlegelmilch. It has not been determined when production at the two factories ceased.

RUSKIN is a Brittish art pottery. The pottery, located at West Smethwick, Birmingham, England, was started by William H. Taylor. His name was used as the mark until around 1899. The firm discontinued producing new pieces of pottery in 1933, but continued to glaze and market their remaining wares until 1935. Ruskin pottery is noted for its exceptionally fine glazes.

SAMPSON WARE dates from the early 19th century. The firm was founded in Paris and reproduced a variety of collectible wares including Chelsea, Meissen and Oriental Lowestoft, with marks which distinguish their wares as reproductions. The firm is still in production.

SATSUMA is a Japanese pottery having a distinctive creamy crackled glaze decorated with bright enamels and often with Japanese figures. The majority of the ware available today includes the mass-produced wares dating from the 1850s. Their quality does not compare to the fine early examples.

SEWER TILE — Sewer tile figures were made by workers at sewer tile and pipe factories during the late nineteenth and early twentieth centuries. Vases and figurines with added decorations are now considered folk art by collectors.

SHAWNEE POTTERY — The Shawnee Pottery Company was founded in 1937 in Zanesville, OH, The plant closed in 1961.

SHEARWATER POTTERY — was founded by G.W. Anderson, along with his wife and their three sons. Local Ocean Springs, MS, clays were used to produce their wares during the 1930s, and the company is still in business.

SLEEPY EYE — The Sleepy Eye Milling Company, Sleepy Eye, MN, used the image of the 19th century Indian chief for advertising purposes from 1883 to 1921. The company offered a variety of premiums.

SPATTERWARE is a softpaste tableware, laboriously decorated with hand-drawn flowers, birds, buildings, trees, etc., with "spatter" decoration chiefly as a background. It was produced in considerable quantity from the early 1800s to around 1850.

To achieve this type of decoration, small bits of sponge were cut into different shapes—leaves, hearts, rosettes, vines, geometrical patterns, etc.—and mounted on the end of a short stick for convenience in dipping into the pigment.

SPONGEWARE, as it is known, is a decorative white earthenware. Color—usually blue, blue/green, brown/tan/blue, or blue/brown—was applied to the white clay base. Because the color was often applied with a colorsoaked sponge, the term "spongeware" became common for this ware. A variety of utilitarian items were produced—pitchers, cookie jars, bean pots, water coolers, etc. Marked examples are rare.

STAFFORDSHIRE is a district in England where a variety of pottery and porcelain wares has been produced by many factories in the area.

STICKSPATTER — The term identifies a type of decoration that combines hand-painting and transfer-painted decoration. "Spattering" was done with either a sponge or brush containing a moderate supply of pigment. Stickspatter was developed from the traditional Staffordshire spatterware, as the earlier ware was time consuming and expensive to produce. Although most of this ware was made in England from the 1850s to the late 1800s, it was also produced in Holland, France and elsewhere.

TEA LEAF is a lightweight stone china decorated with copper or gold "tea leaf" sprigs. It was first made by Anthony Shaw of Longport, England, during the 1850s. By the late 1800s, other potters in Staffordshire were producing the popular ware for export to the United States. As a result, there is a noticeable diversity in decoration.

TECO POTTERY is an art pottery line made by the Terra Cotta Tile works of Terra Cotta, Illinois. The firm was organized in 1881 by William D. Gates. The Teco line was first made in 1885 but not sold commercially until 1902 and was discontinued during the 1920s.

UHL POTTERY — This pottery was made in Evansville, IN, in 1854. In 1908 the pottery was moved to Huntingburg, IN, where their stoneware and glazed pottery was made until the mid-1940s.

UNION PORCELAIN WORKS — The company first marked their wares with an eagle's head holding the letter "S" in its beak in around 1876; the letters "U.P.W." were sometimes added.

VAN BRIGGLE POTTERY was established at Colorado Springs, Colorado, in 1900 by Artus Van Briggle and his wife, Anna. Most of the ware was marked. The first mark included two joined "As," representing their first two initials. The firm is still in operation.

VILLEROY & BOCH — The pottery was founded in 1841 at Mettlach, Germany. The firm produced many types of pottery including the famous Mettlach steins. Although most of their wares were made in the city of Mettlach, they also had factories in other locations. Fortunately for collectors, there is a dating code impressed on the bottom of most pieces that makes it possible to determine the age of the piece.

VOLKMAR pottery was made by Charles Volkmar, New York, from 1879 to around 1911. Volkmar had been a painter, therefore many of his artistic designs often look like oil paintings drawn on pottery.

WALRATH — Frederick Walrath worked in Rochester, NY, New York City, and at the Newcomb Pottery in New Orleans, LA. He signed his pottery items "Walrath Pottery." He died in 1920.

WARWICK china was made in Wheeling, WV, in a pottery from 1887 to 1951. The most familiar Warwick pieces have a shaded brown background. Many pieces were made with hand painted or decal decorations. The word ILGA is sometimes included with the Warwick mark.

WEDGWOOD POTTERY was established by Josiah Wedgwood in 1759 in England. A tremendous variety of fine wares has been produced through the years including basalt, lusterwares, creamware, jasperware, bisque, agate, Queen's Ware and others. The system of marks used by the firm clearly indicates when each piece was made.

Since 1940 the new Wedgwood factory has been located at Barleston.

WELLER POTTERY — Samuel A. Weller established the Weller pottery in 1872 in Fultonham, Ohio. In 1888 the pottery was moved to Piece Street in Putnam, Ohio—now a part of Zanesville, Ohio. The production of art pottery began in 1893 and by late 1897 several prestige lines were being produced including Samantha, Touranda and Dicken's Ware. Other later types included Weller's Louwelsa, Eosian, Aurora, Turada and the rare Sicardo which is the most sought after and most expensive today. The firm closed in 1948.

WHEATLEY — Thomas J. Wheatley worked with the founders of the art pottery movement in Cincinnati, Ohio. He established the Wheatley Pottery in 1880, which was purchased by the Cambridge Tile Manufacturing Company in 1927.

A-MA Aug. 1996   Rafael Osona

Worchester China, Eng., ca. 1807-13, partial set shown, each piece finely painted w/ approx. 70 differing centering shells in gilt & seaweed against white ground, surrounded by cobalt band borders of gilt vine-work comprising 100 pcs. $10,000.00

A-NH Aug. 1996   Northeast Auctions

Chinese Export Porcelain Dinner Service, each decor. w/ figures & scrolls in black & orange w/ gilt highlights. Comprising: 2 rec. cov. veg. dishes, 2 oval cov. veg. dishes, 2 shaped serving dishes, large well & tree platter, platter w/ strainer, 3 nested platters, cir. deep dish, oval deep platter, leaf dish, 18 dinner, soup, luncheon plates and side dishes $7000.00

A-MA Aug. 1996   Northeast Auctions

Canton
Row 1
Strap-Handle Coffeepot w/ teapot & creamer $1,150.00
Two Strap-Handle Mugs, largest 5½" H $550.00
Canton Pitcher, 6" H $650.00
Row 2
Salad Bowl, sq. cut, 9½" L . .$800.00
Two Similar Trencher Salts, 3½" $850.00
Rectangular Ice Cream Tray, 14" L $2,600.00
Square Salad Bowl, 10" . . .$900.00
Row 3
Seven Hot Water Plates, w/ 8 domed covers & pod finals .$3,000.00
Rectangular Covered Brush Box, 8" L $1,700.00
Rectangular Covered Brush Box, 8" L $1,900.00
Octagonal Platter, 17" L .$1,000.00

A-MA Aug. 1996   Robert C. Eldred Co., Inc.

Chinese Export Porcelain Soup Tureen w/ yellow on salmon decor., two blue dot bands & sepia landscape medallions $2,530.00

A-MA Aug. 1996   Robert C. Eldred Co., Inc.

Chinese Export Covered Tureen, blue & white w/ monogrammed armorial-type shields, 14½" L . . .$1,760.00

A-MA Aug. 1996   Robert C. Eldred Co., Inc.

Canton Candlesticks, one w/ repr. & one w/ chip, 9½" H $1,540.00
Canton Covered Boxes, set of three, largest 4½" H, smallest 2½" H $357.50
Chinese Export Salt w/ floral decor, 3¼" L $132.00
Chinese Export Master Salts, two, blue & white, 12½" diam. . . .$302.50
Fitzhugh Platter, 12 1/2" diam $286.00

A-OH May 1996   Garth's Auction

Gaudy Dutch

Row 1, Left to Right

Waste Bowl, dove, wear & stains, 6½"
D, 3¼" H $825.00

Toddy Plate, carnation, rim has minor
enamel flaking, 6½" D $935.00

Row 2, Left to Right

Plate, rose, wear & scratches, 9⅞"
D $550.00

Plate, war bonnet, wear, scratches,
stains & gr. enamel is flaked .$550.00

A-MA Dec. 1995   Skinner, Inc.

Thirty Piece Pink Lustre Partial Dessert Service, (9 illus.) Eng., 1815 c., Spode
of Wilson, each with Greek key border, classical subject and gilt trim, consisting
of seventeen 8" plates; three oval serving dishes, 11" L; four square serving dishes, 8½" L; two shrimp dishes, 7¾" L; two oval sauce tureens w/ covers and underplates, 7" handle to handle; two covered fruit coolers with insert bowls and lin-
ers, 12" H $6,325.00

A-MA Dec. 1995   Skinner, Inc.

Moorcroft Anemone Design Vase, Eng., ca. 1932, blue ground, impressed mark
and paper label, 4" H $316.25

Moorcroft Blue Ground Pansy Vase, Eng., ca. 1930, signed and impressed
marks, 6" H $172.50

Moorcroft Florian Ware Vase, Eng., ca. 1900, blue decorated poppy design,
signed and printed marks, 5½" H $747.50

Macintyre Moorcroft Aurelian Ware Vase, Eng., ca. 1897, underglazed blue
transfer print enhanced with red enamel and gilding, printed mark, 9" H $517.50

Moorcroft Pansy Vase, Eng., ca. 1930, blue ground, signed and impressed marks,
7" H $345.00

Moorcroft Leaf and berry Vase, Eng., ca. 1945, green ground, signed and
impressed marks, 6¼" H $287.50

A-OH Nov. 1995   Garth's Auction

Canton

Left to Right

Row 1

Plates, (1 of 4), Nanking pattern, 1 w/
chip, 9" D $220.00

Posset Cup, w/ mismatched cover, 2
pcs., 3½" H $385.00

Serving Plate, Nanking patt. w/ gilded
rim, 9⅞" W, 10½" L $385.00

Plate, minor edge flakes & short hairline, 9¼" D $16.50

Row 2

Oval Dish, 10⅜ D $330.00

Pitcher, w/ edge flakes,
6¾" H $797.50

Platter, 12¼" L $660.00

Teapot, worn gilding, 5¼" H .$550.00

Vegetable Dish, w/ cover (not pictured), 11⅜" L $440.00

A-PA Nov. 1995   Pook & Pook Inc.

Spatter Plate, red & blue rainbow, 9"
dia., chips, together w/ blue spatter
decor. plate w/ centered red flower,
9¾" dia. $125.00

A-MA Aug. 1996 Robert C. Eldred Co., Inc.

Delft Charger, w/ yellow edge & blue floral decor., 13½" diam. $330.00

A-OR Aug. 1996 O'Gallerie, Inc.

Belleek Nautilus on Coral, faint 1st blk. mark & incised "Belleek Co., Fermanagh" on base, 8" H $375.00

Belleek Nautilus on Coral, w/ 1st mark in blue & incised "Belleek, Co., Fermanagh" on base, 8" H . . .$425.00

A-OR Aug. 1996 O'Gallerie, Inc.

Belleek Aberdeen Vases, left & right, 2nd blk. mark, 6" H . . .$425.00

Belleek Flower Pot, w/ applied roses & shamrocks, 2nd blk. mark, 4¼" H $425.00

A-MA Aug. 1996 Robert C. Eldred Co., Inc.

Oyster Plates, 1 of 5 w/ fish decor. $412.00

Clamshell-Form Plate, w/ painted & raised decor. for 4 oysters & scallop, mkd. Union Porcelain Works, 8½" L $104.50

Limoges Shellfish Plates, 1 of 5 w/ gold decor., 8½" Diam. $357.50

A-OR Aug. 1996 O'Gallerie, Inc.

Belleek Tri-Dolphin Comport, 1st blk. mark w/ incised "Belleek Co., Fermanagh, 5⅛" H $1,100.00

Belleek Thorn Tea Ware Triple Bucket, w/ Mop finish, 1st mark (1863-1890) in blue, 5½" H .$1,400.00

A-MA Aug. 1996 Robert C. Eldred Co., Inc.

Vienna Porcelain Fish Service, includes 14 9½" dinner plates, 11" covered dish, 11 6" bone dishes, sauce boat w/ undertray & ladle, & serving platter 23½" L, 2 handles damaged $495.00

A-MA Aug. 1996 Robert C. Eldred Co., Inc.

Faience Pottery Wine Ewer, decor. w/hand painted grape leaves & clusters, 30" H $385.00

A-MA Aug. 1996 Robert C. Eldred Co., Inc.

Meissen
Footed Fenestrated Compote, in blue & white, crossed swords mark, 9" H, 9½" Diam. $275.00

Handled Platter, in blue & white w/ gilt edge, crossed swords mark, 19¼" L $330.00

Covered Soup Tureen, in blue & white, crossed swords mark, 13" L $330.00

A-MA Aug. 1996 Robert C. Eldred Co., Inc.

Quimper Lavabo, 3 pcs., w/ floral decor. on yellow ground, mkd. "Henriot Quimper France", 14¾" H $247.50

A-MA Oct. 1995   Skinner, Inc.

Left to Right

148-Blue Fitzhugh Oval Platter, w/ mis-matched inset, chips, 17¼" L . . . . .NS
160A-Canton Tile, China, 19th c., rim chips, 7"x7". $402.50
149-Nanking Cider Jug, China, 19th c., repr. to base, 11" H $920.00
521-Sauce Tureens, (2nd, bottom left), blue & white, 19th c., one w/ mismatched cover, 7¾"-8"L $402.50
Canton Syllabub Cup, no reference
153-Canton Fruit Basket, w/ mismatched undertray, China, 19th c., minor chips, 4¾" H, 11" L, 9¾" W. . . . . .NS
149A-Imperial Nanking Teapot, China, 19th c., hairlines to cover, 7" H $345.00
150-Blue Fitzhugh Shrimp Dish, China, 19th c., rim chips, 10½" L $488.75
150-Blue Fitzhugh Covered Sugar Bowl, China, 19th c., 7" dia. $488.75

A-MA Dec. 1995   Skinner, Inc.
Left to Right
Four-Piece Assembled Etruscan Teaset, PA, ca. 1880, Griffen, Smith &

Hill Potteries, covered teapot, slight nick to spout, small line at rim, int. cover chip, 5⅜" H, covered sugar, 5⅜" H, cream pitcher, rim chips, 3½" H; bowl, slight hairline, 5" dia. .$1092.50
Four Etruscan Majolica Shell and Seaweed Items, PA, 1880 c., Griffen, Smith and Hill Potteries, footed bowl, rim chip, 8" dia., spooner, 3½" H, two butter pats, one damaged, 3" dia. $690.00

A-OH Nov. 1995   Garth's Auction

Row 1, Left to Right
Spatterware Handleless Cups, (4) miniatures, 1 w/ blue spatter, 3 w/ red & gr. rainbow spatter, wear, stains & flakes $264.00
Row 2
Spatterware Saucer, green w/ peafowl decor. in red, bl., yellow, & blk., stains, 4½" D $192.50
Staffordshire Cup Plate, dark bl. transfer, "Broadlands, Hampshire, R. Halls Scenery", 4" D $187.00
Spatterware Creamer, blue & white, stain on handle, sm. flakes on foot, 4½" H $60.50
Spatterware Saucer, w/ peafowl decor. in red, bl., yellow & blk., stains, 4½ D $203.50
Row 3
Spatterware Handleless C/S, mismatched, w/peafowl decor., cut w/ sm. edge flakes. $220.00
Spatterware Creamer, blue w/ 4 part flower in red & gr., stains, glaze flakes & crack in base of handle, 4½ H $126.50
Spatterware Handleless C/S, w/ peafowl decor. in bl., yellow, gr. & blk., chips on saucer. $165.00
Spatterware Creamer, blue w/ stenciled bl. flower, stains & hairlines, 4½ H $71.50
Spatterware Handleless C/S, red w/ stains, wear & hairline $60.50

A-OH Nov. 1995   Garth's Auction

Ovoid Stoneware Jug W/ Strap Handle, incised eagle & shield with arrows & olive branch & highlighted in cobalt blue, chips & hairlines in base, handle is restored, 14" H $385.00

A-MA Oct. 1995   Skinner, Inc.

Marblehead Pottery Sailing Ship Bookends, pr., blue, dark blue, light blue, red, black & mustard/green, one chip to back edge, 5½" H, 5½" W $460.00

Pottery Workshop of Boston Vase, Boston, 1921-27, inscribed P.W. of B., 8¾" H, 5¾" D . . . .$NS

Paul Revere Pottery Vase, Boston, 1926, inscribed date, 4¼" H, 5¼ D $488.75

Saturday Evening Girls Pottery Pitcher, Boston, 1926, 7½" H, 5⅛" D $862.50

Chelsea Keramic Art Works Lamp Base, Chelsea, MA, ca. 1880, drilled center bottom, 7¼" H, 4¾" D $172.50

A-MA Dec. 1995   Skinner, Inc.

Minton Pate-Sur-Pate Lawrence Birks Vase, Eng., 1893, soft salmon-colored ground with brown ground oval medallions, farming implements in white relief on opp. side, artist signed, 7¾" H $2530.00

Minton Pate-Sur-Pate Louis Solon Hildesheim Tray, Eng., 1878, mfg. for the Paris Exhib. of 1878, deep brown ground w/ white relief, artist signed & dated, two rim chips, 13"L .$4255.00

Minton Pate-Sur-Pate Covered Vase, Eng., late 19th c., cream ground w/ brn. ground oval medallions and wht. relief, slight gilt loss to cover rim, 9¼" H $2760.00

A-MA Oct. 1995   Skinner, Inc.

Hampshire Pottery

Vase, 6⅝" H, 3¾" D $517.50

Double Handle Vase, 5½" H, 7¾" L $230.00

Melon Pitcher, unsigned, interior spout staining, 8" H $258.75

Chamberstick, 5½" H, 4⅞" D .$201.25

Vase, 6¾" H, 3¾" D $373.75

A-MA Oct. 1995   Skinner, Inc.

Teco Pottery Vase, Terra Cotta, designed by William J. Dodd, 11⅝" H, 4¼" D $5,750.00

A-MA Dec. 1995   Skinner, Inc.

Belleek Covered Oval Openwork Basket, Ire., 1885 c., three strand plaiting, applied floral dec. ribbon mark, (sm. chips to relief), 12¼" L $2185.00

Belleek Covered Oval Openwork Basket, Ire., ca. 1885, three strand plaiting, applied floral dec. ribbon mark, (sm. chips to relief), 11¼" L $1955.00

A-MA Aug. 1995   Skinner, Inc.

Blue Onion Pattern Porcelain Dinner Service, 19th/20th c., mostly Meissen, some other manuf., service for 12 w/ approx. 15 service pieces $8,337.50

A-MA Oct. 1995   Skinner, Inc.

Rose Mandarin Punch Bowl, China, 19th c., 14½" dia. $1840.00

A-MA Dec. 1995   Skinner, Inc.

Belleek Finner Flower Pot, Ire., ca. 1905, second black mark, (chips to relief), 6⅜" H, 11" handle to handle. $1265.00

Belleek Two-Handled Sydenham Basket,, mid 20th c., four strand plaiting with all over pearl glaze and painted floral decoration, impressed pads marked, 10¾" dia. $690.00

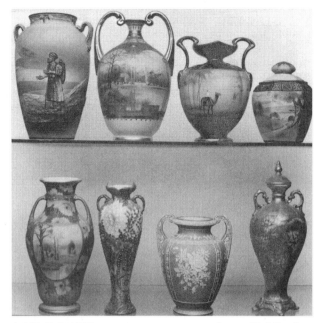

A-MA Oct. 1995   James D. Julia, Inc.

Nippon

Row 1

Vase, matt finish, green "M" mark, 10" H $1,250.00

Scenic Vase, jade/green border w/ landscape design, green "M" mark, 10½" H $350.00

Cobalt Blue Egyptian Scene Vase, matt finish, green "M" mark, 9" H, 5" W $550.00

Covered Humidor w/ landscape scene done in shades of pink & cream w/ green and brown, green "M" mark, 7" H, 6" W $125.00

Row 2

Scenic Vase, matt finish, brown & beige background w/ yellow flowers & gold trim, 11" H, 6" W $150.00

Vase, jeweled purple & white Chrysanthemum, all over gold jewels in a banded & circle patt., blue leaf mark, 11" H $325.00

Jasper Style Vase, royal blue background w/ all over white floral & geometric decor., daisy & peony, green "M" mark, 8" H, 6" W $300.00

Covered Urn, gold enamel decor. & white Carnation like flowers against a green background, blue leaf mark, 13" H $450.00

A-MA Aug. 1996   Robert C. Eldred
                                          Co., Inc.

Canton

Gravy Boat, 19th C., 7" L . . .$165.00
Globular Teapot, 5½" H . . .$302.50
Octagonal Platter, 17½" x 14½" $577.50
Hot Water Dish, 19th C., 9¼" diam. $176.00
Drum-Form Teapot, 19th C., 6" H $412.50

A-MA Aug. 1996   Robert C. Eldred
                                          Co., Inc.

Chinese Porcelain Garden Seats, 19th C., 19" H $2,970.00

A-MA Aug. 1996   Robert C. Eldred
                                          Co., Inc.

Japanese Garden Seats, 18½" H $440.00

A-MA Aug. 1996   Robert C. Eldred
                                          Co., Inc.

Famille Rose Bowl, w/ allover flowering vines on yellow ground, circular panels depict dragons & phoenix, 6" H, 15" diam. , , ,$1,155.00

A-MA Aug. 1996   Robert C. Eldred
                                    Co., Inc.

Quimper Candlesticks, (L & R), blue & maroon w/ floral decor., mkd. "HB Quimper, France", 8¾" H $99.00
French Faience Charger, bird & vase decor. on blue ground w/ scallop edge, chips, 13¾" diam. $220.00
Malicorne Scallop-Edged Pottery Platter, ca. 1890, 11½" L, 8¼" W $440.00

A-OH   Jan. 1996 Garth's Auction

Row One, Left to Right,

Bennington Candlestick, olive mottled glaze, lip has old prof. repr.. 8¾" H $357.50

Bennington Candlestick, flint enamel glaze, 6⅞" H $715.00

Bennington Candlestick, flint enamel glaze, 6⅝" H $462.00

Bennington Candlestick, Rockingham glaze, 7¾" H $357.50

Bennington Candlestick, Rockingham glaze, 8" H $467.50

Row Two, Left to Right,

Bennington Pitcher, w/ "1849" mk., alternate rib patt. in flint enamel that is yell., blk., and brn., very minor wear and pinpoint flake, 8" H $940.00

Bennington Tulip Vase, flint enamel but green is a black olive, pinpoint flakes, 10" H $907.50

Bennington Hound Handled Pitcher, w/ molded vintage, hounds and stag, Rockingham glaze, 9½"H $605.00

A-MA Mar. 1996   Skinner, Inc.

Sevres Style Painted Porcelain & Gilt Metal Mounted Potpourri Urns, pr., ca. 1880, painted on both sides w/ figural & landscape panels on cobalt blue ground, 18½" H $2,530.00

A-MA Jan. 1996   Skinner, Inc.

Clarice Cliff Pottery

Row 1, left to right

Coral Fins Vase, 8¼" H $690.00

Salad Bowl, w/ serving pcs. w/ yel. & orange flowers, br. stems, 4" H .$230.00

"Windmills" Vase, w/ tree band in yel., red., gr., bl., & blk., sign., 8" H . . . .NS

Row 2, left to right

Corset Vase, w/ floral sprays in gr., bl., yel. & br., 9¼" H $805.00

"Harvest Teapot", w/ fruit & florals, 6½" H $230.00

Inspiration Vase, w/ flower frog & floral bouquets on sides, hairline, 4¾" H NS

Row 3

Inspiration Lily Vase, purple lilies over blue/green ground, 7" H $373.75

Row 4, left to right

Autumn Lotus Jug, w/ landscape scene of trees, house in yel. & orange, 11¾" H $575.00

Delicia Citrus Vase, blue & green drips surrounding oranges & lemons, 7¾" H $805.00

Row 5, left to right

Fantasque Pitcher, orange & bl. flowers, 7¾" H $747.50

Circular-Form Vase, w/ white & red striping, 6" H . . . . .NS

Circular Vase, w/ bands of orange, yel. & bl., 8" H $230.00

A-MA Oct. 1995   Skinner, Inc.

Rookwood Pottery Vase, Matt A. Daly, 1886, incised artist's initials, 7" H, 8" D $345.00

Bisque Finished Reversible Lidded Potpourri Jar, Artus Van Briggle, 1887, incised artist's initials/S, 6" H, 6¼" D $690.00

Iris Glaze Vase, Carl Schmidt, 1900, incised artist's cipher and W, 8⅝" H, 4¼" D $1,150.00

A-PA Nov. 1995   Pook & Pook Inc.

Spatter Covered Sugar Bowl, red & green, 4½" H $200.00

A-MA Oct. 1995   Skinner, Inc.

Row 1

Clarice Cliff Pottery
Gardenia Lotus Jug, Eng., org., blue, black, purple, rust & shades of green, 11⅜" H, 7⅛" D $1,265.00
Vase, Eng., gilt stars & blue planets, 16¼" H, 9¾" D .NS
Delicia Citrus Lotus Jug, Eng., stylized fruit in org., yellow, blue & green, 11⅝" H, 7¼" D $517.50

Row 2

Crocus Lotus Jug, Eng., org., blue, purple, greens, yellow & rust, 11⅜" H, 7⅛" D $690.00
Coral Firs Lotus Jug, Eng., org., red, yellow & shades of brown, with black outlining, 11⅝" H, 7¼" D $805.00
Aurea Lotus Jug, Eng., blended green, blue, brown, gray, yellow and rose, 11¼" H, 7⅛" D $920.00

Row 3

Anemone Lotus Jug, Eng., shades of blue with black, pale pink & green, 11⅝" H, 7¼" D $345.00
Rhodanthe Pitcher, Eng., blended orange, yellow, brown and gray, 6⅝" H, 3⅝" D $431.25
Secrets Pitcher, Eng., stylized landscape in yellow, rust, brown and shades of green, 7"H, 4" D $517.50
Rhodanthe Bowl, Eng., blended orange, yellow, gray, brown & black, 2⅞" H, 7⅝" D $373.75
Secrets Lotus Jug, Eng., stylized landscape in yellow, rust, brown and shades of green, 11⅜" H, 7¼" D $1,380.00

A-MA Oct. 1995   Skinner, Inc.

Rookwood Pottery
Standard Glaze Vase, Mary Nourse, 1893, incised artist's initials, 7⅜" H, 5¼" D $575.00
Standard Glaze Vase, Clara C. Lindeman, 1906, incised artist's initials, crazing, 7" H, 3¼" D $460.00
Light Standard Glaze Vase, Artus Van Briggle, 1887, incised artist's initials and L, crazing, 8¼" H, 4" D $517.50
Limoges Style Jug, Albert R. Valentien, 1882, incised G & artist's initials, 4⅝" H, 2¾" D $488.75
Bowl & Creamer, sage green, standard glaze, Mary A. Taylor, 1886, incised artist's cipher & initials, 2⅝" H, 5" D; & 2¾" H, 4" D $373.75

A-MA Dec. 1995   Skinner, Inc.

Sunderland Pink Lustre Puzzle Jug, Eng., ca.1820, rim chip, small edge chip to one nozzle, 6½" H $747.50
Staffordshire Pink Lustre Lion-Form Furniture Rests, Eng., ca. 1820, one with hairlines, 3¾" H $1092.50
Pink Resist Lustre Quintal Flower Holder, Eng., ca. 1815, fluted spouts w/ blue trimmed scalloped rims, rim chip repairs, 7¾" H $575.00

A-MA Dec. 1995   Skinner, Inc.

Etruscan Majolica Shell and Seaweed Serving Dish, PA, ca. 1880, Griffen, Smith and Hill Potteries, impressed mark, rim chips, hairline, 13¾" L $488.75
Two Etruscan Majolica Shell and Seaweed Pitchers, PA, ca. 1880, Griffen, Smith and Hill Potteries, 5, 5¾" H $747.50
Etruscan Majolica Shell and Seaweed Bowl, PA, ca. 1880, Griffen, Smith and Hill Potteries, rim chips, 8½ dia....................$143.75

A-MA Dec. 1995   Skinner, Inc.

Left to Right
Copeland Majolica Pitcher, Eng., ca. 1877, impressed mark and registry code, hairline to handle, 7½" H $1495.00
Copeland Majolica Centerpiece, Eng., ca. 1875, base modeled with coral, impressed mark, rim chip repair, 12" H $977.50
Majolica Pitcher, Eng., late 19th c., brown leaf molded body, impressed mark, slight rim lines, 5½" H $143.75

A-MA Oct. 1995   Skinner, Inc.
Left to Right
George Ohr Pottery Vase, Biloxi, MI, ca. 1901, incised signature, 6" H, 5¾" D $1,495.00
Newcomb College Pottery
Scenic Vase, Anna Frances Simpson, ca. 1915, 7¼" H, 4" D $2,185.00
Low Bowl, Henrietta Bailey, ca. 1915, hairline, 2⅜" H, 6¾" D $488.75
Bowl, Sadie Irvine, ca. 1910, 4⅛" H, 8⅜" D $1,092.50
Bowl, possibly Sadie Irvine, ca. 1920, 3" H, 5" D $862.50
Vase, ca. 1915, Sadie Irvine, 4⅝" H, 2" D $747.50

A-MA Aug. 1995   Skinner, Inc.

Nodders
Left to Right
Bisque, Chinese, early 20th c., 9" H ....$NS
Porcelain figure, Chinese, early 20th c., 19½" H $1,840.00
Bisque Figure, Chinese, early 20th c., 6¾" H $172.50
Chinese Style Figures, pr., .$977.50

A-MA Dec. 1995   Skinner, Inc.

Staffordshire Pink Lustre Quintal Vases, Eng., ca. 1820, wear to spout rims, 7½". $920.00
Pink Lustre Egg Cup Stand, Eng., ca. 1825, possibly Swansea, 8¼", and six egg cups, one repaired, 1¾". $690.00

A-OH Mar 1996   Garth's Auction
Row 1
Mocha Pitcher, w/ tooled bands in blue, black & tan stripes & blue band w/ earthworm, short hairlines on bottom and in handle, pinpoint edge flakes, 6¾" H $1,155.00
Pearlware Plate w/ Green Feather Rim, leeds eagle decor. in black, blue, green and yellow ochre, wear, minor glaze flakes, 8⅛" D $660.00
Parian Bust of John Milton, wear, 7½" H $55.00
Row 2
Staffordshire Soup Plates, (1 of 3), light blue transfer "Japanese", one w/ chip on table ring, 10⅛" D ...$247.00
English Porcelain Cups & Saucer, (2 Of 5), black classical design & Gaudy Welsh are pictured, others are pink luster, oriental transfer & oriental transfer w/ polychrome, minor damage..................$165.00
Staffordshire Soup Plates, (1 of 3) one red transfer w/India landscape, 10⅝" D and 2 light blue "Grecian Scenery", 1 has light stain, 10¼" D $214.50

A-PA May 1996   Skinner, Inc.

Left to right

Whieldon Ware Cauliflower Creamer & Cover, Eng., late 18th C., green glazed leaves, 5½" H $1,265.00

Whieldon Ware Cauliflower Teapot, Eng., 18th C., green glazed leaves, spout repair, 4½" H $805.00

Whieldon Ware Cauliflower Tea Canister, Eng., 18th C., green glazed leaves, rim chips & repair, 3⅝" H $230.00

Whieldon Ware Pineapple Covered Sugar Bowl, Eng., ca. 1765, translucent green & yellow glazes, restored, 4¼" H $805.00

A-PA May 1996   Skinner, Inc.

Wedgwood Black Basalt

Row 1, left to right

Bull Dog, Eng., ca. 1915, w/ glass eyes, marked, 5" L $258.75

Squirrel, Eng., ca. 1915, marked, 2½" H $690.00

Row 2

Poodle, Eng., ca. 1918, w/ imp. mark, 3" H $373.75

Elephant, Eng., ca. 1918, imp. mark, 3½" H .690.00

Bear, Eng., ca. 1915, imp. mark, 2½" H 747.50

A-PA May 1996   Skinner, Inc.

Wedgwood Moonlight Lustre

Left to right

Cup & Saucer, Eng., ca. 1810 w/imp. marks, glaze wear $230.00

Caudle Cup & Saucer, Eng., ca. 1815, imp. marks, cup 3¾" H . . .$316.25

Pink Lustre Pitcher, 3⅛" H, cup, pitcher, 3½" H w/spout chip, rest., marked $402.50

A-PA May 1996   Skinner, Inc.

Wedgwood Black Basalt

Row 1, left to right

Miniature Teapot, Eng., ca. 1860 w/ enamel floral decor, marked, 2⅛" H $460.00

Vase, w/ enamel decor, Eng., mid 19th C., w/ enamel floral decor., marked, foot rim chip, 4" H $431.25

Row 2

Club Pitcher, Eng., ca. 1870, w/ floral sprays, body hairlines, marked, 7½" H $230.00

Teapot w/ cover, Eng., ca. 1850, w/ floral sprays, marked, 4" H . .$460.00

Teapot w/ cover, Eng., ca. 1850, w/ floral spray, marked, int. strainer damage, 7" H $632.50

A-PA May 1996   Skinner, Inc.

Wedgwood Caneware

Row 1, left to right

Glazed Teapot & Cover, Eng., ca. 1820, arabesque molded w/ spaniel finial, imp. mark, spout & cover chip, 5" H $230.00

Vase, Eng., early 19th C., w/rosso antico leafy vinework, imp. mark, repr. to relief, no cover, 5¾" H $115.00

Crater Urn & Cover, Eng., early 19th C., rosso antico foliate reliefs, imp. mark rest. to base, insert cover missing, 5¼" H $575.00

Row 2

Circular-Form Game Pie Dish, Eng., ca. 1820, fruiting grapevine relief, imp. mark, w/ slight rim nicks, 3½" dia. . . $632.50

Inkwell, Eng., ca. 1800, black basalt foliate relief decor., handles rest., imp. mark, 2¼" H $373.75

Two Items, Eng., 19th C., each w/ drab relief decor., bowl w/fern decor., 5¼" dia., mkd., rim reprs., chip to cover, vase w/classical decor., mkd., no cover, 3⅜" H $316.25

A-PA May 1996   Skinner, Inc.

Left to right

Wedgwood Light Blue Jasper Dip Clock Case, Eng., late 19th C., white classical relief, firing lines, slight relief loss, 6¼" H $287.50

Wedgwood Three-Color Jasper Dip Jam Pot, Eng., mid 19th C., white classical relief w/figures & horses to a dark blue ground centering light blue borders, silver plated lid, impressed mark, 3⅜" $460.00

Wedgwood Lilac Jasper Dip Covered Jar, Eng., ca. 1869, white relief of trophies, impressed marks, rim nick to cover, 5" H $517.50

Wedgwood Light Blue Jasper Dip Portland Vase, Eng., late 19th C., white classical relief, 5" H . . .$345.00

Wedgwood Green Jasper Dip Covered Tobacco Jar, Eng., late 19th C., white relief portrait medallions of Lafayette, Franklin & Washington, 7½" H $517.50

A-PA Dec. 1995   Horst Auction Center

Historic Blue Staffordshire,

Row 1, left to right

Platter, "Landing of Lafayette", Clews, 12½" x 9¼" $375.00

Mug, lt. blue, unidentified scenic patt., 5⅝" H $85.00

Row 2

Platter, "Beauties of America, St. Paul's Church, Boston", mkd. J&W Ridgway, 9½" x 6¾" $600.00

Plate, "Beauties of America, Library, Phil.", mkd. J&W Ridgway, 10½" dia. $290.00

A-PA May 1996   Skinner, Inc.

Five Stoneware Wine Cask Labels,
Eng., 19th C., 4 mkd. Wedgwood titled
Maderia, Port, Moselle & Sherry
Copeland titled Champagne w/imp.
mark, 5¾" L $632.50

A-PA May 1996   Skinner, Inc.

Wedgwood Three-Color Jasper

Vases, pr., (1st & 3rd in photo), Eng.,
mid 19th C., classical, foliate & trophy
reliefs in green & lilac, marks, top rims
& socles restored, 6¼" H . .$1,265.00

Clock Case, Eng., late 19th C., white
body w/ applied green roliate reliefs
surrounding lilac figural reliefs of
Father Time & Domestic Employment
subjects, titled motto in relief "Tempus
Fugit", mark, surface staining, foot rim
chip, 8" H $920.00

Vase, Eng., late 19th C., white ground
w/ green & lilac classical foliate reliefs,
restorations, 5⅛" H $460.00

Vase & Cover, ca. 1885, green & lilac
foliate reliefs to white ground, marked,
7" H $1,265.00

A-PA May 1996   Skinner, Inc.

Wedgwood Black Jasper
Left to right

Portland Vase, Eng., ca. 1895, white
classical relief, marked 7" H .$805.00

Chamberstick & Miniature Jug,
(2nd item & back row), Eng., late
19th/early 20th C., white classical
reliefs, 2¼" & 2½" H, marked, $488.75

"Harry Barnard" Creamer, Eng.,
late 19th C., white stylized floral slip,
artist signed, marked, 4⅝" L .$977.50

Covered Teapot, Eng., late 19th C.,
white classical & foliate relief, marked,
4½" H $977.50

A-PA May 1996   Skinner, Inc.

Wedgwood Jasper
Row 1, left to right

Crimson Dip Vase, Eng., ca. 1920,
w/impressed mark, 5" H $920.00
Row 2

Brown Jasper Dip Club Pitcher,
Eng., 19th C., w/impressed mark, 5"
H $977.50

Crimson Jasper Dip Covered Box,
Eng., ca. 1920, w/ imp. mark, 3"
H $862.50

Crimson Jasper Dip Pitcher, Eng.,
ca. 1920, w/imp. mark, rest., 4¾"
H $632.50

A-PA May 1996   Skinner, Inc.

Wedgwood
Left to right

Potpourri Vase & Cover, Eng., ca.
1861, queen's ware body w/hand
painted polychrome enamels, artist
sgn. & makd., 9" H $862.50

Tray, Eng., ca. 1864 w/hand painted
enamel landscape, artist sgn, mkd.
16½" L $862.50

Dish, Eng., ca. 1866 w/enamel decor.,
figural landscape, artist sgn., mkd., 5"
$201.25

A-PA Oct. 1995   Pook & Pook, Inc.

Puzzle Mug, w/relief decor on handle, dark br. glaze, mkd. E.E. OHR, ca.
1900, 3½" H $550.00

A-PA May 1996   Skinner, Inc.

**Wedgwood Majolica Argenta Ware
Stick Stand,** Eng., ca. 1882, hexago-
nal-form w/ raised floral paneled sides
to a cell ground, marked, slight glaze
wear, 21¾" H $2,070.00

A-PA May 1996   Skinner, Inc.

**Wedgwood Hummingbird Lustre
Trumpet Vases,** pr., Eng., ca. 1920,
w/mottled blue exterior & orange interior, flying geese border, printed marks,
6" H $747.50

**Wedgwood Mixed Blue Lustre Cov-
ered Inkwell,** Eng., ca. 1920, gilt
dragon & cloud motifs, window finial
to cover, w/ insert pot, printed marks,
covered restored, 4" H $488.75

A-PA May 1996   Skinner, Inc.

Wedgwood Fairyland Lustre

Bowl, w/ Poplar Trees, Eng., ca. 1920,
black ext., elves & bell branch int.,
mother-of-pearl ground, printed mark,
9⅛" dia. $2,300.00

Octagonal "Firbolgs II" Bowl, Eng.,
ca. 1920, green ground ext., w/ gilt
outlined black figures, Thumbelina
motif int., mother-of-pearl ground,
printed mark, gilt wear, center restoration, 6¼" dia. $345.00

Bowl, w/ Leapfrogging Elves, Eng., ca.
1920, black ext., mother-of-pearl int.
w/ elves on a branch, printed mark,
4⅜" dia. $920.0

A-MA Aug. 1996   Robert C. Eldred
Co., Inc.

Whieldon Plate, w/ scalloped edge, 9½" diam. \$220.00
Whieldon Plate, w/ gadroon & scalloped edge, greem, brown & yellow glaze 209.00

A-MA Aug. 1996   Robert C. Eldred
Co., Inc.

English Blue & White Pearlware, 2 plates 10" diam. & bowl, 7" diam. \$407.00
Liverpool Pitcher, w/ Masonic decor. & restor., 8" H \$192.50

A-MA Aug. 1996   Robert C. Eldred
Co., Inc.

Staffordshire
Row 1, Left to Right
Castle, w/ polychrome bocage & soldier decor., ca. 1860, 9" H . . .\$275.00
Castle, w/ gr. bocage & rust decor. on tan ground, ca. 1860, 8½" H .\$220.00
Castle, w/ gr. bocage & polychrome floral decor., on white ground, ca. 1860, 7" H \$275.00
Castle, w/ polychrome vine decor., stairs & clock, ca. 1860, 8¾"H .\$137.50
Row 2, Left to Right
Cottage, w/ gr. landscape & gr. & orange bocage, ca. 1860, 5½" H .N/S
Cottage, pagoda-form w/ gr. bocage decor., orange & gold highlights, ca. 1880-1900, 6½" H \$154.00
Bank, in form of cottage w/ orange & gr. decor., ca. 1880, 5" H \$192.50
Cottage, w/ pink roof & two ducks in front, ca. 1860-1880, 6¼" H .\$220.00

A-MA Aug. 1996   Robert C. Eldred
Co., Inc.

Left to Right
Eng. Cream Pitcher, possibly Newhall w/ guilted body, red & blue decor., 4½" H \$88.00
Lustre Creamer, w/ pink & gr. highlights & dog decor., 5" H \$187.00
Staffordshire Pottery Teapot, w/ raised strawberry decor., chipped, 6" H \$247.50
Lustre Milk Pitcher, w/ gr. & pink color & dog decor., 6" H \$247.50
Pink Lustre Pitcher, w/ raised ship decor., cherub & ram decor., 6" H \$275.00

A-MA Aug. 1996   Robert C. Eldred
Co., Inc.

Staffordshire Figure, girl carrying wheat & a man w/ wine jug, ca., 1860, 12¼" H \$143.00

A-MA Aug. 1996   Robert C. Eldred
Co., Inc.

Staffordshire
Figural Vase, ca. 1860-80, "Dog Tray", dog w/ red spots, master w/ gr. cape, repr. 12¼" H \$121.00
Figure, "Christ Restoring the Sight to the Blind", w damage, 10½" H \$143.00
Figural Vase, "Robin Hood", 14¾" H \$121.00

A-MA Aug. 1996   Robert C. Eldred
Co., Inc.

Spatterware
Row 1, Left to Right
Sugar Bowl, w/ floral decor., br. & blk. ground, restor., 4" H \$192.50
Plate, mkd. "Meakin", 9½" diam. \$412.50
Cups & Saucers w/ Teapot, (teapot in row 2) Peafowl patt. \$473.00
Handleless Cup & Saucer, pink spatter, cup has reprs. \$27.50
Row 2, Left to Right
Creamer, Peafowl patt., 3" H .\$88.00
Teapot, blue & white w/ house decor., 4½" H \$220.00
Cream Pitcher, blue w/ gr. & red flower design, 3¾" H \$77.00

A-MA Aug. 1996   Robert C. Eldred
Co., Inc.

Staffordshire Spaniels
Pr. in White, w/ gold spots & orange muzzles, ca. 1860, 12¾" H . .\$550.00
Pr. in White, w/ red spots & traces of gold paint, ca. 1850 - 1860, 9¼" H \$495.00
Pr. in White, w/ worn gold lustre highlights, 1 w/ hairline on base, ca. 1870-1890, 8½" H \$220.00
Pr. in White, w/ red spots, 1 w/ foot chip, ca. 1840, 6¼" H \$242.00

A-MA Aug. 1996   Robert C. Eldred
Co., Inc.

Staffordshire
Figural Vases, cows w/ calves & traces of gilt, 11" H, pair \$495.00
Figure, "Suffer Little Children to Come Unto Me", 10⅛" H \$154.00

A-OH Sept. 1995   Garth's Auction

Row 1

Rookwood Horse Head Bookends, pair w/ deep celadon gr. glaze, mkd. "M.H. McDonald", 1954 mark, 6¼" H $275.00

Row 2

Rookwood Vase, salmon pink, & br. pine leaf on a white craquelle ground w/ blue rim, mkd. 1906 & "S. Sax", 9¼" H $1,760.00

Moorcraft Vase, polychrome lotus flower, script signature, 6⅜" H$577.50

Weller Art Pottery Ewer, dk. br. shading to olive w/ flowers, mkd. "Louwelsa Weller", 7" H $154.00

Rookwood Vase, gr. & white Canterbury bells on a white craquelle ground that shades to blue, 1903 mark, 5½" H $462.00

A-MA May 1996   Skinner, Inc.

Van Briggle Art Pottery

Bulbous Vase, w/ embossed leaves & blossoms, mottled green matte glaze, sgn., 9½" H $1,092.50

Ovoid form vase, w/ stylized stems, powdery white matte glaze, obscured mark, 7" H $690.00

Lorelei Vase, ca. 1920's w/ mermaid around top, mulberry glaze, sgn., 10" H $230.00

Vase, w/ 2 handles, green glaze, ca. 1904, mkd., hairlines, 5" H ......N/S

Tapering Vase, w/ leathery deep bronze glaze, sgn. 1906, 8"H .$575.00

A-MA May 1996   Skinner, Inc.

Two Hampshire Pottery Items, vase w/ mottled green glaze, 4½" H, mkd. & large bulbous vase w/ mottled aqua glaze, 8" H $805.00

Hampshire Vase, w/ heavily embossed leaves, green matte glaze, mkd. 8¼" W $575.00

A-MA Aug. 1996   Robert C. Eldred Co., Inc.

Chinese Export Porcelain Drum-form Teapot w/ figural decor., 5½" H $632.50

Drum-Form Teapot, w/ monogram, blue & white, 6" H $247.50

Drum-Form Teapot, w/ Am. eagle decor., 5½" H $687.50

A-MA Aug. 1996   Rafael Osona

Chinese Export Blue & White Vase, early 19th C., decor. w/ panels of birds, butterflies & branches, 13¼"H .$300.00

Chinese Export Blue & White Tureen, 19th C., decor. w/ flowers & butterflies, 7½" H, 12" diam. .$300.00

A-MA Mar. 1996   Skinner, Inc.

A-MA June 1996   Skinner, Inc.

Earthenware Figure, tin glazed peddler, probably France, 19th C., boy w/ lamb in a basket, repr. 8½"H .$316.25

Earthenware Plaque, Prattware polychromed, Eng., late 18th C., depicting a bacchanalian scene, minor chips, hairlines, 10½" H $747.50

A-MA Mar. 1996   Skinner, Inc.

Chinese Hawthorne Temple Jars, pair, 19th C., on hardwood stands, minor chips, 17½" H $2,760.00

A-MA Mar. 1996   Skinner, Inc.

Porcelain Cottage Vases, pair, attrib. to Bennington, mid 19th C., minor chip, gilt wear, 8⅞" H $460.00

Liverpool Creamware Jug, transfer printed, Eng. early 19th C., decor. w/ Masonic symbols, reverse w/ symbols & Masonic motto, chips, cracks, 11¾" H $575.00

Liverpool Creamware Mug, transfer printed, Eng. 19th C., "Come Box the Compass", minor chips & hairlines, 4¾" H $488.75

Liverpool Creamware Jug, transfer printed, Eng. early 19th C., "The Sailor's Return,", chips, crack, 7⅝" H .$632.50

A-MA Oct. 1995   Skinner, Inc.

Row 1t

Spatterware Low Bowls, 4 pcs., 19th c., w/ central floral reserves, minor chips, rim wear, staining, 10¾"-10⅞". $632.50

Flow Blue Charger, 19th c., minor glaze and base chips, knife marks, 17¾" dia. $431.25

Polychrome Decorated Earthenware Plates, 4 pcs. Adams, Eng., 19th c., marked on bases, chips, hairlines, knife marks, 10½"-10⅝". $115.00

Bottom Left

Row 2

Spatterware Items, 12 pcs., 19th c., six cups, four saucers, and two plates w/ peafowl and floral dec, minor imperf.. . . . .$805.00

Bottom Right

Child's Peafowl Spatterware Tea Set, 19th c., tea pot, covered sugar, creamer and three cups, restoration $575.00

A-MA Dec. 1995   Skinner, Inc.

Moorcroft Anemone Decorated Vases, pr. Eng., mid 20th c., dark blue ground, signed and impressed marks, 12" H $460.00

Moorcroft Pansy Two-Handle Vase, Eng., 1930 c., blue ground, signed and impressed marks, 8" H $546.25

A-MA Dec. 1995   Skinner, Inc.

Wedgwood Crimson Jasper Dip Jardiniere, Eng., 1920 c., white classical relief, impressed marks, slight relief loss, 9" H $1265.00

Wedgwood Crimson Jasper Dip Tea Cannister and Cover, Eng., 1920 c., ball finial missing, 5¼" $920.00

Wedgwood Crimson Jasper Dip Pitcher, Eng., 1920 c., 3½" H $747.50

Wedgwood Crimson Jasper Dip Three Handled Mug, Eng., 1920 c., 4¼" H $1035.00

A-MA Dec. 1995   Skinner, Inc.

Wedgwood Fairyland Lustre Punch Bowl, Eng., ca. 1925, pattern Z 4968, hairlines and rim chip restored, gilt wear, 11¼" dia. $1380.00

A-MA Dec. 1995   Skinner, Inc.

Minton Pate-Sur-Pate Louis Solon Plaque, Eng., Last qtr. 19th c. dark brn. ground w/ wht. relief, artist signed, 8½" x 15¾". $8625.00

A-OH Nov. 1995   Garth's Auction

Row 1

Redware Plate, prob. by Jacob Medinger, Montgomery County, PA, 1856-1932, sgraffito design w/ drummer & fife player w/ stylized flowers in white slip w/ green & brown, coggled rim, 8½" D $990.00

Early Bronze Candlestick W/ Scalloped Base, underside is engraved "F.I.M.", 5¾" H $220.00

Stoneware Pitcher, w/ strap handle, brushed cobalt blue floral design, mottled & spotted grey salt glaze, hairline in base & small chips on spout, 8⅝" H $412.50

Redware Plate, yellow slip decoration, 9¼ D $495.00

Row 2

Stoneware Jug, w/ strap handle, impressed label "Fort Edward Pottery Co." & quill work wreath & 1858 in cobalt blue slip, very minor flakes, 11" H $770.00

Tin Lamp, w/ old green paint, side mounted reservoir or font w/ brass wick adj. knob & air vent stem, has ring for 4⅛" shade-no shade, 9¾" H overall. $275.00

Stoneware Ovoid Jar, incised designs w/ bird on one side & stylized foliage design w/ ring on the other, ring design is highlighted in cobalt blue, chips & hairlines, 9¼" H $330.00

Wrought Iron Rush Light Holder, w/ candle socket counter weight, three feet & twisted detail, 9½" H $385.00

Ovoid Stoneware Pitcher, w/ Strap Handle, impressed "1" in circle on neck near handle, cobalt blue brushed floral design, 10⅞" H $880.00

A-OH Oct. 1995   Garth's Auction

Historical Blue Staffordshire

Row 1, Left to Right

Med. Blue Transfer Plate, "City Hall New York", minor scratches, 9¾" D $148.50

Med. Blue Transfer Cup & Saucer, handleless, vase of flowers & bird, chips on rim of cup $104.50

Med. Blue Transfer Pitcher, Boston State House / City Hall N.Y., sm. chips & hairline, in base, 6⅞" $412.50

Med. Blue Transfer Plate, "Fair Mount Near Phila.", mkd. "Stubbs", minor wear, 10¼" D $165.00

Row 2, Left to Right

Dk. Blue Transfer Soup Plate, arms of "New York", mkd. "Mayer", rim flakes, 10" D $632.50

Dk. Blue Transfer Vegetable Dish, "A Ship of the Line in the Downs", w/ a mismatched cover , lid has hairline & flakes, 9⅝" L $907.50

A-OH Oct. 1995   Garth's Auction

All Blue & White Sponge Spatter

Row 1, Left to Right

Two Plates, w/ molded rims, 9¼" D $220.00

Two Plates, w/ molded rims that match above, 7½" D $165.00

Two Mini, Pitchers, bulbous porcelain, 2½" H, & paneled, minor stains, 3½" H $209.00

Water Pitcher, bulbous, 7½"H $192.50

Row 2, Left to Right

Pitcher, rim chip & minor flakes on base, 9" H $275.00

Barrel Shaped Pitcher, 8⅜"H $220.00

Water Pitcher, short hairline in foot & minor stains, 9¾" H $55.00

Pitcher, w/ bulbous base & cylindrical neck, chips, 8⅞" H $220.00

A-OH Oct. 1995   Garth's Auction

Row 1, Left to Right

Two Pieces Sponge Spatter, blue, butter crock (pictured), 6" D & salt crock w/ molded basket weave & vintage, 5¾" D, both have hairlines $137.50

Sponge Spatter Bowls, three blue & white w/ tan stripes, largest has wear, 4⅛", 8¼" & 9⅛" D $357.50

Row 2

Stoneware Bean Pot, blue & white w/ high relief designs of two children and "Boston Baked Beans", 7½" H .$330.00

Stoneware Pitcher, blue & white molded w/ tree bark & flowers, 7½" H $165.00

Sponge Spatter Sugar Bowl, blue & white, attrib. to Buford Brothers, East Liverpool, Ohio, Lid has prof. repr., 7½" H $165.00

Stoneware Covered Jar, blue & white molded w/ stippled surface & flowers, has holes for wire bale handle, chips, 7½" D, 7" H $66.00

Row 3

Sponge Spatter Pitcher, blue & white w/ molded rose, minor open surface blisters, 8⅞" H $357.50

Stoneware Pitcher, blue & white molded w/ relief designs of Teutonic royalty w/ German inscriptions & dolphin handle, 9¼" H $165.00

Molded Stoneware, blue & white w/ sponged borders & blue flowers, hairline, 9" H $82.50

Sponge Spatter Pitcher, blue & white, hairline & minor flakes, 9⅛" H $330.00

A-MA June 1996   Skinner

Canton Tank, China, 19th C., on mahogany veneer stand, imperf. to stand, 7½" H, 25½" D $4,312.50

A-OH Oct. 1995   Garth's Auction

Row 1, Left to Right

Pearlware Bowl, blue & white oriental decor., "S" mark Salopian, wear & slightly yellowed rim repr., 9¼" D, 4" H $165.00

Two Waste Bowls, Pearlware w/ blue floral transfer, chips on table ring & wear 6" D, & Eng. porcelain w/ polychrome floral enameling, minor wear, 4⅝" D $170.50

Gaudy Welsh Porcelain, 2 pcs., waste bowl, 6⅛" D, pitcher, 5⅜" H ...$440.00

Row 2, Left to Right

Demi-Tasse Cup & Saucer, porcelain, blue & white oriental transfer w/ gilt, Worcester mark $192.50

Gaudy Welsh Creamer, porcelain, 4" H $137.50

Gaudy Cup & Saucer, ironstone handleless, urn patt., saucer has minor flaking & sm. chip on back edge of rim $104.50

Staffordshire Dog w/ Pup, sanded, prof. repr., on base, 4⅛" H ...$181.50

Pearlware Leaf Shaped Dish, blue transfer scene & serrated edge w/ molded veins on back, Worcester crescent mark, clear glaze has streak of amber ash, sm. edge flakes, 5⅛" L ...$214.50

Demi-Tasse Cup & Saucer, porcelain $192.50

Row 3, Left to Right

Queensware Plates, two similar, mkd. "Wedgwood", floral transfer w/ landscape designs on polychrome enamel & brick red stripes, minor wear & enamel flaking, 9⅞" & 10⅜" D $187.00

Teapot w/ Under Tray, porcelain, impressed crown, Grisaille classical scenes & gilt, edge damage, 7¼" H $330.00

Gaudy Staffordshire Plate, floral designs in red, purple, yellow gr. & blk., stains & wear w/ chips on table ring, 10½" D $82.50

Porcelain Teapot, attrib. to Coalport, cobalt blue underglaze w/ red floral enameling & gilt, gilt has wear and finial repr., 6" H $357.50

A-OH Oct. 1995   Garth's Auction

Row 1

Gaudy Stick Spatter Plates, two w/ floral designs & red borders, one mkd. "Edge Malkin & Co.", 8¾" D, & minor stains, 8⅞" D $187.00

Spatterware Toddy, red design spatter border w/ blue stripe & viola in purple, gr., yellow ochre & blk., pinpoint flakes, 5¾" D $176.00

Mini. Cup & Two Saucers, ironstone handleless, stick spatter floral border n red, gr. & yellow, blue stripes, very minor flakes $88.00

Spatterware Cup & Saucer, blue handleless, saucer has blk. deer, cup is badly damaged & poorly glued, saucer has chip & hairline $330.00

Row 2

Gaudy Stick Spatter Soup Plate, w/ center flower & rim swags, wear & minor damage, 9⅜" D $165.00

Spatterware Cup & Saucer, purple, handleless $220.00

Two Plates, w/ spatter borders in red, gr. & blue, sm. also has blk. & is mkd. "Elsmore & Foster", stains, wear & larger has two rim chips, 7½" & 6⅝" D $143.00

Cup & Saucer, handleless w/ mismatched peafowl decor. in red, blue, gr., yellow ochre & blk., minor stains & short hairlines $49.50

Spatterware Soup Plate, red design spatter border w/ blue stripes & thistle & lily of the valley in purple, blue, red, gr., & blk., stains & crazing w/ some glaze wear on rim, 9⅞" D $170.50

A-NH Aug. 1996   Northeast Auctions

A-OH Oct. 1995   Garth's Auction

Historical Blue Staffordshire

Dk. Blue Transfer Plate, "Marine Hospital, Louisville, Kentucky", mkd. "E. Wood & Sons", wear, pinpoint flakes & chip on back side of rim, 9¼" D $302.50

Dk. Blue Transfer Cups & Saucers, six handleless, "Castle Toward" by "J. Hall", sm. chips mostly on table rings of saucers, light stains $1,023

Dk. Blue Transfer Soup Plate, "Landing of Gen. Lafayette...", mkd. "Clews", rim chips, 9⅞" D . . .$275.00

Dk. Blue Transfer Plate, "Transylvania University, Lexington", mkd. "Wood", wear and light scratches, 9½" D $357.50

Dk Blue Transfer Plate, "Landing of Gen. Lafayette..." wear, scratches and some painted over rim chips, mkd. "Clews", 10" D $302.50

Dk Blue Transfer Soup Plate, "Pine Orchard House, Catskill Mountains", mkd. "Wood", minor wear & light scratches, 9 3/8" D $522.50

Dk Blue Transfer Plate, "Commodore MacDonnough's Victory", mkd. "Wood", rim glaze flakes, 10¼" D $357.50

Canton

Row 1

Pitcher, w/ bamboo-form handle, 15" H $3,000.00

Two Footed Egg Cups $150.00

Cut-Corner Bowl, 9" L $800.00

Well & Tree Platter, 17" L .$650.00

Row 2

Two Square Covered Vegetable Dishes, w/ pod finials $500.00

Helmet-Form Creamer, 4½" H $500.00

Oval Reticulated Fruit Bowl & Tray, 11" L $700.00

Cider Pitcher, 6½" H $400.00

Row 3

Two Canton Shrimp Dishes, 10" L $1,000.00

Nanking Oblong Platter & Strainer, 15½" L $1,000.00

Two Hot Water Plates, . . .$450.00

A-OH Oct. 1995   Garth's Auction

Row 1, Left to Right

Porcelain Cups & Saucers, four, Eng. w/ reddish br. landscape transfer w/ pink luster trim, one cup has rim chip $110.00

Spatterware Cup & Saucer, gr. handleless, peafowl in red, blue, yellow & blk., gr. varies, minor flakes .$330.00

Row 2, Left to Right

Gaudy Sugar Bowls, two blue & white pearlware, rectangular one is mkd. "Wood", both have chips, 4½" & 5¾" H $330.00

Copper Mirror Holders, pair of Battersea type enameled, polychrome mourning scenes w/ tomb & classically attired woman, "Sacred to Friendship", one has damage to brass edging & cracks in enamel, slight variation in brass trim, 2" D $220.00

Spatterware Teapot, blue w/ thistle in red & gr., yellowed repr. to base of handle & tip of spout, sm. chips & lid is mismatched, 6⅛" H $550.00

Chelsea Creamer, gilded trim & date "1835", 5¼" H $77.00

Row 3, Left to Right

Mocha Pitcher, w/ molded leaf handle, blue bands & gr. stripes, wear, crow's feet & hairline in base of handle, 7" H $302.50

Gaudy Dutch Soup Plate, butterfly patt., wear & scratches w/ hairline in rim, 8½" D $495.00

Eng. Pitcher, white salt glaze, minor stain, 7¾" H $71.50

Pratt Pitcher, pearlware w/ molded designs, yellow, gr., tan, blue & br., chips on handle & spout & short hairline, 7¼" H $533.50

A-OH Nov. 1995   Garth's Auction

Row 1, Left to Right

Treenware Tea caddy, pear shape, orig. finish & lock, escut. missing, 6¼" H $1595.00

Redware Flower Pot w/ attached saucer base, clear glaze w/amber, br. & gr. glaze, chips & wear, 5"H . .$247.50

Treenware Tea Caddy, apple shape w/ lock & escut., varnish finish, hole in bottom, 4⅝" H $1,155.00

Row 2

Pitcher . . . . .N/S

Redware Pie Plate, w/3 lines of yellow slip decor., wear, chips & hairline, 9½" D $330.00

Redware Teapot, w/ molded ribbed detail, orange & dark br. splotches, chips, finial glued, 7⅛" H . . .$385.00

Redware Ovid Jar w/ rope twist handles, amber glaze, brown sponging w/gr. dots & br. flecks, wear & flakes, chip on base, 7" H $1,815.00

A-OH Nov. 1995   Garth's Auction

Rockingham
Row 1, Left to Right

Plates, 2 pcs., w/ scalloped rims & rayed senters, 8" D 220.00

Mug & Footed Salt, 2 pcs., mug, 3" H, & footed salt, 2⅞" D $148.50

Oblong Octagonal Vegetable Dish, wear & edge flakes, 10⅜" L . . .$137.50

Mugs, 2 pcs., one has small flakes on base, 3¼", 3⅜" H $170.50

Row 2

Pie Plates, 2 pcs., 10" D $209.00

Oblong Octagonal Vegetable Dish, hairline, 12½" L $170.50

Pitcher, 8" H $49.50

A-OH Nov. 1995   Garth's Auction

Row 1, Left to Right

Spatterware Plate, blue w/ tulip in red, gr., yellow & blk., imp. "Cotton & Barlow", 8¾" D $412.50

Spatterware Sugar Bowl, blue w/ tulip decor., rim hairline & chips, 5¼" H $247.50

Pottery Parrot, white clay w/ gr. & brn. glaze, wear to top & beak, 7¾" H $60.50

Spatterware Sugar Bowl, purple w/ small flakes & minor bruise in edge of lid, 5¼" H $192.50

Rainbow Spatterware Plate w/ bull's eye center, red & gr. w/ rim flake & stains, 8¼" D $770.00

Row 2

Spatterware Plate, blue w/ peafowl decor., imp. "Pearl Stoneware, P.W. & Co." mark, stains & wear, 8⅛" D $357.50

Staffordshire Toby Jug, figure w/ pitcher, hat has prof. repr., minor crazing, chips, 9¾ H $330.00

Spatterware Sugar Bowl, blue w/ fining bank, in gr., red & blk., wear, flakes, mismatched lid, 7⅝" H $192.50

Spatterware plate, blue w/ peafowl decor., edge wear & stains, 8⅜" D $302.50

A-PA May 1996   Skinner, Inc.

Wedgwood Vitreous Stoneware
Left to right

Mortar & Pestle, Eng., ca. 1900, w/ wood handle pestle, mortar imp. "Best Composition" & factory marks, 4" dia. $258.75

Mortar & Pestle, Eng., 19th C., wood handle pestle mkd. #3, 8¼" L, mortar 6½" dia. w/int. rim chip, mkd.$287.50

Mortar & Pestle, Eng., ca. 1800, wooden handled pestle, 7⅞" L, mortar w/rim chips, hairline, marked, 8½" dia. $287.50

A-OH Nov. 1995   Garth's Auction

Gaudy Staffordshire
Adam's Rose Pattern
Left to Right, Top to Bottom

Cups & Saucers W/ Scalloped Rims, 6 pcs., slight variation in pattern, saucers marked "Adams", minor chips. $1155.00

Waste Bowl & Sugar, 2 pcs., wear, stains, crazing & chip on lid, 5" H $412.00

Plates w/ Molded Beaded Edge, 5 pcs., stains, small chips, one has hairlines, 7" D $137.50

Cups & Saucers, w/ Smooth Rims & Black Rim Stripe, 3 pcs., one cup has hairlines, slight variation, one saucer marked "Adams". $181.50

Plates W/ Molded Beaded Edge, 4 pcs., two marked "Adams", small flakes, 8" D $93.50

Bowl W/ Scalloped Rim, chips & hairlines, 8½" D $715.00

Plates, 6 pcs., "Adams", chips & hairlines, 8½" D $159.50

Plates, 4 pcs., three marked "Adams", chips, one has hairlines, 9½" D .$115.50

Plates W/ Molded Beaded Edge, 3 pcs., two marked "Adams", some damage, 9¼" D $11.00

Plates, 4 pcs., two marked "Adams", one has chips & hairlines, 10¾" D . $225.50

Plates, 6 pcs., "Adams", very minor flakes, 9½" D $429.00

Large Soup Plates, 4 pcs., three marked "Adams:, minor damage, 10½" D $330.00

Platter, "Adams", stains & minor crazing, 15¼ L $577.50

Covered Vegetable, "Adams", molded rim & finial designs, lid has edge chip, 12½" L $2530.0

A-PA May 1996   Pook & Pook, Inc.

PA Decorated Chalkware

Pineapple Mounted on Pedestal, polychrome decor., mid 19th C., 9½" H, together w/ chalkware fruit arrangement, 11½" H $1,400.00

Pair of Doves, polychrome decor., 19th c., 10" H $1,100.00

Floral Arrangement, polychromed, mid 19th C., w/ pomegranate ferns, etc., 14¾" H $1,200.00

Standing Poodle, mid 19th C., retaining much of orig. paint decor., 7¼" H $400.00

Seated Cat, polychrome decor,, mid 19th C., 9¼" H $650.00

Seated Cat, polychrome decor., mid 19th C., 5½" H $800.00

A-MA Aug. 1996   Robert C. Eldred Co., Inc.

Royal Worcester

Row 1, Left to Right

Pitcher, w/ raised gold floral decor., 9" H $220.00

Pitcher, w/ fern decor., 7½"H $187.50

Pitcher, w/ gilt & floral decor., w/ mask-form spout, 7¾" H $264.00

Ewers, pair, gilt & floral decor. on cream ground, 8¾" H $275.00

Row 2, Left to Right

Biscuit Jar, w/ ribbed body, artist signed on cover, 7½" H $242.00

Pitcher, w/ floral & gilt decor. on cream ground, w/ snake-form handle, 7" H $187.50

Two-Handled Vase, 9¼" H .$143.00

Milk Pitcher, w/ gilt & floral decor., 6½" H $242.00

A-MA Aug. 1996   Robert C. Eldred Co., Inc.

Rose Mandarin

Vase, 10⅜"H $357.00

Creamer, 4" H $165.00

Lighthouse Form Teapot, 7¼" H $412.50

Creamer, 4" H $143.00

Candlestick, w/ sm. glaze check, 9¾" H $357.50

A-MA Aug. 1996   Robert C. Eldred Co., Inc.

Two Staffordshire Plates, in "King's Rose" patt., mkd. "Rogers", 8½" & 8¼" diam. $187.00

Spatterware Plate, w/ red border & central gr. eagle on shield transfer decor., 9" diam. $209.00

Brown Spatterware Cup, handless cup, in Tulip patt. $44.00

A-PA May 1996   Pook & Pook, Inc.

Redware Pie Plate, early 19th C., PA., w/ yellow squiggle slip decor., 11¼" dia., together w/ a smaller example, 9¾" dia. $375.00

Redware Charger, early 19th C., bearing initials "G.R." in cream & mottled gr. slip decor., minor losses, 14½" dia. $1,900.00

Continental Redware Deep Plate, 19th C., w/ circular yellow squiggle decor., 16¾" dia. $250.00

Redware Pie Plate, early 19th C., PA., w/ trailing slip decor., 9¾" H .$450.00

Redware Jar, early 19th C., PA., w/ blk. manganese decor., 6¾" H . . .N/S

Redware Mug, early 19th C., PA., w/ blk. splash manganese decor., 5¾" H, together w/ redware ovoid form double handled jar, 19th C., 5¾" H 350.00

Redware Ovoid Jar, 19th C., w/ rope twist handles w/ gr. & orange mottled glazing, 7½" H $950.00

A-MA Aug. 1996   Robert C. Eldred Co., Inc.

Eng. Soft Paste Teapot, oyster & rose patt., 6½" H $687.50

Eng. Soft Paste Handleless Cups & Saucers, Strawberry patt., 1 cup & saucer w/ hairline, Peafowl patt. $198.00

Eng. Spatterware Cup & Saucer, Peafowl patt. $110.00

Eng. Soft Paste Covered Sugar Bowl, Strawberry patt. $187.00

Eng. Pottery Mug, canary yellow w/ inscrip., 2" H $242.00

A-PA May 1996   Pook & Pook Inc.

Rockingham Glazed Pitcher & Bowl, by Norton & Fenton Pottery Co., Bennington, VT, 1849 w/ gr./br. & ochre marbelized glazing, 14½" H . . . . . .N/S

Bennington Flask, br. & yellow mottled, mid 19th C., 7¾", ...$800.00

Bennington Titled Book Flask, br. & yellow mottled, mid 19th C., together w/ similar example, each 6" H . . .$800.00

Bennington Standing Lion, mid 19th C., w/ coleslaw mane & front paw resting on a ball, 7½" H., 10" W .$2,800.00

Rockingham Br. Glased Coffee Pot, late 19th C., w/ goose necked spout, colonial gentlemen form, 10" H, together w/ an earthenware tobacco jar in farm woman form, chips/losses to paint, 9½" H $375.00

A-PA May 1996   Pook & Pook Inc.

Small Stoneware Pitcher, 19th C., w/ exten. cobalt floral decor., 7¼" H $1,700.00

A-OH APR. 1996   Garth's Auction

Row 1, Left to Right
Gaudy Ironstone Handleless Cup & Saucer, strawberry dec. w/ flowers on saucer, mismatched, stains & cup has hairline $165.00
Blue & White Canton Sauce Tureen, w/ undertray, boar's head handles, rim bruise, 7½" L . . .$495.00
Row 2, Left to Right
Crown Derby Figures of Youth Maiden, mark, polychrome & gilt, minor edge damage, 8⅞" H . .$550.00
Gaudy Ironstone Plate, Strawberries & flowers, impressed "Thos Walker", minor stains, 9⅞" D $275.00

A-OH June 1996   Garth's Auction

Row 1, Left to Right
Pitcher, molded cattle in oval, sm. chips & interior crazing, 8" H $192.50
Pitcher, molded leaping stags in oval, sm. surface flakes, 8"H $214.50
Pitcher, molded eagles & shields in ovals, minor crazing, 8" H . . .$385.00
Row 2, Left to Right
Pitcher, molded swans in ovals, short hairline in spout & minor surface chips, 8" H $275.00
Pitcher, molded Indian heads in circles, sm. chips & some in the making defects, 8¼" H $412.50
Pitcher, molded cherries, prof. repr., 8" H $77.00
Row 3, Left to Right,
Pitcher, molded butterflies in circles, prof. repr., 8¼" H $192.50

Pitcher, molded roses, sm. edge flakes, 9" H $440.00
Pitcher, molded vintage, star mark on bottom, sm. edge flakes, 9¼"H $176.00
Pitcher, molded leaping stags in ovals, pinpoint flakes on spout, 8" H $357.50

A-OH June 1996   Garth's Auction

Row 1, Left to Right
Pitcher, molded cattails, 7"H $192.50
Pitcher, molded windmills, shallow flake on table ring & smaller flake on spout are both in the making, 7¼" H $192.50
Pitcher, molded boy & girl, hairline & chip at base of handle, 6⅛" H .$55.00
Row 2, Left to Right
Pitcher, molded flying birds (swallows), sm. edge flakes, 7⅞" H $572.00
Pitcher, molded roadway lined w/ trees, rim chips, 7⅝" H $192.50
Pitcher, molded shield, hairline in handle & prof. repr., 8" H . . .$225.50
Row 3, Left to Right
Pitcher, molded leaping deer in one oval & swan in the other, 8" H $550.00
Pitcher, molded brick arches & pillars, 8¾" H $440.00
Pitcher, molded doe & fawn, minor chips & hairlines, 8¼' H $165.00
Pitcher, molded pinwheels, 8¼" H $192.00

A-OH June 1996   Garth's Auction

Blue and White Spongeware Unless Otherwise Described

Row 1, Left to Right
Miniature Cuspidor, blue stripes, repr. rim chips, 3¼" D $275.00

Three Cups & Saucers, (2 pictured), dk. blue, similar but not matching, cups have stains & crazing & one has rim chip $115.50
Miniature Teapot, sm. flakes & handle has prof. repr., 4¼" H $577.50
Miniature Covered Dish, lid, 3¼" D $935.00
Row 2, Left to Right
"Butter" Crock, w/ wire bail & wodden handle, no lid, 6" D $77.00
Miniature Blue & White Salt Box, w/ sm. rim flake, 3" D, 3⅜" H $324.50
Teapot, lid is chipped & glued, 5½" H $632.50
Small Creamer, prof. repr., 3⅜" H $302.50
Butter Crock w/ Lid, dk. blue, three rim hairlines, 5½" H $110.00
Row 3, Left to Right
Milk Pitcher, w/ bulbous base w/ dk. greyish blue, 5⅝" H $412.50
Small Bowl, w/ blue & br. sponging, 5" D, 2⅝" H $104.50
Bottle Shaped Bank, w/ blue polka dots, lip chips, 6" H $742.50
Old Sleepy Eye Creamer, sm. flakes on bottom, 3⅞" H $440.00
Milk Pitcher, dk. blue, stain, 5¾" H $330.00

A-OH Nov. 1995   Garth's Auction

Row 1
Redware Ovoid Jar, w/ Tooled Lines, Applied Handles & Flared Lip, wear & chips & hairline around foot, 8¾" H . $275.00
Redware Jar, w/ Tooled Band & Slightly Protruding Lip, mottled amber glaze, old label on base, 8⅜" H $192.50
Redware Ovoid Jar, w/ Tooled Lines, Applied Shoulder Handles & Flared Lip, wear & chips, 8¼" H $275.00

Row 2
Rockingham Pitcher w/ Lid, molded sheaf & grain, small flakes & lid has chips on underside of lip, 10" H overall. $220.00
Redware Pitcher, w/ Unglazed White Slip, impressed "Bell & Son, Strasburg", small chips, 9¾" H $16.50
Rockingham Teapot, molded figure of Chinaman on each side, chips, 9½" H overall. $165.00

A-OH Jan. 1996   Garth's Auction

All pottery banks unless noted

Row One

Pig, brn. and blue sponging on a cream colored ground, old chips, 5⅝" L . .$137.50

Two Banks, "Acorn Stove's..." in grn., 3" H and blk. boy in blue, chips at coin slot, 2⅞" H $165.00

Hen on Nest, two tone brn. and wht., 4¾" L $159.50

Two Banks, D. yellow w/ running grn., hairlines and small chips, 6" L, and "Razor Back" pig w/ Rockingham glaze, glued, not pictured, 6" L $192.50

Stoneware Beehive, two tone greyish bisque and brown metallic, Albany slip, incised "A penny saved is a penny earned", 4¾" D. 3⅛" H $187.00

Row Two

Two Banks, cat in bag in yel. w/ running grn., chips at coin slot, 3¾" H, and frog in gr., 4" H $275.00

Two Banks, red clay, incised "X's" and black glaze, 4⅞" H, and jug w/ red and gold paint, chips at coin slot, 4⅞" H $176.00

Two Banks, Indian head in Rockingham glaze, incised "1815" (but not date), 4¼" H, and bison in olive brn. w/ greenish blue strip on back, 5⅞" L, both have small chips. $99.00

Seated pig, yel. w/ brn. splotches and bluish grn. sponging on base, minor damage at coin slot, 5½" L $192.50

Row Three

Two Barrel Shaped Banks, in colorful running glaze colors of grn., amber and brn., sm. flakes, 5", 5½" H $220.00

Two banks, bear w/ dk. brn. glaze, 5⅝" H and stoneware elephant w/ blk. shiny glaze, 4" H, both have small chips and elephant has shallow flake on base, 3⅞" H $275.00

Three Banks, Rockingham glaze, possum has prof. restor., 5½" H, owl has chips, 6¼" H, monkey is 4⅞" H $247.50

Two Painted Banks, red clay w/ red and yel. running glaze and polychrome flowers, 4¼" H, and wht. clay w/ bluish grn. and bird's nest w/ pink blossoms, 5" H, both have sm. flakes. $192.50

A-MA Oct. 1995   Skinner, Inc.

21A-Child's Mug, canary yellow transfer decor., 19th c., chips, .$460.00

220-Children's Mugs, (3 of 10), 19th c., transfer printed, lusterware & enamel decor., imperfections. $546.25

215-Children's Mugs, (2 of 4), 19th c., minor chips. $920.00

217-Children's Mugs, (4 of 5), minor chips, hairlines. $747.50

A-OH July 1996   Garth's Auction

Row 1

Salopian Handleless Cup & Saucer, pearlware w/ blk. transfer of deer w/ polychrome enameling, cup has hairline & pinpoint flakes on table ring $104.50

Mocha Handleless Cup & Saucer, tooled rims w/ gr., blk. seaweed decor. on orange ground, sm. edge chips, saucer has hairlines $550.00

Row 2

Gaudy Dutch Handleless Cup & Saucer, rose pattern, sm. edge flakes $412.50

Gaudy Dutch Waste Bowl, rose patt., wear, hairlines & stains w/ flake on table ring & glaze flakes on rim, 5½" D $357.50

Gaudy Dutch Handleless Cup & Saucer, rose pattern, close mismatch, hairlines, sm. chips, some enamel flaking $275.00

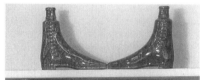

A-OH July 1996   Garth's Auction

Row 1

Rockingham Shoe Bottles, pinpoint flakes, 6⅝" H $220.00

Row 2, Left to Right

Bennington Book Flask, Rockingham glaze w/ edge chips from kiln adhesion $770.00

Bennington Covered Soap Dish, molded alternate rib pattern, flint enamel glaze, "1849" mark, chips on edge of lid, 5⅝" L $880.00

Bennington Pie Plate, Rockingham glaze w/ yellow highlights, "1849" mark, wear & scratches, 11" D $715.00

Two Pieces of Rockingham, book flask, chips 5¼" H & round soap dish, 5⅛" D $198.00

A-PA May 1996   Pook & Pook Inc.

PA. Sheraton Cherry Tall Case Clock, ca. 1810, 93" H $2,300.00

A-PA May 1996   Pook & Pook Inc.

PA. Poplar Tall Case Clock, early 19th C., w/ works by J. Weiss, Bethlehem, PA., retains traces of old red stain, 98" H $4,000.00

A-MA June 1996   Skinner

Cherry Tall Case Clock, Asa Hopkins, Litchfield, CT., 1820-30, w/ thirty-hour wooden pull-up weight driven movement, ref., imperf., 91½" H . .$2,990.00

A-OH May 1996   Garth Auctions

Sheraton Grandfather's Clock, refin. cherry w/ curly walnut & curly maple, wag-on-the-wall works, not orig. to clock, reprs. and finials missing, 93½" H $2,750.00

A-OH APR. 1996   Garth's Auction

Tall Clock, cherry w/ some curl & old dk finish, w/ weights & pendulum, case has some old pieced repair to moldings & bonnet has some repairs, edge chip on bonnet door, 89½" H $7,425.00

A-MA June 1996   Skinner

Tall Case Clock, painted pine, Riley Whiting, Winchester CT., C. 1830, case painted red w/ freehand floral & foliate devices & sim. stringing in gold & blk., imperf., 83" H $4,887.50

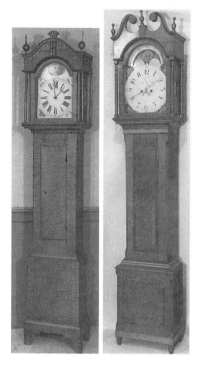

A-OH July 1996   Garth's Auction

Tall Case Clock, curly maple w/ tiger grain, dovetailed bracket feet, wag on the wall works w/ painted face, restur., 90" H $5,610.00

Tall Case Clock, ref. cherry w/ figured cherry, crossbanded mahogany veneer & bird's eye maple veneer, brass works w/ painted metal face that has calendar movement, second hand & phases of the moon dial, minor age cracks, 96¼" H $4,675.00

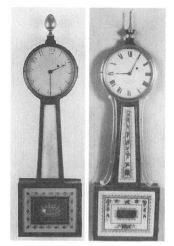

A-MA June 1996   Skinner

Left

Banjo Timepiece, federal mahogany & mahogany veneer, Boston, C. 1820, w/ eight-day weight driven movement, "T" bridge suspension, imperf., 33½" H $3,105.00

A-MA Aug. 1996   Robert C. Eldred Co., Inc.

Right

Banjo Clock, custom-made, sign. "Elmer O. Stennis, Weymouth", cherry, reverse-painted throat & tablet, 32" H $1,430.00

A-MA Aug. 1996   Robert C. Eldred Co., Inc.

English Long Case Clock, oak, wooden finial, painted dial, by Robert J. Amlwch., 85" H $770.00

A-OH APR. 1996   Garth's Auction

Pillar & Scroll Shelf Clock, mahogany case w/ orig. reverse painting, wooden works, mkd. "Patent Clocks by E. Terry & Sons", minor repairs $1,980.00

A-OH June 1996   Garth's Auction

Tall Case Clock, ref. curly maple w/ walnut moldings, wag on the wall works w/ worn painted wooden face, brass gears & wooden plates, age crack in base & finials repl. w/ weight and pendulum, 88¾" H $2,090.00

A-OH July 1996   Garth's Auction

Pillar & Scroll Shelf Clock, mahogany & mahogany veneer case, brass works, orig. weights, key & pendulum, reverse painting is a replm., paper label reads "Clocks made & sold by Seth Thomas, Plymouth, Conn." $1,210.00

A-OH Mar. 1996   Garth's Auctions

Tall Case Clock, pine w/ old worn reddish brown grained finish, dovetailed base, wooden works w/ painted wooden face that has Masonic decoration & is mkd. "S. Hoadley, Plymouth", second hand is missing, pendulum & weights repl., 83" H $1,870.00

A-OH Mar. 1996   Garth's Auctions

Tall Case Clock, cherry w/ weights, pendulum & key, center brass finial repl. & side finials are missing, age cracks in case, 90½" H $5,555.00

A-PA Nov. 1995   Pook & Pook Inc.

Chippendale Tall Case Clock, PA, walnut, 30 hr. works & painted white dial signed Jacob Young, Allentown w/ calendar hand, ca. 1780, 95" H $4,250.00

A-PA Apr. 1996   Pook & Pook Inc.

Tall Case Clock, works, sgn. by Daniel Flint, Philadelphia, ca. 1800, 103" H $7,000.00

A-PA Nov. 1995   Pook & Pook Inc.

Grain Painted Tall Case Clock, 30 hrs. works, by Daniel Christ of Kutztown, PA, ca. 1820, 92½" H .2,250.00
Cherry Tall Case Clock, herringbone inlay & painted face, ca. 1820, 89" H $2,750.00

A-PA Nov. 1995   Pook & Pook Inc.

Chippendale Tall Case Clock, Pa. Lehigh Co., w/ 30 hr. works, painted dial signed Peter Miller, old red stained surface, late 18th C., 93" H .$5,800.00

A-MA June 1996   Skinner

Pillar & Scroll Shelf Clock, federal mahogany & mahogany veneer, Seth Thomas, Plymouth, CT., C. 1818, w/ thirty-hour strap wood movement, restored, 30¼″ H, 17″ W . . .$3,105.00

A-MA Aug. 1996   Robert C. Eldred Co., Inc.

Shelf Clock, by C. & N. Jerome, Bristol, CT, mahogany veneers w/ blk. & gilt painted dial & 2 reverse painted tablets $990.00

A-MA June 1996   Skinner

Pillar & Scroll Shelf Clock, mahogany & birch veneer, E. Terry & Son, Plymouth, CT. C. 1818-24, w/ thirty-hour wooden weight driven movement, ref., restored, imperf., 31¼″ H, 17¼″ W $1,380.00

A-MA June 1996   Skinner

Pillar & Scroll Shelf Clock, mahogany & mahogany veneer, Erastus Hodges, Torrington Hollow, CT., C. 1830, w/ thirty-hour wooden weight driven movement, restored 29″ H, 13¼″ W $3,220.00

A-PA Nov. 1995   Aston Auctioneers & Appraisers

Tall Case Clock, 8-day w/ moon phase, Berks Co., PA., ca. 1830, flame cherry case $5,600.00

A-MA June 1996   Skinner

Parcel Gilt Triple Decker Shelf Clock, mahogany & mahogany veneer, Chauncey & Lawson C. Ives, Bristol, CT., C. 1830-38, w/ eight-day brass strap movement, imperf., 36″ H, 17⅜″ W $805.00

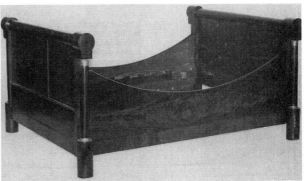

A-NH Aug. 1996   Northeast Auctions

Classical-Revival Bedstead, Am., mahogany w/ head-board & footboard flanked w/ brass capitals & bases, 64" W, 82" L $2,750.00

A-MA Aug. 1996   Robert C. Eldred Co., Inc.

Sheraton Tester Crib, mahogany, 24" W, 41" L . . . $1,320.00

A-NH Aug. 1996   Northeast Auctions

Mahogany Tall-Post Bedstead, Am. w/ elaborate pineap-ple carving, 8" H $3,500.00

A-NH Aug. 1996   Northeast Auctions

Portsmouth Sheraton Bedstead, carved mahogany & flame birch canopy, chamfered headposts, reeded footposts w/ acanthus leaf carving, 62½" H, 42" W, 77" L $4,800.00

A-NH Aug. 1996   Northeast Auctions

Federal Carved Mahogany Tall-Post Beadstead, NY, posts turned & reeded w/ acanthus leaf & swag carving, 85" H, 80" L, 61" W $3,250.00

A-MA Oct. 1995   Skinner, Inc.

Smoke Grained Child's Chest over Drawer, N. Eng., 1830's, with recessed panel sides, original surface and wooden pulls, (minor surface imperfections), 24½" H, 31" W, 16¾" D $1380.00

A-MA Oct. 1995   Skinner, Inc.

Small Grain Painted Pine Dome-Top Box, N. Eng., early 19th c., with original red and cream vinegar paint, 12" H, 24" W, 13" D $431.25

A-MA Oct. 1995   Skinner, Inc.

Grain Painted Poplar Six Board Chest, PA, 1830-40, w/ molded top and lidded till, early graining simulates tiger maple, (imperfections), 24¼ H, 42" W, 20" D $805.00

A-MA Jan. 1996   Skinner, Inc.

Shaker Three-Drawer Blanket Box, N.H., ca. 1848 . . . .$125,000.00

A-PA Dec. 1995 Horst Auction Center

Paint Box, PA, early 19th C., nailed construction, paint appears to be of later date, initialed "A.E." on side, red ground w/ yellow, red & black design, brass hinges, iron lock plate, int. lined w/paper, 12" W x 7⅝" D, 7¼" H . .$300.00

A-PA Dec. 1995 Horst Auction Center

Weber Box, PA, w/hinged lid & bracket feet, dk. gr. ground w/ hand painted stylized flower design, two-story house, wire hinges, orig. tin hasp, pegged const., 9⅞" W, 5⅛" D, 5" H, minor wear $14,000.00

A-VA Aug. 1995 Ken Farmer Auctions

Bucher Dome Top Box, ca. 1810-40, w/ orig. salmon floral paint, mustard banded borders, org. untouched surface, 5" H, 10½" W, 6¾ D . .$5,525.00

A-MA June 1996   Skinner, Inc.

Six Board Chest, paint decor., N. Eng., 1820-30, top & sides painted yellow w/ smoke decor., bordered by blue-gr. striping, minor restored to paint, 27" H, 47" W, 20½" D $3,737.50

A-MA Jan. 1996   Skinner, Inc.

Shaker Three-Drawer Blanket Box, ca. 1848, w/ mortised paneled lid, pine, orig. red-org. paint, iron hinges and lock, brass escutcheon, dovetailed case w/ applied broken ogee shaped bracket base, 3 dovetailed drawers w/ hardwood pulls, 29¼" H, 49⅝" L, 21⅝" D $140,000.00

A-VA Aug. 1995 Ken Farmer Auctions

Blanket Chest, PA, ca. 1820-50, white pine w/ orig. red & mustard paint, black highlights, 28⅜" H, 42½" W, 23½" D $2,750.00

A-PA Dec. 1995   Alderfer Auction Co.

"Deep Run Decorator" Chest, w/ 2 drawers, Sechstern device on lid, tulip on ends & eyes on front, salmon decor. w/ yellow moldings, poplar, from Bedminister, Bucks, Co., 38½ W, 20" D, 28" H $22,000.00

A-MA June 1996   Skinner, Inc.

Six-Board Chest, grain painted pine, 1825-40, orig. mustard & burnt sienna paint to resemble mahogany, minor imperf., 24½" H, 35½" W, 18½" D $1,035.00

A-PA Apr. 1996   Pook & Pook Inc.

Q.A. Mahogany Bonnet Top High-boy, Goddard Townsend School, New-port, RI, ca. 1770, 84½" H, 36" W, 19" D $30,000.00

A-PA Oct. 1995   Pook & Pook, Inc.

Q.A. Cherry Highboy, NJ, ca. 1760, 70¼" H, 39½" W $7,500.00

A-MA Aug. 1996   Robert C. Eldred Co., Inc.

Q.A. Highboy, maple w/ pine sides, repl. brasses, restor., 70½" H, 30" W, 20" D $2,640.00

A-MA Jan. 1996   Skinner, Inc.

Q.A. Highboy, maple, MA, ca. 1760, old ref., replm. brasses, 73" H, 37" W, 21" D $9,200.00

A-MA Mar. 1996   Skinner, Inc.

Q.A. High Chest, walnut inlaid, MA., ca. 1750-70, old ref., repl. brasses, imperf., 67½" H, 36½" W, 19¼" D $11,500.00

A-PA Nov. 1995   Pook & Pook Inc.

Chippendale Style Centennial Highboy, PA, mahogany bonnet top, 91½" H, 42" W $5,500.00

A-OH June 1996   Garth's Auction

Queen Anne Highboy, curly maple w/ traces of old finish, top case is dovetailed & has molded cornice, chestnut secondary wood, orig. brasses, attrib. to Rhode Island, minor pieced repr. to one corner of molding, apron drops are replaced & minor edge damage, 36" W, 71" H $13,750.00

A-MA Mar. 1996   Skinner, Inc.

Q.A. Tiger Maple High Chest, North Shore, MA. ca. 1740-60, old repl. brasses, old ref., minor lip losses, 73" H, 39" W, 19¾" D $17,250.00

A-MA Mar. 1996   Skinner, Inc.

Chippendale Base to High Chest, cherry carved, Connecticut, late 18th C., old ref., repl. brasses, repl. top, other imperf., 35½" H, 36¾" W, 18¾" D $2,185.00

A-PA Apr. 1996   Pook & Pook Inc.

Canton Covered Soup Tureen, 19th C. $1,400.00
Chippendale Lowboy, Delaware Valley, walnut, ca. 1780, repr., period brasses, 29¼" H, 35¾" W, 21" D . .$17,500.00

A-MA Jan. 1996   Skinner, Inc.

Bow-Front Bureau, mahogany w/ mahogany veneer, MA, ca. 1820, old ref., imperfections, 44½" H, 42" W, 22½" D $2,070.00

A-OH Mar. 1996   Garth's Auction

Queen Anne Highboy, curly maple refinish w/ reddish brown stain. Pine secondary wood, brasses old replms., minor repair & age cracks, 34½" W, 67¾" H $9,350.00
Stoneware Ovoid Jug w/ Strap Handle, cobalt blue brushed floral decor. w/ "3", chip on lip, 15" H $247.50

A-MA Mar. 1996   Skinner, Inc.

Q.A. Carved Maple High Chest, maple, CT., 18th C., some orig. brass, old ref., 72¼" H, 38" W, 18¾" D $14,950.00

A-PA Nov. 1995   Pook & Pook Inc.

High Chest of Drawers, walnut, Chester County PA double panel sides case w/ berry line inlay on 2 drawers, sgn. S.M. & dated 1758, w/ provenance, 54½″ H, 38″ W, 21″ D $17,000.00

A-VA Sept. 1995 Ken Farmer Auctions

Chest of Drawers, walnut w/ yellow pine secondary, E. TN, ca. 1820, 44″ H, 35″ W, 16¾″ D $1,210.00

A-MA Jan. 1996   Skinner, Inc.

Tall Chest of Drawers, maple, late 18th c., ref., old brasses, imperfections, 49¾″ H, 36″ W, 17¼″ D $3,335.00

A-MA Jan. 1996   Skinner, Inc.

Tall Chest of Drawers, MA, ca. 1790, maple, restoration, 57¼″ H, 36¾″ W, 17¼″ D $5,462.50

A-PA Oct. 1995   Pook & Pook, Inc.

Chippendale High Chest of Drawers, PA, walnut, ca. 1780, 59″ H, 38″ W $4,500.00
Delft Charger, blue & white, ca. 1750, 13¼″ diam. $400.00

A-OH Jan. 1996   Garth's Auction

Chippendale High Chest, maple w/ old mellow ref., old but not orig. brasses, age cracks, shims added to feet, 35⅝″ W, cornice 19¼″ x 38½″, 54½″ H $4,180.00
Decorated Bride's Box, bentwood pine w/ worn orig. decor., laced seams, 15¼ L $660.00

A-MA Aug. 1996   Robert C. Eldred Co., Inc.

Hepplewhite Bowfront Chest, cherry w/ line inlay to top & drawer fronts, orig. brasses, 38" H, 41" W, 20½" D $1,760.00

A-OH June 1996   Garth's Auction

Chippendale High Chest, PA., walnut w/ old ref., dovetailed case, & drawers, repl. brasses & top drawers have had added locks removed, minor reprs., minor edge damage & age cracks, 39" W, 67" H $5,775.00

A-OH May 1996   Garth's Auction

Hepplewhite Tall Chest, cherry w/ old refin., orig. oval brasses w/ wheat design, feet replaced, minor edge damage & sm. reprs., poplar secondary wood, 40" W, cornice is 22¼" x 42¼", 67¼" H $4,070.00

A-MA June 1996   Skinner, Inc.

Chest Over Drawers, N. Eng., w/ blue paint, early 19th C., the old blue is over an earlier blue-gr. paint, 37" H, 38" W, 18" D $6,900.00

A-MA June 1996   Skinner, Inc.

Bow-Front Bureau, federal cherry & tiger maple veneer, 1800-15, w/ top edge & cockbeaded drawers outlined in crossbanded mahogany veneer & stringing, old repl. brasses & ref., 46½" H, 40" W, 21½" D $8,050.00

A-MA June 1996   Skinner, Inc.

Carved Dressing Bureau, mahogany & mahogany veneer, C. 1825, ref., imperf., 60" H, 38" W, 20" D . .$805.00

A-MA June 1996   Skinner, Inc.

Carved Bureau, mahogany, cherry & mahogany veneer, C. 1825, ref., minor imperf., 51½" , 47" , 22"D . . .$632.50

A-MA June 1996   Skinner, Inc.

Carved Bureau, mahogany & mahogany veneer, C. 1820, ref., repl. brasses, minor imperf., 46" H, 40" W, 20" D $3,105.00

A-MA Aug. 1996   Robert C. Eldred Co., Inc.

Sheraton Chest, cherry w/ paneled ends, 47½" H, 46" W, 21" D . .$880.00

A-MA Aug. 1996   Robert C. Eldred Co., Inc.

Chippendale Two-Part Cupboard/ Bureau, PA., cherry, orig. brasses, restor., 73" H, 51" W, 19½" D $2,420.00

A-MA Mar. 1996   Skinner, Inc.

Inlaid Serpentine Chest of Drawers, federal cherry & cherry veneer, Rhode Island, ca. 1810, repl. brasses, ref., feet repl., other minor imperf., 37" H, 44⅞" W, 22½" D $9,775.00

A-MA Aug. 1996   Robert C. Eldred Co., Inc.

Sheraton Chest, mahogany w/ cookie corners, cockbeaded drawers, 39½" H, 43" W, 20" D $715.00

A-MA Mar. 1996   Skinner, Inc.

Chest of Drawers, federal cherry inlaid, Rowan County, N.C., ca. 1800-10, old ref., imperf., 44½" H, 43½" W, 20" D $1,380.00

A-MA June 1996   Skinner, Inc.

Carved Chest of Drawers, federal mahogany veneer, N. Eng., early 19th C., old ref., repl. brasses, height loss, veneer patches, 35"H, 37¼"W, 18"D . .$575.00

A-MA Aug. 1996   Robert C. Eldred Co., Inc.

Sheraton Bureau, mahogany w/ 3 stepped drawers above 4 "D" form drawers w/ cockbeading & inlaid fronts, cookie corners, 48" H, 45" W, 23" D $770.00

A-MA Aug. 1996   Robert C. Eldred Co., Inc.

Sheraton Bureau, mahogany, repl. brasses, 44" H, 45" L, 22" D $467.50

A-MA June 1996   Skinner, Inc.

Chippendale Chest of Drawers, tiger maple, late 18th C., ref., old repl. brasses, imperf., 42" H, 36" W, 18¾" D $1,955.00

A-MA Jan. 1996   Skinner, Inc.

Double Cupboard Over Case of Drawers, ca. 1840, pine, orig. brn. paint, replm. hardwood pulls, 37¼″ H, 36½″ W, 17⅛″ D $27,600.00

A-MA June 1996   Skinner, Inc.

Chippendale Walnut Chest on Chest, PA., 1760-90, orig. brass, old surface, feet cut, 75″ H, 40½″ W, 21½″ D $6,900.00

A-PA Apr. 1996   Pook & Pook Inc.

Chippendale Mahogany Chest on Chest, Philadelphia, ca. 1775, repr. to drawer fronts & feet, 95½″ H, 43¼″ W, 22″ D $21,000.00

A-OH APR. 1996   Garth's Auction

Sheraton High Chest, cherry w/ orig. finish, orig. brasses, pine secondary wood, age cracks in side panels, 39″ W, 66¾″ H $6,600

A-OH Mar. 1996   Garth's Auction

Chippendale High Chest, PA., walnut cleaned down to old natural patina, dovetailed case & drawers, pine secondary wood, replaced brasses, minor drawer edge damage & some age cracks, 42¾″ W, 61″ H $3630.00

A-PA May 1996   Pook & Pook Inc.

Chippendale Mahogany Chest on Chest, N.Y., ca. 1780, retains orig. brasses, 78″H, 48″W, 23¾″D .$8,000.00

A-PA Mar. 1996   Horst Auctioneers

Corner Cupboard, PA, grain painted, 2 pc. $6,100.00

A-PA Mar. 1996   Horst Auctioneers

Dutch Cupboard, 2pc. w/ red, blue, & yellow decor. Berks Co. PA, ca. 1841 . . . .$30,000.00

A-OH Nov. 1995   Garth's Auction

Chippendale 2 Pc. Architectural Corner Cupboard, Walnut w/ old finish, orig. brass bales and "H" hinges, one hinge is damaged, four panes of glass cracked, turned finials are old replm. and one is missing plinth, pine secondary wood,minor damage and small repairs, 50" W, 51" at cornice, 99" H. $15,950.00

A-VA Aug. 1995 Ken Farmer Auctions

Corner Cupboard, NC, ca. 1780-1800, walnut w/ poplar secondary, replm. hinges & ref., 90½" H, 49" W, 26" D $4,400.00

A-PA Oct. 1995   Pook & Pook, Inc.

Q.A. Corner Cupboard, Delaware Valley, pine & Popular, ca. 1760, 83¼" H, 34" W $4,500.00

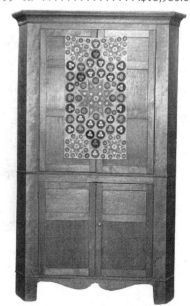

A-OH Jan. 1996   Garth's Auction

One Piece Corner Cupboard, cherry w/ old mellow ref., minor edge damage & sm. pieced repr. to ends of cornice, 50½" W x 54½" W at cornice, 85½" H $2,750.00

Applique Rug, stars, circles & three leaf clovers in blues, olive, grey, white, red & brown, on goldenrod ground, wear, stains, small holes & tears, 19" x 36" $440.00

A-VA Sept. 1995 Ken Farmer Auctions

Painted Linen Press, GA, ca. 1840, yellow pine w/ old red paint 63½" H, 43" W, 17¼" D $1,210.00

A-PA Oct. 1995   Pook & Pook, Inc.

Q.A. Slant Front Desk, Delaware Valley, walnut, fully fitted, ca. 1760, 42½" H, 36¼" W $7,000.00

A-PA Oct. 1995   Pook & Pook, Inc.

KAS, pine painted blue, late 18th c., 81¾" H, 61½" W $3,250.00

A-PA Oct. 1995   Pook & Pook, Inc.

Chippendale Linen Press, NJ, gum wood, 2 parts, ca. 1780, 74½"H, 46" W $4,000.00

A-OH Jan. 1996   Garth's Auction

Chippendale Secretary, 2 pc., ref. cherry, reprs. & replm., pine & walnut secondary wood, 39¾" W, desk is 22" x 40½", 80" H, 31" writing ht. . .$3,575.00
Canada Goose, Chesapeake Bay, MD, mid 20th c., orig. paint, crack in neck, 24" L $247.50

A-OH Mar 1996   Garth's Auction

Eastlake Victorian Two Piece Cylinder Top Secretary, walnut & burl veneer, old refinishing, minor veneer damage & some moldings replaced, 41¾" W, 96¾" H . .$2090.00

A-MA Mar. 1996   Skinner, Inc.

Desk & Bookcase, federal mahogany inlaid, MD. or southern U.S., ca. 1790, top drawer fitted w/ fold-out writing surface & desk compartments, ref., repl. brasses, loss of height, other imperf., 104" H, 46¼" W, 21" D $4,887.50

A-MA Aug. 1996   Robert C. Eldred Co., Inc.

Hepplewhite Secretary, mahogany w/ line inlays, 72" H, 36" W, 19" D $1,760.00

A-PA Nov. 1995   Aston Auctioneers & Appraisers

Corner Cupboard, flame-cherry, PA, ca. 1830 . . . .$6,700.00

A-OH July 1996   Garth's Auction

One Piece Corner Cupboard, curly maple & old ref., cut down from the bottom end & bracket feet repl., 43½" W 47" W at cornice, 77" H .$2,860.00

A-MA Aug. 1996   Robert C. Eldred Co., Inc.

Blind-Front Corner Cupboard, in cherry, one piece, 76" H, takes a 36" corner $2,145.00

A-MA Mar. 1996   Skinner, Inc.

Chippendale Walnut Corner Cupboard, late 18th C., old finish, imperf., 84" H, 41" W, 20" D $4,887.50

A-MA June 1996   Skinner, Inc.

Wm. & Mary Slant Lid Desk, walnut inlaid & maple, Boston, early 18th C., w/ contrasting stringing, old ref., engraved brasses, restored, 40" H, 34" W, 17½" D $4,887.50

A-MA June 1996   Skinner, Inc.

Chippendale Slant Lid Desk, tiger maple, last quarter 18th C., old finish, imperf., 40" H, 35¾" W, 18" D . .$5,462.50

A-OH Mar. 1996   Garth's Auction

Eastlake Cylinder Top Secretary, 2 pc., walnut & burl veneer w/minor damage, 41¾" W, 96¾" H . .$2,090.00

A-MA Mar. 1996   Skinner, Inc.

Chippendale Slant Lid Desk, carved mahogany, Newport, R.I., ca. 1750-70, old ref., reprs., 41½" H, 38" W, 20¾" D $6,900.00

A-MA Mar. 1996   Skinner, Inc.

Tambour Lady's Desk, federal mahogany inlaid, North Shore, MA. ca. 1790, old ref., old brasses, restored, 43½" H, 37¾" W, 21¼" D . . .$5,750.00

A-OH Mar. 1996   Garth's Auction

Chippendale Oxbow Slant Front Desk, mahogany w/ old finish & claw feet, dovetailed case, four dovetailed drawers in beaded frames, & filled interior w/ pigeon holes, eight drawers & two pullout letter drawers w/ half columns, lid has restored hinge rail & repaired splits, interior is partially rebuilt, feet old replacements, pine secondary wood, repl. brasses, 42" W, 20½" D, 42¼" H $4070.00

A-MA Mar. 1996   Skinner

Slant Lid Desk, federal walnut inlaid, Piedmont, N.C. area, 19th C., repl. brasses, ref., reprs., 41¾" H, 36¼" W, 18" D $4,600.00

A-MA June 1996   Skinner, Inc.

Chippendale Slant Lid Desk, maple, N. Eng., C. 1760, old ref., repl. brasses, reprs. to base, 41¾" H, 36¼" W, 17½" D $3,105.00

A-OH July 1996   Garth's Auction

Two-Piece Chippendale Secretary, MA, walnut w/ banded inlay & old finish, restor. 38" W, 21½" D, 31 . . .$17,600.00
Pair of Brass Queen Anne Candlesticks, 7¼" H $2,200.00

A-OH APR. 1996   Garth's Auction

Ohio Two Piece Corner Cupboard, refinished cherry, w/ two dovetailed drawers in base, one hinge on top door reset & hardware replaced, attributed to Delaware County, 44½" W, 88½" H $4,290.00

A-IL Apr. 1996   Olivers

Cupboard, w/2 doors, boot jack ends, orig. slamon red w/ dark gr. paint, 75¼" H, 40½" W, 12 ¾" D .$9,000.00

A-MA June 1996   Skinner, Inc.

Six-Board Chest, painted, N. Eng., C. 1800, w/ covered till & shaped ends w/ orig. blue paint, imperf., 25½" H, 44¼" W, 18½" D $1,035.00

A-OH APR. 1996   Garth's Auction

One Piece Open Pewter Cupboard, w/ architectural detail, pine w/ old mellow refinishing, step back top has fluted pilasters, repairs to cornice, 41½" W, 84" H $1,980.00

A-MA Mar. 1996   Skinner, Inc.

Six-Board Chest, painted, N. Eng., ca. 1790, old light blue paint, 26" H, 38¾" W, 20" D $2,300.00

A-OH Sept. 1995   Garth's Auction

Country two piece secretary, cherry, 2 dovetailed drawers & slant top, fold down lid w/ pigeon hole interior in base. Top & base are mismatched & base has been rebuilt to fit top, 41"W. Cornice 13½" x 44¼", 79½" H $550.00

GA9-10b
A-OH Sept. 1995   Garth's Auction

English Campaign Wardrobe, mahogany w/ brass flush hardware, dovetailed drawers, top, frame & back are hinged to fold down flat, 3 modern interior shelves, minor repr. & feet replm., 55" W, cornice is 20½" x 58", 75" H $1,705.00

A-MA Mar. 1996   Skinner, Inc.

Walnut Vernacular Sideboard, Meckremburg Co., N.C., early 19th C., imperf., 41" H, 52" W, 17¼" D $1,610.00

A-MA June 1996　　　　Skinner, Inc.

Carved Sideboard, mahogany veneer, mid-Atlantic states, 1830's, old finish, repl. pulls, imperf., 49" H, 48" W, 22" D $862.50

A-MA June 1996　　　　Skinner, Inc.

Pine Corner Cupboard, 18th C., old ref., 81" H, 57" W, 22" D . . .$3,680.00

A-MA Jan. 1996　　　　Skinner, Inc.

One-Door Cupboard, ca. 1790, pine, old blue paint over red, iron hinges, brass pull, 37¼" H, 36½" W, 17⅛" D $17,250.00

A-MA Aug. 1996　　　　Robert C. Eldred Co., Inc.

Sheraton Mini. Bureau, w/ grain-painted decor. simulating mahogany & tiger maple, 16½" H, 8" D $2,860.00

A-PA Nov. 1995　　　　Aston Auctioneers & Appraisers

Miniature Empire Chest of Drawers, tiger maple & maple . . .$400.00

A-PA May 1996　　　　Pook & Pook Inc.

Western PA. Chippendale Secretary, walnut, ca. 1780, 83½" H, 38½" W $3,800.00

A-MA Aug. 1996　　　　Robert C. Eldred Co., Inc.

Mini. Cabinet, walnut, flanked by Ionic columns, top w/ star inlay, ivory, 17" H, 11¾" W, 9½" D $1,045.00

A-PA May 1996　　　　Pook & Pook Inc.

Phil. Mahogany Veneered Work Table, ca. 1830, w/ lift lid center section enclosing a writing surface flanked by two oblong lift ild compartments w/ ebonized maple spindles enclosing silk bags, 30" H, 27¼" W $850.00

A-OH APR. 1996　　　　Garth's Auction

Kas, Gumwood w/ old mellow ref., orig. "H" hinges, poplar secondary wood, old repairs, 56¼" W, 73½" H $4,730.00

A-MA Oct. 1995   Skinner, Inc.

Federal Sideboard, mahogany veneer, N. Shore, MA, ca. 1800, old ref., repl. brasses, repr., 40½" H, 55½" W, 17" D $7,475.00

A-MA Mar. 1996   Skinner, Inc.

Sideboard, federal mahogany & mahogany veneer inlaid, MA. or N.H., ca. 1800, w/ pictorial inlaid oval outlined in stringing on the facade of the butler's desk, repl. brasses, imperf., 38" H, 64¼" W, 22¾" D $9,200.00

A-MA Mar. 1996   Skinner, Inc.

Three-Part Dining Table, federal mahogany turned & carved, North Shore, MA, ca. 1820, w/ beaded edge outlining the table top & skirt, 29" H, extends to 103" W, 50" D   . .$5,462.50

A-OH Nov. 1995   Garth's Auction

Hepplewhite Sideboard, w/ deep serpentine curve, mahogany w/ figured veneer and old finish, veneer and edge damage w/ age cracks w/ small sections of veneer missing on rails, poplar secondary wood, old but not orig. brasses, 72½"W, 29⅝"D, 40½"H. . .$4,400.00

A-MA June 1996   Skinner, Inc.

Sideboard, federal mahogany veneer, N. Eng., 1790-1810, w/ stringing outlining drawers, cupboards & legs, cuff inlay, ref., repl. brass, restored, 40¾" H, 71" W, 24½" D $4,887.50

A-MA Mar. 1996   Skinner, Inc.

Dining Table, mahogany, N. Eng., 1815-20, old ref., minor imperf., 28" H, extended 66¼" W, 47½" D .$1,035.00

A-PA Oct. 1995   Pook & Pook, Inc.

Federal Mahogany Sideboard, w/ ovals having inlaid trailing vines, reprs, ca. 1790-1800, 39" H, 70½" L . . . .
. . . .$32,500.00

A-OH April 1996   Early Auction Co.

Curio Cabinet
w. serpentine glass door & sides, gilt fleur-de-lis & acanthus leaf trim, 48" H $950.00

A-OH April 1996   Early Auction Co.

Vernis Martin Curio Cabinet w/ courtyard scene on front & scenic landscape sides, mirrored back & floral garnitures on legs & around glass, 72" H $1,500.00

A-PA Oct. 1995   Pook & Pook, Inc.

Chippendale Side Chairs, Phil., mahogany, ca. 1770, ...$37,500.00
Chippendale Arm Chair, mahogany, ca. 1790 . . . .$1,700.00

A-OH Nov. 1995   Garth's Auction

Chippendale Side Chair, PA, walnut w/ old dark finish, slip seat has new frame and is upholstered in ivory brocade, 38¾" H. $1,650.00

A-MA Aug. 1996   Robert C. Eldred Co., Inc.

Chippendale Side Chair, mahogany w/ slip seat, 18 C. $770.00

A-PA Oct. 1995   Pook & Pook, Inc.

Chippendale Side Chairs, pr., mahogany, ca. 1770 . . . .$13,000.00
Philaelphia Q.A. Armchair, walnut, ca. 1765 . . . .$3,250.00

A-OH Nov. 1995   Garth's Auction

Chippendale Side Chair, PA, walnut w/ old dk. finish, cabriole legs w/ ball and claw feet, molded edge seat frame, slip seat, pierced splat w/ Gothic tracery and shaped crest, some edge damage to back legs an seat frame, slip seat upholstered in ivory brocade, 37¾" H. $3,410.00

A-MA Oct. 1995   Skinner, Inc.

Set of Four Mahogany Chippendale Side Chairs, (2 illus.) Boston, MA area, ca. 1750-80, old refinish, minor imperfection, 36½" H $9200.00

A-PA Oct. 1995   Pook & Pook, Inc.

Georgian Chippendale Chairs, set of 6, mahogany w/ribbon backs, together w/2 matching side chairs of later date (not shown), ca. 1780 . . . . .$8,000.00

A-OH Nov. 1995   Garth's Auction

Q.A. Armchair, NH, maple w/ old refinishing, old rush seat has worn paint,44" H. $16,500.00

A-MA June 1996   Skinner, Inc.

Q.A. Walnut Side Chairs, Boston area, 1730-60 w/ balloon seats, old ref., reprs, 39½" H $13,800.00

A-MA Mar. 1996   Skinner, Inc.

Q.A. Side Chairs, pair, turned and carved maple, MA., late 18th C., old red stained finish, 40¾" H $2,530.00

A-MA Mar. 1996   Skinner, Inc.

Q.A. Side Chairs, pair, turned and carved, MA, late 18th C., old red stained finish, 41" H $4,025.00

A-MA Mar. 1996   Skinner, Inc.

Q.A. Maple Side Chair, MA., late 18th C., old ref., minor imperf., 40" H $632.50

A-MA Mar. 1996   Skinner, Inc.

Q.A. Side Chair, walnut carved & veneered, Newport, R.I., ca. 1750-65, attrib. to the shop of John Goddard, old ref., minor imperf., 41¾" H $10,350.00

A-MA Mar. 1996   Skinner, Inc.

Side Chairs, pair, federal carved mahogany, Salem, MA., ca. 1790, imperf., 36" H $7,475.00

A-MA Mar. 1996   Skinner, Inc.

Q.A. Carved & Turned Side Chairs, assembled set of four, stained maple & ash, N. Eng., 18th C., old ref., imperf., w/ additional similar side chair, 42¾" H $4,312.50

A-MA Mar. 1996   Skinner, Inc.

Shield-Back Carved Side Chairs, set of four, federal mahogany, Salem, MA., ca. 1800, old surface, 37¾"H $9,200.00

A-MA Mar. 1996   Skinner, Inc.

Fancy Chairs, set of six, N. Eng., ca. 1810-20, w/ orig. background w/ gold & yellow decor., old cane seats, some paint & other imperf., 35" H .$747.50

A-MA Mar. 1996   Skinner, Inc.

Q.A. Walnut Easy Chair, Boston, mid 18th C., imperf., 48" H, 32½" W $11,500.00

A-OH Nov. 1995   Garth's Auction

Federal Wingback Armchair, reeded mahogany frame, 42¼ H on brass casters. $7,150.00

A-MA Oct. 1995   Skinner, Inc.

Q.A. Side Chair, MA, ca.1730-50, w/ old raw umber and sienna graining, replm. seat, surface imperf., 41½" H $1,840.00

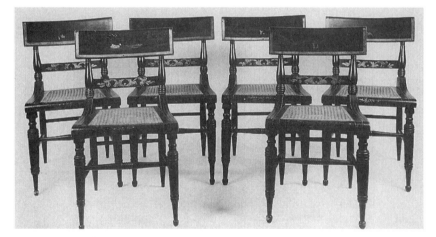

A-MA Jan. 1996   Skinner, Inc.

Side Chairs, 6 classical painted and gilded, NY, ca. 1820, w/ various scenes, seat 18" H, 31½" H $3,335.00

A-OH Nov. 1995   Garth's Auction

PA Q.A. Side Chair, eastern, walnut w/ old finish, one front foot and one end of crest below ear have old pieced repr., back glue blocks removed and strips added to side of frame to support seat, one back foot has old edge damage, one front glue block replaced, frame of slip seat has wooden braces added, 41" H. $2,970.00

A-OH Nov. 1995   Garth's Auction

Q.A. Side Chair, Philadelphia, walnut w/ old finish, minor repairs and age cracks but no replm. except for glue blocks in seat frame, chip on inside edge of one top leg post at seat, seat frame has had angle irons added and removed, slip seat upholstered in gold damask, 39" H. $3,520.00

A-MA Oct. 1995   Skinner, Inc.

Left to Right

Shaker Rocker, Maple, Enfield, NH, ca. 1840., old ref., losses and repr., 39½"
H $143.75

Shaker Rocker, maple, Mt. Lebannon, NY, 1875-1942 production, mkd. #1, ref.,
reprs., 28¾" H $115.00

Shaker Rocker, maple, Mt. Lebanon, N.Y., 1875-1942 production, mkd. #5, , minor
imperfections, 38½" H $431.25

Shaker Rocker, maple, Mt. Lebanon, N.Y., 1875-1942 production, mkd. #7 w/
decal, orig. varnish, minor imperf., 42" H $431.25

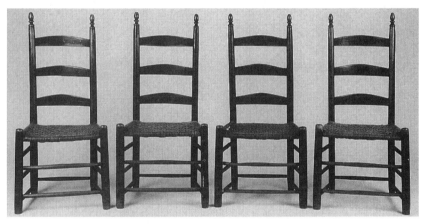

A-MA Jan. 1996   Skinner, Inc.

Shaker Slat Back Side Chairs, N. Eng., 4, maple & ash painted, late 18th c.,
minor imperfections, seat 16" H, 39½" H $920.00

A-MA Oct. 1995   Skinner, Inc.

**Assembled Set of Four Maple Slat-
Back Side Chairs,** (2 illus.) Berks
County, PA, 1750-70, replaced rush
seats, old refinish, 41½" H . . .$2185.00

A-MA Oct. 1995   Skinner, Inc.

Shaker Rocker, maple, Canterbury,
NH, ca. 1850, ref., 46½" H .$19,550.00

A-MA Jan. 1996   Skinner, Inc.

Side Chair, maple, brn. stain, woven
tape seat, one replm. tilter .$1,035.00

Rocking Chair, maple, woven multi-
colored tape seat, seat 14" H, 39½"
H $920.00

Side Chair, maple, pink & green woven
tape seat with fabric lining, replm tilters,
seat 15¼" H, 40⅞" H $805.00

A-MA Jan. 1996   Skinner, Inc.

Shaker Armchair w/ Rockers, ca.
1880, maple, black paint, replm. seat,
seat 15⅛" H, 41¾" H $1,380.00

Armchair, ca. 1930, maple, old brn.
stain, splint seat, seat 18⅞" H, 41⅛" H
. . . .$690.00

Rocking Chair, maple, ebony stain, red &
olive tape seat covered w/ olive velveteen
seat, seat 15" H, 34¾" H $402.50

A-MA Jan. 1996   Skinner, Inc.

Thumb-Back Windsor Side Chairs, 4, N. Eng., early 19th c., painted red, org., & brn., w/ metallic & grn. stenciling, imperfections, seat 17" H, 33¾" H ...$1,725.00

A-MA Oct. 1995   Skinner, Inc.

Set of Six Rod-Back Windsor Side Chairs, (3 illus.) N. Eng., early 19th c., old ref., 34" H $3450.00

A-VA Sept. 1995 Ken Farmer Auctions

Left to right
Sack Back Windsor Chair, CT, ca. 1780, shaped arms w/ "H" stretcher, old green paint $1,430.00
Rod Back Windsor Arm Chair, red paint, shaped seat $412.50

A-MA Oct. 1995   Skinner, Inc.

Set of Six Painted Rod-Back Windsor Side Chairs, (3 illus.) MA, 1800-20, old black paint, wear, 34½ H .$3105.00

A-MA Oct. 1995   Skinner, Inc.

Pair of Painted & Decor. Step Down Windsors, N. Eng., early 19th c., orig. blk. paint w/ floral leaf decor. on crests & stiles, minor paint wear, 36" H $1150.00

A-MA Oct. 1995   Skinner, Inc.

Windsor Comb-Back Armchair, PA, 1765-80, refinished, repairs, 40" H $4312.50

A-MA Oct. 1995   Skinner, Inc.

Set of Five Painted Rod-Back Windsor Side Chairs, (3 illus.) MA, ca. 1800-20, old black paint, wear, 35" H $1840.00

A-OH Jan. 1996   Garth's Auction

Philadelphia Windsor Armchair, old ref. good color, two back spindles & 1 arm vary in type of wood & color, 44¾" H $1,430.00

A-OH July 1996   Garth's Auction

Fanback Windsor Armchair, old gr. repaint, feet ended out, 17½" seat, 40" H $1,430.00

A-MA Mar. 1996 . . . . . . .Skinner, Inc.

Step Down Windsor Side Chairs, set of five, maple, pine & oak, PA., ca. 1830, old ref. minor imperf., 35" H. $1,150.00

A-PA May 1996   Pook & Pook Inc.

NE Windsor Rodback Settee, ca. 1800, retains br. surface w/ ylw. floral decor. & pinstriping, 78" W   .$5,500.00

A-MA Mar. 1996   Skinner, Inc.

Fan-Back Windsor Side Chair, branded "J.C. Tuttle," Salem, MA., late 18th / early 19th C., minor traces of orig. red paint, old ref., 36" H $373.75

A-MA June 1996   Skinner, Inc.

Fan-Back Windsor Armchair, maple, ash & pine, N. Eng., late 18th C., old finish, minor imperf., 38½" H   .$3,737.50

A-PA May 1996   Pook & Pook Inc.

Phil. Windsor Bench, ca. 1800, w/ bowback, bamboo turnings & plank seat, old finish, 37½" H, 77¼" W $2,500.00

A-MA Mar. 1996   Skinner, Inc.

Sack-Back Windsor Armchair, painted, R.I. or MA., ca. 1780, old blk. paint over earlier gr. paint, minor imperf., 39" H $4,887.50

A-MA June 1996   Skinner, Inc.

Sack-Back Windsor Chair, R.I. or MA., 1770-90, old dk. gr. paint, 36" H $5,175.00

A-MA Aug. 1996   Robert C. Eldred Co., Inc.

Windsor Armchair, w/ old blk. paint, back height 41½" $440.00

A-MA Mar. 1996   Skinner, Inc.

Gilt Gesso Looking Glass, MA., ca. 1820, minor imperf., 42" H, 21" W $3,450.00

A-MA Mar. 1996   Skinner, Inc.

Looking Glass, federal gilt & Elgomise panel, Providence, R.I., ca. 1800-10, 37¼" H, 15¼" W $5,175.00

A-MA Mar. 1996   Skinner, Inc.

Wall Mirror, federal mahogany inlaid & parcel gilt, N.Y. City, ca. 1800, old surface, imperf., 50½"H, 21½"W $6,325.00

A-MA Mar. 1996   Skinner, Inc.

Chippendale Mahogany Veneer & Parcel Gilt Mirror, late 18th. C., w/ scrolled crest & gilt incised vines, old surface, imperfections, 41" H, 22¼" W $1,840.00

A-MA Mar. 1996   Skinner, Inc.

Chippendale Mirror, mahogany veneer & parcel gilt, Eng., 18th C., old surface, minor reprs., 43" H, 22½" W $6,325.00

A-MA Mar. 1996   Skinner, Inc.

Chippendale Mirror, mahogany & mahogany veneer & parcel gilt, Eng., 18th C., imperf., 31"H, 17"W .$1,150.00

A-MA Mar. 1996   Skinner, Inc.

Chippendale Mirror, mahogany & mahogany veneer & parcel gilt, Am. or Eng., 18th C., 45" H, 25" W .$2,300.00

A-MA Mar. 1996   Skinner, Inc.

Chippendale Mirror, mahogany & mahogany veneer parcel gilt, Am. or Eng., third quarter 18th C., restored, 45½" H, 23" W $1,840.00

A-MA Mar. 1996   Skinner, Inc.

Chippendale Mirror, walnut veneer & parcel gilt, Am. or Eng., third quarter 18th C., old surface, imperf., 39½" H, 21½" W $1,725.00

A-OH July 1996   Garth's Auction

Chippendale Scroll Mirror, w/ figured walnut veneer, gilded leaves & phoenix crest, reprs., repl. mirror, 43½" H, 24" W $990.00

A-MA June 1996   Skinner, Inc.

Federal Mirror, Baltimore, C. 1801, w/ gilt, reverse painting on glass, orig. condition, minor imperf., 42½" H, 26½" W $18,400.00

A-MA Aug. 1996   Northeast Auctions

Federal Giltwood & Eglomise Wall Mirror, w/patriotic white & gold panel, 44" H $1,600.00

A-OH Jan. 1996   Garth's Auction

Empire Architectural Mirror, gilded gesso on wood w/ acorn cornice, acanthus & floral designs w/ orig. reverse painting, some edge damage, 25" W, 46" H $412.50

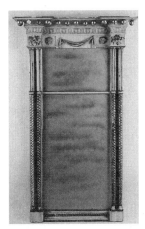

A-MA June 1996   Skinner, Inc.

Carved Gilt & Painted Mirror, N. Eng., 1815-25, imperf., 57¾" H, 35¼" W $2,185.00

A-MA Aug. 1996   Robert C. Eldred Co., Inc.

Convex Mirror, shell-form pendiment flanked by two dolphins gushing water, 2 candle arms, 29" H, 29" W .$4,400.00

A-OH APR. 1996   Garth's Auction

Federal Mirror, mahogany w/ old alligatored varnish finish, orig. mirror discolored, 37⅞" H, 17¾" W .$770.00

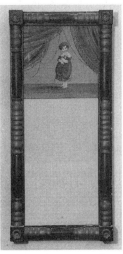

A-OH APR. 1996   Garth's Auction

Empire Mirror, w/ old blk. & gold repaint, brass rosettes in corner blocks, orig. reverse glass painting, orig. mirror, 29¾" H, 14" W $440.00

A-MA Aug. 1996   Northeast Auctions

Federal Giltwood Convex Mirror, w/ eagle & bellflower carving, 38" H $2,000.00

A-OH May 1996   Garth's Auction

Victorian Sofa, refin. carved walnut frame, reupholstered in gold floral brocade, 76" L $220.00

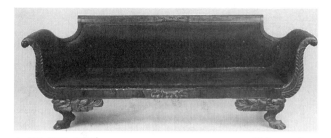

A-MA Mar. 1996   Skinner, Inc.

Carved Sofa, mahogany & mahogany veneer, MA., C. 1820-30, castors missing, imperf., 91" L $1,725.00

A-OH May 1996   Garth's Auction

Victorian Settee, medallion back, refin. finger carved walnut frame, reupholstered in deep pink velvet w/ tufted back, 59½" L $440.00

A-OH APR. 1996   Garth's Auction

Philadelphia Sheraton Sofa, mahogany frame w/ old finish, reupholstered, one back leg is braced, 76" W, 25½" D, 34⅜" H $4,400.00

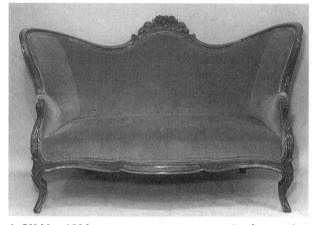

A-OH May 1996   Garth's Auction

Victorian Sofas, pair, (1 of 2), refin. walnut frame w/ well detailed rose carved crest, reupholstered in deep mauve velvet, 61" L $990.00

A-MA Aug. 1996   Robert C. Eldred Co., Inc.

Classical-Style Sofa, mahogany w/ bird's head scrolls at back, 70" L $2,200.00

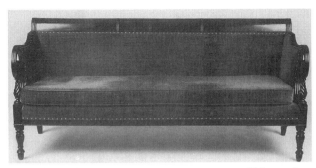

A-MA Oct. 1995   Skinner, Inc.

Classical Carved Mahogany Veneer Settee, ca. 1810, w/ scrolled arms and turned legs on castors, imperfections, 36¾" H, 74" L $1955.00

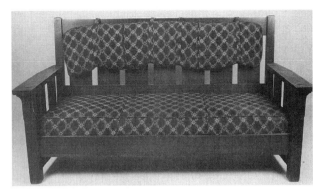

A-MA Oct. 1995   Skinner, Inc.

Lifetime Oak Settle, ca. 1910, Hastings, MI, orig. Med. finish & spring cushion seat, 40"H, 75½"L, 29½"W . . .$1,955.00

A-MA Oct. 1995   Skinner, Inc.

Classical Carved Mahogany Veneer Small Settee, Boston area, third quarter 19th c., w/ veneered seat rail, old surface, 32" H, 53½" L, 20½" D $2070.00

A-OH Nov. 1995   Garth's Auction

Sheraton Bamboo Windsor Settle Bench, old worn dark-brown finish, some edge damage and one back spindle is missing, 73" L $4,620.00

A-MA Jan. 1996   Skinner, Inc.

Sofa, carved mahogany & veneer, N. Eng., ca. 1825, old ref., some repr., 36⅛" H, 93¼" W, 25¾" D $1,265.00

A-MA Dec. 1995   Skinner, Inc.

Rococo Revival Seating Furniture, 2 pcs., (one pict.), mid 19th C., rosewood settee & similar walnut armchair $4,600.00

A-MA Jan. 1996   Skinner, Inc.

Dining Table, Queen Anne, painted red, cherry & birch, 18th c., minor imperfections, 28½" H, 40½" W, 36" D $20,700.00

A-MA Oct. 1995   Skinner, Inc.

Q.A. Drop Leaf Table, New Eng., mahogany, 18th c., ref., w/ restoration, 28½" H, 45½" W, 14½" D $2875.00

A-MA June 1996   Skinner, Inc.

Q.A. Maple Dining Table, N. Eng., C. 1760, old ref. minor imperf., 26¼" H, 47" D, 46" W $6,325.00

A-MA Aug. 1996   Robert C. Eldred Co.,   Inc.

English Pembroke Table, mahogany w/ 1 real and 1 false drawer, inlaid legs, 37½" L, 29" H $550.00

A-MA June 1996   Skinner, Inc.

Q.A. Maple Dining Table, N. Eng., C. 1760, old ref., imperf., 27½" H, 43½" D, extended 44⅜" W $5,462.50

A-MA Mar. 1996   Skinner, Inc.

Tilt Top Stand, federal mahogany carved, attrib. to Joseph Short, Newburyport, MA., ca. 1800, imperf., 27½" H, 23½" W, 17¾" D $4,600.00

A-MA Mar. 1996   Skinner, Inc.

Q.A. Mahogany Stand, R.I., ca. 1770, 26¾" H, 22" D $1,265.00

A-IL Apr. 1996   Olivers

Chippendale Pie Crust Tea Table, w/ball & claw feet, N. Eng., top diam. 35", 28" H $6,500.00

A-MA Mar. 1996   Skinner, Inc.

Chippendale Walnut Stand, Phil. ca. 1760-90, 28¾" H, 18" D . . .$24,150.00

A-MA Jan. 1996   Skinner, Inc.

Painted Candlestand, NH, birch, red, old ref., imperfections, 26½" H, 16½" W, 16⅛" D $2,875.00

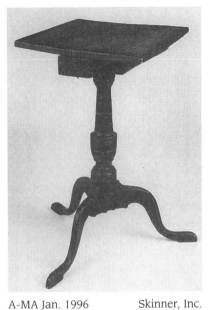

A-MA Jan. 1996   Skinner, Inc.

Chippendale Candlestand Cherry, w/drawer, late 18th c., old black paint & gilt striping, 25½" H, 14¾" W, 15¼" D $2,990.00

A-KY Oct. 1995 Ken Farmer Auctions

Paint Decor. Candle Stand, PA, Lancaster Co., ca. 1820-1840, salmon squiggle decor., 29" H, 18" W, 11" D $1,100.00

A-MA Mar. 1996   Skinner, Inc.

Mahogany Candlestand, probably MA., late 18th C., old finish, imperf., 27½" H, 23" W, 18" D $2,530.00

A-MA Aug. 1996   Robert C. Eldred Co., Inc.

Q.A. Tilt-Top Tea Table, cherry & maple, 28" H, 31½" Diam. ...$605.00

A-MA Oct. 1995   Skinner, Inc.

Chippendale Dish-Top Tea Table, N. Eng., w/ birdcage, mahogany, 18th c., old ref., imperf., 28" H, 36½" D $3220.00

A-MA Aug. 1996   Robert C. Eldred Co., Inc.

Tilt-Top Tea Table, w/ birdcage, cherry, 36" diam., 26" H $880.00

A-MA June 1996   Skinner, Inc.

Candlestand, maple & birch, N. Eng., C. 1800, old ref., minor reprs, 28½" H, 15⅝" D $1,495.00

A-MA Mar. 1996   Skinner, Inc.

Chippendale Tilt-Top Tea Table, mahogany carved, N. Eng., late 18th C., ref., imperf., 27" H, 34⅝" D .$1,092.50

A-MA Aug. 1996   Robert C. Eldred Co., Inc.

Hepplewhite Three-Part Banquet Table, mahogany w/ mahogany veneers, restor. $2,420.00

A-MA Mar. 1996   Skinner, Inc.

Inlaid Card Table, federal mahogany, Boston, ca. 1810, minor imperf., 28½" H, 36" W, 17½" D $5,750.00

A-MA Mar. 1996   Skinner, Inc.

Q.A. Mahogany Tea Table, MA., ca. 1760, old ref., restored, 26½" H, 29" W, 19½" D $14,950.00

A-MA Mar. 1996   Skinner, Inc.

Demi-Lune Card Table, federal mahogany & mahogany veneer, Concord, N.H., ca. 1810, w/ stringing in outline & inlaid oval paterae at the top of each leg, imperf., 28½" H, 36" W, 17" D $1,380.00

A-MA Mar. 1996   Skinner, Inc.

Card Table, federal mahogany inlaid, attrib. to the Seymour workshop, Boston, ca. 1800-10, old ref., 29½" H, 36" W, 17¼" D $6,325.00

A-MA Jan. 1996   Skinner, Inc.

Tea Table, NH, maple, painted red, 18th c., imperfections, 26" H, 33" W, 22¾" D $3,737.50

A-MA Mar. 1996   Skinner, Inc.

Chippendale Carved Card Table, mahogany, Newport, R.I. ca. 1760-80, attrib. to John Townsend, old ref., minor imperf., 28" H, 33¾" W, 16¾" $8,625.00

A-MA Mar. 1996   Skinner, Inc.

Card Table, federal mahogany veneer carved, attrib. to Samuel McIntire workshop, Salem, MA. ca. 1800-10, old surface, imperf., 29½" H, 36¼" W, 17¾" D $21,850.00

A-MA Jan. 1996   Skinner, Inc.

Drop Leaf Dining Table, mahogany, N. Eng., ca. 1830, old ref., 28" H, 20" W, ext. 71¼" W, 43¾" D $690.00

A-MA Mar. 1996   Skinner, Inc.

Pembroke Table, federal mahogany & mahogany veneer, N.Y., early 19th C., old ref., minor imperf., 28¾" H, 21½" W, 38¾" D $862.50

A-MA June 1996   Skinner, Inc.

Mahogany Pembroke Table, N. Eng., late 18th C., w/ beaded drawer & molded Marlborough legs, w/ pierced brackets, ref., repl. brackets, 27½" H, 18" W, 32¾" D $1,380.00

A-MA Mar. 1996   Skinner, Inc.

Federal Mahogany Breakfast Table, N.Y. or CT. late 18th C., orig. brass on single drawer w/ scratch bead, old ref., old repl. stretchers, 28⅛" H, 19⅝" W, 29⅛" D $1,495.00

A-MA June 1996   Skinner, Inc.

Tavern Table, pine & maple, N. Eng., 18th C., oval top, molded stretcher, 23⅝" H, 28" W, 21¼" D $4,887.50

A-MA Mar. 1996   Skinner, Inc.

Maple & Pine Chair Table, N. Eng., ca. 1800, old ref., 28½" H, 47½" D $3,737.50

A-MA Jan. 1996   Skinner, Inc.

Wm. & Mary Butterfly Table, Maple, N. Eng., 18th c., ref., 24¾" H, 28" W, 33" D $1,150.00

A-MA Mar. 1996   Skinner, Inc.

William & Mary Side Table, walnut & yellow pine, Piedmont area, southern states, 18th C., orig. pulls ref. w/ traces of red paint, 27¾" H, 26¾" W, 16⅝" D $5,175.00

A-MA Mar. 1996   Skinner, Inc.

Tavern Table, painted, turned, N. Eng. 18th C., painted off white over earlier red, imperf., 26½" H, 30 " W, 26" D $4,600.00

A-MA June 1996   Skinner, Inc.

Walnut Side Table w/ Drawer, Lancaster County, PA., mid 18th C., old finish, minor imperf., 30" H, 38" W, 27¼" D $3,737.50

A-MA June 1996   Skinner, Inc.

Card Table, carved mahogany veneer & brass, N.Y. or N.J., 1820's w/ swivel top, veneered skirt & brass paw feet, old ref., imperf. 31" H, 35¾" W, 18⅜" D $2,300.00

A-MA Oct. 1995   Skinner, Inc.

Classical Gaming Table, mahogany, ca. 1825, old finish, minor imperfs., 29½" H, 36" W, 18" D $460.00

A-MA Oct. 1995   Skinner, Inc.

Classical Sofa Table, ca. 1820-40, mahogany veneer, w/ 2 cockbeaded drawers, orig. brass, old ref, 31¼" H, 23⅜" W, 39¾" D $4025.00

A-MA June 1996   Skinner, Inc.

Sewing Stand, mahogany & mahogany veneer carved, attrib. to Isaac Vose & Issac Vose Jr., Boston, C. 1824, old fin., minor imperf., 30¼" H, 20½" W, 18½" D $3,737.50

A-MA Oct. 1995   Skinner, Inc.

Classical Card Table, mahogany veneer, imperfs., 28½" H, 36¼" W, 17¾" D $632.50

A-MA June 1996   Skinner, Inc.

Sewing Stand, federal mahogany & flame birch veneer inlaid, Boston or Salem, MA., 1790-1800, old ref., repl. bag, imperf., reprs., 29¼" H, 21" W, 16" D $3,450.00

A-MA Oct. 1995   Skinner, Inc.

Classical Work Stand, MA, ca. 1815-25, mahogany vaneer, old refinish, imperfs., 27½" H, 19¼" W, 18" D $690.00

A-MA Oct. 1995   Skinner, Inc.

Stand Table, NH, early 19th c., birch & tiger maple, orig. brasses, old ref., 29¼ H, 18½" D $2,300.00

A-MA Mar. 1996   Skinner, Inc.

Sewing Stand, federal mahogany & flame birch veneer, Boston or Salem, MA., ca. 1800-10, ref., imperf., 27½" H, 16⅞" W, 15½" D $2,990.00

A-KY Oct. 1995 Ken Farmer Auctions

Writing Arm Windsor Rocker, half arrow slats in bac, old green paint, early 19th C, 43" H $385.00
Windsor Side Chair, ca. 1780-1800, traces of old red paint $192.50

A-PA Oct. 1995   Pook & Pook, Inc.

Chippendale Side Chairs, pr., Delaware Valley, walnut, ca. 1770 . .$16,000.00
Q.A. Drop Leaf Table, PA, walnut, ca. 1770, 28¾" H, 45¾" W $4,000.00

A-MA Jan. 1996   Skinner, Inc.

Side Chair, maple, olive colored taped seat, salmon paint, old repr., seat 16½" H, 40¾" H, ...$977.50

One-Drawer Table, ca. 1840, curly birch and pine, old red wash, 26¾" H, 36" W, 22¾" D $8,050.00

Side Chair, maple, multi-colored tape seat, red stain, tilters, repr. break to top slat, leather thongs on tilters replm., seat 14¾" H, 40¾" H $805.00

A-MA Jan. 1996   Skinner, Inc.

Dining Chairs, 6, N. Eng., classical tiger maple, ca. 1830, old ref., imperfections, seat 17½" H, 43¼" H $2,185.00

A-KY Oct. 1995 Ken Farmer Auctions

Windsor Side Chairs, pr., PA, bamboo turnings, 2nd qtr. 19th C., orig. black sponge on red paint decor. w/ mustard high-lights on crest, 34½" H $605.00
Table, PA, 19th C., w/ old black paint over poplar & pine, oval top w/ straight edge on back, dovetailed drawer, 30" H, 41" W, 21 " D$2,200.00

A-IA July, 1996   Gene Harris Auction

Ornate High Back Chair w/ rolled arms & back. $150.00
Ornate Magazine Rack, . . .$150.00
Rolled Back Side Chair, stick & ball dec. $175.00
Ornate Triple Shelf Stand, $550.00

A-IA July, 1996   Gene Harris Auction

Diamond Back Flare-Sided Rocker, ...$125.00
Rolled Edge Diamond Back Flare-Sided Rocker, ...$200.00
Full Skirted Diamond Back Chair, ...$70.00
Chaise Lounge, ...$475.00

A-IA July, 1996   Gene Harris Auction

Flat Sided Rocker, ...$275.00

A-IA July, 1996   Gene Harris Auction

Blue Platform rocker w/ rabbit ear & charm decoration, rolled arms.$500.00

A-IA July, 1996   Gene Harris Auction

Ornate Spiderweb Back Rocker, ...$300.00
Two Tier Magazine Stand, .$400.00
High Back Ornate Chair w/ Rabbit Ear, spider web back. $200.00

A-IA July, 1996   Gene Harris Auction

2 Pc. Stick & Ball Cradle, .$125.00

A-IA July, 1996   Gene Harris Auction

Settee, lift top seat, skirted. .$250.00
Wicker Wheel Chair, black. $150.00

A-IA July, 1996   Gene Harris Auction

Natural Wicker Couch & Chair Set w/ upholstered back & seat. .$600.00

A-IA July, 1996   Gene Harris Auction

Pair of Spring Chairs $300.00

A-IA July, 1996   Gene Harris Auction

Wooden-Base Wicker-Shade Lamp $140.00
Tea Cart $250.00
Large Floor Lamp $575.00
Ornate Stick & Ball Chair .$200.00
Tea Cart w/ Glass Top $375.00
Magazine Holder . . . . .N/S
Low Green Ferner $120.00
Wicker Ottoman w/ Padding $150.00

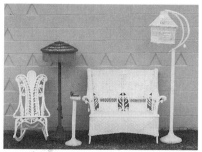

A-IA July, 1996   Gene Harris Auction

Ornate Rocker $175.00
Floor Lamp w/ Fringed Shade $200.00
Floor Model Ashtray $50.00
High Back Settee, rolled arms & back. $475.00
Bird Cage on Stand $200.00

A-IA July, 1996   Gene Harris Auction

Scale $30.00
Wicker Table w/ Two Shelves $80.00
Oak Top Wicker Base Oval Table $225.00
Drop Leaf Oak Top Table w/ wicker base. $550.00
Tightly Woven Table, drape to legs. $70.00
Oval Wicker Table $75.00
Wooden Top Table $65.00

A-IA July, 1996   Gene Harris Auction

3 Pc. Heywood Wakefield Bamboo Set, two chairs & round table. $700.00

A-IA July, 1996   Gene Harris Auction

Rolled Edge Rocker . . . . .N/S
Settee w/ Small Rolled Edge . . . .
. . . .$175.00
Barrel Chair $50.00

A-IA July, 1996   Gene Harris Auction

Scrolled Photographers Corner Chair $300.00

A-IA July, 1996   Gene Harris Auction

Ornately Decorated Lounge Chair
. . . .$800.00

A-IA July, 1996   Gene Harris Auction

Ornate Triple Shelf Stand .$550.00
Two Tier Magazine Stand .$400.00

A-OH APR. 1996   Garth's Auction

Decorated Pennsylvania Settle Bench, orig. yellow paint w/ br. & blk. striping & stenciled & freehand flowers w/ angel wings, mkd. "J. Swint, chair maker", has some wear but yellow is very bright, 78½" L . .$9,900.00

A-MA Aug. 1996   Robert C. Eldred Co., Inc.

Corner Chair, w/ rush seat, old br. finish, back 30" H $385.00

A-OH June 1996   Garth's Auction

Decorated Kas, poplar w/ old polychrome floral repaint on ivory panels w/ red moldings and blue ground, three sections, case w/ removable doors & interior shelves & wide molded cornice, repl. feet, minor edge wear & age cracks, repl. brasses, 56" W, 71¼" H $2,750.00

A-MA Aug. 1996   Robert C. Eldred Co., Inc.

Sheraton / Victorian Whatnot Stand, mahogany w/ mahogany veneers, w/ inlay, 58½" H, 24" W, 17" D $880.00

A-VA Aug. 1995 Ken Farmer Auctions

Carved Q.A. Corner Chair, walnut, ca. 1730-1750, minor patches to rear seat rail & one foot, knee responds missing, seat 17" H, 32" H, 25" W, 25" D $4,125.00

A-CT May 1996   Craftsman Auctions
Hexagonal Table, Stickley Bros. . . .
. . . .$950.00

A-CT May 1996   Craftsman Auctions
Bookcase, Limbert, orig. finish &
branded, 57" x 48" x 14" . . .$2,500.00

A-CT May 1996   Craftsman Auctions
2 Drawer Nightstand, L&JG Stickley,
new finish, 29½" x 20" x 14"$1,350.00

A-CT May 1996   Craftsman Auctions
Morris Chair, L&JG Stickley, orig. finish, slats to seat signed
"Handcraft" decal $3,450.00

A-CT May 1996   Craftsman Auctions
Early Arm Chair, Gustav Stickley, orig. finish, 39" x 31" x
28" $1,900.00

A-CT May 1996   Craftsman Auctions
Triple Door Bookcase, Limbert, orig. finish, 57" x 66" x
14" $4,000.00

A-CT May 1996   Craftsman Auctions
Roll top Desk, Gustav Stickley, new dark brown finish,
some restoration & minor roughness, missing locks on interior drawers $3,750.00

A-CT May 1996   Craftsman Auctions

Arts & Crafts Oak Twin Beds, pr., ca. 1912, orig. med./light finish, headboard & foot board, 54⅞" H, 79¼" L, 42¼" W $575.00

A-CT May 1996   Craftsman Auctions

Dining Table, Limbert, w/ four leaves, orig. finish, branded, 48" D . .$2,250.00

A-MA May 1996   Skinner, Inc.

Breakfront Sideboard, walnut & oak, w/ enameled copper trim, amber glass door panels & center mirror, English Arts & Crafts, 83" H, 85" W, 28" D $7,475.00

A-MA Oct. 1995   Skinner, Inc.

Arts and Crafts Oak Tall Case Clock, Colonial Mfg. Co., Zeeland, MI, orig. medium finish, 88½" H, 20⅝" W, 13½" D $1,610.00

A-CT May 1996   Craftsman Auctions

Arm Settle, Lifetime, orig. finish, paper label, cushion replaced, 36" x 78" x 31½" $2,750.00

A-CT May 1996   Craftsman Auctions

Double Door Bookcase, Limbert, has cut-outs, new red-brown finish, 47" x 32" x 11" $2,850.00

A-MA Oct. 1995   Skinner, Inc.

Lifetime Oak Two Door Bookcase,
Hastings, MI, ca. 1912, orig. med./dark
finish, brass hardware & glass, 56¾" H,
48½" W, 14⅝" D $1,380.00

A-MA Oct. 1995   Skinner, Inc.

**Gustav Stickley Oak Two-Door
Bookcase,** ca. 1912, light finish, ref.,
44¼" H, 36" W, 12⅛" D $3,565.00

A-MA Jan. 1996   Skinner, Inc.

Lifetime Oak Slant Lid Desk, Lifetime decal, minor imperfections, 43½"
H, 32" W, 16" D 920.00

A-MA Oct. 1995   Skinner, Inc.

**L. & J.G. Stickley Oak Two-Door
China Cabinet,** ca. 1912, orig. med.
finish and hammered copper hardware, roughness, imperfections, 66½"
H, 49" W, 15" D $8,337.50

A-MA Oct. 1995   Skinner, Inc.

**Arts & Crafts Oak, Leaded Glass &
Mirrored Sideboard,** Eng., ca. 1905,
orig. light finish, central leaded glass,
mirror-backed shelves & backsplash,
69¾" H, 60" W, 22¾ D $1,092.50

A-MA Oct. 1995   Skinner, Inc.

Limbert Oak Single Drawer Desk,
Holland, MI, ca. 1912, medium finish,
ref. top, 29¾" H, 42" L, 28" W $1,092.50

A-MA Oct. 1995   Skinner, Inc.

**Gustav Stickley Oak Spindle
Library Table,** ca. 1908, med. finish,
13 spindles, water rings on top, 28¾"
H, 36" L, 23⅞" W $3,737.50

A-MA Oct. 1995   Skinner, Inc.

**L. & J.G. Stickley Oak Occasional
Table,** ca. 1907, med. finish, some
later finish, 29¼" H, 36" D .$1,725.00

A-MA Oct. 1995   Skinner, Inc.

**L. & J.G. Stickley Oak Trestle
Table,** ca. 1910, orig. med. finish, 29¼"
H, 54" L, 32" W $3,105.00

A-OH Mar. 1996   Garth's Auctions

Mission Style Sofa Bench, oak w/ old
finish, cushion reupholstered in brown
leather finish vinyl, 78 L $357.50
Fireplace Fender, brass rails & steel
wire mesh, 37¼" L $137.50

A-MA Oct. 1995　　　Skinner, Inc.

Gustav Stickley Oak V Back Chairs, pr. orig. med., dark finish, one w/ later finish, 35¾ H, 18¾" W $1,092.50

Gustav Stickley Oak Tabouret, ca., 1905, orig., med. finish, 18⅛" H, 16" D $1,150.00

Early Gustav Stickley Oak Footstool, ca. 1902, med. finish, brick Naugahyde upholstery, 4⅞" H, 13⅝" W $575.00

A-MA Oct. 1995　　　Skinner, Inc.

Shop of the Crafters Oak Arm Chair, Cincinnati, ca. 1910, light finish, straight ladder-back w/tapering back post, ref., replm. seat, 42" H, 28¼ W $977.50

Oak Smoker's Cabinet w/ Cutouts, orig., med. finish & brass pull, side separation repair, 38⅞" H, 14" W, 12⅛" D $747.50

A-MA Oct. 1995　　　Skinner, Inc.

Oak Slat Sided Arm Rocker, Frank S. Harden Co., Connellsville/Camden, NY, orig. med. finish & leather upholstered box spring seat, 36" H, 27¼" W $373.75

Oak Book Stand, Frank S. Harden Co., Connellsville/Camden, NY, orig. finish w/ some finish loss on top shelf, 41¼" H, 20¼ L, 16" W $345.00

A-MA Oct. 1995　　　Skinner, Inc.

Arts & Crafts Oak Arm Rocker, Harden or J.M. Young, Camden, NY, ca 1910, orig. med. finish, 35¾" H, 27" W $345.00

J.M. Young Oak Footstool, orig. med. finish & leather upholstery, 16⅝" H, 18" L, 12¾" W $115.00

Arts & Crafts Oak & Leather Upholstered Arm Chair, Camden, NY, orig. med. finish & leather, 38⅛" H, 26" W . . . .$NS

A-MA Oct. 1995　　　Skinner, Inc.

Gustav Stickley Oak Chalet Desk, ca. 1907, med. finish, int. drop-front water mark, 45¾" H, 22⅛" W$1,840.00

L. & J.G. Stickley Onondaga Shops Oak Side Chair, ca. 1905, med. finish, missing seat cushion, 37¼" H, 19⅜" W $287.50

A-MA Jan. 1996　　　Skinner, Inc.

J.M. Young Oak Rocker & Chair, w/ paper labels, orig. finish, 35" H & 39½" H $747.50

A-MA Oct. 1995　　　Skinner, Inc.

Left to Right

Gustav Stickley Oak Spindle Arm Chair, ca. 1907, med. finish, 47¾" H, 27⅜" W $7,475.00

Gustav Stickley Oak Spindle Arm Chair, ca. 1904, med. finish, back seat apron imperfections, 47¾" H, 27⅜" W $4,312.50

A-MA Oct. 1995　　　Skinner, Inc.

L. & J.G. Stickley Oak Rocking Morris Chair, ca. 1912, orig. med. finish, spring cushion seat, adjustable back, 38½" H, 29½" W $1,495.00

L. & J.G. Stickley Oak Rocking Morris Chair, ca. 1912, mahogany finish, orig. spring cushion, adjustable back, 38½" H, 29½" W $1,495.00

A-MA Oct. 1995　　　Skinner, Inc.

L. & J.G. Stickley Oak Slat Sided Morris Chair, ca. 1907, orig. med. finish & spring cushion seat, adjustable back, replm. bar, 42½" H, 31½" W $2,760.00

AGATA GLASS was patented by Joseph Locke of the New England Glass Company of Cambridge, Massachusetts, in 1877. The application of a metallic stain left a mottled design characteristic of agata, hence the name.

AMBER GLASS is the name of any glassware having a yellowish-brown color. It became popular during the last quarter of the 19th century.

AMBERINA GLASS was patented by the New England Glass Company in 1833. It is generally recognized as a clear yellow glass shading to a deep red or fushcia at the top. When the colors are opposite, it is known as reverse amberina. It was machine-pressed into molds, free blown, cut and pattern molded. Almost every glass factory here and in Europe produced this ware; however, few pieces were ever marked.

AMETHYST GLASS — The term identifies any glassware made in the proper dark purple shade. It became popular after the Civil War.

ART GLASS is a general term given to various types of ornamental glass made to be decorative rather than functional. It dates primarily from the late Victorian period to the present day and, during the span of time, glassmakers have achieved fantastic effects of shape, color, pattern, texture and decoration.

AVENTURINE GLASS — The Venetians are credited with the discovery of aventurine during the 1860s. It was produced by various mixes of copper in yellow glass. When the finished pieces were broken, ground or crushed, they were used as decorative material by glassblowers. Therefore, a piece of aventurine glass consists of many tiny glittering particles on the body of the object, suggestive of sprinkled gold crumbs or dust. Other colors in aventurine are known to exist.

BACCARAT GLASS was first made in France in 1756 by La Compagnie des Cristelleries de Baccarat—until the firm went bankrupt. Production began for the second time during the 1820s and the firm is still in operation, producing fine glassware and paperweights. Baccarat is famous for its earlier paperweights made during the last half of the 19th century.

BOHEMIAN GLASS is named for its country of origin. It is ornate, overlay, or flashed glassware, popular during the Victorian era.

BRISTOL GLASS is a lightweight opaque glass, often having a light bluish tint, and decorated with enamels. The ware is a product of Bristol, England—a glass center since the 1700s.

BURMESE — Frederick Shirley developed this shaded art glass at the now-famous old Mt. Washington Glass Company in New Bedford, Massachusetts, and patented his discovery under the name of "Burmese" on December 15, 1885. The ware was also made in England by Thomas Webb & Sons.

Burmese is a hand-blown glass with the exception of a few pieces that were pattern molded. The latter are either ribbed, hobnail or diamond quilted in design. This ware is found in two textures or finishes: the original glazed or shiny finish, and the dull, velvety, satin finish. It is a homogeneous glass (singlelayered) that was never lined, cased or plated. Although its color varies slightly, it always shades from a delicate yellow at the base to a lovely salmon-pink at the top. The blending of colors is so gradual that it is difficult to determine where one color ends and the other begins.

CAMBRIDGE glasswares were produced by the Cambridge Glass Company in Ohio from 1901 until the firm closed in 1954.

CAMEO GLASS can be defined as any glass in which the surface has been cut away to leave a design in relief. Cutting is accomplished by the use of hand-cutting tools, wheel cutting and hydrofluoric acid. This ware can be clear or colored glass of a single layer, or glass with multiple layers of clear or colored glass.

Although cameo glass has been produced for centuries, the majority available today dates from the late 1800s. It has been produced in England, France and other parts of Europe, as well as the United States. The most famous of the French masters of cameo wares was Emile Gallé .

CANDY CONTAINTERS were used for holding tiny candy pellets. These were produced in a variety of shapes—locomotives, cars, boats, guns, and such, for children.

CARNIVAL GLASS was an inexpensive, pressed iridescent glassware made from about 1900 through the 1920s. It was made in quantitites by Northwood Glass Company, Fenton Art Glass Company and others, to compete with the expensive art glass of the period. Originally called "taffeta" glass, the ware became known as "carnival" glass during the 1920s when carnivals gave examples as premiums or prizes.

CORALENE — The term coralene denotes a type of decoration rather than a kind of glass—consisting of many tiny beads, either of colored or transparent glass—decorating the surface. The most popular design used resembled coral or seaweed, hence the name.

CRACKLE GLASS — This type of art glass was an invention of the Venetians that spread rapidly to other countries. It is made by plunging red-hot glass into cold water, then reheating and reblowing it, thus producing an unusual outer surface which appears to be covered with a multitiude of tiny fractures, but is perfectly smooth to the touch.

CRANBERRY GLASS — The term "cranberry glass" refers to color only, not to a particular type of glass. It is undoubtedly the most familiar colored glass known to collectors. This ware was blown or molded, and often decorated with enamels.

CROWN MILANO glass was made by Frederick Shirley at the Mt. Washington Glass Company, New Bedford, Massachusetts, from 1886-1888. It is ivory in color with a satin finish, and was embellished with floral sprays, scrolls and gold enamel.

CROWN TUSCAN glass has a pink-opaque body. It was originally produced in 1936 by A.J. Bennett, president of the Cambridge Glass Company of Cambridge, Ohio. The line was discontinued in 1954. Occasionally referred to as Royal Crown Tuscan, this ware was named for a scenic area in Italy, and it has been said that its color was taken from the fresh-colored sky at sunrise. When transilluminated, examples do have all of the blaze of a sunrise—a characteristic that is even applied to new examples of the ware reproduced by Mrs. Elizabeth Degenhart of Crystal Art Glass, and Harold D. Bennett, Guernsey Glass Company of Cambridge, Ohio.

CUSTARD GLASS was manufactured in the United States for a period of about 30 years (1885-1915). Although Harry Northwood was the first and largest manufacturer of custard glass, it was also produced by the Heisey Glass Company, Diamond Glass Company, Fenton Art Glass Company and a number of others.

The name custard glass is derived from its "custard yellow" color which may shade light yellow to ivory to light green—glass that is opaque to opalescent. Most pieces have fiery opalescence when held to the light. Both the color and glow of this ware came from the use of uranium salts in the glass. It is generally a heavy type pressed glass made in a variety of different patterns.

CUT OVERLAY — The term identifies pieces of glassware usually having a milk-white exterior that have been cased with cranberry, blue or amber glass. Other type examples are deep blue, amber or cranberry on crystal glass, and the majority of pieces has been decorated with dainty flowers. Although Bohemian glass manufacturers produced some very choice pieces during the 19th century, fine examples were also made in America, as well as in France and England.

DAUM NANCY is the mark found on pieces of French cameo glass made by August and Antonin Daum after 1875.

DURAND ART GLASS was made by Victor Durand from 1879 to 1935 at the Durand Art Glass Works in Vineland, New Jersey. The glass resembles Tiffany in quality. Drawn white feather designs and thinly drawn glass threading (quite brittle) applied around the main body of the ware, are striking examples of Durand creations on an iridescent surface.

FLASHED WARES were popular during the late 19th century. They were made by partially coating the inner surface of an object with a thin plating of glass or another, more dominant color—usually red. These pieces can readily be identified by holding the object to the light and examining the rim, as it will show more than one layer of glass. Many pieces of "rubina crystal" (cranberry to clear), "blue amberina" (blue to amber), and "rubina verde" (cranberry to green), were manufactured in this way.

FINDLAY or ONYX art glass was manufactured about 1890 for only a short time by the Dalzell Gilmore Leighton Company of Findlay, Ohio.

FRANCISWARE is a hobnail glassware with frosted or clear glass hobs and stained amber rims and tops. It was produced during the late 1880s by Hobbs, Brockunier and Company.

FRY GLASS was made by the H.C. Fry Company, Rochester, Pennsylvania, from 1901, when the firm was organized, until 1934 when operations ceased. The firm specialized in the manufacturing of cut glassware. The production of their famous "foval" glass did not begin until the 1920s. The firm also produced a variety of glass specialties, oven wares and etched glass.

GALLÉ glass was made in Nancy, France, by Emile Gallé at the Gallé Factory founded in 1874. The firm produced both enameled and cameo glass, pottery, furniture and other art nouveau items. After Gallé 's death in 1904, the factory continued operating until 1935.

GREENTOWN glass was made in Greentown, Indiana, by the Indiana Tumbler and Goblet Company from 1894 until 1903. The firm produced a variety of pressed glasswares in addition to milk and chocolate glass.

GUNDERSON peachblow is a more recent type art glass produced in 1952 by the Gunderson-Pairpoint Glass Works of New Bedford, Massachusetts, successors to the Mt. Washington Glass Company. Gunderson pieces have a soft satin finish shading from white at the base to a deep rose at the top.

HOBNAIL — The term hobnail identifies any glassware having "bumps"—flattened, rounded or pointed—over the outer surface of the glass. A variety of patterns exists. Many of the fine early examples were produced by Hobbs, Brockunier and Company, Wheeling, West Virginia, and the New England Glass Company.

HOLLY AMBER, originally known as "golden agate," is a pressed glass pattern which features holly berries and leaves over its glossy surface. Its color shades from golden brown tones to opalescent streaks. This ware was produced by the Indiana Tumbler and Goblet Company for only 6 months, from January 1 to June 13, 1903. Examples are rare and expensive.

IMPERIAL GLASS — The Imperial Glass Company of Bellaire, Ohio, was organized in 1901 by a group of prominent citizens of Wheeling, West Virginia. A variety of fine art glass, in addition to carnival glass, was produced by the firm. The two trademarks which identified the ware were issued in June 1914. One consisted of the firm's name, "Imperial," and the other included a cross formed by double-pointed arrows.

The latter ll of their present production—including reproduced carnival glass.

LATTICINO is the name given to articles of glass in which a network of tiny milk-white lines appear, crisscrossing between two walls of glass. It is a type of filigree glassware developed during the 16th century by the Venetians.

LEGRAS GLASS, cameo, acid cut and enameled glasswares were made by August J.F. Legras at Saint-Denis, France, from 1864-1914.

LOETZ GLASS was made in Austria just before the turn of the century. As Loetz worked in the Tiffany factory before returning to Austria, much of his glass is similar in appearance to Tiffany wares. Loetz glass is often marked "Loetz" or "Loetz-Austria."

LUTZ GLASS was made by Nicholas Lutz, a Frenchman, who worked at the Boston and Sandwich Glass Company from 1870 to 1888 when it closed. He also produced fine glass at the Mt. Washington Glass Company. Lutz is noted for two different types of glass—striped and threaded wares. Other glass houses also produced similar glass and these wares were known as Lutz-type.

MARY GREGORY was an artist for the Boston and Sandwich Glass Company during the last quarter of the 19th century. She decorated glassware with white enamel figures of young children engaged in playing, collecting butterflies, etc., in white on transparent glass, both clear and colored. Today the term "Mary Gregory" glass applies to any glassware that remotely resembles her work.

MERCURY GLASS is a double-walled glass that dates from the 1850s to about 1910. It was made in England as well as the United States during this period. Its interior, usually in the form of vases, is lined with flashing mercury, giving the items an all over silvery appearance. The entrance hole in the base of each piece was sealed over. Many pieces were decorated.

MILK GLASS is an opaque pressed glassware, usually of milk-white color, although green, amethyst, black, and shades of blue were made. Milk glass was produced in quantity in the United States during the 1880s, in a variety of patterns.

MILLEFIORI — This decorative glassware is considered to be a specialty of the Venetians. It is sometimes called "glass of a thousand flowers," and has been made for centuries. Very thin colored glass rods are arranged in bundles, then fused together with heat. When the piece of glass is sliced across, it has a design like that of many small flowers. These tiny wafer-thin slices are then embedded in larger masses of glass, enlarged and shaped.

MOSER GLASS was made by Kolomon Moser at Carlsbad. The ware is considered to be another type of art nouveau glass as it was produced during its heyday—during the early 1900s. Principal colors included amethyst, cranberry, green and blue, with fancy enameled decoration.

MOTHER-OF-PEARL, often abbreviated in descriptions as M.O.P., is glass composed of two or more layers, with a pattern showing through to the other surface. The pattern, caused by internal air traps, is created by expanding the inside layer of molten glass into molds with varying design. When another layer of glass is applied, this brings out the design. The final layer of glass is then acid dipped, and the result is mother-of-pearl satinware. Patterns are numerous. The most frequently found are the diamond quilted, raindrop and herringbone. This ware can be one solid color, a single color shading light to dark, two colors blended or a variety of colors which include the rainbow effect. In addition, many pieces are decorated with colorful enamels, coralene beading, and other applied glass decorations.

NAILSEA GLASS was first produced in England from 1788 to 1873. The characteristics that identify this ware are the "pulled" loopings and swirls of colored glass over the body of the object.

NEW ENGLAND PEACHBLOW was patented in 1886 by the New England Glass Company. It is a single-layered glass shading from opaque white at the base to deep rose-red or raspberry at the top. Some pieces have a glossy surface, but most were given an acid bath to produce a soft, matte finish.

NEW MARTINSVILLE PEACHBLOW GLASS was produced from 1901-1907 at New Martinsville, Pennsylvania.

OPALESCENT GLASS — The term refers to glasswares which have a milky white effect in the glass, usually on a colored ground. There are three basic types of this ware. Presently, the most popular includes pressed glass patterns found in table settings. Here the opalescence appears at the top rim, the base, or a combination of both. On blown or mold-blown glass, the pattern itself consists of this milky effect—such as Spanish lace. Another example is the opalescent points on some pieces of hobnail glass. These wares are lighter weight. The third group includes opalescent novelties, primarily of the pressed variety.

PEKING GLASS is a type of Chinese cameo glass produced from the 1700s, well into the 19th century.

PHOENIX GLASS — The firm was established in Beaver County, Pennsylvania, during the late 1800s, and produced a variety of commercial glasswares. During the 1930s the factory made a desirable sculptured gift-type glassware which has become very collectible in recent years. Vases, lamps, bowls, ginger jars, candlesticks, etc., were made until the 1950s in various colors with a satin finish.

PIGEON BLOOD is a bright reddish-orange glassware dating from the early 1900s.

POMONA GLASS was invented in 1884 by Joseph Locke at the New England Glass Company.

PRESSED GLASS was the inexpensive glassware produced in quantity to fill the increasing demand for tablewares when Americans moved away from the simple table utensils of pioneer times. During the 1820s, ingenious Yankees invented and perfected machinery for successfully pressing glass. About 1865, manufacturers began to color their products. Literally hundreds of different patterns were produced.

QUEZAL is a very fine quality blown iridescent glassware produced by Martin Bach, in his factory in Brooklyn, New York, from 1901-1920. Named after the Central American bird, quezal glassware has an iridescent finish featuring contrasting colored glass threads. Green, white and gold colors are most often found.

ROSALINE GLASS is a product of the Steuben Glass Works of Corning, New York. The firm was founded by Frederick Carter and T.C. Hawkes, Sr. Rosaline is a rose-colored jade glass or colored alabaster. The firm is now owned by the Corning Glass Company, which is presently producing fine glass of exceptional quality.

ROYAL FLEMISH ART GLASS was made by the Mt. Washington Glass Works during the 1880s. It has an acid finish which may consist of one or more colors, decorated with raised gold enameled lines separating into sections. Fanciful painted enamel designs also decorate this ware. Royal Flemish glass is marked "RF," with the letter "R" reversed and backed to the letter "F," within a four-sided orange-red diamond mark.

RUBINA GLASS is a transparent blown glassware that shades from clear to red. One of the first to produce this crystal during the late 1800s was Hobbs, Brocunier and Company of Wheeling, West Virginia.

RUBINA VERDE is a blown art glass made by Hobbs, Brocunier and Company, during the late 1800s. It is a transparent glassware that shades from red to yellow-green.

SABINO GLASS originated in Paris, France, in the 1920s. The company was founded by Marius-Ernest Sabine, and was noted for art deco figures, vases, animals, nudes and animals in clear, opalescent and colored glass.

SANDWICH GLASS — One of the most interesting and enduring pages from America's past is Sandwich glass produced by the famous Boston and Sandwich Glass Company at Sandwich, Massachusetts. The firm began operations in 1825, and the glass flour-ished until 1888 when the factory closed. Despite the popularity of Sandwich Glass, little is known about its founder, Deming Jarvis.

The Sandwich Glass house turned out hundreds of designs in both plain and figured patterns, in colors and crystal, so that no one type could be considered entirely typical—but the best known is the "lacy" glass produced there. The variety and multitude of designs and patterns produced by the company over the years is a tribute to its greatness.

SILVER DEPOSIT GLASS was made during the late 19th and early 20th centuries. Silver was deposited on the glass surface by a chemical process so that a pattern appeared against a clear or colored ground. This ware is sometimes referred to as "silver overlay."

SLAG GLASS was originally known as "mosaic" and "marble glass" because of its streaked appearance. Production in the United States began about 1880. The largest producer of this ware was Challinor, Taylor and Company, The various slag mixtures are: purple, butterscotch, blue, orange, green and chocolate. A small quantity of pink slag was also produced in the inverted fan and feather pattern. Examples are rare and expensive.

SPANISH LACE is a Victorian glass pattern that is easily identified by its distinct opalescent flower and leaf pattern. It belongs to the shaded opalescent glass family. ·

STEUBEN — The Steuben Glass Works was founded in 1904 by Frederick Carter, an Englishman, and T.G. Hawkes, Sr., at Corning, New York. In 1918 the firm was purchased by the Corning Glass Company. However, Steuben remained with the firm, designing a bounty of fine art glass of exceptional quality.

STIEGEL-TYPE GLASS — Henry William Stiegel founded America's first flint glass factory during the 1760s at Manheim, Pennsylvania. Stiegel glass is flint or crystal glass; it is thin and clear, and has a bell-like ring when tapped. The ware is quite brittle and fragile. Designs were painted freehand on the glass—birds, animals and architectural motifs, surrounded by leaves and flowers. The engraved glass resulted from craftsmen etching the glass surface with a copper wheel, then cutting the desired patterns.

It is extremely difficult to identify, with certainty, a piece of original Stiegel glass. Part of the problem resulted from the lack of an identifying mark on the products. Additionally, many of the craftsmen moved to other areas after the Stiegel plant closed—producing a similar glass product. Therefore, when one is uncertain about the origin of this type ware, it is referred to as "Stiegel-type" glass.

TIFFANY GLASS was made by Louis Comfort Tiffany, one of America's outstanding glass designers of the art nouveau period, from about 1870 to the 1930s. Tiffany's designs included a variety of lamps, bronze work, silver, pottery and stained glass windows. Practically all items made were marked "L.C. Tiffany" or "L.C.T." in addition to the word Favrile".

TORTOISESHELL GLASS — As its name indicates, this type glassware resembles the color of tortoiseshell and has deep rich brown tones combined with amber and cream-colored shades. Tortoiseshell glass was originally produced in 1880 by Francis Pohl, a German chemist. It was also made in the United States by the Sandwich Glass Works and other glass houses during the late 1800s.

VAL ST. LAMBERT Cristalleries, located in Belgium, was founded in 1825 and the firm is still in operation.

VASA MURRHINA glassware was produced in quantity at the Vasa Murrhina Art Glass Company of Sandwich, Massachusetts, during the late 1900s. John C. DeVoy, assignor to the firm, registered a patent on July 1, 1884, for the process of decorating glassware with particles of mica flakes (coated with copper, gold, nickel or silver) sandwiched between an inner layer of clear or transparent colored glass. The ware was also produced by other American glass firms and in England.

VASELINE GLASS — The term "vaseline" refers to color only, as it resembles the greenish-yellow color typical of the oily petroleum jelly known as Vaseline. This ware has been produced in a variety of patterns both here and in Europe—from the late 1800s. It has been made in both clear and opaque yellow, vaseline combined with clear glass, and occasionally the two colors are combined in one piece.

VERLYS GLASS is a type of art glass produced in France after 1931. The Heisey Glass Company, Newark, Ohio, produced identical glass for a short time, after having obtained the rights and formula from the French factory. French-produced ware can be identified from the American product by the signature, the French is mold marked, whereas the American glass is etched script signed.

WAVECREST GLASS is an opaque white glassware made from the late 1890s by French factories and the Pairpoint Manufacturing Company at New Bedford, Massachusetts. Items were decorated by the C.F. Monroe Company of Meriden, Connecticut, with painted pastel enamels. The name wavecrest was used after 1898 with the initials for the company "C.F.M. Co." Operations ceased during World War II.

WEBB GLASS was made by Thomas Webb & Sons of Stourbridge, England, during the late Victorian period. The firm produced a variety of different types of art and cameo glass.

WHEELING PEACHBLOW — With its simple lines and delicate shadings, Wheeling Peachblow was produced soon after 1883 by J.H. Hobbs, Brockunier and Company at Wheeling, West Virginia. It is a two-layered glass lined or cased inside with an opaque, milk-white type of plated glassware. The outer layer shades from a bright yellow at the base to a mahogany red at the top. The majority of pieces produced are in the glossy finish.

A-MA Oct. 1995 Skinner, Inc.

Left to right

Quezal Art Glass Stick Vase, transparent ambergris, inscribed "Quezal", 9⅞"
H $345.00
Gold Quezal Glass & Bronze Trumpet Vases, pr., ambergris cones w/ gold
irid. surface, inscribed "Quezel", 9" H $977.50
Quezal Gold Irid. Vase, inscribed "Quezal", 7" H $488.75
Blue Irid. Art Glass Candlesticks, pr., inscribed "Quezal",
8½" H $517.50
Art Glass Vase, robin's egg blue w/ aubergine heart and vine, fake mark of
Durand, 12" H $920.00
Imperial Free Hand Art Glass Vase, blue transparent body w/ opaque white
decor., orig., Imperial label, 5¾" H $517.50
American Art Glass Floriform Vase, green & gold pulled feather decoration,
fake mark incised on base, 6" H, 7" D $402.50
Kew Blas Vase, Union Glass Co, green & gold pulled feather w/ deep orange
irid. interior, inscribed "Kew Blas", 5¼" H $747.50

A-MA Oct. 1995 Skinner, Inc.

**Tiffany Favrile Glass & Metal
Snuff/Scent Jar,** gold & silvered, w/
"TG&D Co" paper label, 3" H $1,955.00

A-MA Oct. 1995 Skinner, Inc.

Left to Right

Daum Nancy Glass

Gilt Metal Piano Lamp, single socket, marked "Daum Nancy France", 12"
H $747.50
Cordial Tumblers, 8, bubbled orange, engraved "Daum (cross) Nancy France",
3" H $460.00
Butterfly Vase, shaded apricot-pink-yellow in white, engraved "Daum Nancy
(cross)" 7¾" H $2,530.00
Berluze Vase, incised mark "Daum Nancy", 14½" H $345.00
Cameo Glass Enameled Coverd Jar, yellow-purple body, gold marked, base rim
chip restored, 4⅝" H $1,380.00

A-MA Oct. 1995 Skinner, Inc.

Left to Right

Tiffany Favrile

Gold Heart & Vine Vase, gold irid.
luster, green heart-shaped leaves &
vines, inscribed "L.C. Tiffany Favrile,
14½" H $1,495.00
Gold Applied Vase, engraved "L.C.
Tiffany Favrile", 4½" H $1,035.00
Opal Glass Vase, irid. gold & green
pulled feather, inscribed L.C. Tiffany
Favrile, 5" H $1,437.50
Freeblown Vase, inscribed on base
"L.C. Tiffany Favrile", 3"H $2,070.00
Gold & Green Loving Cup, inscribed
"L.C. Tiffany Favrile", 5" H . . .$920.00
Twisted Candlesticks, pr., inscribed
"L.C.T.", 7" H . . . . .NS

A-OH April 1996   Early Auction Co.

Row 1, Left to Right

314-Mt. Washington Cracker Jar, yellow poppies w/ leaves, red ground, 5″ H $450.00

557-Handel Lamp, w/ reverse painted shade, woodland scene, 16″ diam., overall 23″ H $2,750.00

733-M.O.P. pink herringbone ewer w/ camphor handle, 8″ H . . .$175.00

623-Iridescent Vases, bluish gold, embedded in leather bases, 17½″ H $1,400.00

778-Miniature Opaque Lamp w/ blue shade, base decor. w/ flowers & cupis, 8¼″ H $270.00

469-Lamp w/reverse painted shade, 18″ diam., wooded landscape, w/paper label of Incandescent Lamp Co., 26″ H $1,350.00

341-Prussian Blue Pitcher, w/ enamel decor., 9½″ H $325.00

Row 2, Left to Right

470-Rosaline Covered Dresser Box w/ alabaster knob & base $625.00

305-Scent Container w/ twig handle, 3½″ H $650.00

297-Lotusware Cracker Jar w/ netted panels, 6½″ H $550.00

599-French Cameo Vase w/ blue leaves, islands & snow capped mtns., sgn. deVez, repr. 8″ H $850.00

775-End-of-Day Pitcher w/ burnt orange gold mica, melon body, reeded handle, 9″ H $165.00

Row 3, Left to Right

619-Pairpoint Bouboir Lamp w/ reverse painted scenic shade, mkd $1,400.00

466-French Cameo Vase, purple morning glories & leafy vines, chartreuse ground, sgn. Arsall, 12½″ H $800.00

551-Mt. Washington Cracker Jar, molticolor pansies against biscuit ground, 5″ H $500.00

533-Crown Milano Pitcher, multicolor tapestry style w/ floral blossoms, egg color ground, w/ gilt, 10½″ H $950.00

542-French Cameo Vase w/ autumn colors, yellow ground, sgn. Legras, 23½″ H $1,200.00

519-English Cameo Vase, red w/ white apple blossoms & leafy branches, 7¼″ H $1,000.00

Row 4, Left to Right

774-Triple Overlay Pcs., trumpet form vase w/ raised gold decor. 8¼″ H; cylindrical container w/ silver, 4¼″ H, ea. cut pink, white to clear $440.00

298-Chocolate Pot, mkd. K.T. & K., 9″ H $350.00

550-Wavecrest Helmschmied Swirl Dresser Box, blue w/ floral enamel decor., 7″ diam. $475.00

671-Mont Joye Vase, w/ enamel violets & gilt leaves, 11½″ H $275.00

780-Peking Cameo Vases, w/ orange finches onfloral branches, white ground, 8″ H $410.00

A-OH April 1996 — Early Auction Co.

Row 1, Left to Right
620-Amber Overshot Pitcher w/ applied prussian blue handle, 8¾″ H $400.00

611-Lamp w/ reverse painted shade 16″ diam., w/ summer landscape, black base, 21″ H $850.00

694-Imperial Iridescent Vase, frosty finish w/ ruby heart & vines, 8″ H $625.00

316-Victorian Lustres, emerald green w/ white star flowers, gold bars, 14½″ H $250.00

456-Lamp w/ reverse painted shade, fall foliage decor., 18″ diam., overall 24″ H $2,000.00

610-Loetz-Type Compote, iridescent blue, ribbed, 9″ H $400.00

Row 2, Left to Right

621-Mary Gregory Tea Wermer, lavender insert decor., pierced metal frame, 4½″ H $250.00

731-Loetz Vase, iridescent royal blue w/ textured patt., 10″ H $325.00

518-Peachblow M.O.P. Ewer, rainbow Herringbone patt., 6¾″ H $400.00

Row 3, Left to Right
649-Lamp w/ reverse painted shade, summer landscape, 14″ diam., copper color base, 21″ H $1,250.00

729-Loetz Bowl, Emerald Green, Embedded in Brass, 7″ diam., 6½″ H $275.00

P-10-Rookwood Vase, w/ insects, floral blossoms, mkd. Rookwood, 1883 kiln insignia, 21″ H $3,200.00

480-Pate-Sur-Pate Plaques, pair w/ different white figures on blue ground, mkd. Limoges, Marchal. image 5½″ X 7½″ $1,100.00

Row 4, Left to Right
95-French Cameo Vase, large purple br. stylized flowers & leaves, sgn. Deque, 20″ H $2,600.00

727-Victorian Epergne, chartreuse opalescent, 20″ H $500.00

516-Hobnail Bride's Bowl, attrib. to Hobbs, 1 hob missing, 11″ diam $350.00

449-Porcelain Ewer, w/ gold dragon handle, salmon & burgandy flowers/green leaves, 11″ H $180.00

458-Webb Peachblow Stick Vase w/ enamel decor., 14″ H $375.00

A-OH April 1996   Early Auction Co.

Facing Page

Row 1, Left to Right

531-Mt. Washington Crown Milano Vase w/ serpent coil around neck & enamel decor., 10¾" H $1,850.00

563-Quezal Vase w/ irid. opal body & decor. w/ pulled leaves/outlined in gold, 5½" H $850.00

504-Lamp w/ leaded green holly leaves & berries, 24" diam., bronze base, overall ht. 25" $2750.00

556-N.E. Plated Amberina Bowl, 3¾" H, 8" diam. $5,750.00

650-French Cameo Vase, sgn. Daum Nancy, decor. w/ leaves, branches & insects, blue & burgandy/ground, 13" H $2,750.00

569-Tiffany Favrile Vase w/ iridescent gold ribbed body, sgn., 15" H . . . $1,350.00

567-Durand Rose Bowl, iridescent bluish black, gold base, decor. w/ vines & leaves, sgn., 5" H $1,650.00

523-Tiffany Miniature Vase, bl. emerald gr. w/ iridescent blue pulled feathers, sgn. LCT, 2" H $1,500.00

540-Crown Milano Stick Vase, gilt w/ floral decor., sgn., 15" H .$900.00

664-Steuben Cluthra Vase, pink w/ opalescent "M" handles, 10" H $330.00

537-Kew Blas Vase w/ pulled decor., iridescent gold ground, 10" H . .$700.00

Row 2, Left to Right

536-English Cameo Vase, pink ground w/ flowers, buds & butterfly, 8¾" H $3,000.00

85-Wavecrest "Collars & Cuffs" Hinged Box, maroon, white & gr. decor., 7½" H $1,000.00

209-Burmese Vase, Webb, ruffled petal top, scalloped ft., 4" H . .$300.00

479-Baccarat Vase, gilt decor., opalescent body, brass ball feet, chip on base, 8½" H $1,600.00

565-Durand Vase, red & opalescent pulled feathers, 9" H $850.00

89-French Cameo Vase, dark red trees, ginger sky, & islands, sgn. Galle, 9¾" H $1,000.00

568-English Cameo Stick Vase, tangerine & white decor., lemon ground, 5½" H $1,900.00

203-Tiffany Master Sale, irid. reddish, sgn. L.C.T., 1½" H $200.00

530-Nailsea Fairy Lamp, blue satin, Clarke's insert, 6½" H $600.00

549-Mt. Washington Peachblow Creamer, w/ applied handle, 2½" H . $1,200.00

Row 3, Left to Right

579-Cologne, ivory "Cantalope", stamped Thomas Webb & Sons, Ltd., silver onion cap. $2,000.00

244-French Cameo Vase w/ enameled red berries & autumn branches, orange to purple ground, sgn. Daum Nancy, 9¼" H $1,900.00

583-N.E. Plated Amberina Vase, 3½" H $3,200.00

Durand Rose Bowl w/ iridescent gold on bluish gold base, 5¼" H . . .$700.00

86-Kelva Hinged Box, decor. w/ pink & maroon flowers, white ground, 3" H $550.00

654-French Cameo Vase, pastel pink with spring blossoms, satiny almond ground, sgn. Galle, 14" H $9,750.00

472-Nailsea Fairy Lamp, red w/ camphor feet, 6" H $450.00

663-Webb Plate, ivory w/ elaborate decor., mkd. Thomas Webb & Sons, Ltd., 9" diam. $1,300.00

204-Master Salt, iridescent reddish gold, sgn. L.C.T., 1¼" H $250.00

539-Mt. Washington Crown Milano Sweetmeat, gold sea urchins on wheat ground, 3" H $750.00

652-Favrile Vase, w/ olive gr. leaves & entwined vines w/ yellow blossoms, sgn. L.C.T., 6" H $6,500.00

318-Webb Burmese Vase w/ lavender flowers on leafy vine, 2½" H $375.00

561-Tiffany Vase w/ iridescent gold pulled feathers w/ lime green tips, sgn. L.C.T., 11" H $1,500.00

260-Quezal Vase, miniature, King Tut patt., amber, blue, irid. opal., 4" H $1,000.00

Row 4, Left to Right

219-Steuben Decanter, reddish gold, flame stopper, sgn. Aurene, 10" H $800.00

560-Mt. Washington Cracker Jar, w/ decor., children & flowers, molded cover, 5" H $600.00

552-Crown Milano Cologne, black & golden apple blossoms w/ gold on creamy ground, 5" H $800.00

257-Quezal Vase w/ irid. golden leaves w/ swirled tips on opal ground, sgn., 9"H $2,000.00

271-Mt. Washington Fig Shaker w/ pink & blue floral clusters on apricot textured ground. $200.00

232-French Cameo Stick Vase decor. w/ enameled violet bouquet & bold leaf, sgn. Mont Joye, 7½" H $350.00

564-Durand Console Set, cobalt blue w/ opal pulled feathers w/ yellow bases, bowl 13¼" diam., candlesticks 3" H $1,700.00

267-Amberina Mustard Pot w/ hinged top, 3" H $450.00

651-French Cameo Decanter, clear body decor. w/ orange & white grape pods, 8" H, sgn. Galle, $1,200.00

Row 5, Left to Right

237-French Tumbler w/ enamel decor. & cranberry spatter, mkd. Cristalleri Emile Galle Nancy. $800.00

205-Tiffany Nut Bowl, iridescent bluish gold, sgn. L.C.T., 1" H .$190.00

535-Mt. Washington Burmese Tankard Creamer w/ acid finish, 5½" H $450.00

115-Steuben Aurene Calcite Sherbet, blue w/ underplate & paper label, 4" H $750.00

202-Tiffany Cordials, 4 w/ iridescent reddish finish, sgn. L.C.T., 2" H $800.00

259-Durand miniature vase w/ opal leaves, carmel tips on vines, irid. blue ground, 4¼ H $600.00

483-Satin Glass Rainbow Salt & Pepper Shakers, 3¾" H . .$1,700.00

116-Steuben Aurene Calcite Sherbet & Underplate, gold finish, 4" H . $450.00

264-Wavecrest Helmschmied Swirl Muffineer w/ colorful arrow leaves, blue ground, 2¾" H $525.00

261-Durand Ruby Creamer w/ opal pulled leaves, applied white handle, 4" H $1,300.00

A-MA Oct. 1995   James D. Julia, Inc.

Holly Amber Glass Unless Noted

Row 1

Covered Compote, 8″ H, w/ slightest edge roughage on int. of lid $750.00
Tumbler, 4″ H $300.00
Greentown Beverage Set, 9 pc. in chocolate glass, 8 mugs 4½″ H w/ cavalier scene including a castle, w/ a large 8¾″ pitcher showing drinking scene $900.00

Row 2

Water Pitcher, 9″ H $1,500.00
Large Covered Compote, 9¼″ H x 6″ W, w/ int. flake on cover rim $1,050.00
Pedestal Sugar Bowl, 7″ H, 4¼″ across, 3½″ crack in body of sugar bowl $925.00
Open Compote, unusual form consisting of 2 inverted covers, 6″ H, 7″ across, base rim flake $1,250.00

Row 3

Vase, 6¼″ H, 3″ across $400.00
Covered Jelly Compote, 8″ H $850.00
Vase, 6¼″ H, 3″ across $400.00
Covered Sugar Bowl, 7¼″ H $850.00
Vase, 6″ H, w/ slight edge roughage $400.00
Toothpick Holder, 2½″ H x 3″ W $350.00

A-MA Oct. 1995   James D. Julia, Inc.

Cut Glass of the Brilliant Period

Left to right

Bowl, triple layer type, diamond & hobstar cutting w/ hobstar cut bottom, 4″ H, 8″ dia. . . . . .NS
Red-Cut-To-Clear Pedestal Bowl, cut in a Russian variant patt., w/ ray cut base, 5″ H, 9½″ dia. $1,550.00
Pedestal Champagne Pitcher, w/ all over Hobstar & Diamond cutting and cut foot, applied notched handle, 14½″ H $1,600.00
Three Part Punch Bowl, Poinsettia & Harvard patt., 16″ H, 14″ dia. $4,600.00
Three Handled Loving Cup, w/ silver rim, 9½″ H $1,500.00

A-MA Oct. 1995   James D. Julia, Inc.

Galle Cameo Glass

Row 1

Vase, signed Galle, brilliant yellow background w/ purple floral design, 4½″ H, 3″ W $650.00
Vase, signed Galle, pale yellow & amethyst background w/ floral decor., 4″ H $350.00
Bulbous Vase, large brown cameo cut flowers against a mottled yellow ground, 3¾″ H $550.00

Row 2

Vase, brilliant yellow/orange frosted background w/ deep red fern design, 9¾″ H $2,000.00
Banjo Vase, light green cameo cut blossoms & leaves against a frosted white shading to peach ground, 7″ H $520.00
Vase, purple floral cameo cutting against a frosted pink ground, 5½″ H $450.00
Vase, deep apricot orange floral decor. against a frosted clear & pink opalescent background, signed Galle w/ star, 7¼″ H, 3½″ W $750.00
Water Lily Vase, purple cameo cut water lilies against a frosted yellow shading to pink ground, 10″ H . . .$1,650.00

A-MA Oct. 1995   James D. Julia, Inc.

Wavecrest Open Bowl, w/ glossy royal blue background, blown-out floral design with pink wild rose decor., pink banner mark, 2½" H, 5½" W $150.00

Wavecrest Egg Crate Pattern Hinged Jewel Box, w/ purple scrolls, w/ blue & yellow beaded floral decor., purple & gold highlights, 6" W, 3¾" H $650.00

Wavecrest Footed Toothpick Holder, signed, yellow & pink pansy decor., orig., brass metal work, 2¼" H .$200.00

Wavecrest Open Bowl, pale pink & white background w/ blue painted and enameled flowers, signed w/ pink banner mark, 2" H, 4½" W $70.00

Row 2

Wavecrest Egg Crate Double Handled Open Nappi, pink & white enamel floral decor., 2¼" H, 4" L $75.00

Wavecrest Open Handled Nappi, swirl design w/ floral painted & enamel decor., 1¾" H, 4" W $60.00

Wavecrest Open Handled Nappi, swirl design w/ floral painted & enamel decor., 1¾" H, 4" W $95.00

Wavecrest Footed Jewel Box, pale yellow background w/ blue & maroon floral decor., fancy metal work, signed, 3½" H, 3¼" W, wear on lid, orig. lining $200.00

Wavecrest Open Nappis, pr., floral decor., metal handle on one is off and the other is missing metal rim . . .$70.00

Row 3

Wavecrest Plain Card Holder, signed, pale blue background w/ pink rose decor., 2½" H, 4" L $95.00

Wavecrest Footed Pin Tray, Roccocco design w/ floral decor., fancy cast foot $175.00

Nakara Footed Oval Box, green & pink shaded background w/ pink & white enameled roses, brown leaves, footed hardware, 3½" H, 5½" L $400.00

Kelva Covered Box, signed, deep green background w/ pink & white rose decor., 3" H, 4½" W $350.00

Mt. Washington/Smith Bros, Rose Bowl, pale blue & lavender pansy decor., against a soft beige background w/ white enamel beaded top, signed, 4" H, 4" W $150.00

Row 4

Wavecrest Toothpick w/ Metal Base, white background w/ pale blue floral design, 3¾" H, 3" W $225.00

Nakara Indian Portrait Humidor, signed, glossy brown background w/ a full face portrait of an Indian chief $850.00

Wavecrest Cracker Jar, signed, pale yellow background w/ pink & blue wild rose floral decor., 7" H, 6" W, cover not orig. $175.00

Smith Bros, Covered Biscuit Jar, signed, pale beige background w/ gold ivy decor., & gold floral and vine design, 7" H, 6" W $500.00

A-MA Oct. 1995   Skinner, Inc.

Left to Right

Galle Cameo Glass

Vase, peach & colorless body, mkd. "Galle", 17½" H $2,185.00

Double Bulbed Cameo Vase, frosted body layered in ruby red, mkd. "Galle", 9¾" H $1,380.00

Decorative Bowl, pink & green, mkd. "Galle", 4½" H $1,495.00

Verre Parlant Seashell Dish, pearlescent pink, mkd., 2" H, 6¼" L$1,092.50

Vase, pink & rasperry, mkd. "Galle", 18¾" H $2,760.00

Polished Cameo Glass Vase, mkd. "Galle", 8" H $1,035.00

A-MA Oct. 1995   James D. Julia, Inc.

Cut Glass of the Brilliant Period

Left to right

Basket, w/ notched applied handle & floral acid etched & cut design, ray cut bottom, 17" H $1,100.00

Vase, in Greek Key & multiple hobstar patt., 20½" H $7,250.00

A-MA Oct. 1995   James D. Julia, Inc.

Loetz Vase, signed, gold/purple iridescent finish w/ a translucent gold oyster background color, 5¾" H, 6" W $1,700.00

Loetz Vase, signed, olive/green glass w/ deep brown pulled wave patt, & gold iridescent surface, sterling overlay design, 9" H $5,350.00

A-OH Apr.1996   Early Auction Co.

Row 1, Left to Right

105-Durand Vases (1 of 2), blue irid., 12″ H $2,200.00

113-Quezal Shades w/ pulled green feathers on opal ground, 5½″ H & attached to triple column wrought iron bases, overall H-16″, (1 w/ fitter chips) $400.00

182-Kelva Box w/ rose decor., 4½″ D $400.00

176-Steuben Vase, rose lotus pod & leaf design on textured alabaster, 12″ H $1200.00

120-Steuben Vase. blue irid. ribs w/ waisted body, sign., 6″ H . . .$1,100.00

142-Burmese Pickle Jar, melon ribbed body, decor. w/ enamel flowers, sgn. Barbour Bros. $700.00

112-Quezal Vase w/ pulled gr. feathers, golden tips on opal, irid. foot, 14″ H $1,300.00

102-Durand Vase, irid. blue w/ opal "King Tut" design, 7″ H $1,000.00

185-Kelva Vase w/ ormolu mounts, purple tulips on blue, 11″ H . .$750.00

Row 2, Left to Right

166-Libbey Amberina Vase, ribbed w/ fold-down top, 6½″ H . .$1,100.00

188-Cameo Vase, Art Deco w/ red poppies on yellow ground, sgn. LeVerre, 13½″ H $1,000.00

144-Burmese Vase, Mt. Washington, salt & pepper, each w/ painted flowers, Pairpoint holder $275.00

111-Nash Center Bowl w/ gold irid. decor., 11″ diam., 3½″ H $375.00

190-Wheeling Peachblow Vase w/ shiny finish, sm. nick., 9½″ H .$375.00

117- Steuben Aurene Compote, bluish gold w/ stretched ruffled rim, 7¼″ diam., 7½″ H $800.00

184-Kelva Fernery, pink wild roses on mottled olive gr. ground, mkd., 8″ diam $475.00

174-Steuben Cluthra Fan Vase, pink, sgn., 8″ H $1,200.00

101-Durand Lamp, w/ gold feather design & threading, 10″ H . . .$800.00

Row 3, Left to Right

181-Wavecrest Vase, w/ pink flowers, ormolu handles, mkd., 6½″ diam $500.00

140-Mt. Washington Burmese Biscuit Jar w/ acid finish, 9″ H . . .$450.00

179-Wavecrest Dresser Box w/ fern decor., 7½″ diam. $650.00

183-Kelva Box "Cigars" w/ gold, pink wild roses on blue ground, 5″ H $500.00

137-Mt.Washington Shakers, three w/ red carnations, enamel berries & leaves $225.00

119-Steuben Aurene Bowl, gold center, sgn., 11½″ diam., 4½″ H . .$800.00

172-Steuben Verre de Dole Sherbets w/ underplates, two, 5½″ H . . . $400.00

138-Mt. Washington Burmese Shakers, Lay-Down w/ enameled flowers. $220.00

122-L.C. Tiffany Favrile bluish gold pitcher, sgn., 7½″ H $1,000.00

177-Moss Agate Vase, Stevens & Williams w/ applied ring, 4½″ H$900.00

103-Durand Vase, blue w/ hearts & vines, sgn., 9½″ H $800.00

Row 4, Left to Right

127-Mt. Washington Ostrich Egg Muffineer, decor. w/ pastel nasturtiums, 4″ H $250.00

128-Mt. Washington Ostrich Egg Muffineer w/ blue cornflowers on opal ground, 4″ H $275.00

129-Mt. Washington Ostrich Egg Muffineer, fall leaves w/ raspberry on yellow ground, 4″ H $275.00

130-Mt. Washington Ostrich Egg Muffineer w/ blue cornflowers opal ground, 4″ H $400.00

131-Mt. Washington Ostrich Egg Muffineer w/ pansies on blue ground, 4″ H $350.00

125-Mt. Washington Biscuit Jar w/ enamel spider mum decor., 7½″ H $550.00

139-Mt. Washington Melon Ribbed Shakers w/ raised gold flowers, $230.00

132-Mt. Washington Ostrich Egg Muffineer w/ enamel flowers, 4″ H $310.00

133-Mt. Washington Ostrich Egg Muffineer w/ arrow form lids, Burmese tint ground, 4″ H . . .$325.00

134-Mt. Washington Ostrich Egg Muffineer w/ nasturtiums on pink/ orange ground, 4″ H $350.00

135-Mt. Washington Ostrich Egg Muffineer w/ maiden hair fern, mkd. pat'd., 4″ H $250.00

136-Mt. Washington Ostrich Egg Muffineer w/ small flowers on gr. ground, 4″ H $175.00

Row 5, Left to Right

143-Mt. Washington Burmese Ribbed Shakers in silverplated holder, 2″ H $425.00

123-L.C. Tiffany Vase w/ gold irid., blue zipper patt. on corset body, sgn., 6½″ H $900.00

121-Tiffany Favrile Finger Bowls w/ underplates (1 of 3), ea. sgn., plates 11½″ diam. $1050.00

139-Mt. Washington frosted melon shakers w/ gold flowers. $230.00

187-Smith Bros. melon ribbed bowl, 5½″ diam. $325.00

137-Mt. Washington Shakers (1 of 3) w/ red carnations, enamel berries & leaves. $225.00

191-Agata, N. England, tri-con toothpick, 2½″ H $525.00

126-Crown Milano Bowl w/ sq. top, painted raspberry & leaf decor., 4½″ H $450.00

186-Smith Bros. Biscuit Jar w/ pink roses & green leaves outlined in gold, 7″ diam. $800.00

A-OH Mar. 1996   Garth's Auctions

Row 1

Clear Blown Ewer w/ Sixteen Ribs, midwestern, applied handle, some wear, 9″ H, plus eight rib stopper. $55.00

Two Clear Blown Pittsburgh Flint Pillar Mold Vases w/ applied foot & baluster stem, stain in one, 9½″ H $220.00

Clear Blown Double Gemel Bottle, w/ white looping, applied foot & rigaree & applied peacock blue lips, 9¾″ H $247.50

Clear Blown Flint Compote, applied foot, hollow baluster stem, bowl w/ four panels & folded over rim w/ cut foliage band, wear on foot, 10¾″ D, 10¼″ H $715.00

Row 2

Clear Blown Covered Jar, applied foot, hollow hourglass stem & thirteen panels on bowl, lid has twelve panels & applied finial, finial has large chip, 16½″ H $165.00

Clear Blown Lace Maker's Lamp, 10″ H $247.00

Clear Blown Bellows Shaped Vase, w/ applied foot & rigaree, opalescent looping, 16¼″ H $247.50

Clear Blown Flint Vase, cut panels, oval bull's eyes, etc., rayed foot has probably been recut, rim has some grinding, 11¾″ H . . . . .NS

A-MA Oct. 1995   Skinner, Inc.

Left to Right

N. Eng. Glass, two pieces, green opaque vase w/ vivid blue decoration above gold borderline, 4¼″ H; Agata finger bowl w/ deep raspberry w/ decoration, 5″ D $805.00
Greentown Holly Amber Compote, raised on conical pedestal foot, 4¼″ H, 7¼″ L $230.00
Locke Art Etched Crystal Goblets, 12, w/ poppy decoration, ea. signed, 3 chipped, 6½″ H 862.50
Greentown Findlay Onyx Pitcher, 7¾″ H, cracked across base, ...$NS
Agata Vase, N. Eng., Glass Co. 6½″ H 977.50

A-MA Oct. 1995   Skinner, Inc.

Left to Right
Plated Amberina
Cruet, N. Eng., Glass Co., fuchsia red shaded to amber, heat check at top w/ chip, 6¾″ H $1,150.00
Lily Vase, N. Eng. Glass Co., w/ pin-point impurities in glass, 9″ H$2,415.00
Tumbler, N. Eng. Glass Co., 3¾″ H $920.00

A-MA Oct. 1995   Skinner, Inc.

Left to Right
Coralene Satin Glass Fairy Lamp, turquoise blue, 5½″ H $373.75
Coralene Opal Glass Vase, minor coralene loss, 7″ H $172.50
Coralene MOP Vase, shaded pink satin w/ D.Q. patt., w/ yellow decor., 6¼″ H $230.00

A-MA Oct. 1995   Skinner, Inc.

Left to Right
Tiffany Favrile Bowl, blue irid., inscribed "LCT Favrile 1925", 2″ H, 6″ D .$690.00
Tiffany Cordials, pr., gold irid., inscribed "LCT Favrile", 5½″ H $460.00
Tiffany Favrile Heart Vase, blue shaded to purple, green & black leaves, inscribed "L.C. Tiffany Favrile 1503L" 2⅝″ H, 3¼″ D $2,185.00
Tiffany Favrile Glass Vase, dark cobalt blue, inscribed "L.C. Tiffany Favrile", 12″ H $977.50
Tiffany Favrile Vase, cobalt blue, inscribed "L.C. Tiffany - Favrile", 6¼″ H $2,070.00
Tiffany Bowl, blue irid., inscribed "L.C. Tiffany Inc. Favrile 4403M", some scratches to int. iridescence, 3″ H, 8¾″ D $575.00
Tiffany Favrile Miniatures, 3, gold iridescence, inscribed w/ Tiffany marks, 1¾″ - 4¾″ H $977.50

A-OH Mar. 1996   Garth's Auctions

Clear Blown Pillar Mold Vase w/ applied amethyst on ribs & rim, eight swirled ribs, 8″ H $605.00
Clear Blown Pittsburgh Flint Pillar Mold Goblet Shaped Vase w/ applied foot & rim, 8⅝″ H $55.00
Two Pieces of Clear Blown Glass: decanter w/ three applied rings & white looping, slight grinding on applied foot, 8⅛″ H, plus mismatched stopper & pitcher w/ applied handle & white threading, 6¼″ H . . . . .NS

A-MA Oct. 1995 — Skinner, Inc.

MOP Satin Glass Vases, D.Q. patt., pink 10" H, apricot 11" H $258.75

Jewel Casket, 1" crack inside cover, 5¼" x 3½" 5" H, ...$172.50

Fairy Lamp, rose nailsea patt., minor chips at top of base, 5½" H $316.25

Rosebowls, four, rainbow satin glass w/ decor.................$230.00

Satin Glass Vase, yellow w/ enamel decor., 9½" H $172.50

Satin Glass Vase, honeycomb patt., amber w/ enamel decor., 5" H $172.50

A-MA Oct. 1995 — Skinner, Inc.

Opal Glass Cigar Box, w/ ormolu decor., 5½" H ....NS

Wavecrest Glass Vase, w/ ormolu decor., 13¾" H $977.50

Mt. Wash. Crown Milano Sweet-meat Jar, bead loss, 4½" H ..$488.75

Mt. Wash. Crown Milano Pansy Vase, 9" H $1,150.00

Mt. Wash. Crown Milano Swirled Vase, 6" H $546.25

Mt. Wash. Crown Milano Vase w/ Handles, 9" H $1,840.00

Mt. Wash. Crown Milano Jar, 5½" H $460.00

Opal Glass Jewel Box, w/ ormolu decor., damage, 6" H $517.50

A-MA Oct. 1995 — Skinner, Inc.

Peachblow Satin Glass Perfume, rose to red, top frozen, sgn. Thomas Webb & Sons, 5½" H $431.25

Cameo Vase, Ivory, sg. Thomas Webb & Sons, 5" H $1,035.00

Cameo Vase, Thomas Webb & Sons, sapphire blue, 4½" H $690.00

CameoVase, blue w/ enamel decor., sign. Thomas Webb & Sons, 7½" H $1,265.00

English Cameo Rosebowl, D.Q. M.O.P., lime yellow, w/ damage, 3" H, 4" D ..NS

Cameo Glass Bowl, w/ morning glory decor., rose red overlaid in white, 4½" H, 10" D $1,150.00

A-MA Oct. 1995 — Skinner, Inc.

New Eng. Amberina Castor Set, Mount Washington Glass Co., 14" H $1,495.00

A-OH Apr. 1996   Early Auction Co.

Row 1, Left to Right

224-Loetz Vase, Austria, ribbed w/ silvery blue waves, sgn. 5″ H . . .$1,100.00

100-Pairpoint Lamp w/ reversed painted shade sgn. C. Durand, 12″, overall ht. 18″. $1,650.00

59-Sauce Dish, fuchsia amberina, 4″ diam. $125.00

366-Custard Glass Toothpick Holder, Argonaut Shell patt., 3″ H $300.00

666-Plaque on Copper, w/ enameled fall foliage, cottages, etc., sgn. Faure, Limoges. $2,100.00

201-Kew Blas Vase w/ opal pulled feathers upon gold ground, sgn., 6½″ H $650.00

60-Toothpick Holder, Aberina, D.Q. patt., 2½″ H $175.00

97-Schneider Glass Bowl, reddish orange & cobalt on amethyst foot, sgn. 6¼″ H $550.00

218-Steuben Decanter, reddish gold, flame stopper, sgn. Aurene, 10″ H $1,250.00

275-Lamp w/ reverse painted shade, autumn colors, shade 18″ diam., overall 24″ H $1,000.00

274-Cruet, fuchsia amberina, Inverted Thumbprint patt., 5½″ H $350.00

368-Custard Glass Tooth Holder, Chrysanthemum Sprig patt., 2¾″ H $275.00

269-Tiffany Vase, iridescent gold, sgn. L.C. Tiffany Favrile, 15″ H $1,350.00

Row 2, Left to Right

266-Wavecrest Vase, pastel pink & blue flora, gilt rim, 6¼″ H . . .$300.00

321-Kelva Box, w/ pink floral cover, dark gr. mottled ground, sgn. 4½″ diam. $350.00

79-Crown Milano Cracker Barrel, decor. w/ raised spider mums/ leaves & buds, 5″ H $950.00

362-Amberina Stork Vase by Joseph Loche, 3¾″ H $1,750.00

233-French Cameo Vase, w/ lavender flower & vine on white and lavender ground, 7½″ H $800.00

71-French Cameo Base, olive gr. seed pods on light gr. & pink ground, sgn. Galle, 6½″ H $700.00

371-Mt. Washington salt & pepper shakers w/ enamel flowers, gr. ground, 1¾″ H $200.00

534-Mt. Washington Burmese Stick Vase w/ enamel decor 8″ H . . .$975.00

248-Quezal Sherbet, iridescent opal w/ enamel decor., gold interior, 3¾″ H $200.00

122-Tiffany Pitcher, bluish gold, sgn. L.C. Tiffany Favrile, 7½″ H $1000.00

347-Spatter Hobnail Basket w/ thorn handle, 5″ H, 6½″ D . . .$125.00

76-Cut Velvet Vases (1 illus.) D.Q. patt., pink; 2nd vertical ribbed, 7½″ & 6″ H $320.00

370-Coin Spot M.O.P. blue salt & pepper shakers, 3½″ H $600.00

215-Smith Bros. Vase, daisies on leafy stems, gilt & enamel, 4½″ H $200.00

Row 3, Left to Right

65-Mt. Washington Burmese Toothpick, acid finish, 2″ H .$200.00

168-Steuben Blue Aurene Calcite Compote, 6¼″ H $800.00

169-Steuben Gold Aurene Calcite Compote, 6¼″ H $700.00

73-French Cameo Bowl, dr. gr. foliage w/ grass & trees, sgn. Daum Nancy, 4″ diam. $1,200.00

247-French Cameo Vase, golden orange w/ brown & yellow decor., sgn. Carder, LeVerre Francais, 6½″ H $775.00

334-N.E. Peachblow Pear w/ long stem, 5½″ L $150.00

655-French Cameo Bowl, burgundy fronds w/ seed capsules, blue, yellow opal ground, 11″ H, 18″ diam. made by Galle, paper label "Varese Hnos". . . . $11,500.00

332-Findlay Onyx Spooner, 4″ H $350.00

333-Findlay Onyx Creamer, 4″ H $375.00

171-Steuben Selenium Finger Bowl, red w/ underplate. . . .$500.00

Row 4, Left to Right

653-French Cameo Vase, w/ purple leaves & floral pods, pink & white flowers, sgn. St. Louis Nancy, 3¾″ H $675.00

66-Burmese Melon Ribbed Toothpick w/ floral decor. 1¾″ H . . .$750.00

345-Burmese Fairy Lamp, acid finish on clear Clarke's base on acanthus leaf metal stand, 2½″ H $325.00

323-Wavecrest Box, bl. gr. corners w/ pastel ferns, metal rim, 5″ H . . .$450.00

344-D.Q.M.O.P. Tazza, red w/ camphor trim, attached to silver plated base, 10″ H $375.00

118-Steuben Aurene Bowl, reddish gold center, button feet, 10″ diam., 2″ H $350.00

273-Amberina Lily Vase, 9″ H $350.00

234-French Cameo Vase, chocolate br. foliage, yellow sky w/ birds, sgn. Galle, 6½″ H $800.00

365-Pomona Toothpick Holders, D.Q., 2¼″ H-2nd shown in row 5. . . . . .$260.00

359-Amberina Tankard Pitcher, Daisy & Button patt.,amber handle w/ heat check, 5″ H $250.00

Row 4, Left to Right

159-Silhouette Bear Claret, black, 5½″ H $155.00

160-Kangaroo Cocktail, ruby experimental, 6″ H $325.00

562-Tiffany Bowl, iridescent blue w/ wavy rim, sgn. L.C.T. Favrile, 6½″ diam. $825.00

70-French Cameo Vase, maroon w/ floral clusters on frosty pale pink ground, sgn. Galle, base chip, 5¾″ H $525.00

84-Wavecrest Box, Collars & Cuffs, maroon & white daisies, gr. foliage, 7″ H $700.00

369-Frosted 3-Face salt & pepper shakers, 2½″ H, pr. $100.00

265-Wavecrest Box, orange & yellow floral bouquets w/ pink enamel edging. $650.00

365-Pamona Toothpick Holder, D.Q., 2½″ H, #1 shown in row 4, price for two. $260.00

58-Libby Vase, fuchsia amberina, ribbed, 4¼″ H $215.00

A-OH May 1996   Garth Auctions

Mini. on Ivory Portraits, pair, Napoleon & Josephine, signed w/ matching inlaid tortoise shell & engraved brass frames, 5½″ H, 4¼″ W $330.00

Wavecrest Jar, white & pale blue w/ delicate enameled flowers, 3½″ D $221.00

Oval Cameo Jar, pink & clear floral design, "Val St. Lambert", pinpoint flakes, 3¾″ L $192.50

French Cameo Jar, pale pink flowers w/ traces of gilt, sgn. "Daum Nancy", w/ silverplated lid w/ flower, 3⅜″ D $137.50

Mini. on Ivory Portraits, five, young women, engraved ivory frames have minor damage, similar but no matching, 4″ H, 3½″ W $687.50

Dresser Jars, three enameled, yellow gr. w/ gilt & cherub, 3⅜″ D; pale pink frosted w/ flowers, 5″ D & pale pink frosted w/ art nouveau flowers in gold, white, blue & yellow, 3¾″ D, all have brass fittings $280.50

Dresser Box, blue jasper dip w/ white classical decor., mkd. "Wedgwood, Made in England, 4″ x 4″ $33.00

Covered Dishes, two of eight porcelain footed w/ serpent handles, each w/ different color & some variations, mkd. "Dresden", 3¾″ D $484.00

Oval Porcelain Brooch, handpainted w/ portrait of woman in plumed hat, metal back, 1⅝″ H, 1¼″ W $16.50

A-OH April 1996   Early Auction Co.

Facing Page
Row 1, Left to Right

343-Durand Vase w/ iridescent gold body w/ threading, sgn. V. Durand, teakwood base, 7½" H $700.00

658-French Cameo Vase, peach frosty ground, w/ tulips, fading from burgandy to salmon & amber, sgn. Galle, 15" H $5,500.00

262-Webb Vase, pink all-over cut to opal, w/ flocks of birds, 8" H $1,100.00

206-Tiffany Finger Bowl, irid. gold w/ underplate, sgn. L.C.T. . . .$400.00

656-French Cameo Vase, honey amber pods on opal, pink & chartreuse ground, sgn. Galle, 18" H $2,500.00

533-Crown Milano Pitcher, multi-color tapestry w/ flowers, leaves & gilt, 12" H $950.00

81-English Cameo Vase w/ fuchsia blossom & vine, red ground, sgn. Thomas Webb & Sons, Cameo, 6" H $2,000.00

78-Pairpoint Lamp w/ directoire shade, 16" diam. w/ floral scrolls, bl. marble base, 26" H $2,700.00

538-Durand Vase, iridescent blue, gold foot, sgn. V. Durand, 8¼" H $1,250.00

Row 2, Left to Right

141-Mt. Washington Burmese Bisquit Jar w/ pink enameled flowers, 6½" H $400.00

246-French Cameo Atomizer w/ raspberries & leaves, sgn. Richard, metal mounts, 12" H $700.00

94-L.C. Tiffany Favrile Vase w/ iridescent blue, sgn. 13½" H . .$1,150.00

662-Pate-de-Verre Tray w/ butterfly, pine needles & cones, mkd. A. Walter, Nancy, 7" diam. $2,000.00

559-Mt. Washington Lava Vase, bl. body w/ colorful inclusions, 4½" H $2,900.00

91-English Cameo Vase w/ sunbursts, branches & insects, chip on base, sgn. Webb, 8¾" H . . .$1,000.00

525-Flemish Cracker Jar, gold w/ bl. Roman coins & flowers, 5¾" H $1,200.00

76-Cut Velvet Vases, 6" & 7½" H, w/ verticle rib & D.Q. patt. $320.00

Quezal Footed Sherbet w/ irid. opal decor. & gr. pulled feathers, irid. gold int., 3¾" H $1,300.00

236-French Cameo Vase, blue w/ autumn colors, frosty sky, sgn. Galle, 10" H $1,750.00

231-Mont Joye CameoVase, textured gr. body decor. w/ gold spider mum, sgn., 7" H $325.00

Row 3, Left to Right

263-French Cameo Vase, red poppies, black leafy stems, mottled yellow & blue, frosty ground, 5¼" H, sgn. Muller Fres Luneville. $2,100.00

80-Tiffany Favrile Tumbler w/ irid. gold surface, sgn., 4" H $525.00

657-French Cameo Ink Well, w/ vine & grape leaves, pods against gr. & org. speckled ground, sgn. Daum Nancy 4½" H $2,300.00

510-Tiffany Favrile Aqua Place Setting, 5 pc. shown, includes 9 plates, stemware & sherbets, sgn. . .$1,125.00

67-Mt. Washington Burmese Toothpick, acid finish, 2¼" H $200.00

207-Tiffany Favrile Vase, irid. gold w/ gr. leaves & gold vines, sgn. 6" H $1,500.00

258-Durand Vase, w/ opal leaves & entwined vines on irid. blue ground, sgn. 7¼" H $1,200.00

243-French Cameo Cologne Bottle, purple & burgandy orchids, sgn. Daum Nancy, 5¼" H $2,250.00

222-Wheeling Peachblow Tumbler w/ glossy finish, 4'H $350.00

69-Webb Peachblow Vase w/ multicolor hummingbird on gold leaf & berry branch, 9" H $260.00

Row 4, Left to Right

570-Tiffany Favrile Bowl, gold w/ green leaf pods, vine & frog, sgn. $1,500.00

61-Amberina "Stork" Vase, by Joseph Locke, 4½" H $1,200.00

526-Mt. Washington Cracker Jar, bisquit color ground w/ fall colors & gold, 6½" H $550.00

661-Webb Burmese Epergne stamped "Queen's Burmese Thomas Webb & Sons & Clarke's Fairy, w/ beveled mirror, 14" diam, 8" H $3,500.00

322-Kelva Box w/ pink floral w/ gr. ground, 2½" H $375.00

72-Cameo Vase w/ gr. leaves & holly berries, gilt, sgn. Valleysthal, 6½" H . . $375.00

221-Stevens & Williams M.O.P. Vase, butterscotch, 7" H $450.00

Row 5, Left to Right

335-Vasa Murrhina Satin Rose Bowl, 3" H $140.00

83-Tiffany Vase, Irid. Reddish Gold, sgn. L.C.T., 3½" H $500.00

235-French Cameo Vase, lavender-blue violets on yellow & blue ground, sgn. Galle, 3½" H $650.00

242- Tiffany Bowl, irid. bluish gold sgn. L.C.T. Favrile, 7¾" diam., 3½" H $1,100.00

216-Steuben Perfume, iridescent blue, sgn. Aurene, 6" H $1,300.00

217-Steuben Perfume, iridescent reddish gold, sgn. Aurene, 6" H $1,000.00

270-Mt. Washington Muffineer, pastel blue flowers & leaves, biscuit body, 2½" H $425.00

62-Webb Peachblow Sweetmeat, shiny finish, w/ raised gold floral decor., 2½" H $300.00

A-OH May 1996   Garth Auctions

Paperweights by Ronald Hansen, Makinaw City, MI, ca. 1910 & either have engraved signature or "H" cane.

Row 1, Left to Right

Green Snake, on beige ground, "H" cane, 2⅝" D $110.00

Pink & White Snake on gr. ground, engraved signature, 2½" D $55.00

Flower, in red, white, gr. yellow & blue on br. striated ground & ringed w/ red canes, "H" cane, cut facets, 2⅝" D $275.00

Row 2, Left to Right

Cherries, red & gr. on blue ground, engraved signature, 2⅜" D . .$165.00

Flower, pink & gr. on a blue ground, "H" cane, 2½" D $137.50

Flower, red, gr. & yellow on a cobalt blue ground, "H" cane, cut facets, 2½" D $165.00

Flower, pink & gr. on a blue ground, "H" cane, cut facets, 2½" D . .$165.00

Row 3, Left to Right

Flower, blue & gr. on a yellow ground, "H" cane, 2¼" D $104.50

Flowers, multi-colored on a blue ground, "H" cane, cut facets, 2⅛" D $165.00

Flower, blue & gr. on a orange ground, engraved signature, 2⅜" D . .$121.00

Row 4, Left to Right

Bell-Like Flowers, white & gr. on red ground, "H" cane, 2⅜" $275.00

Paperweight Perfume, blue & orange snake on clear crystal, dated 1977 . . . .$11.00

Three Paperweights, blue bird on branch, unsigned & two½" diam. miniatures, 1 blue, 1 pink . . .$357.50

A-OH Apr.1996 Early Auction Co.

Row 1, Left To Right

358-Amberina Toothpick, footed, Daisy & Button patt., 3" H . . .$275.00
208-D.Q.M.O.P. Vase, pink w/ raised gold bird, floral branches, camphor handles, 9½" H $1,000.00
25-Cruets, 2 Prussian blue, each 7½" H $170.00
26-Blurina Cruet w/ reeded handle & faceted stopper, 6½" H $200.00
96-Schneider Majorelle Vase, mottled tangerine & cobalt, sgn., 9¾" H $2000.00
27-Cruet, Prussian blue opalescent, seaweed blue handle, 6" H . .$200.00
64-D.Q. Burmese Toothpick, shiny surface w/ squared rim, 2½" H .$300.00
74-Webb Peachblow Vase, decor. w/ bouquet of yellow roses w/ foliage, 13" H $200.00
75-Webb Vase, blue satin decor. w/ gold lotus blossoms, leaves & floral branch, 9½" H $225.00
367-Findlay Onyx Toothpick Holder, 2½" H $500.00
29-Cruets, 1 blue w/ beaded ovals, 7" H, 2nd Scroll w/ Acanthus patt, aqua, 5" H $180.00

Row 2, Left to Right

30-Cruets, 2 Prussian blue, ea. w/ white enamel decor, D.Q. 8" H, bulbous, 6" H $150.00
31-Cruets, 2 Prussian blue, 1 w/ assorted enamel flowers, 6" H, 2nd Inv. Thumb. Patt. 5½" H $300.00
32-Cruets, 2 cased pink, "Bulging Loops" w/ mica spatter, 2nd opalescent. $350.00
69-Webb Peachblow Vase, decor. w/ hummingbird, branches & gold leaf, 9" H $260.00
63-Webb Burmese shiny nut bowl w/ yellow floral design, 2¼" H $250.00
33-Cruets, 1 w/ mica spatter, 6" H, 2nd Sandwich Peachblow w/ enamel decor. 6½" H $600.00
56-Rubina Verde D.Q. Pitcher, w/ white enamel flowers & butterfly, 7¼" H $500.00
34-Cruets, 1 pink overlay w/ blue enamel design, 6½" H, 2nd mingled red & yellow, 5½" H $600.00

Row 3, Left to Right

38-Cruets, pink satin glass, Florette patt. & Guttate patt., each 5" H .$340.00
36-Cruet, Croesus patt., emerald gr. w/ fan patt. stopper, 6½" H . .$200.00
37-Cruet, Royal Ivy patt., pink cased spatter, 6½" H $275.00
404-Cruet, Webb Peachblow, decor. w/ fall color leaves & assorted flowers, 6½" H $450.00
407-Cruet, pink & white w/ clear handle, 6½" H $500.00
408-Cruet, pink cut velvet D.Q. patt., clear handle, 6" H $425.00
413-Cruet, pink M.O.P. Herringbone patt., shades to white, 5½" H .$400.00
414-Cruet, Apricot D.Q.M.O.P., camphor reeded handled w/ ball stopper, 6" H $375.00
415-Cruet, pink M.O P. Coin Spot patt., w/ camphor reeded handle, marriage stopper, 6½" H $300.00
416-Cruet, Webb w/ glossy finish, decor w/ blue & white enamel designs, 6" H $875.00

Row 4, Left to Right

417-Cruets, 2 spatter glass w/ pink, amber, burgundy & opal, 7" & 6" H $300.00
418-Cruets, Bohemian, 1 w/ gilt tracings on ruby, 6½" H, 2nd ruby cut to clear D.Q. 6" H $400.00
419-Cruets, Bohemian, 1 of 3, ruby w/ etched to clear floral, gilt panels $300.00
420-Cruet, D.Q.M.O.P., pink w/ camphor handle, marriage faceted stopper, 5" H $375.00
421-Cruet, D.Q.M.O.P., blue w/ camphor handle, facted stopper . .$400.00
422-Cruet, M.O.P., pink, w/ camphor handle & ball stopper, 6¾" H .$250.00
423-Cruet, M.O.P., amber Coin Spot patt. w/ camphor reeded handle, marriage stopper, 7" H $250.00

Row 5, Left to Right

1-Tumblers, 1 pink & 1 cranberry Hobnail patt., open areas in base $120.00
2-Tumblers, 1 pink reverse swirl, 1 burgundy & white swirl $90.00
5-Tumblers, 2 New England Agata glass $650.00
6-Tumbler, Holly Amber patt. .$450.00
8-Tumblers, 1 blue M.O.P. Herringbone & 1 D. Q. patt. $130.00
10-Tumblers, 1 red Herringbone M.O.P., 1 yellow spatter, 1 red & white spatter w/ mica. $210.00

Row 6, Left to Right

13-Tumblers, 1 Webb pink cased, 2 satin w/ enameled flowers . .$480.00
15-Peachblow Tumblers, 2 w/ shiny surface $400.00
16-Burmese Tumblers, 2 w/ acid finish. $240.00
17-Vasa Murrhina Tumblers, rainbow colors $170.00
18-Wheeling Peachblow Tumblers, minor inside rim roughness. . .$220.00
19-M.O.P. Coin Spot Tumbler, pastel colors. $275.00
20-Holly Amber Tumbler. $525.00
21-M.O.P. Coin Spot Tumbler, red to white & yellow cased. $210.00
23-Tumblers (1 of 3), cranberry thumbprint w/ D.Q., Amberina & Pomona tumblers. $210.00

A-OH July 1996 Garth's Auction

Stiegel Type Blown Glass w/ Polychrome Enamel Decoration

Row 1, Left to Right

Tumbler, flowers and man on horseback, 3⅝" H $632.50

Bottle w/ Pewter Top, (no cap), flowers w/ vase in oval, 5¼" H . . .$385.00

Tumbler, flowers & bird, shallow flake on lip, 4" H $330.00

Tumbler, flowers & bird, lip chip, 3⅛" H $137.50

Jigger, joined hands w/ heart & love birds, Ger. inscription w/ date "1720", 2½" H $330.00

Row 2, Left to Right

Mug, w/ applied handle, flowers & rooster, 5" H $632.50

Bottle, w/ half post neck, flowers & woman w/ Ger. inscription, pewter top (no cap), 5⅝" H $330.00

Mug, w/ applied handle, floral band, 4¼" H $55.00

Bottle, w/ half post neck & pewter top w/ screw cap, floral, interior stain & amethystine tint, 5⅞" H $330.00

Mug, w/ applied handle, floral band w/ love birds, colors have faded look & there is a check at base of handle, 4⅜" H $330.00

Row 3, Left to Right

Tumbler, floral w/ bird on heart, 4/3¼" H $522.50

Bottle, w/ half post neck & pewter top w/ screw cap, floral, interior stain w/ residue, 5⅝" H $275.00

Bottle, w/ half post neck & pewter top (no cap), floral, 6" H $385.00

Pair of Bottles, w/ half post necks & pewter tops w/ screw caps, man & woman w/ flowers & Ger. inscription, second period, 6⅛" H $385.00

Tumbler, woman & heart in hand & flowers, 4¼" H $467.50

A-OH Apr. 1996   Early Auction Co.

Facing Page

Row 1, Left to Right

487-Steuben Green Jade Urn w/ alabaster "M" handles 9¾" H .$900.00

315-Pickle Castor w/ frosted insert, silver plated frame, matching cover $250.00

670-Mont Joye Vase, green w/ enamel floral decor., golden leaves. . . . .NS

492-Steuben Compote, green jade w/ swirl patt., alabaster ft.. mkd., 4" H $300.00

455-Steuben Lamp, pink Aurene w/ irid. bluish gold veins, floral silk shade, 18" H $1,500.00

498-Moser Vase, Alexandrite ribbed, 8½" H $450.00

584-N.E. Peachblow Creamer w/ white enamel daisies on leafy stems, 2½" H $550.00

497-Cluthra Vase, blue w/ clear foot, sgn. Mimball, 12" H $425.00

459-Mt. Washington Vase, yellow coralene w/ assorted designs on pink, white & yellow ground, 7" H .$675.00

702-Steuben Vase, green jade w/ alabaster foot, 8" H $200.00

Row 2, Left to Right

555-French Cameo Vase w/ enameled burgundy florals on frosty ground, sgn. Legras, 7¾" H $550.00

462-Northwoods Vase w/ camphor leaf handles, pink, yellow & white, 8½" H $325.00

457-Webb Satin Vase, yellow to white ground w/ roses, insects & leafy decor., 18" H $550.00

600-French Cameo Vase, maroon fishing harbor & sailing vessels, citron sky, sgn. Galle, 7¾" H $2500.00

693-Fenton Mosaic Vase, mandarin red & carmel designs against dark threading, irid., 8" H $1600.00

592-Cameo Vase, red w/ white stalks of foxglove & leaves, drilled for lamp, 11¾" H $1,800.00

290-Ewer, brilliantly colored w/ floral bouquet & gold enamel, mkd. Rudolstadt, Germany, R.W., in diamond w/ crown, 16½" H $300.00

590-Wheeling Peachblow Tumbler w/ shiny surface, 3¾" H $250.00

Row 3, Left to Right

575-Durand Iridescent Bluish Gold Vase, sgn. V. Durand, 16" H $1,400.00

585-Mt. Washington Burmese Creamer w/ shiny finish, wishbone feet, 3½" H $700.00

590-Wheeling Peachblow Tumbler w/ shiny finish, 3¾" H $250.00

608-Lalique Bowl w/ tied prussian blue frost glass fabrique-like wreath, 6" H, script sgn. $1,750.00

437-Overlay Vase, English, pink rim w/ amber edge, applied flower & leaves, 10½" H $160.00

291-French Vase, lemon yellow w/ splotches of autumn colors, sgn. Lorraine, 9" diam. $225.00

699-Amberina Pitcher, Inverted Thumbprint patt., clear reeded handle, 5½" H $200.00

Row 4, Left to Right

618-Covered Urn, English satin glass, decor. w/ plum color enamel flowers, almond to burnt orange ground, 10½" H $1,000.00

509-French Cameo Box, w/ enamel decor., silver embossed rim, sgn. Daum Nancy, 4" H., 7" L . .$1,850.00

529-French Cameo Pottery Wall Pocket, sgn. Galle Nancy, 12" H $700.00

607-Steuben Verre-de-Sole Compote, frosty celeste blue twist stem, 7" H $700.00

544-Coralene Seaweed Vase, yellow, 10½" H $450.00

695-Amberina D. Q. Celery w/ scalloped edge, 6½" H $275.00

588-Mt. Washington Burmese Tumbler, acid finish, 3¾" H .$135.00

613-Loetz Vase, iridescent green, melon ribbed, 6½" H $300.00

Row 5, Left to Right

614-Loetz Circular Bos w/ hinged cover, iridescent blue w/ chartreuse vines, 3½" H 450.00

486-Steuben Gold Calcite bowl, 2½" H, 5½" diam. $375.00

601-Smith Brothers Container, decor. w/ autumn leaves & gold vines, 3½" H $575.00

708-Loetz Ink Well, iridescent green, w/ brass, 2¾" H $550.00

587-Coralene Seaweed Vase, blue w/ amber branch feet, 6½" H $375.00

701-Steuben Compote, gold calcite w/ rolled rim, 3¼" H $325.00

A-OH May 1996   Garth Auctions

Row 1, Left to Right

Satin Glass Biscuit Jars, pair, pink w/ diamond quilted bowls & silver plated fittings, 8" H $330.00

Kettle Stove, w/ Mary Gregory type insert & white enameling on mauve glass, nickel plated fitting & font w/ burner, 5" D $192.50

French Cameo Bowl, violets in purple, gr. & red on a blue & frosted ground, scalloped rim, mkd. "Daum Nancy", 8" D $2,310.00

Row 2, Left to Right

Bride's Basket, clear deeply scalloped bowl w/ red & opal looping, cased in opal, silver plated frame, 9½" D, 12" H $247.50

Two Decanter Sets, w/ floral enameling, one is blue egg, 10" H, & the other is clear, 11" H, both made to hold sm. decanter & wines, clear one is complete but one wine is broken, blue one has no decanter & only five of six wines, mismatched, ...$137.50

Silver Plated Butter Dish, w/ domed top supported by cherubs, insert missing as is butter knife, 12¼" H .$203.50

A-OH July 1996   Garth's Auction

Large Clear Blown Jar, w/ applied base & applied ring near lip, lid has folded rim, but panels & applied & cut finial, 21¾" H $660.00

Clear Blown Trumpet Vase, w/ applied foot & wafer stem, 17½" H $495.00

Clear Blown Witch Ball, w/ opaque white looping, 7" H $495.00

Clear Blown Pittsburgh Pillar Mold Jar, applied foot & stem w/ applied lip on bowl, 17" H $687.50

A-OH Apr.1996   Early Auction Co.

Row 1, Left to Right

Rookwood Vellum Vase, 10½" H, ca. 1930, sgn. E.T. Hurley $1,800.00

Tiffany Lamp w/ leaded turtle-back shade, bronze base, mkd. Tiffany Studios, N.Y. $6,000.00

Cameo Vase, cocoa br. w/gr. foliage, apricot sky, sign Galle, 9¾" H $2,300.00

Wheeling Peachblow Toothpick Holder, 2¼" H $900.00

Royal Flemish Vase, pale yellow w/ raised gold rays, crown rim decor. w/ br. spirals $5,000.00

Federzeichnung Vase w/ pearlized scrolled trails, rich br. borders, gilt, 8½" H $2,100.00

French Cameo Vase, lavender & olive gr. on apricot grown, sgn. Galle, 11¾" H $700.00

Row 2, Left to Right

Crown Milano Pitcher, lavendar blue w/ rose shrubbery, gold twisted handle, 10½" H $3,000.00

French Cameo Bowl, grey gr. branches w/ fruit, apricot frosty ground, sgn. Daum Nancy, 5½" h, 8" D $1,500.00

Rookwood Vase, gold foliage, bl. background, ca. 1930, sgn. E.T. Hurley $2,350.00

Plated Amberina Tumbler, 3¾" H $1,700.00

Rozane Ware Pitcher, br. ground, mkd. & sgn. W. Myers, 14½ H, 14" H $1,800.00

English Cameo Rose Bowl, yellow ground, sgn. Thomas Webb & Sons Gem Cameo, 4" H $1,300.00

Cameo Vase w/ white decor. on red satin ground, sgn. Thomas Webb & Sons, 8¼" H $2,250.00

Row 3, Left to Right

Tiffany Vase w/ irid. gold, br., opal, green, sgn. L.C. Tiffany Favrile, 4½" H $2,300.00

Durand Vase w/ irid. gold, pulled feathers & gold threading, sgn. 10½" H $1,600.00

English Cameo Vase w/ white decor. on blue ground, 10" H $2,250.00

Crown Milano cov. container, white body decor. w/ multicolor ground, mkd., 3" H $625.00

Burmese Epergne, decor. w/ ivy, crystal rigaree tooled leaves, sgn. Queen's Burmese, Thomas Webb & Sons, 12" H $4000.00

Tiffany Vase, irid. gold body w/ lattice network, sgn. L.C. Tiffany, Favrile. $2,600.00

French Cameo Vase w/ black & blues, yellow sky, sgn. Galle, 9¾" H $1,750.00

A-MA Oct. 1995   Skinner, Inc.

170-Sandwich Glass Amethyst Pressed Glass Tulip Vase, Boston and Sandwich Glass Co., mid 19th c., (very minor chips to base), 9½". $805.00

172-Sandwich Glass Amber Spooner, attrib. to Boston and Sandwich Glass Co., mid 19th c., (chips and scratches), 4¾" H. $862.00

171-Sandwich Glass Blue Loop Cologne, attrib. to Boston and Sandwich Glass Company, mid 19th c., (chips), 8¼" H. $1265.00

175-Sandwich Glass Green Canary Oval Panelled Frame Cologne, Boston and Sandwich Glass Co., mid 19th c., with lily stopper, (minor chips), 6⅝" H $546.25

181-Five Sandwich and Sandwich-type Glass Items, 19th c., opaque light blue hour glass cologne, emerald cologne, clambroth cologne, deep ruby cologne and cobalt three-blown mold sunburst in square open salt, (imperfection), 2¾"-7⅞" H $1725.00

180-Two Sandwich Glass Amber Colognes, attrib. to Boston and Sandwich Glass Co., (minor chips), 5½" and 7¾" H $546.25

182-Sandwich-Type Glass Medium Blue Diamond Pattern Glass Spoon Holder, Amer, mid 19th c., 5" H $488.75

A-MA Oct. 1995   Skinner, Inc.

Left to Right

Steuben Celeste Blue Glasses, 6 cordials & 6 wines, 4¼" H & 5" H $460.00

Steuben Celeste Blue Bowls, two, 7⅜" H, 11¾" D $488.75

Steuben Celeste Blue Candlesticks, pr., 15" H $805.00

Steuben Celeste Blue Compotes, 3, graduated sizes, 2¾" H, 3½" H, 3¼" H $373.75

A-MA Oct. 1995   Skinner, Inc.

Austrian Threaded Red Glass Vase, attributed to Pallme - Koning & Habel, 12" H $402.50
Loetz Glass Shades, pr., amber conical body w/ red pulled feather & green leaf & vine, several chips on top and base rims, 4" H, 2¼ D $747.50
Loetz-Type Austrian Green Fan Vase, 10" H, 9½" W $373.75
Austrian Metal Mounted Art Glass Items, 2, Loetz-type syrup jar, 4¼" H; handled irid. dish, 5" H $345.00
Silver Overlay Glass Vase, impressed "L. Sterling", 6¾" H $1,265.00
Gold Irid. Silver Overlay Vase, inscribed "L. Sterling", 2½" H $747.50
Gold Irid. Silver Overlaid Vase, Loetz-style glass, 3⅞" H $805.00
Bohemian Glass Jar, twisted blue-grey opal glass w/ shiny metal rim, 6" H, 4¾" D $172.50

A-MA May 1996   Skinner, Inc.

Orrefors Swedish Ariel Bowl, by Edvin Ohrstrom, w/ air trip bubbles & aubergine stripes, sgn., 8" D $690.00

A-MA Oct. 1995   Skinner, Inc.

Steuben Deco. Aurene Shades, pr., gold int. & feathers on white irid., marked on rim, 5¼" H, 2¼" D $316.25
Steuben Ivrene Shades, pr., white shades w/ irid. surface, minor chips at collet rim, 3¼" H $230.00
Steuben Gold Aurene Shades, pr., bright orange tone coloring, silver Steuben fleur de lis mark at rim, 2½" H, 6" D $373.75
Steuben Gold Aurene Glass Shades, pr., marked w/ silvered fleur de lis stamp at rim, 5" H, 2¼" D $316.25

A-MA Oct. 1995   Skinner, Inc.

Left to Right
Loetz Papillon Vase, green, engraved w/ crossed arrows mark & "Austria", 3¾" H, 6" D $431.25
Loetz Glass Rosebowl, brilliant blue w/ gold irid. papillon spotted surface, 5¼" H, 7" D $690.00
Loetz-Type Glass Vase, 4⅝" H $1,380.00
Loetz Glass Bowl, design of Edward Prochaska, interior water stain, 3½" H, 5½" D $632.50

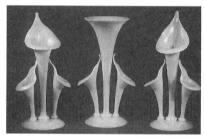

A-MA Oct. 1995   Skinner, Inc.

Left & Right
Steuben Ivrene Triple Lily Vases, pr., irid. surface, ea. inscribed "Steuben", 12½" H $2,070.00
Center
Steuben Ivrene Triple Lily Trumpet Vase, inscribed "Steuben", faintly spotted irid. surface, 12" H $862.50

A-MA Oct. 1995   Skinner, Inc.

Steuben Decorated Gold Aurene Vase, platinum irid. surface w/ six green pulled and hooked feather elements, 4" H $1,265.00

A-MA Oct. 1995   James D. Julia, Inc.

Holly Amber Glass Unless Noted

Row 1, back
Tray, 8" across, w/ one rim flake $850.00
Relish, 9" L, slight edge roughage $375.00

Row 1, front
Bowls, 3 pcs., 1 shown, 4¼" $450.00
Berry Bowl, 4" W $150.00
Berry Bowl, 4" W $150.00
Berry Bowl, 4" W $175.00

Row 2
Handled Mug, 4" H $400.00
Bowl, 7½" L, 4½" W $425.00
Berry Bowl, 4" W $150.00
Berry Bowl, 4" W $150.00
Jelly Compote, 3½" H, 4¾" W $700.00

Row 3
Covered Butter Dish, 6½" H $900.00
Master Berry Bowl, 8½" W, minute flake on rim .$300.00
Berry Bowl, 4" W $150.00
Tumbler w/ Beaded Rim, 3½" H $600.00

Row 4
Covered Butter Dish, 5" H, 5" W $950.00
Cream Pitcher, 4½" $450.00
Greentown Chocolate Glass Compote, Cactus Pattern, 5½" H $125.00
Spooner, 4" H, w/ edge roughage $450.00
Greentown Chocolate Glass Salt & Pepper, Cactus Pattern red Agate, 3¼" H $175.00

Row 5
Plate, 7½" $400.00
Plate, 7½" $400.00
Plate, 7½" $400.00

A-MA Oct. 1995   James D. Julia, Inc.

Loetz Glass Vase, pale green/blue w/ sterling silver overlay, 4½" H, 4" W $1,300.00

A-MA Oct. 1995   James D. Julia, Inc.

Galle Cameo Glass
Row 1
Vase, deep purple Crocus patt. against a frosted yellow & purple background, 6½" H $1,700.00

Vase, olive/brown glass w/ carved & enameled floral & thistle patt. w/ gold highlights, signed Galle on base, 4¾" H, 5" W $1,250.00
Stick Vase, deep orange apricot floral cameo design against a frosted white background, signed Galle, 6¾" H . .$800.00
Row 2
Vase, yellow frosted & brown background w/ an all over landscape design of lake w/ trees, 8¼" H, 3" W .$1,900.00
Banjo Vase, signed Galle w/ star, bright pink background w/ green & brown, 7" H $1,400.00
Flask Vase, deep amethyst Wisteria decor. on frosted clear & pink background, signed Galle w/ star, 5¾" H, 4¾" W . . $1,300.00
Banjo Vase, signed Galle, landscape & lake design, deep yellow frosted opalescent background w/ brown overlay, 7" H $1,400.00
Vase, teardrop from w/ brown floral cutting against a frosted yellow ground, 8¼" H $1,600.00

A-MA Oct. 1995   James D. Julia, Inc.

Mt. Washington Royal Flemish

Row 1

Vase w/ unusual flying bird decor., soft beige background w/ gold sections & stars, 6" H $1,250.00

Brides Bowl/Centerpiece, signed, pairpoint silver plated stand of a full figured cherub. Bowl decor. w/ elaborate all over chrysanthemum pattern in shades of blue, purple, pink & yellow w/ green, maroon & gold leaves, all over gold "sections". Maroon border w/ gold trim. Signed w/ monogram, bowl 4" H, 11" dia, overall ht. 16½", slight rim flake on int. of bowl. $3,000.00

Bulbous Stick Vase w/ snail handles, Roman coin decor., panels painted in shades of lavender, pale blue & tan, gold "sections" w/ maroon jewels, neck w/ lavender & gold winged Griffin design, 13¾" H, 7¼" W $3,700.00

Miniature Banquet Lamp w/ decor. of seagulls in flight w/ sea plants, sea creatures against a frosted background w/ decor. in shades of pale blue, green w/ white & bluish-grey birds. Gold highlights, lamp in 3 parts, orig. metal hardware, signed w/ monogram & numbered. 22½" H, 7½" shade dia., restor. near rim of shade $4,000.00

Row 2

Double Handled Open Sugar Bowl w/ apple blossom decor. in pink & yellow, gold sectioning w/ pale lavender & beige background, 2¾" H, 4" W $550.00

Biscuit Jar, all over circle decor. in various sizes against a deep maroon/brown background, circles dine in shades of pale green, pale brown, mustard. Gold chrysanthemum decor. w/ green & brown leaves, signed in cover "MW", 7¾" H, 5¾" W $2,200.00

Bulbous Vase w/ purple, blue & yellow pansy decor. w/ all over leaf & vine background design. 6½" H, 7" W $1,950.00

Roman Coin Biscuit Jar, deep beige, tan & rust background w/ silver & gold coin, orig. metal hardware, 8¼" H, 5½" W $1,700.00

A-OH Sept. 1995   Garth's Auction

Row 1, Left to Right

Clear Crystal Paperweight, Pink & White swirls w/ center cane in red, white & gr., 2½" D $1,017.50

Clear Crystal Paperweight, Baccarat cut faces w/ floral canes in pink, white, blue & purple w/ gr. foliage, 2⅝" D $990.00

Clear Crystal Paperweight, sm. Baccarat w/ floral canes in white, purple, gr. & pink, surface bruises, 1¾" D . . . $385.00

Clear Crystal Paperweight, pear weight in orange & amber w/ pink stem & clear base, 2⅝" D . . .$660.00

Clear Crystal Paperweight, eagle & shield sulfide, minor wear, 2¼" D $275.00

Clear Crystal Paperweight, cut flutes w/ multi-colored floral canes, minor wear & pinpoint flakes, 2½" D $275.00

Row 2, Left to Right

Clear Crystal Paperweight, clichy w/ multi-colored floral canes, surface chips & bruises, 2⅞" D $605.00

Clear Crystal Paperweight, central flower w/ white cane center & gr. leaves, wreath of red & white floral canes, cut star, 2⅞" D $2,145.00

Clear Crystal Paperweight, sandwich w/ red & gr. flower w/ cane center on a white latticinio ground, wear & minor chips, 3¼" D $550.00

Clear Crystal Paperweight, floral design in canes of red, white blue & gr., sm. flakes on bottom, 3¼" D .$495.00

Clear Crystal Paperweight, Baccarat w/ cut facets & jumbled candy canes, 3" D $357.50

Row 3, Left to Right

Clear Crystal Paperweight, St. Louis w/ red, yellow & green fruit on a white latticinio ground, minor wear, 3" D $880.00

Clear Crystal Paperweight, Bristol w/ floral design in multi-colored canes, sm. flakes & surface scratch, 2¾" D . $275.00

Clear Crystal Paperweight, footed weight w/ concentric circles of canes in white, pink, gr., red, blue, etc., 3¾" D $330.00

Clear Crystal Paperweight, pansy in deep purple, white & yellow w/ gr. foliage & cane center, wear & scratches, 2⅝" D $660.00

A-OH Jan. 1996   Garth's Auction

Left to Right

Ancient Tripod Pottery Vessel, prob. Mesoamerican, two legs restored, damage to rim, 4½" D, 6¾" H $5.50
Hohokam Pottery Jar, red over buff is very faded, broken and restored, 4½" D, 3½" H $38.50
Anasazi Pottery Bowl, St. John's polychrome, redware w/ wht. diamond design on outside and black design, crack and chips to rim, 10 ⅛" D, 4 ⅛" H . . .$333.00
Anasazi Pottery Ladle, blk. on grey, handle broken and chips to rim, numbers and "Red Lake Ariz" on back, 3¾" W, 6" L $71.50
Southwest Pottery Bowl, prob. Mogollon, outer surface red negative over buff grey, broken, repr. and kill hole filled, 7"D, 3¼" H $27.50
Anasazi Pottery Bowl, polychrome umber and red ochre design on orange, Pinedale?, hazing, glued hairline crack and loop handle broken off, 8½" D, 4½" H $93.50

A-OH Jan. 1996   Garth's Auction

California Indian Basket, collected as Mono-Tulare, prob. Mono or Yokuts, missing rim stitches, two on outer body, 21½"D, 12" H $4400.00
Papago/Pima Model Basketry Kiaha, lace coil burden basket w/ faded red and blue design, late 19th c., 13 ½" D, plus sticks. $660.00
Papago Basket, D. oval willow bowl w/ martynia zoomorphic figures around sides, early 20th c., 10¼" x 13⅜", 6½" H $357.50
Two Pottery Bowls, polychrome over wht. slip, one marked "Laguna, N. Mex" has rim chip and hairline, inner yel. slip goes over side, 7⅜" D., 5⅛" H, ohter is Isleta in Laguna style, minor rim wear, 1880-1910, 6¾"D, 3¾"H $187.00
Hupa Basketry Tray, 17¾" D, 6" H $330.00
Hopi Pottery, umber on smoked orangy slip, jar marked "Hopi", 3¾" D, 7" H, bowl sgn. "E. Chapella" w/ minor scratching, 4⅞" D, 2½" H, bowl sgn. "Nellie Nampeyo", wear and chips to rim, 4¼" D, 2 ⅛" H $192.50

A-OH Mar. 1996   Garth's Auction

Plains Style Parfleche Rifle Case, red, blue, yellow and green geometric design, red wool binding w/ long buckskin fringe, 43" L $93.50
Pipe Bag, Cheyenne design in black & white pony beads on maroon red trade cloth w/ long buckskin fringe, beads appear to be old but rest is recent, 20" L plus fringe. $82.50
Pima Basketry Tray, whirling fret design in martynia & willow, 3¾" H, 12⅜" D $440.00
Blackfoot Gauntlets or Gloves, cuffs & back of hand beaded in blues, oranges & reds, elkhide, 14" L$440.00
Hopi Basketry Bowl, coil w/ yellow, brown & black design encircling body, 4" H, 9" D $93.50
Sioux Women's Leggings, classic design in green, white heart red & blue on white bead ground, replaced ties, leather wear & repair, some missing beads, 11¼" x 12⅜". $660.00
Sioux Moccasins, beaded in green & white w/ detailing in blue, yellow & white heart pinks & orangy/red trade cloth around cuff, leather damage, slight bead damage, 10⅜" L . .$247.50
Small Pima Basketry Tray, geometric design in martynia & willow, one rim stitch missing, 6¼" D $121.00
Plains Style Tobacco Bag, strip at bottom beaded in pink, blue, maroon, yellow, green & red then attached to bag, tin cone & brass bead dangles, red & yellow ochre stained bag, 14" L plus dangles. $104.50
Plains Sioux Moccasins, sinew sewn beading in green, orangy/red and white w/ pale blue details, yellow cloth cuff binding, minute bead loss, large size, wearable, 11" L $275.00

A-MA Aug. 1996   Robert C. Eldred
Co., Inc.

Apache Basket, ca. 1900 w/floral & figural design, 3¼"H, 18" Dia. $3,850.00

A-OH Jan. 1996 Garth's Auction

Apache Burden Basket, old style w/ red cloth and leather bottom, red dye and martynia design, missing fringes, 16¾" D, 12¾" H $935.00

Pima Basketry Tray, radiating stepped design in martynia and willow, 15¾" D, 4" H $605.00

Hopi Shallow Pottery Tray, ochre and umber design on creamy slip, pierced clay tab for hanging, old paper tab on back reads "Nampeyo", glaze chip at rim and slight wear to design, 1890-1920, 9⅜" D, 2" H $2,640.00

Hopi Pottery Bowl, avian design in red ochre and umber on an orangy slip, sgn. "Ruth Paymella", glaze hairline and scrape, ca. 1940, 6" D, 5⅜" H $77.00

Santa Domingo Pottery Olla, strong red ochre and umber design on a creamy grey slip over a red slightly concave bottom, early 20th c., minute wear, 9½" D, 10" H $1430.00

Hopi Pottery Bowl, ca. 1930, red ochre and umber design over creamy orange slip has wear, hairline crack, sm. blk. spots on int., 8⅝" D, 3¼" H $220.00

Hopi Shallow Pottery Tray, umber avian design on orangy slip, "Alva Rowena" penciled on back, minor wear to design in one area and sticker mark, 9¼" D, 1⅞" H $165.00

Papago Basket, yucca w/ human and animal figures in martynia, 12" D., 14¼" H $286.00

A-OHJan. 1996 Garth's Auction

Row One, Left to Right,

Washoe/Paiute Burden Basket Model, twill weave, some widely spaced rim stitches are missing, early 20th c., 10¾ D, 12¾" L $247.50

Paiute Basketry Parching Tray, twined willow, old tag "Pur from Lucy Markan", early 20th c., wear and scorching, 14¼" W, 17⅞" H $77.00

Jicarilla Apache Basketry Water Jar, pitched inside, horsehair and rawhide attachment, old label "Belonged to Bert C. Phillips founder of Taos Art Colony", ca. 1890, 12" D $935.00

Paiute Basketry water Jar, red ochre stained, pitched and w/ horsehair and string handles, third of rim stiching is missing, late 19th c., 8" D, 11¾" H $192.50

Santo Domingo Pottery Water Olla, polychrome floral design in red ochre and blk. on a buffish slip, early 20th c., small poorly repr. rim chip and crack at base, 10⅜"D, 9¾" H $1,045.00

Santo Domingo Pottery Pitcher, polychrome red ochre and blk. on creamy ground, broken and repr., hairline visible by handle, 6 ⅛" D, 8⅞" H $110.00

Santo Domingo Pottery Water Olla, black design on an orangish slip over a red ochre concave base, wear from use, rim chips and calcifying from water at base, 19th c., 11 ⅛" D, 10⅝" H $1,265.00

Santo Domingo Pottery Bowl, blk. design on greyish slip, red int. and worn base, sm. rim chips, hairline and "50" scratched through slip, 9¼" D, 6" H $220.00

Santo Domingo Pottery Jar, blk. design on creamy slip over a red ochre concave bottom, minor wear, ca. 1900, 5¾" D, 4¾" H $385.00

A-OH Jan. 1996   Garth's Auction

Row 1

Mission Indian Basketry Bowl, So. Calif. Cahuilla, Agua Caliente w/ fine patina to juncus body, minor rim damage, 5" H, 13½" D $137.50

Hopi Pottery Jar, curvilinear avian design, umber w/ red ochre on a cream to orangy slip polished body, wear on rim, ca. 1920, 4½"H, 5⅝"D $49.50

Large Acoma Water Jar, medium brown & ochre design over white slip body above ochre bottle bottom, wear, small chips & some peeling of ochre design, ca: 1940, 9" H, 10" D .$269.50

Hopi Coiled Basket, brown step design around deep bowl shape, 5" H, 7" D $49.50

A-OH Mar. 1996   Garth's Auctions

Row 1

Navajo Gallup Yei Weaving, russet, brown and reds on natural background, pea size hole, 17¼" x 38" $49.50

Early Papago Basketry Tray, stepped whirling fret design in martynia & willow, minor rim damage, 3½" H, 14" D $148.50

Zuni Pottery Jar, umber & red ochre heartline deer & sunflower medallion on white slip, slight wear & dry clay crazing on inside bottom, 5" H, 6¼" D $159.50

Algonquin Bark Canoe Model, 19¾" L $27.50

Two Hopi Pottery Jars, umber designs on a polished red/orange body, both made by Sunbeam David, 3½" H & 3¾" H $99.00

Acoma Pottery Jar, umber & red ochre geometric design over white slip, early 1900's, 8" H, 9½" D . .$1,210.00

Hopi Pottery Seed Jar, Hano Sikyati Revival on dark orange body, wear to bottom, 6" hairline above shoulder, 7" H, 13" D $1,595.00

Row 2

Santo Domingo Pottery Jar, black design on cream slip over red concave bottom, glued break & chip at rim, 8¾" H, 7" D $82.50

California Mission Basket, cupeno, simple design w/ juncus coil, damage, 2⅜" H, 9" D $27.50

Hopi Pottery Jar, second mesa, umber on polished orange body, signed w/ corn emblem for Lena Chio, minor spaling, 6¼" H, 6½" D $225.50

Hopi Pottery Bowl, second mesa, dark umber & red ochre on creamy white polished slip, signed w/ corn emblem for Lena Chio, scratch on side, minute flaking, 5¼" H, 8¼" D $247.50

Pima Basket Tray, martynia & willow, ca: 1920, minor rim damage, 2⅜" H, 12½" D $115.00

Three Hopi Vessels, all umber on creamy orange slip, slight wear, one pencil signed "Erma Jawyewa", 2½", 2½", 3½" L $66.00

Row 2

Two Northwestern Berry Baskets, Salishan (missing rim attachments), 26½" H, 7½" D and Wakeshan (not pictured), 3½" H, 8" D $44.00

Four Santo Domingo Pottery Pieces, early tourist ware, red ochre & black on cream: two containers; pitcher & tray, all have minute slip crazing, 2" to 6" H $60.50

Acoma Pottery Double Spout Wedding Jar, ochre & umber avian design on white slip, 1930's, roughness & wear at spout tips, 12" H, 5¾" D $220.00

Jicarilla Apache Basketry Vessel, traditional deep oval w/ faced aniline red & green zig zag design, 8½" H, 19¼" L $214.50

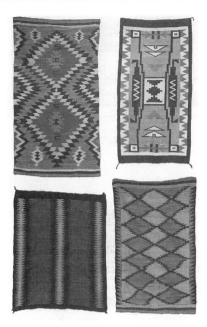

A-OH Jan. 1996   Garth's Auction

Row 1

Navajo Rug, ca. 1900, red, carded grey dk. brn., and natural hand carded wool, two corner tasels worn, several selvage yarn breaks and slight soiling, 2'7"W, 4'10"L, ...$660.00

Navajo Rug, W. Reservation storm pattern hand carded red, blk., grey and natural, stain or soiling at one end, 3'11" W, 6'8" L $275.00

Row 2

Navajo Rug, finely carded and woven natural brn., tan and wht. wool, ca. 1910, unused condition, 3'10" W, 4'8" L $935.00

Navajo Rug, serrate diamond Toadlena area, ca. 1900, slight staining, two areas thin and worn and break at one end, all sides blanket-stitched (possible damage underneath), 4'5" W, 6'10" L $247.50

A-MA Aug. 1996   Robert C. Eldred Co., Inc.

Pima Basket, w/ geometric design, ca. 1900, 5" dia., 5" H $1,760.00

A-MA Aug. 1996   Robert C. Eldred Co., Inc.

Granado-Type Navajo Rug, red & white w/brown medallion design, 6'6" x 4'4", ca. 1920 . . . .$440.00

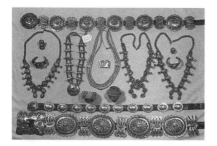

A-OH Mar. 1996   Garth's Auction

Navajo Concho Belt, w/ turquoise blue center stones on black leather, belt is 51" L $467.50

Navajo Turquoise & Sterling Silver Squash Blossom Necklace, Bracelet & Ring, turquoise is robin's egg blue w/ black veining. . .$330.00

Navajo Chip-Inlay Necklace, coral & turquoise squash blossom style w/ birds for blossoms, signed. . .$110.00

Two Pieces of Indian Jewelry, A Santo Domingo three strand turquoise he-shi necklace w/ shell spacers & Navajo sterling rainbow god & stone inlay belt buckle signed. $275.00

Navajo Coral & Sterling Silver Squash Blossom Necklace, stones surrounded by silver leaf $308.00

Navajo Turquoise & Sterling Silver Squash Blossom Necklace, Bracelet & Ring, greenish turquoise. . .$385.00

Two Miniature Baskets, both finely woven, pima w/ step design, and Wakeshan basket w/ birds around circumference, 2" H $231.00

Navajo Sterling Silver Concho Belt, ten finely wrought & stamped conchos, plus buckle, belt is 51½" L $440.00

Navajo Concho Belt, Oval & Butterfly Shape, stamped nickel silver conchos set w/ turquoise blue stones, plus buckle, belt is 38" L $231.00

A-OH Mar. 1996   Garth's Auction

Native America Rugs
Yei Weaving, white figures on grey ground, ca: 1970, 2'8½" x 3'3". $60.50

A-OH Mar. 1996   Garth's Auctions

Plains Parfleche Container, buffalo hide w/ red, blue, yellow & green geometric design, red wool edge binding, 14¼" H, 16" W $110.00

Plains Hairpipe Dance Ornament, bone leather, brass beads w/ ribbon, beads & velvet, restrung, 24½" L, framed, 34" H, 18½" W $82.50

Plains Twin Tab Tobacco Bag, simple lazy stitch bands in sky blue, dark blue, white-heart red, metallic gold & orangy white-heart red beads, ca: 1890-1900, 13" L plus fringe. .$176.00

Two Headbands, plateau woman's headband, Nez Perce/Yakima type worn by Pendleton Roundup Indian Princesses, multi-color beading on leather, 20¼" L and a red, blue and white loom beaded headband w/ leather ties, 19" L $27.50

Southwestern Anasazi Pottery Bowl, black and buff design on polished red interior, has two 1" hairlines, 2¼" H $49.50

Plains Cree Woman's Hightop Moccasins, classic floral multi-color beading on yellow ochre stained hide, some wear to leather, & repair, 12" H$555.50

Sioux Child's Moccasins, sky blue, cheyenne pink, white-heart red & yellow beads, sinew sewn, 6" L .$357.50

Plains Moccasins, leather w/ multi-color mix beads & areas of cut faceted metallic beads, ca: 1920, 9½" L$137.50

Navajo, probably Crystal area, deep red, dark brown & carded grey handspun wool w/ fine sheen, ca: 1910-15, selvage wear and one warp break, 4'6" x 7'. $478.50

Navajo, transitional period serrate diamond, red, black, grey & natural wool, unused condition, corner tassels, minute bleeding, 3'9" x 5'3". .$137.50

Navajo, serrate diamond design, red, browns & natural, ca: 1920, minor wear to corners & edges, 3'10" x 6'. $440.00

A-OH Mar. 1996   Garth's Auctions
Small Navajo Pictorial Rug, six pointed star in dark red centered w/ whirling log design w/ arrows, 23" x 25½" $77.00

Cheyenne Moccasins, pine tree green, white-heart red, dark blue & light blue beads on a white bead ground, buffalo hide uppers have nicks out of each heel flap, bead loss, 10" L $555.50

Plateau Pouch, Blackfoot, floral design in blue, yellow, translucent maroon, white & green beads, 1" missing bead edging on flap, 5" x 5½" $22.00

Arapaho Moccasins, typical cross design in green, yellow, dark navy blue & white beads on soft buckskin, seam separations & break to one leather tie, 10¼" L $137.50

Plateau/Northern Woodlands Baby Wrap, black velvet body w/ colorful spot stitch floral beading, leather lacing, 24" L $159.50

Easter Woodland-Algonquin Pouch, multi-color beaded floral design on black velvet w/ replaced blue ribbon edging, bead loss, 6⅛" x 6" $27.50

Two Pair of Beaded Armbands, Old Plains Sioux, red, blue & white beads, leather ties missing, 13" L, plateau armbands beaded (not pictured), 11½" L $49.50

Northern Plains/Plateau Moccasins, graphic lead design in pink, yellow, red, green & blue, calico flap binding, ca: 1890, 9½" L $412.50

Eastern Woodland/Northern Algonquin Moccasins, moosehide w/ multi-color floral beading, thread worn at top of tongue, worn silk cord detailing, 9¼" L $137.50

Navajo, ganado serrate zig-zag, red, blue, black, brown & natural bleeding made pink, ca: 1925, 2'10" x 4'10". $192.50

Navajo, West Reservation, finely woven stripe & band in gold, red, black, grey & natural, 2'10" x 6". $357.50

Navajo, natural color stepped terrace w/ unusual green center, several small holes & wear at one end, ca: 1925, 3'3" x 4'11". $412.50

A-MA Oct. 1995   Skinner, Inc.
Reverse Painted Scenic Table Lamp, pebbled surface Phoenix-type glass shade, Moe Bridges urn form base, 24" H, 17" D $977.50

A-MA Oct. 1995   Skinner, Inc.
Phoenix-type Reverse Painted Nautical Lamp, puffed surface on domed glass shade, mounted on urn form gilt metal cast base, small rim chip, platform foot base gilt worn off, 24" H, 17" D $1,265.00

A-MA Oct. 1995   Skinner, Inc.
Handel Reverse Painted Tropical Island Scenic Lamp, bell-shaped glass dome, signed "Handel 3310", mounted on three socket bronzed metal base, 20" H, 15" D . . .$3,335.00

A-MA Oct. 1995   Skinner, Inc.
Reverse Painted Scenic Table Lamp, Phoenix-type pebble surface glass dome shade, 22" H, 17" D $690.00

A-MA Oct. 1995   Skinner, Inc.
Duffner & Kimberly Peony Leaded Glass Lamp, conical shade w/ dropped apron, mounted on four-light Duffner cast bronze base w/ elaborate acanthus leaf ribbing, 29" H, 24" D . . $14,950.00

A-MA Oct. 1995   Skinner, Inc.
Handel Reverse Painted Scenic Lamp, conical Teromo glass dome, signed at rim "Handel", 3 socket bronzed metal base w/ integrated faux teakwood platform foot, 23" H, 18" D $5,750.00

A-MA Oct. 1995   Skinner, Inc.
Bent Panel Slag Glass Table Lamp, attributed to Frankel Light Co, Cincinnati, elaborate urn-decorated metal frame, 21" H, 19" D $690.00

A-MA Oct. 1995   Skinner, Inc.
Quezal Four-Arm Table Lamp, sculptural base w/ cast metal female portraits, 4 bell-shaped gold iridescent shades marked "Quezal", some chipping to shade rims, lamp shaft repainted, 20" H $805.00

A-MA Oct. 1995   Skinner, Inc.
Seuss Ornamental Glass Co Dogwood Lamp, shaped umbrella dome shade of leaded glass segments, raised on three-socket bronze base, 21" H, 20" D $2,300.00

A-MA Oct. 1995   James D. Julia, Inc.

Pairpoint Puffy Table Lamp, Stratford shade w/ border of white roses, dogwood blossoms & hummingbirds against a deep pink background w/ floral scrolling, on bronzed metal art Nouveau base, not Pairpoint, shade dia. 14", 22" H $3,500.00

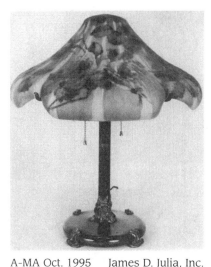

A-MA Oct. 1995   James D. Julia, Inc.

Pairpoint "Genoa Rose" Table Lamp, Genoa shade painted on int. w/ large deep pink roses, green leaves & stems against a green ground w/ white striping, on copper finished Art Nouveau base, shade dia. 16", 21" H . .$8,500.00

A-MA Oct. 1995   James D. Julia, Inc.

Slag Panel Hanging Fixture, border w/ an overlay of a desert oasis scene, 24" dia. $450.00

A-MA Oct. 1995   James D. Julia, Inc.

Art Nouveau Slag Panel Hanging Hall Fixture, 16" H $200.00

A-MA Oct. 1995   James D. Julia, Inc.

Pairpoint Puffy Gladiola Table Lamp, Stratford shade painted on the int. w/ gladiolas & foliage in colors of orange, yellow, pink & blue against a frosted white ground, on a copper finished fluted candlestick base, shade dia. 14", 22" H $7,000.00

A-MA Oct. 1995   James D. Julia, Inc.

Pittsburgh Reverse Painted Table Lamp, Domical shade in "chipped" glass painted on the int. w/ a tropical scene of palm trees, blue shading to amber sky, bronze metal Arts & Craft style base, shade dia. 14", 22" H $700.00

A-MA Oct. 1995   James D. Julia, Inc.

Handel Leaded Glass Table Lamp,

A-MA Aug. 1996   Robert C. Eldred
Co., Inc.

Pairpoint Lamp, w/ shaped ribbed blown-out shade decor. w/ roses, brass base, shade 16″ diam., 21″ H $3,360.00

A-OR Aug. 1996   O'Gallerie, Inc.

Tiffany Table Lamp, w/ stained & leaded glass shade in "Swirling Leaf" patt., mkd. Tiffany Studios NY, 21½″ H $9,000.00

A-MA Aug. 1996   Robert C. Eldred
Co., Inc.

Leaded Glass Table Lamp, shade in caramel w/ floral band, bronze base, shade 16″ diam., 23″ H $1,540.00

A-ME May. 1996   Skinner, Inc.

Fulper Pottery Leaded Glass Lamp, w/ mushroom shade w/ green & ochre slag glass inserts, mkd., 16″H .$11,500.00

A-ME May. 1996   Skinner, Inc.

Tiffany Nautilus Lamp, on dragonfly enameled base w/ shell shade & silvered rim, sgn. 15″ H $4,830.00

A-ME May. 1996   Skinner, Inc.

Reverse Painted & Stenciled Glass Shade, w/ Arts & Crafts stylistic border in amber brown & orange, 16" diam. $575.00

A-ME May. 1996   Skinner, Inc.

Handel Desk Lamp, w/ rolled cylinder of green Teroma glass cased to white, w/ sgn. "Handel" fabric label, 16"H $1,265.00

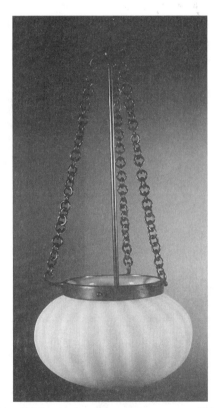

A-ME May. 1996   Skinner, Inc.

Quezal Bronze & Art Glass Chandelier, w/ sgn. "Quezal" elongated iridescent glass shades of brilliant fiery green-amber, herringbone patt., 40" H, 36" W, shade diam. 19" .$12,650.00

A-ME May. 1996   Skinner, Inc.

Tiffany Bronze & Favrile Glass Ceiling Lamp, yellow opal. optic ribbed globe w/ bronze collar, chains & single-socket, sgn L.C.T., 30" H, shade 11½" opening . . .$2,070.00

A-MA Oct. 1995   Skinner, Inc.
Handel Bent Panel Table Lamp,
seven segments of white glass panels
framed by yellow blossom bronzed
metal, three sockets replm., 22" H, 16"
D $2,415.00

A-MA Oct. 1995   Skinner, Inc.
Handel Leaded Glass Pansy Lamp,
drop apron on shaped dome shade,
supported on three socket bronzed
metal ribbed base, 23" H,
18" D $3,737.50

A-MA Oct. 1995   Skinner, Inc.
**Tiffany Bronze & Glass Bellflower
Lamp,** shade impressed "Tiffany Studios NY", damaged, slender urn form
three-light base w/fine patina, 21½" H,
15½" D $7,475.00

A-MA Oct. 1995   Skinner, Inc.
Bent Panel Slag Glass Table Lamp,
eight green-white-amber slag sections
mounted behind gilt metal urn & swag
shade frame, single socket, 21½" H, 17"
D $488.75

A-MA Oct. 1995   Skinner, Inc.
**Tiffany Bronze Peacock Table
Lamp,** leaded Favrile glass, supported
on 3 arm fluid lamp base w/ font, foliate pad platform, all impressed "Tiffany
Studios", some glass segment cracks,
19½" H, 16" D $26,450.00

A-MA Oct. 1995   Skinner, Inc.
Cast Iron & Slag Glass Table Lamp,
pyramidal shade lined w/green slag
glass panels, single socket, 2 shade
panels cracked, 19½" H, 11" D$345.00

A-MA Oct. 1995   Skinner, Inc.
**Leaded Glass Water Lily Table
Lamp,** conical shade with multicolored glass segments, mounted on two
light cast metal base painted green-
black, marked "Jefferson" at base rim,
21½ H, 18" D $3,737.50

A-ME Oct. 1996   James D. Julia Inc.
**Handel "Birds in Flight" Hanging
Fixture,** w/ orig. bronzed hardware,
Globeshaped shade in "chipped"
glass $1,600.00

A-ME Oct. 1996   James D. Julia Inc.
**Obverse Painted Hanging Globe
Fixture,** w/ entire surface painted to
simulate a cage, metal hdw. .$400.00

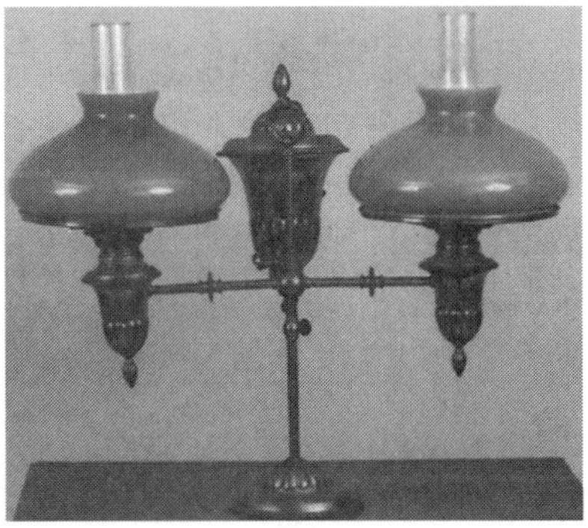

A-IL Apr. 1996 Olivers

Double Student Lamp, copper finish w/camamel cased glass shades, 21¾" H $750.00

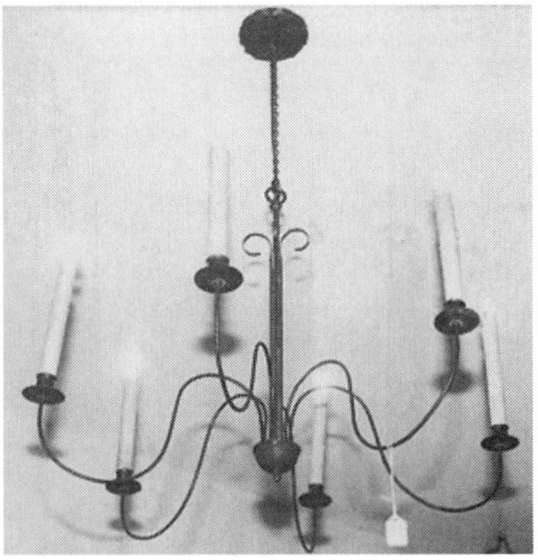

A-KY Oct. 1995 Ken Farmer Auctions

Chandelier, 19th C. style, six stem, electrified, 29" D, 20" H $357.50

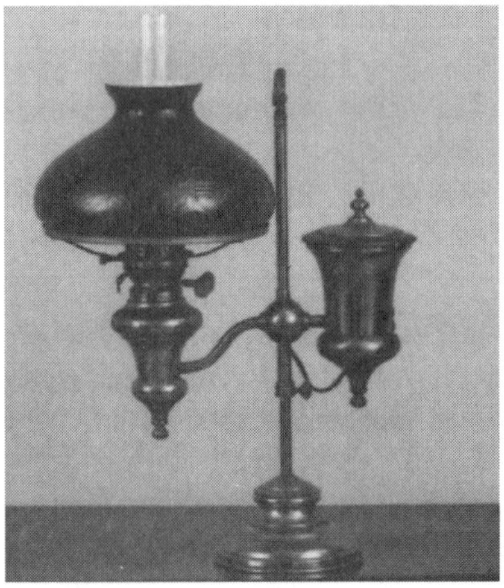

A-IL Apr. 1996 Olivers

Single Student Lamp, brass w/Loetz Iridescent gr. shade, (red when lighted), dents in reservoir, 21¾" H . . .$750.00

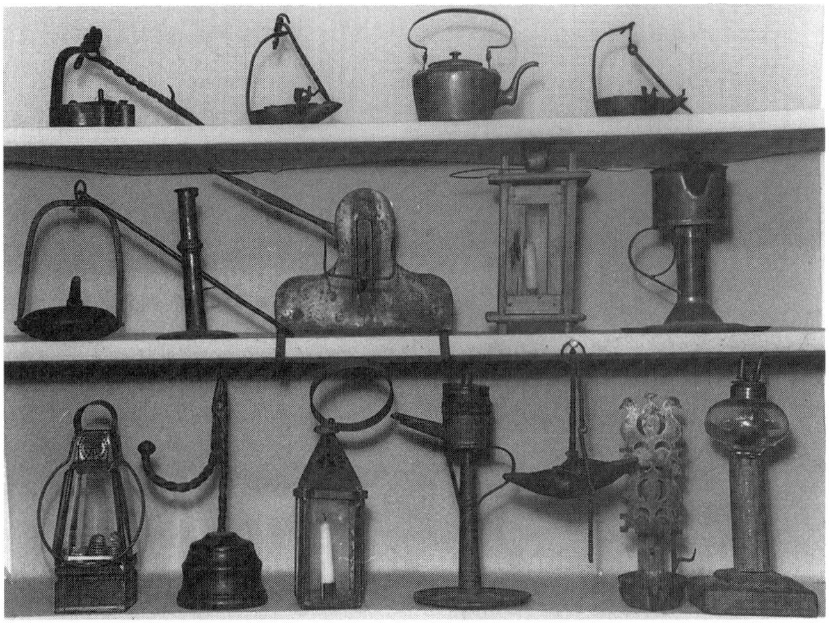

A-OH July 1996 Garth's Auction

Row 1, Left to Right

Wrt. Iron Betty Lamp, w/ heart finial & swivel lid, 4¼" H, plus twisted hanger, pick missing $110.00

Wrt. Iron Betty Lamp, w/ bird finial on lid, 4" H, plus twisted hanger, pick missing $148.00

Miniature Copper Tea Kettle, handmade, 3" H plus swivel handle$412.50

Wrt. Iron Betty Lamp, w/ bird finial on lid, 4" H, plus hanger, pick missing $154.00

Row 2, Left to Right

Wrt. Iron Spout Lamp, w/ bale, 6" H plus hanger $192.50

Hogscraper Candlestick, w/ lip hanger & pushup mkd. "ONE", brass ring is battered, tin foot is an old replm., 6½" H $99.00

Wrt. Iron Fireside Spit, w/ geared lever action, 8" L $302.50

Wooden Barn Lantern, pine & beech w/ natural patina, glass sides & door w/ handmade iron fittings, glued age cracks in top plate, 7½" H . . .$440.00

Tin Double Spout Lamp, w/ lid, copper wick supports, 7¾" H $165.00

Row 3, Left to Right

Tin Lantern, w/ beveled glass sides, brass kerosene burner, sm. corner crack in glass is filled w/ solder, 8¾" H $247.50

Wrt. Iron Splint Holder, w/ twisted detail, turned wooden base, 10⅜" H $302.50

Tin Candle Lantern, w/ punched star air holes, mkd. "Parker's Patent 1853, Proctorsville, Vt", repr. 7½" H, plus ring handle $247.50

Tin Spout Lamp, hinged lid on font has socket for taper, 9½" H . .$165.00

Two Grease Lamps, wrt. iron hanging w/ four spouts, 5¾" H plus hanger & double crusie w/ tooled & cutout bird finials, 9" H $330.00

Make Do Lamp, clear font w/ damaged stem on a wooden base, brass collar & brass burning fluid burner w/ snuffer caps, spouts are damaged & one is loose, 11" H 104.50

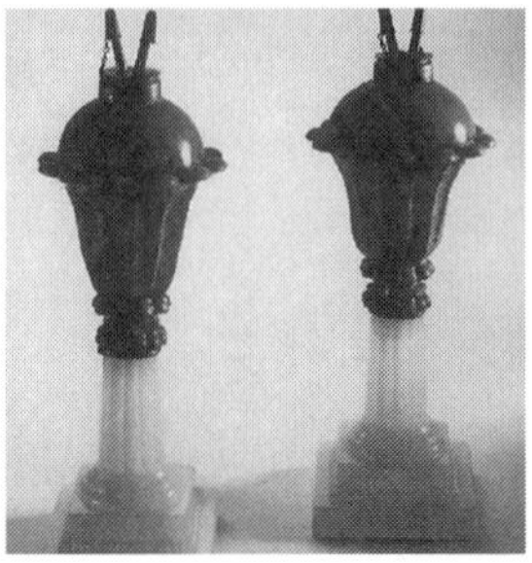

A-MA Aug. 1996 Skinner, Inc.

Sandwich Glass Tulip Lamps, Clambroth & blue pressed glass, 19th C., minor base chips & cracks, 12½" H $1,850.00

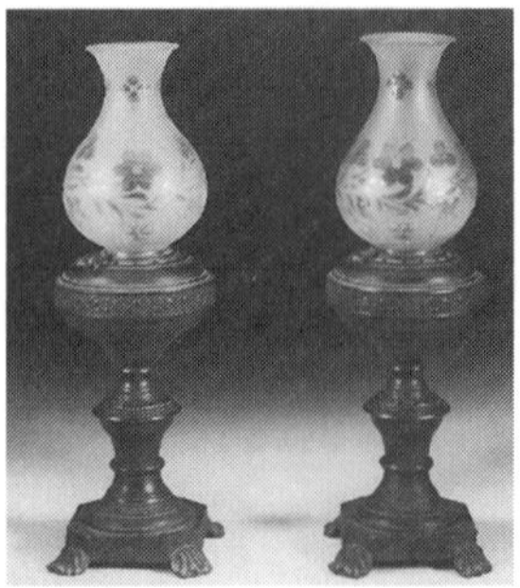

A-MA Aug. 1996 Skinner, Inc.

Patented Metal Oil Lamps, mid 19th C., w/ wheet cut shades, 15⅛" H $1,725.00

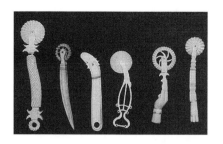

A-NH Aug. 1996   Northeast Auctions

Scrimshaw

Rope-Twist Carved Jagging Wheel
w/ ebony band, 8¾" L $1,900.00

Pie Crimper of tapering fluted form
inlaid w/abalone heart, 7"L . .$500.00

Jagging Wheel w/ fluted wheel, 6"
L $350.00

Jagging Wheel w/ finely shaped &
pierced handle, 6" L $1,000.00

Pie Crimper w/ hand-form handle &
saw-tooth decor. wheel, 6"L $2,300.00

Jagging Wheel inlaid w/ abalone diamond, 6½" L $700.00

A Aug. 1996   Rafael Osona

Whalebone Busk, mid-19th C.,
engraved on both sides including Lady
Liberty w/ anchor & flag, masonic
obelisk depicting naval hero & crossed
Am. flags, compass rose & anthropo-
morphic sun; on reverse side entwined
hearts, foliage, a frigate, barque & a
brig, 15" H $3,300.00

A Aug. 1996   Rafael Osona

Whale Ivory Double Jagging Wheel,
mid-19th C., 6¾" L $3,800.00

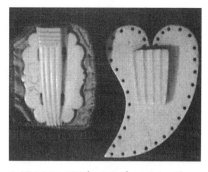

A-NH Aug. 1996   Northeast Auctions

Two Sailor Carved Needle Holders,
mid-19th C., one a carved whalebone
heart, the other noval whale ivory
plaque w/ reeded needle rack, mounted on fabric, 2" & 1½" $350.00

A-NH Aug. 1996   Northeast Auctions

Carved Whale Ivory Sander, mid-
19th C., 24¼" H $400.00

A Aug. 1996   Rafael Osona

Work Box, sailor made w/ ivory inlay,
19th C., w/ ebony dot inlay & fitted lift-
out tray, 4¾" H, 10" W, 6" D $1,300.00

A-NH Aug. 1996   Northeast Auctions

Whalebone Swift, finely carved &
mounted on an inlaid ivory & exotic
wood table grip, 19" H $3,400.00

A-NH Aug. 1996   Northeast Auctions

Whale Ivory Pipe Tamp, mid-19th C,
in form of a woman's leg w/ high button shoe, engraved w/ garter, 2 38"
H $175.00

A-MA Oct. 1995   Skinner, Inc.

Pewter Triple-Belly Coffee Pot, Boardman and Co., Hartford, Conn., 1830 c., marked Jacobs, fig. 39, (minor imperfections), 11½" ht. $862.50

Pewter Three-Quart Flagon, Thomas D. and Sherman Boardman, Hartford, Conn., 1810-30 c., stamped with "BX" quality mark, marked Laughlin fig. 428, (imperfections), 13¾" ht. $747.50

Pewter Deep Dish, samuel Hamlin or Samuel E. Hamlin, Providence, R.I., 1771-1856 c., marked Laughlin, fig. 330,331, (minor pitting, scratches), 13½ dia. . .$488.75

Five-Piece Pewter Communion Set, Leonard, Reed and Barton, Taunton, Mass., 1835-40 c., including ewer, two plates and two chalices, (imperfections), 10" ewer ht. $805.00

Pewter Cann, Thomas D. and Sherman boardman, Hartford, Conn., 1810-30 c., marked Laughlin, fig. 428, (dents, minor pitting and scratches), 4⅝" ht. . .$805.00

Pewter One-Quart Flagon, Boardman and Co., Hartford, Conn., 1825-27 c., marked Laughlin, fig. 431, (minor dents and pitting), 8½" ht. $1955.00

Pewter Porringer, Gershom Jones, Providence, R.I., 1774-1809 c., marked Laughlin, fig. 341, (minor dents and pitting), 4⅜" dia. $1955.00

Pewter One-Quart Flagon, Boardman and Co., Hartford, Conn., 1825-27 c., marked Laughlin, fig. 431, (minor dents and pitting), 8½" ht. $1955.00

Pewter Porringer, Thomas D. and Sherman Boardman, Hartford, Conn., 1810-30 c., marked Laughlin, fig. 428, 5⅜" dia. $690.00

A-OH Nov. 1995   Garth's Auctions

Row 1, Left to Right
Pewter Plate, eagle touch w' "S.D." but w/ smooth oval edge on touch instead of sawtooth, 8" D . . .$110.00
Pair of Pewter Candlesticks, unmarked but attributed to Homan, 7⅜" H $275.00
Pewter Basin, unmarked American, 8" D, 2" H $214.50
Pewter Communion Chalice, 6 7/8" H $27.50
Eng. Pewter Plate, indistinct "London" touch for Robert Bush, Bristol, Eng., minor wear, 7⅞" D $93.50

Row 2
Pewter Plate, eagle touch "Boardman Warranted", J#40, Thomas Danforth Boardman et al, Hartford, minor wear, 8⅝" D $192.50
Pewter Teapot, unmarked American, soldered repairs, 8½" H $38.50
Pewter Tall Pot, lighthouse, "H.B. Ward & Co.", Wallingford, Conn., spout is separating from pot and handle is resoldered, 10⅜" H $71.50
Pewter Teapot, unmarked American, heat damage around bottom edge, 8½" H $71.50
Pewter Plate, eagle touch w/ "G. Lightner, Baltimore", J#205, battered, 8¾" D $220.00

A-PA Dec. 1995 Horst Auction Center
Toleware Coffee Pot, w/hinged lid, black ground w/ red, yellow, gr. decor., 10½" H $950.00

A-PA Dec. 1995 Horst Auction Center
Toleware Coffee Pot w/ hinged lid, stick spout, japanned ground w/yellow, red bl. & gr. decor., 5¾" H $900.00

A-OH Nov. 1995   Garth's Auctions
Pewter Hand Lamp w/ Cast Ear Handle, "M. Hyde" touch, N.Y. City, 3¼" H, plus burning fluid burner w/ snuffers $192.50
Two Similar Eng. Pewter Tumblers W/ Engraved Monogram, faint touch marks, 3⅞" and 4" H . . .$55.00
Pewter Mug W/ Cast Ear Handle, foot is battered, 3⅜" H $16.50
Two Pewter Lamps Both Marked "Capen & Molineux, N.Y.", one is hand lamp w/ cast ear handles, the other conical font, 3⅛" H, 3¼" H, plus burning fluid burners w/ snuffer caps. $302.50

A-OH Jan. 1996 Garth's Auction

Row One, Left to Right,

Cast Iron Betty Lamp, w/ swivel lid on font and brass half circle design w/ engraved "K.F.", 3½" H, plus hanger. $192.50

Two Primitive Betty Lamps, wrought iron, one w/chicken finial has repair. . .$165.00

Two Pieces of Lighting, sm. tin signal lamp w/ bull's eye lens, revolving gr. and red int. lenses, worn blk., 5" H, and tin betty lamp w/ chain and twisted pick, top is loose. $71.50

Ash Tray, brass and wrought steel, w/ cigar cutter and match holder, 8¼" L $137.50

Row Two, Left to Right,

Early Treen Plate, maple w/ old worn patina, 7⅜" x 7½". $440.00

Copper Torch Lamp, wooden handle, filler cup is marked, 4" x 4" x 4¾" plus 10" handle. $27.50

Two Tinder Lighters, in tin boxes, round with steel and rectangular w/ flint and steel, 4" D, 6½" L $203.50

Early Treen Plate, poplar, old worn surface has been varnished, 6¾" x 7". .$330.00

Row Three, Left to Right,

Tin Lard Lamp, on saucer base, 7½" H $154.00

Hogscraper Candlestick, w/ push up and lip hanger, worn tin finish, 5" H $132.00

Punched Tin Foot Warmer, mortised wooden frame w/ traces of old red, tin has some rust, 8" x 9". $143.00

Dovetailed Copper Coffee of Chocolate Pot, side handle w/ heart attachment and hinged lid w/ brass finial, polished, minor dents and lid has some repair, 8" H $165.00

Tin Kettle Lamp, removable font, wick pick on chain, some resoldering, 8½" H $148.50

A-MA June 1996 Skinner, Inc.

Silver Porringer by Paul Revere, Apollos Rivoire, Boston, 1725-54, unusually lg. circular bowl w/ convex sides & slightly raised center, maker's mark REVERE in rectangle stmpd. inside bowl, minor surface imperf., 2" H, 9" L, 6" D 9 troy oz. . . .$10,350.00

A-OH Nov. 1995 Garth's Auctions

Left to Right, Row 1

Tole Tea Caddy, worn orig. gold crystallized paint w/ white and gold edge striping, feet and finial incomplete, int. baffle is loose, 5" H $49.50

Tole Dome Top Deed Box, orig. dk. brn. japanning w/ white band, yellow striping and strawberries in red, grn. and blk, wear, 8" L $330.00

Tole Sugar Bowl, worn orig. dk. brn. japanning w/ floral dec. in red and yel., 3¾" H $275.00

Row 2

Tole Oval Domed Top Box, orig. reddish brn. japanning w/ floral dec. in red, blue, grn. and white, minor wear and soldered repr., 7½" L $165.00

Tole Oval Bread Tray, reticulated sides and open rim handles, orig. red paint w/ floral dec. in yel., white, red and blk, minor wear, 7¼" W, 13¼" L, 3½" H $1,210.00

A-PA Oct. 1995 Pook & Pook, Inc.

Left to right

Candlesticks, Georgian silver w/ shell base, pr. $2,400.00

Capstan Candlestick, Spanish brass, 17th c., 5¼" H $425.25

Candlesticks, Georgian, brass w/ scallop base, ca. 1760, pr., . . .$900.00

Chamberstick, English, brass w/ large flange on candle cup, pierced handle, late 18th c., 4¼" H . . .$300.00

Candlestick, brass, ca. 1780, 8" H, together w/cut corner brass candlestick, 7½" H & a Spanish stick $700.00

Candlesticks, George III, brass, 9¾" H, w/another pr. $500.00

Dutch Tobacco Box, brass w/depiction of a crucifixion, 18th C. . .$475.00

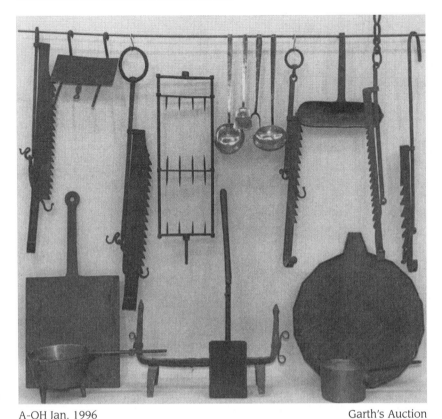

A-OH Jan. 1996   Garth's Auction

Wrought Iron Sawtooth Trammel, simple tooling w/ initials and date "B.S. 1781", adjusts from 36". $165.00

Wrought Iron Kettle Shelf, 10¼" W, 14" L $33.00

Wrought Iron Sawtooth Trammel, found in Missouri, adjusts for 43". .$99.00

Roasting Spit, cast iron w/ wrought spikes, 31" L $165.00

Four Piece Utensil Set, brass and wrought iron, all pieces marked "F.B.S. Canton, O. Pat. Jan. 26, '86" (Frederick B. Smith), polished, width of handles varies slightly, 19" L $385.00

Wrought Iron Sawtooth Tramel, good detail, adjusts from 30". $93.50

Wrought Iron Pan, for soaking rush and splint for lighting devices, edge damage, 14½" W, 14¾" L $385.00

Wrought Iron Sawtooth Trammel, somewhat battered, adjusts from 34", plus hanging chain. $38.50

Wrought Iron Sawtooth Trammel, pitted, 39" L $38.50

Large Heavy Sheet Steel Peel, 16" x 32". $137.50

Cast Brass Cooking Pot, w/ three feet and cast design in handle, minor rim splits, 10¼" D, 12" handle. 192.50

Primitive Wrought Iron Andiron, Ex Roger Bacon, 26½" L $55.00

Wrought and Sheet Iron Coffee Roaster, w/ sliding lid and wooden handle, pan has splits in end, 33½" L $165.00

Cast Iron Griddle, w/ raised rim and spout, some edge damage, found in Adams County, Penn., 22" D $137.50

Dovetailed Copper Sauce Pan, w/ cast iron handle w/ cast label "Wrought Iron Range Co", 7¼" D, 9" handle. $82.50

A-MA Oct. 1995   Skinner, Inc.

Roycroft Hammered Copper Tea & Coffee Service, 6 pc. set, East Aurora, NY, ca. 1909 . . . .$1,610.00

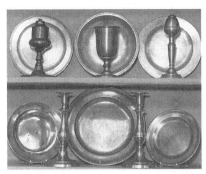

A-OH Nov. 1995   Garth's Auctions

Row 1, Left to Right

Pewter Plate, "Roswell Gleason" touch, J#149, Dorchester, Mass., minor scratches, 9⅜" D $165.00

Pewter Lamp, "Capen & Molineux, N.Y." touch, repl. brass colar, 7⅞" H, plus whale oil burner. $165.00

Eng. Pewter Basin, good clear touch marks for "Townsend & Compton, London", 9⅛" D, 2⅜" H $110.00

Pewter Communion Chalice, "Leonard Reed & Barton", minor dents, 7" H $55.00

Eng. Pewter Plate, "Townsend & Compton, London" touch, wear and scratches, 9¼" D $27.50

Pewter Lamp, unmkd but possibly by J. Warren, Cincinnati, Ohio, 8½" H plus whale oil burner, ...$132.00

Row 2

English Pewter Plate, good clear touch marks for "Richard Yates, Shoreditch, London", some wear and scratches w/ dent at edge of booge, 8½" D $27.50

Pair of Pewter Candlesticks, unmkd. but attrib. to Homan, Cincinnati, Oh, 9¾" H $330.00

German Pewter Charger, double head eagle touch and rim engraved "F.C.C. 1838", wear and scratches, 11½" H $82.50

English Pewter Plate, crowned rose touch w/ "London" for Robert Bush, Bristol, Eng., minor scratches, 7⅞" D $22.00

A-PA Oct. 1995   Pook & Pook, Inc.

Copper Tea Kettle, Am., sgn. W. Heiss, ca. 1820, 6½" H $1,000.00

Cooper Tea Kettle, PA, sgn. B. Harbeson (1765-1823) $3,000.00

Candle Mold, tin w/8-tubes, Bucks Co., PA, sgn. J. Ketterer, 11¼"H $2,200.00

Jan. 1996   Skinner, Inc.

Shaker 57-Long Handled Dipper, hvy. gauge tin, 12¾" H, bowl 4¼" D $345.00

58-Tinware Items, four, cookie cutter; herb tin; pail, w/ wooden handle; biscuit cutter $201.25

33-Tin Carrier, 3" H, 11¼" L, 8" D $345.00

102-Wood Items, six, barrel lid, 28" D, two turned pegs, wooden handle, maple scoop, masher $258.75

87-Small Strainer w/ Handle, formed flared bowl w/ integral punched-screen bottom, 9⅛" H, bowl 4¼" D $46.00

44-Apple Corer & Slicer, riveted const., 4 quarter-round cutting blades, leather guard, 5" H, 4⅝" D $86.25

67-Cream Pitcher, sm. cylindrical vessel, 3¼" H, 2⅞" D $172.50

26-Dust Pan, birch handle, inscribed "Harriet Johns 1880", 13" L, 5" W $3,680.00

53-Cup w/ Lid, domed lid w/ turned wooden know painted blk., 2⅞" H, 4¼ D $258.75

A-OH July 1996   Garth's Auction

Row 1, Left to Right

Pewter Porringer, cast crown handle, split in handle, 4¾" D $137.50

Pewter Porringer, cast old English handle w/ "T.D. & S.B" touch, sm. hole in bowl, 4" D $495.00

Two Pewter Porringers, w/ Lee type handles, 3¼" D & sm. one 2¼" D, both have some battering $88.00

Pewter Ladle, w/ turned wooden handle, engraved initials "H.B." 15" L $165.00

Row 2, Left to Right

Bronze Two Part Mold, for making pewter spoons, 8" L $242.00

Steel Flatware, Twelve pieces w/ antler handles (2 pictured), six forks & six knives mkd. "Marshes & Shepherd, Sheffield" $137.50

Pewter Ladle, w/ curved handle, "T.D. Boardman" touch, 13" L $247.50

Two Pewter Ice Cream Molds, eagle w/ shield 5" & Halloween witch (not shown), 5½" $275.00

Pewter Ice Cream Molds, pr., George & Martha Washington, 5½" H .$247.50

A-OH July 1996   Garth's Auction

Pair of Large Tin Cookie Cutters, man & woman, 11½" $143.00

Large Tin Cookie Cutter, leaping deer, 8" $192.00

Large Tin Cookie Cutter, deer w/ stylized antlers, one section at back of neck is loose, 6½" $159.50

Four Tin Cookie Cutters, heart, bird, figure w/ short arms 5⅜" & elephant 5" L $275.00

Two Tin Cookie Cutters, eagle 4" & lovebirds on heart, 7" $1,292.50

Two Wrt. Iron Trivets, heart shaped, long handle & penny feet, 10"L & scrolled design w/ sm. feet, old break in iron, 6½" $704.00

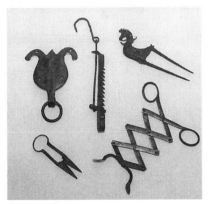

A-PA Nov. 1995   Aston Auctioneers
                     & Appraisers

Conestoga Wagon Toolbox Hasp Plate, tulip-shaped, wrought iron, PA $260.00

Seahorse Cutter, iron $55.00

Toggle Ember Tongs, extension, iron, PA, German $410.00

Weavers Shears, iron $65.00

Trammel, miniature, iron . . . . . .N/S

A-PA Nov. 1995   Aston Auctioneers
                     & Appraisers

Trivet, w/ shoe-on-foot base, wooden handle $925.00

A-PA Nov. 1995   Aston Auctioneers
                     & Appraisers

Roosting Bird Cookie Cutter, tinned sheet-metal $400.00

A-OH APR. 1996   Garth's Auction

Two Tin Cookie Cutters, man w/ hat, 6⅝" H & rabbit, 6" L $198.00

2 Tin Cookie Cutters, stag, 5½" H, & a horse (seam is loose), 4¾" L .$110.00

Three Tin Cookie Cutters, w/ some rust, lrg. leaf 9½" L, chicken 5½" & rooster w/ elaborately crimped detail 6¼" L $396.00

A-OH Mar. 1996   Garth's Auctions

Appliqued Quilt, red, blue & yellow calico, worn & some blues are in tatters, 80" x 92" $715.00

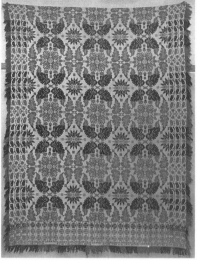

A-OH May 1996   Garth Auctions

Jacquard Coverlet, two piece, single weave, mkd. "Joseph Deavler, Mary Buch, 1841". (Joseph Deavler 1809 - 1886 Lancaster county, Pa.), navy blue, sage gr., red & natural white, 81" x 106" $550.00

A-OH Mar. 1996   Garth's Auctions

Pieced Quilt, monkey wrench in multi-colored calico on a red calico ground w/yellow border stripe, backed w/blue & white homespun, binding is machine sewn, 76" x 82". . . .$286.00

A-OH Mar. 1996   Garth's Auctions

Pieced Quilt, design in green, pink & white calico, backing is blue & white gingham, binding machine sewn, 76" x 90". $269.50

A-OH Mar. 1996   Garth's Auctions

Pieced Quilt, nine patch w/sawtooth border in prints, calicos & solids in shades of red, brown, yellow, green etc., some wear & stains, 70" x 84".$269.50

◄ **Jacquard Coverlet,** two piece, single weave, mkd. "John Rick in Rome, S.C., Ohio, 1854", navy blue, tomato red & natural white, wear & fringe is incomplete, 69" x 82" $412.50

► **Jacquard Coverlet,** two piece, single weave, mkd. "John Hartman, Lafayette, Ohio 1857", navy blue, teal gr., deep red & natural white & olive, very minor stains, 78" x 88" $1,017.50

A-PA Dec. 1995   Alderfer Auction Co.

S.B. Musselman Coverlet, 1842 w/ "Pennsylvan" border, red, blue, green & ivory, 82" x 102" $925.00

A-OH May 1996   Garth Auctions

A-OH May 1996   Garth Auctions

A-PA Apr. 1996   Noel Barrett Antiques & Auctions Ltd.

Row 1
250-Double Decker Bus, lithographed tin, clockwork, excellent, 4¼" .$275.00
251-Chauffeur Driven Saloon Car, lighographed tin, bright colors & detailed embossing, exellent, 4¼" $396.00
252-Closed Sedan, gray w/ black top, lithograhed tin, excellent, 4¼" .$286.00
253-Saloon Car, Yellow w/ black top, lighographed tin, excellent, 4" .$297.00

Row 2
254-Closed Touring Car, brown, lithographed tin, excellent, 4" $253.00
255-Closed Touring Car, pr., lithographed tin, excellent, 3¼" . .$286.00
256-Open Touring Car, two, lighographed tin, excellent . .$302.50
257-Race Car, lighographed tin, excellent, 3" $375.50

Row 3
258-Open Touring Car, tan, lighographed tin, very good (missing driver), 4¼" $77.00
259-Open Touring Car, green, lithographed tin, excellent, 5½" .$412.50
260-Open Touring Car, yellow & black, lithographed tin, very good, 4½" $275.00
261-Open Touring Car, gray, lithographed tin, very good, 4¼" . .$209.00

A-PA Apr. 1996   Noel Barrett Antiques & Auctions Ltd.

Row 1
262-Two Men on Motorcycle, lighographed tin, excellent, 6" $715.00
263-Motorcycle w/ Rider, brightly colored lithographed tin w/ friction mechanism, excellent to near mint, "made in Japan", 3½" $154.00
264-Three Wheeler Motorcycle, lithographed tin, good to very good, 3½" $467.50

Row 2
265-Motorcycle w/ Closed Side Car, highly detailed lithographed tin, very good to excellent, 3½" . .$440.00
266-Triumph Motorcycle, lithographed tin, great color & detail, excellent to near mint, 2¾" $1,155.00
267-Motorcycle #187, lithographed tin, excellent, 2¾" $1,045.50

A-PA Apr. 1996   Noel Barrett Antiques & Auctions Ltd.

Row 1
268-Horse Drawn Postal Van, lithographed tin, excellent, 5½" $247.50
269-Horse Drawn Dray, tan, lithographed tin, nice detail, excellent, 5" $88.00
270-Horse Cart, bright lithography, "made in Italy", near mint, 5" $110.00
Row 2
271-Horse Drawn Dray w/Sidelamps, lithographed tin, excellent, 4½" $187.00

272-Horse Drawn Covered Lorry, lithographed tin, very good to excellent, 5½" $143.00
273-Horse Drawn Cab w/ Driver, lithographed tin, very good to excellent, 4½" $176.00

Row 3
274-Horse Drawn Cab w/ Passengers, highly detail lithography, very good to excellent, 4½" $176.00
275-Girl in Goat Cart, lithographed tin, excellent, 4¼" $165.00
276-Horse Drawn Hansom Cab, lithographed tin, great color, excellent to near mint, 3¾" $203.50
277-Horse Drawn Water Wagon, lithographed tin, very good w/ some surface wear on tank, 4¾" . .$181.50

Row 4
278-Dog Cart, spirit painted tin, very good to excellent w/ wear in cart bed, 5½" $132.00
279-Donkey Cart, lithographed tin donkey, excellent., 4½" $38.50

A-PA Apr. 1996   Noel Barrett Antiques & Auctions Ltd.

Row 1

280-Four Horse Caisson, lithographed tin, very good to excellent w/ some wear on cannon barrel, 7½" $220.00

281-Four Horse Supply Cart, lithographed tin, highly detailed, very good to excellent, 6¾" $275.00

Row 2

282-Horse Drawn Military Boat on Cart, lithographed tin, excellent, 4¾" $192.50

283-Horse Drawn Military Ambulance, lithographed tin, very good to excellent, 4½" $275.00

284-Horse Drawn Flat Bed Wagon, lithographed tin, excellent, 5" $110.00

A-PA Apr. 1996   Noel Barrett Antiques & Auctions Ltd.

Row 1

295-Cow on Platform, lithographed tin, excellent, 3" $220.00
296-Rabbit on Platform, lithographed tin, excellent, 2½" $220.00

297-Goat on Platform, lithographed tin figure on stained tin base, excellent, 3" $308.00

298-Goose on Platform, lithographed tin, excellent, 3½" . .$341.00

Row 2

299-Lion on Platform, lithographed tin, very good to excellent w/ some wear, 3" $99.00

300-Dog on Platform, lithographed tin, brightly colored, excellent to near mint, 2½" $154.00

301-Animated Duck, lithographed tin, very colorful, excellent, 2½" . .$209.00

302-Pecking Geese in Coop, lithographed tin, very good w/ wear on back of coop, 2¼" $104.50

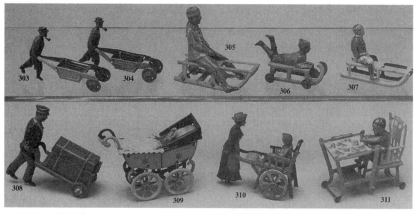

A-PA Apr. 1996   Noel Barrett Antiques & Auctions Ltd.

Row 1

303-Man w/ Wheelbarrow, lithographed tin, excellent, 3" $110.00
304-Man w/ Wheelbarrow, lithographed tin, good to very good, 3" . . .$77.00
305-Boy Seated on Sleigh, lithography, very good to excellent, 3" . .$522.50
306-Boy Lying on Sleigh, lithographed tin, very good to excellent, 2½" .$275.00
307-Boy Seated on Sleigh, nice detail, excellent, 2½" $440.00

Row 2

308-Porter w/ Trunk, great detail, excellent, 3¼" $385.00
309-Baby Carriage, great detail in lighography, excellent, 3½" $385.00
310-Lady w/ Baby Strolling Chair, lithographed tin, excellent, 2¾" $357.00
311-Playtable/Highcair Combination, great detail & intricate design, excellent, 2¾" $247.50

A-PA Apr. 1996 Noel Barrett Antiques & Auctions Ltd.

Left to right

382-Man Swinging Around Pole, painted tin, very good to excellent, replaced flag, 15" $1,650.00

383-Scotchman w/ Bagpipes, painted tin, very good w/ some paint loss, 11" $467.50

384-Man Shooting Rifle, painted tin, excellent to near mint, some damage to box lid edges, no bullets, 9" .$1,870.00

385-Soccer Player, painted tin, very good to excellent w/ some paint loss, some repaint, 8½" $852.50

A-PA Apr. 1996   Noel Barrett Antiques & Auctions Ltd.

Left to right
331-Standing Rooster, Painted tin, wings flap & head rocks, good to very good w/ some paint loss, 9½" tall $275.00

332-Chicken Flapping Wings, Painted tin, wings flap as bird rolls forward, good to very good w/ some paint loss, 6½" $357.00

333-Pigeon, painted tin, good to very good w/ some paint loss, 7¼" $165.00

334-Parrot on Perch, painted tin, nice color, very good to excellent w/ some paint loss, 10" tall $632.50

335-Parrot, painted tin, good to very good w/ some paint loss, 9" $198.00

336-Swan, painted tin, good to very good w/ some paint loss, 6½" $209.00

337-Bird on Branch, painted tin, good to very good w/ some paint loss, 8" $220.00

338-Bird in Trunk, painted tin, excellent w/ some paint loss, 4½" W$385.00

A-PA Apr. 1996 Noel Barrett Antiques & Auctions Ltd.

Row 1
339-Poodle w/ Dog Jumping Rope, painted & lithographed tin, good w/ serious paint loss on poodle, 7" . .$440.00
340-Three Poodles on Round Base, painted tin, very good to excellent w/ some paint loss, 6" tall $632.50
341-Bear w/ Zylophone & Poodle, painted tin, very good w/ some paint loss, 7½" $797.50
Row 2
342-Poodle w/ Revolving Ball, painted tin, very good w/ serious paint loss on dog, 7½" $495.00
343-Bear & Poodle w/ Jump Rope, painted tin, very good to excellent w/ some repaint, 5½" $220.00
344-Elephant w/ Revolving Ball, flocked elephant w/ painted tin hat, lithographed tin ball, very good to excellent, 6½" tall $742.50

A-PA Apr. 1996 Noel Barrett Antiques & Auctions Ltd.

Row 1
404-Large Reindeer, painted tin, excellent, 9" $577.50
405-Standing Bear w/ Rod, painted tin, very good/excellent, 8" . .$308.00
406-Tumbling Bear, painted tin, excellent, repainted, 5" $99.00
407-Bear Twirling Umbrella, painted tin, exc., repaint umbrella, 5" .$330.00
Row 2
408-Fox chasing Goose, painted tin, excellent w/paint loss, 10" . .$412.50
409-Feeding Horse, painted tin, very good/exc., poss. repainted, 8" $412.50
410-Cat w/ Mouse in Cage, painted tin, excellent, 10" $467.50
411-Feeding Donkey, painted tin, good to very good, 6¾" $148.50

A-PA Apr. 1996   Noel Barrett Antiques & Auctions Ltd.

Row 1
345-Clown Pushed by Goat, painted tin, very good to excellent, w/ some paint loss, 7" $852.50

346-Black Clown Pushed by Dog, painted tin, very good, clown repainted, 7" $825.00
347-Bear Riding Irish Mail, painted tin, good w/ some paint loss, 6½" $495.00
348-Boy on Irish Mail, painted tin, good to very good w/ some paint loss, 6¼" $385.00
Row 2
349-Two Boys on Irish Mail, painted tin, good w/ serious paint loss, 6" $495.00
350-Boy in Cart w/ Two Goats, painted tin, good w some paint loss, 6½" $495.00
351-Man in Sulky, painted tin, good to very good w/ some paint loss, 9" $880.00
352-Tricycle Cart w/ Pasenger, painted tin, good w/ some paint loss, 7" $687.50

A-PA Apr. 1996   Noel Barrett Antiques & Auctions Ltd.

Row 1
353-Man w/ Clarinet, painted tin, very good w/ some paint loss, 8" .$742.50

354-Man Doing Splits, painted tin, very good w/some paint loss, 8" $495.00
355-Two Blacksmiths working on Carriage Wheel, painted tin, very good w/ some paint loss, some repaint, 8½" $605.00
356-Chinese Lady w/ Fan, painted tin, fair to good w/ paint loss & erratic mechanism, 7¾" $687.50
357-Chinaman w/ Gong, painted tin, good w/ some paint loss, 7" . .$770.00
Row 2
358-Jumping Man in Tails, painted tin, good w/some paint loss, 6¾" $577.50
359-Lady w/ Parasol & Bustle, painted tin, very good to excellent, w/ some paint loss, 6¾" $907.50
360-Woman Pulling Cart, painted tin, good, w/ some paint loss mostly on figure, 7" $121.00
361-Crawling Soldier, painted tin, very good w/ some paint loss, 10½" $330.00

A-PA Apr. 1996   Noel Barrett Antiques & Auctions Ltd.

Row 1
390-Clown w/ Dog & Monkey, painted tin, good to very good w/ some paint loss on figures & base, 7½" .$1,045.00
391-Clown Trombonist, painted tin, very good to excellent w/ some paint loss, 8½" $990.00
392-Clown Riding Donkey, painted tin, very good, replaced ear on donkey, some paint loss, 6" $550.00
393-Clown w/ Noise Maker & Jumping Jack, painted tin, excellent, figure may be repainted, 8¼" $2,750.00
Row 2
394-Clown on Telephone, painted tin, very good w/ some paint loss, 7" $2,970.00
395-Two Clowns w/ Two Poodles on Ladders, painted tin, good w/ some paint loss, repaint on base, 10½" $742.50
396-Big Clown w/ Little Clown, painted tin, very good to excellent, 10½" $1,870.00
397-Clown w/ Cymbals & Wine Bottles, painted tin, excellent, professionally & beautifully repainted, 12½" .$2,530.00

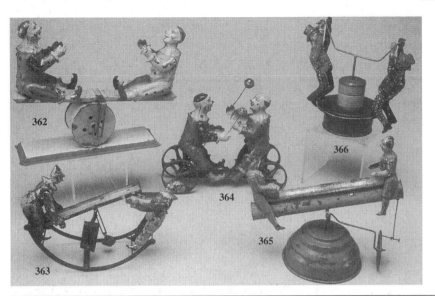

A-PA Apr. 1996 Noel Barrett Antiques & Auctions Ltd.

Left to right

362-Clown Seesaw, painted tin, very good w/ some paint loss, some resoldering, 10" $1,320.00

363-Clowns on Rocking Seesaw w/ rolling Ball, painted tin, good w/ some paint loss, 8" $632.50

364-Two Clowns w/ Bells on Cart, painted tin, very good, repainted, wheels not orig., 7¾" $797.50

365-Clown Seesaw & Ball Roll Roundego, painted tin, good w/ some paint loss, 8½" $687.50

366-Two Men on Roundego, painted tin, good to very good w/ some paint loss, 7½" $687.50

A-PA Apr. 1996 Noel Barrett Antiques & Auctions Ltd.

Row 1

367-Boy Twirling Balls w/ Blond Hair, painted tin, excellent, professionally restored, 8½" $550.00

368-Waltzing Couple, painted tin, excellent, professionally restored, 8" $935.00

369-Jack Sprat & Wife, painted tin, fair to good w/ serious paint loss, 6½" $412.50

370-Boy Twirling Balls w/ Cap, painted tin, excellent, professionally restored, 10" $385.00

Row 2

371-Fat Lady in Blue Dress, painted tin, very good to excellent w/ some paint loss, 6" $412.50

372-Lady Chasing Mouse, painted tin, good w/ serious paint loss, 10" $550.00

373-Lady Feeding Chickens, painted tin, very good to excellent w/ some paint loss, 9" $1,100.00

374-Lady w/ Parasol on Base, painted tin, very good to excellent, some repaint, 6½" $220.00

A-PA Apr. 1996 Noel Barrett Antiques & Auctions Ltd.

Left to right

412-Crawling Beetle, painted tin, excellent to near mint, 7½" $357.50

413-Jumping Frog, cloth & lithographed tin, excellent, 3½" $220.00

414-Crawling Turtle, lithographed tin, excellent, 7½" $467.50

415-Somersaulting Dog, lithographed tin, excellent, 5" $467.50

416-Black Cat w/ Mouse, painted tin, very good to excellent w/ some paint loss, 9¼" $258.50

417-Lobster, painted tin, excellent, 8½" $495.00

A-MA Oct. 1995   Skinner, Inc.

Clockwise

Stump Speaker Mechanical Bank, Shepard Hardware Co., pat. June 8, 1886, painted cast iron, finish very good, crack in base, missing trap door, 9¾" H $1,610.00

Clown on Globe Mechanical Bank, J & E Stevens Co., ca. 1900, painted cast iron, yellow base, finish fair, 9" H $1,610.00

Patty & the Pig Mechanical Bank, J & E Stevens Co., pat. Aug. 8, 1882, painted cast iron, dark blue jacket, Patty's face plate is detached, eyes repr., finish fair to good, 7⅛" H $1,840.00

I Always Did "Spise a Mule" Mechanical Bank, J & E Stevens Co., pat. Jan 6, 1877, painted cast iron, finish poor, 10¼" L, 8⅛" H $517.50

Popeye Knockout Bank, Straits Corp., Detroit, MI, 1930's, lithographed tin, missing trap, very good cond., 4¼" H, 3½" L . . . .$NS

Humpty Dumpty Mechanical Bank, Shepard Hardware Co., pat. June 17, 1884, painted cast iron, fair to good cond., overall paint loss, 7½" H $747.50

Organ Bank Cat & Dog, Kyser & Rex Co., pat. June 13, 1882, painted cast iron, monkey w/ yellow jacket and red pants, finish good cond., 7½" H $805.00

"Tammany" Mechanical Bank, J & E Stevens Co., pat. June 8, 1875, painted cast iron, gray pants, black coat, finish very good, some wear, 5¾" H .$460.00

A-OH   Jan. 1996 Garth's Auction

Row 1

Toy Bed and Similar Doll, N. Eng., wood and bone, minor damage, one leg of doll is loose and bed joints are glued, 6½" L, 5" H $550.00

Four Carved Doll Torsos, painted heads, minor wear and some nose damage, 4"-5½" H $528.00

Apple Pin Cushion, painted silk, some wear, 2¼" H $16.50

Cast Iron Toy Train W/ Engine and Flat Car, "C.P.R.R.," worn black, red and gold, break in engine and one wheel on car is incomplete, $13¾" L $110.00

Row 2

German Toy Show Dog, wood and papier mache w/ paint, white wooly coat, glass eyes, ribbon collar, red top knot and saddle blanket, back legs have damage and touch up paint, muzzle has some damage, 5½" H $137.50

Wooden Alphabet Blocks, twenty-six, worn. $137.50

German Toy Dog W/ Basket, wood and papier mache w/ paint, white wooly coat, glass eyes, ribbon collar, basket loose, body rattles, minor wear. 5⅝" H $330.00

Row 3

Jack-O-Lantern, tin w/ worn orig. oran. paint w/ blk., wooden stem and wire base made to fit a pole, 7" D $742.50

Noah's Ark W/ Two Groups of Animals, ark is pine w/ worn orig polychrome paint, lid hinges are broken, one group worn w/ damage, second group has polychrome paint.14¾" L $330.00

Christmas Tree Fence, cast iron, old green paint, one section damaged, six sections are 11½" L, two sections are 8" L plus gate. $302.50

A-MA Oct. 1995   Skinner, Inc.

Clockwise

Punch & Judy Mechanical Bank, Shepard Hardware Co., pat. July 15, 1884, painted cast iron, very good to exc. cond., 7½" H, 6⅛" W . .$2,530.00

William Tell Mechanical Bank, J & E Stevens Co., pat. June 23, 1896, painted cast iron, very good to exc. cond., 10½" L, 6⅝" H $575.00

Indian & Bear Mechanical Bank, J & E Stevens, Co., ca. 1900, painted cast iron, very good to exc. cond., 10⁵⁄₁₆" L, 7½" H $3,737.50

Dog Tray Bank, Kyser & Red Co., pat. 1880, cast iron, blue building w/ red top and base, gold trim, white dog, good to very good cond., base repr. & chipped, pivot on bottom of dog broken, 4⁵⁄₁₆" L $5,462.50

Bad Accident Mechanical Bank, J & E Stevens, Co., ca. 1900, painted cast iron, exc. cond., minor paint loss & wear $4,600.00

A-MA Oct. 1995   Skinner, Inc.

Santa in Sleigh Pulled by Reindeer, early 20th c., papier mache cloth figure, wicker & wood sleigh, some damage, flannel covered papier mache deer, some damage, glass eyes, clockwork activates nodding head, motor needs adjusting, 36" L $2,300.00

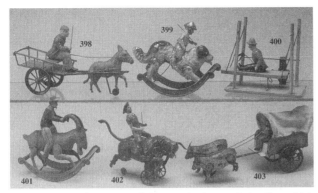

A-PA Apr. 1996   Noel Barrett Antiques & Auctions Ltd.

Row 1

398-Man w/ Donkey Cart, lithographed and painted tin, very good to excellent w/ some paint loss, 10" . . .$330.00
399-Boy Riding Dog on Rockers, painted tin, fair to good w/ some paint loss, 6½" $495.00
400-Man on Swing, painted tin & lithographed tin, good w/ paint loss on figure, 6¼" $247.50
Row 2
401-Man Riding Goat, painted tin, excellent, professionally repainted, 7" $302.50
402-Man Riding Bull, painted tin, very good w/ some paint loss, 8" $357.50
403-Ox Cart, painted tin, very good w/ some paint loss, 10" $165.00

A-MA Oct. 1995   Skinner, Inc.

Left to Right

Candy Container (illus.) & 2 papier mache & cloth Santas
. . . .$258.75
Belsnickle, 6⅜" H, w/ Santa & ornament, damage $258.75
Belsnickles w/ Feather Tree, late 19th c., 11" H . . .$NS
Papier Mache & Cloth Santa, in Cardboard Sled, German
. . . .$86.25
Papier Mache & Cloth Santa, early 20th c., legs loose, 9⅝" H $690.00
Ornament (1 of 4), Santa & three angels $86.25

A-MA Oct. 1995   Skinner, Inc.

Left to Right

Bisque Head Character Baby Doll, Century Doll Co., Kestner head w/molded hair & features, blue glass eyes, cloth body & limbs, composition hands, 11" H . .$258.75
Heubach Bisque Head Toddler, ca. 1920's, sleeping blue eyes, open mouth, light brown mohair wig, bent limb toddler body, restored, 13½" H $258.75
Armand Marseille Bisque Character Head Toddler, sleeping blue glass eyes, open mouth, red mohair wig, fully jointed toddler body, 19" H $460.00
German All Bisque Doll, molded & painted hair & features, impressed Germany mark, jointed at shoulders & hips, molded socks and shoes, 7½" H . . . .$NS
Kestner Painted Black Bisque Head Doll, stationary brown glass eyes, open mouth, fully jointed black painted composition body, damaged & repaired, 12" H . . . ." .$747.50
Bisque Head Character Baby, brown glass sleeping eyes, open mouth, orig. blonde mohair wig, composition toddler body, jointed at shoulders and hips, paint worn, 10½" H $345.00
Revalo Bisque Head Character Doll, molded hair & features, intaglio eyes, open/closed mouth, head by Heubach, fully jointed composition body, some paint damage, 11¼" H $546.25
Bisque No-Snow Boy, Germany, ca. 1910, jointed at shoulders, molded head, winter outfit, 7¾" H $230.00

A-PA Apr. 1996 Noel Barrett Antiques & Auctions Ltd.

386-Lady at Sewing Machine, painted tin, excellent w/ some paint loss, 5" $2,090.00
387-Boys Playing Piggy Back, painted tin, excellent w/ some paint loss, 5¼" $1,650.00
388-Boy on Stilts, painted tin, very good to excellent w/ some paint loss, 9" $1,925.00
389-Lady Ironing Shirt Front & Collar, painted tin, excellent w/ some paint loss, 7¼" $2,145.00

A-PA Apr. 1996   Noel Barrett Antiques & Auctions Ltd.

Clockwise

451-Gun Boat, wht & red lithographed tin, very good to excellent, 11" $577.50

452-Torpedo Boat, painted tin, excellent, 17" $1,265.00

453-Battleship, painted tin, excellent, some prof. repainting, 14" $770.00

454-Leipszig Battleship, painted tin, excellent, 12" $715.00

455-Sidewheeler Boat, painted tin, excellent, missing stack, 8" . . .$1,650.00

456-Four Stack Battleship, lithographed tin, excellent, 6" $660.00

457-Racing Boat, lithographed tin, excellent, 5" $935.00

458-River Launch, lithographed tin, excellent, 7½" $935.00

A-PA Apr. 1996 Noel Barrett Antiques
& Auctions Ltd.

Row 1

459-Squirrel Cage, painted tin, very good to excellent, 9" wide . .$385.00

460-Man on Trike, painted tin & lead, excellent to near mint, 4" $550.00

461-Lady Pushing Cart, painted tin, very good to excellent w/ some paint loss, 6½" $715.00

Row 2

462-Hansom Cab, painted tin, good, 9" $302.50

463-Black Man Pushing Fruit Cart, painted & lithographed tin, good to very good w/ some paint loss, 8" .$962.50

A-PA Apr. 1996 Noel Barrett Antiques
& Auctions Ltd.

Early Bi-Wing Airplane, lithographed tin, excellent $2,860.00

◄**471-Boy on Scooter,** painted tin, very good to excellent, 9" .$1,375.00

472-Pigeon, painted tin, very good, 8" $121.00

Row 2

473-Side Dumping Truck, painted embossed tin, very good to excellent, some scratched, 7¾" $440.00

474-Tractor, painted embossed tin, good to very good, 6" $137.50

475-Tractor w/ Covered Trailer, very good to excellent, some surface wear, 14" $357.50

Row 3

476-Chinaman Pulling Rickshaw, painted composition & tin, orig. box, near mint, 6½" $385.00

477-Woman Pushing Fruit Cart, painted composition & tin, orig. box, near mint, 6" $330.00

A-PA Apr. 1996   Noel Barrett Antiques & Auctions Ltd.

Row 1

470-Lady Pushing Baby Carriage, painted tin, wire, & lead, excellent, baby not orig., mainspring broken, 7" tall $1,045.00

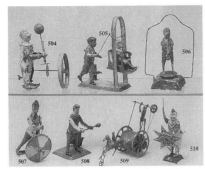

A-PA Apr. 1996 Noel Barrett Antiques & Auctions Ltd.

Row 1

504-Clown w/ Hoop & Wooden Ball, painted tin, good, weak paint, 5½" $275.00

505-Two Boys w/ Swing, painted tin, good w/ some paint loss & repaint on base, 6¾" $550.00

506-Twirling Boy, painted tin, poor to fair, 7" $275.00

Row 2

507-Clown w/ Twirling Parasol, painted tin, very good w/ some paint loss, 5½" $467.50

508-Strong Man, painted tin, excellent, repainted, 5" $467.50

509-Acrobat Cart, painted tin, good w/ some paint loss, 6" $275.00

510-Small Clown w/ Twirler, painted tin, good w/paint loss, 5" $522.50

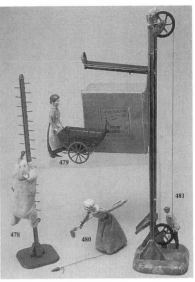

A-PA Apr. 1996 Noel Barrett Antiques & Auctions Ltd.

Left to right

478-Bear Climbing Pole, painted tin w/ cloth covered bear, excellent, 14" $1,870.00

479-Woman Pushing Cart, painted tin, wire & lead, excellent to near mint, 7" $1,045.00

480-Lady Chasing Mouse, painted tin, wire & lead, exc., 8" . .$2,200.00

481-Gravity Marble Toy, painted tin & lead, very good to exc., 26" $687.50

A-PA Apr. 1996   Noel Barrett Antiques & Auctions Ltd.

Left to right

525-Two Skiers, celluloid & tin, excellent to near mint, 6½" $385.00

526-Cowboy & Indian, "Horse Racing", celluloid & tin, orig. box, excellent, 4"
. . . .$275.00

527-Cowboy Chasing Cow, "Western Hero", celluloid & tin, orig. box, excellent, 6½"
. . . .$275.00

528-Clown Standing on Hands, celluloid & tin, very good to excellent, 8½"
. . . .$121.00

529-Monkey Guitarist, celluloid & tin, excellent, 7½" $187.00

530-Clown on Donkey, celluloid & tin, very good to excellent, 8" . . .$209.00

531-Covered Wagon, celluloid & tin, excellent, 8½" $104.50

532-Pig w/ Horn & Chicks, celluloid & tin, excellent, 9½" $38.50

533-Man & Woman Pulled by Donkey, celluloid & tin, excellent to near mint, mechanism overwound, 8¼" $99.00

534-Two Horseback Riders, celluloid & tin, excellent, 6" $104.50

535-Walking Drummer Boy, lithographed tin figure w/ celluloid head, excellent, 8¾" $220.00

A-OH July 1996   Garth's Auction

The following 5 items are a five-piece "Golden Age of the Circus" train w/ animals by "Steiff".

Row 1

Calliope Wagon, w/ battery powered music box & pulled by elephant w/ bear driver in clown costume, 21" L, overall $907.50

Wagon, w/ two bears & flag "Steiff Circus", 9" L plus tongue $220.00

Row 2

Wagon w/ Tiger, 9" L plus tongue . .
. . . .$363.00

Wagon w/ Giraffe, 9" L plus tongue
. . . .$165.00

Wagon w/ Lion, 9" L plus tongue . .
. . . .$341.00

Row 1

Tin Lamp Posts, 4 (2 pic.), by Fallows, American Tin Company (unmarked), worn japanning, some damage, 7¾" H $44.00

Cast Iron Mechanical Bank, "Speaking Dog", Norman 5170A, orig. polychrome paint has wear but is colorful, some touch up paint on face & hands, key lock top has edge damage & is not an exact match, 7⅛" L $687.50

Miniature Tole in Original Paint w/ Stenciled Presentation Labels such as "MyGirl", "My Boy", "A Present", "Little Pet", etc., 7 pcs., five cups and two pails w/ lids, three are red and four are green, very worn, 1½" to 2⅛" H $198.00

Toy Train, w/ Live Steam Engine in Tin & Brass & Two Tin Passenger Cars, "G.C. & Co." (Carette), some wear & damage, 18" L overall. $192.50

Row 2

Tin Horse Toys, 2, one w/ buggy, the other w/ open cart, very worn orig. poly-chrome paint & some repair, attributed to George Brown, 6½" & 7¾" L .$242.00

Building Shaped Banks, two, tin, Cupalo in green, red & black, 4½" H & peaked roof in red & silver, 4¼" H, both are worn. $77.00

Building Shaped Banks, 4, tin, worn red w/blue & bold, 3½" to 4¼" H $198.00

Row 3

Toy Train, w/ Cast Iron Electric Engine Marked "Bing" & Tin Tender, Two Passen-ger Cars Marked "Pennsylvania Lines" & one "Baggage/Mail" Car All Marked "W.B. Germany", worn original black, red, brown & yellow paint, 31½" L overall. $220.00

Row 4

Train Set Buildings, 2, tin, garage like shed w/ track initialed on interior, embossed detail & worn polychrome, marked "G.B.N. Bavaria" (pictured), 10" L & one in a curved design w/ four tracks & worn orig. polychrome, one set of doors missing & track mostly missing, attrib. to Marklin, 24" L $82.50

Toy Train, w/ Cast Iron Electric Engine & Three Tin Passenger Cars, worn orig. black, green, brown, yellow, white & red, all marked "New York Central" by Bing, cars marked "W.B. Germany", 28" L overall. $247.50

Bell Toys, 2, cast iron & bell metal, smallest has heart wheels, 3½" & 5" D$143.00

Toonerville Trolley "Crackerjack" Toy, amazing detail, great lithography, near exact miniature of the classic tin toy, near mint, 1¾" $632.50

Row 1

Buddy "L" Hydraulic Dump Truck, ca. 1935, pressed steel, black cab, red dump body, seat missing good cond., 25" L $546.25

Row 2

Kingsbury Zypher Coupe & Boat Trailer, ca. 1936, pressed steel, wind-up, orange w/ rubber wheels, no boat, exc. cond., 20½" L $345.00

Toy Trucks, 2, Tonka, stake truck, ca. 1955, org. box, mint cond., 16" L, Marx mobile guided missile unit truck, org. box, exc. cond., box missing two flaps, 13" L $546.25

Wyandotte Streamline Coupe & Trailer, 1930's, painted pressed steel, orange, wooden wheels, exc. cond., 11½" L $287.50

Row 3

Keystone Locomotive, Sit & Ride, ca. 1930's, pressed steel, electric head-light, black & red, fair to good cond., surface rust, 26" L $345.00

A-OH Mar. 1996   Garth's Auctions

Row 1
"World Educator" Game, Wooden Box w/ Colorful Chromolitho on Paper, "W.S. Reed Toy Co. Leominster, Mass.", ext. worn & end of box missing, 15¾"L $55.00
"Fire Engine Picture Puzzle", wood & cardboard box w/ colorful chromolitho on paper, "McLoughlin 1887", two pieces are missing, minor wear, 12¼" L . . .$137.50
"Locomotive Picture Puzzle", cardboard box w/ colorful chromolitho on paper, "Parker Brothers 1894", 9½" L $137.50

Row 2
Three Piece Wooden Train, Colorful Chromolitho Decoration, mkd. "R. Bliss Mfg. Co." Engine "U.S. Grant", tender "Golden Gate Special" & passenger car "American Palace Car" (w/ wooden blocks), wear & edge damage, 36" L $1,210.00

Toy Piano, Shaped Like A Church w/ Steeple At One End & Keyboard at the Other, wood w/ chromolitho paper covering, wear, plays, 12¾" L $220.00

Row 3
Wooden Blocks, set of 8 that Stack to Form an Obelisk but Also Nest Together for Storage, colorful chromolitho paper covering is worn & varnished, 33¾" H $550.00

Toy Battleship Gunboat, wood & cardboard box w/ chromolitho paper covering seven sailors, disassembles, damage & wear w/ some missing pieces, 36L $550.00

"Locomotive Picture Puzzle", wood & cardboard box w/ colorful chromolitho on paper, "McLoughlin Bros. 1901", minor wear, 18¼" L . .$313.00

Toy Cargo Ship, wood w/ chromolitho on paper covering, "Ocean Wave" (Pat 1877, 1882) w/ five bales (blocks) & one seaman, wear & some wooden parts have been restored, 28½" L $1,210.00

"The New Pretty Village" Folding Cardboard Building & Wood & Cardboard Box, All w/ Colorful Chromolitho Paper Covering, "McLoughlin Bros. 1897, wear damage, 20½" L $82.50

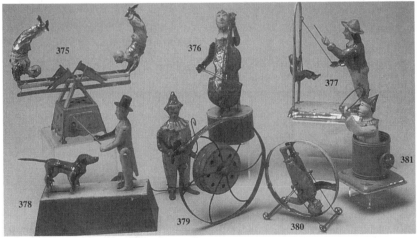

A-PA Apr. 1996   Noel Barrett Antiques & Auctions Ltd.

Row 1
373-Two Clowns on Ladder, painted tin, good to very good w/ some paint loss, 8½" $1,760.00
376-Clown Playing Base Fiddle, painted tin, good w/ serious paint loss, 8" $467.50
377-Monkey on Swing w/ Clown, painted tin, very good, arm resoldered, 7½" $495.00

Row 2
378-Man w/ Performing Dog, painted tin, good to very good w/ some paint loss, 7" $440.00
379-Clown w/ Large Hoop, painted tin, good w/ some paint loss, 6" $220.00

380-Clown in Hoop, painted tin, very good w/ some paint loss, 5" $632.50
381-Clown w/ Hoop in Barrel, painted tin, steam accessory, exc., 6" $467.50

A-PA Apr. 1996 Noel Barrett Antiques & Auctions Ltd.

Left to right
559-Clown w/ Monkey, celluloid & tin, near mint, 7½" $220.00
560-Clown w/ Elephant on Wheels, celluloid & tin, excellent, 12½" $330.00
561-Bareback Rider & Clown, celluloid, excellent, 10" $632.50
562-Musicians w/ Revolving Canopies, pr., excellent, 7½" $220.00
563-Kittens at Play Roundego, "Jolly Cat", celluloid, excellent to near mint, 9" $330.00

A-PA Apr. 1996   Noel Barrett Antiques & Auctions Ltd.

418-Cat Pushing Mouse Cage, painted tin, good w/ some paint loss, 8½" $1,045.00
419-Rabit Violinist, lithographed tin, good, surface stained, 10" $907.50
420-Mother w/ Baby Pig, painted tin, excellent w/ some professional restoration on surface & mechanical, 6" $990.00
421-Dog Violinist, painted tin, good to very good w/paint loss, 6½" .$605.00
422-Dog Drummer w/ Cymbals, painted tin, excellent, professionally repainted, 6½" $660.00
423-Frog w/ Parasol, painted tin, good to very good w/ some paint loss, 8½" $1,265.00
424-Drummer Cat, painted & lithographed tin, good to very good w/ some paint loss, 6" $522.50
425-Frog w/ Cane, painted tin, good w/ paint loss, 6¼" $742.50
426-Walking Cat w/ Glasses, painted tin, very good w/paint loss, 6" $357.50

A-PA Apr. 1996 Noel Barrett Antiques & Auctions Ltd.

427-Donkey Playing Mandolin, painted tin, good to very good w/ some paint loss, 8¾" $687.50
428-Standing Bird w/ Cane & Fly, painted tin, very good w/ some paint loss, 7½" $1,650.00

A-PA Apr. 1996 Noel Barrett Antiques & Auctions Ltd.

Car w/ Bull, painted & lithographed tin, very good to excellent, minor paint loss, 11" $3,630.00

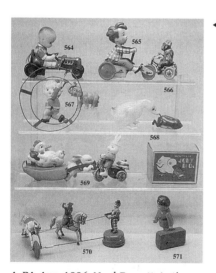

A-PA Apr. 1996 Noel Barrett Antiques & Auctions Ltd.

Row 1
564-Boy Driving Race Car, lithographed tin, excellent, 6" $71.50

◀**565-Boy on 3 Wheel Irish Mail,** lithographed tin, excellent to near mint, 6" $220.00
566-Monkey Tricycle, lithographed tin, exc.. to near mint, 3½" . .$165.00

Row 2
567-Girl in Hoop & elephant, celluloid, very good to exc., 6" .$132.00
568-Duck & Frog, celluloid & lithographed tin, near mint, 7¾" . .$88.00

Row 3
569-Easter Toys, celluloid & tin, excellent, "Made in Japan", the larger is 7" $121.00

Row 4
570-Toys w/ Horses, lithographed tin horse w/ composition cowboy, very good to excellent, 3½", composition and tin clown w/ performing horse, excellent $187.00
571-Boy w/ Suitcase, celluloid & tin, 4½" $132.00

A-PA Apr. 1996 Noel Barrett Antiques & Auctions Ltd.

Paya Touring Car, box stained, ...$55.00
Paya 3 Wheel Auto, 5" $44.00
Paya Seaplane, box stained, 12" wingspan $176.00
Paya Race Car, 14" $99.00
Paya Fire Trucks, pr., 3¼" . .$66.00

A-NH Aug. 1996   Northeast Auctions

Hepplewhite Inlaid Mahogany Knife Boxes w/ serpentine-front, shell inlay & fitted interior, 14" H $4,750.00

A-MA Aug. 1996   Skinner, Inc.

Slat-Back Armchair, NH, old bl. paint w/ gold highlights, 45½" H .$3,105.00

A-NH Aug. 1996   Northeast Auctions

Weathervane, Am. copper full-bodied horse & sulky by Fisk, in mustard paint, 38" L $8,000.00

Blanket Chest, N. Eng., w/ flame graining on an ochre ground, bootjack ends, 43" L $1,600.00

A-MA Aug. 1996   Skinner, Inc.

Roundabout Chair, N. Eng., 18th C., w/ dark gr. paint, old rush seat, minor repairs, 30¾" H $1,725.00

A-MA Aug. 1996   Skinner, Inc.

Federal Corner Cupboard, w/ orig. red wash, early 19th C., minor imperf., 90" H, 43" W, 20" D $7,475.00

A-MA Aug. 1996   Skinner, Inc.

Pine Paneled Cupboard, N. Eng., painted, 19th C., old blk. paint, 77¼" H, 47" W $1,840.00

A-MA Aug. 1996   Skinner, Inc.

Paneled Pewter Dresser, pine, painted, N. Eng. or Canada, 18th C., surface imperf., 7½"H, 71½"W, 16"D .$5,462.50

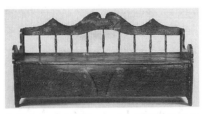

A-MA Aug. 1996   Skinner, Inc.

Decorated Settle/Bed, grain painted, Scandinavia, ca. 1830, paint wear, 36½" W, 70¾" D, 67" W $1,092.50

A-MA Aug. 1996   Skinner, Inc.

Pine Chest, N. Eng., 2nd half 18th C., old refinish, lacks pulls, 44" H, 37½" W $517.50

A-MA Mar. 1996   Skinner, Inc.

Rosewood Grained Banjo Clock, Howard & David, Boston, ca. 1840-59, eight-day weight driven movement, very minor imperf., 31¾" H .$1,955.00

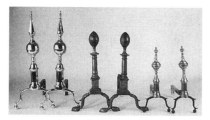

A-MA Mar. 1996   Skinner, Inc.

Brass Steeple Topped Andirons, pair, Am. early 19th C., polished, 24½" H $977.50
Brass Lemon Top Andirons, pr., Am. late 18th / early 19th C., missing one logstop, other damage, 19"H .$632.50
Brass Urn Andirons, pair, Am. 19th C., w/ matching shovel & tongs, alterations, 16" H $431.25

A-MA June 1996   Skinner, Inc.

Chippendale Slant Lid Desk, maple & tiger maple, late 18th C., ref. repl. brasses, imperf. $4,887.50

A-PA Nov. 1995   Aston Auctioneers & Appraisers

Mennonite Quilt, ...$250.00

A-MA Mar. 1996   Skinner, Inc.

Gilt Copper Weather Vane, Am., late 19th C., imperf., 38"H, 44"L .$4,025.00

A-MA Mar. 1996   Skinner, Inc.

Chippendale Cherry Tall Case Clock, Nathan Howell, New Haven CT., ca. 1741-84, old ref., minor imperf., 81½" H $6,325.00

A-MA Mar. 1996   Skinner, Inc.

Mahogany Banjo Clock, J.L. Dunning, Burlington, VT., ca. 1820, eight-day weight driven movement, imperf., 30¾" H $2,300.00

A-MA Aug.   Robert C. Eldred Co., Inc.

Hepplewhite Fall-Front Desk, NY, early 19th C., mahogany w/ mahogany veneers, banded inlays, some rest. $2,750.00

A-MA Aug. 1996   Skinner, Inc.

Federal Lady's Desk, N. Eng., mahogany & mahogany veneer, ca. 1800, replaced brasses, old refinish, 47" W, 42" W, 22" D $1,150.00

A-OH July 1996   Garth's Auction

Drafting Table, cast iron frame w/ tripod feet, pedestal w/ adjustable arm that has an oak shelf w/ cubby hole, drawing board is also oak & has adjustments for height & tilt, board is 21" x 26" $990.00

Blown Glass Bell, opaque white w/ red looping & applied red rim, mercury glass handle has been reattached, no clapper, 10" H $275.00

Needlework Panel, silk on linen homespun, four story house w/ trees, surrounded by flowering vines w/ birds, signed "Eufemea Moore, August 28th, 1816", colors are teal, pale gr., shades of gold, br., yellow white & red, some stains & fading but good overall condition, 21½" H, 18" W . .$3,685.00

A-OH May 1996   Garth's Auction

Stoneware

Row 1, Left to Right

Canning Jar, w/ cobalt blue stenciled cherries & leaf, minor flakes, 8" H $852.50

Canning Jar, w/ cobalt blue stenciled mkd. "S. & L. Vicker's, rim chips, 6⅜" H $550.00

Flask, cobalt blue brushed leaf & stripes, faint hairline in base, 9⅛" H $990.00

Conical Canning Jar, w/ tan glaze on grey clay w/ br. stenciled mkd. "John Hunts Premium Cider Apple Butter", shallow lip flakes, 6" H $605.00

Canning Jar, w/ cobalt blue brushed name w/ polka dots, "James Dunn", chips & surface flakes, 7¼" H $550.00

Row 2, Left to Right

Pitcher, cobalt blue brushed floral decor., sm. chips & hairlines in bottom, 8¾" H $605.00

Canning Jar, w/ cobalt blue stenciled pear w/ leaves, 6⅝" H $687.50

Bottle, w/ cobalt blue brushed flower, 7⅜" H $247.50

Pitcher, w/ cobalt blue brushed floral designs, glazed over chip on handle, 7" H $660.00

Canning Jar, w/ cobalt blue brushed flowers & stripes, 8¼" H . . .$1,650.00

A-OH July 1996   Garth's Auction

Pewter Cupboard, one piece, open, walnut w/ old worn finish, w/ one board ends, renailing & reprs., age cracks & edge damage, 46" W, 16½" D, 79¼" H $2,200.00

Copper Skillets, four similar, w/ cast iron handles, 1 lid, 8" to 10" D $319.00

Copper Sauce Pans, five similar, w/ cast iron handles, four are dovetailed & all have lids, one pot & one lid are by "Temple & Crook, Metcomb ST. S.W.", 4" to 7½" D $550.00

Copper Sauce Pans, five similar w/ cast iron handles, four are dovetailed all have lids, three pots & three lids are signed either by "Lewis & Conger, New York" or "Temple & Crook", one lid is oversize, 5" to 7½" D $412.50

Copper Sauce Pans, graduated set of seven similar w/ cast iron handles, all have lids, but several are mismatched, one lid has "Paris" label, 4" to 9" D $440.00

A-OH July 1996   Garth's Auction

Watercolor on Paper, landscape w/ town, river, cows, etc, signed "Malton 1823", w/ rosewood veneer frame, 19⅜" H, 23⅜" W $1,045.00

Watercolor Theorem on Paper, cucumber, raddish & blossoms, mkd. "Marion L. Fowler", light stains & old gilt frame, 9" H, 11" W $467.50

Country Sheraton Stand, curly maple w/ old mellow ref., one dovetailed drawer & two board top, poplar secondary wood, top has age crack & sm. corner split, 18" x 23½", 30" H .$660.00

Bowback Windsor Armchair, Old worn ref., w/ knuckle arms, 37¼" H $3,300.00

Lighting Device, wrt. iron candle arm w/ two sockets on adjustable threaded rod, wooden base, 17½" H $770.00

A-OH May 1996   Garth's Auction

Crock, mkd. "W.T. Moore, Middleburg, Summit Co. Ohio", cobalt blue brushed flower & "3", 11¼" H $330.00

A-MA Mar. 1996   Skinner, Inc.

Regency Terrestrial & Celestial Library Globes, pr., Cary's of London, ca. 1805, the first corr. to 1805, the second to 1799, mahogany tripod base w/ spade feet, lacking compasses, overall 43" H, 19" D $24,150.00

A-OH Mar 1996   Garth's Auction

Early Mirror, mahogany on pine, 14½" H, 9½" W $60.50

Two Cut Black Paper Silhouettes: Gentleman initialed "R.B" and lady signed in ink "Harriot Camm", not a pr. but in matching ebonized frames w/ gilded liners, 7½" H, 6½" W . .$440.00

Black Duck, balsa w/ wooden head, orig. paint & glass eyes, 14½"L $121.00

Shorebird w/ orig. paint & replaced beak, 10½" H $302.50

Paint Grained Case w/ Seven Dovetailed Drawers, poplar w/ orig. curly maple graining, case dovetailed, 8½" x 21", 4¾" D $412.50

A-OH April 1996   Early Auction Co.

Imperial Synphonion Music Box, double cone, mahogany case w/ pressed trim, sits on mahogany cabinet w/ shelf, approx. 29-15½" discs. $3,750.00

A-OH Mar 1996   Garth's Auction

Three Primitive Wooden Kraut Cutters, two walnut, one poplar all w/ old worn patina, largest has branded label "J. Schisghka", 24½" to 29" L .$115.50

Country Table w/ maple base & pine bread board top, dovetailed drawer, filled age cracks in top, 27" x 46½", 27¼" H $522.50

Two Cast Iron Eagle Snow Birds, 6½" $55.00

Dome Top Hide Covered Trunk w/ tin corners, leather trim and brass tacks, mkd. "London", damage, 14" L $121.00

Primitive Sausage Grinder, hard & soft wood w/ old patina, wrought iron hooks hold case, 22" H $11.00

All Wooden Lodge Axe, "Blue grass" on blade, from Woodmen's Society, Bloomington, Indiana, 47½" L .$82.50

A-IL Nov. 1995   James D. Julia, Inc.

Symphony Coin-Operated Piano, early 20th c., made by the Marquette Piano Co., Chicago, 61" H, 30" W, 59" L. $7000.00

A-IL Nov. 1995   James D. Julia, Inc.

Cremona Coin-Operated Piano, early 20th c., made by the Marquette Piano Co., Chicago, 64" H, 29" W, 60" L. $3750.00

A-OH May 1996   Garth's Auction

Lithograph, by "Kellogg & Comstock", handcolored, "Son of Temperance", good color, stains, beveled frame in old red, 17" H, 13" W .$82.50

Chalk Horse Head Plaque, w/ orig. red & blk. paint, wear, chips & old repr., 9" H $236.50

Empire Chest of Drawers, refin. cherry & curly maple w/ shiny varnish finish, dovetailed drawers, feet have edge chips, 42" W, top is 21¾" x 42¾", 47¼" H $687.50

Ovoid Stoneware Jar, w/ cobalt blue striping & stenciled "Wm. Hallage & Co. Groceries and Tea Dealers No. 18 Deamon, Pittsburgh, Pa.", 8¾" H . .$330.00

Ovoid Stoneware Jar, cobalt blue brushed decor., rim chips & hairlines, 9¼" H $192.50

Ovoid Stoneware Jar, Impressed mkd. "Cowden & Wilcox, Harrisburg, Pa." & brushed cobalt blue tulip, rim chips, 9½" H $214.50

Ovoid Stoneware Jar, cobalt blue stripes & stenciled mkd. "Jas Hamilton Co. Greensboro, Pa 2", 10" H .$165.00

Ovoid Stoneware Churn, w/ cobalt blue quill work, flower & "8", edge chips, 19" H $385.00

Ovoid Stoneware Churn, w/ cobalt blue stenciled # "6" in wreath, rim chips, 18" H $258.50

A-OH May 1996   Garth's Auction

Ovoid Jar, mkd. "S. Hart, Fulton", cobalt blue brushed tulip, foliage & "3", rim chips & hairlines, 12½" H $330.00

A-OH May 1996   Garth's Auction

Welsh Cupboard, pine w/ dk. br. finish, two piece constr., handmade repro., 60" W, 16¾" D, 83" W .$715.00
Note: the redware is contemporary by PA Dutch folk potter Lester Breininger, Robesonia PA.. His pieces are marked with date. Sgraffito pieces have yellow slip w/ gr. splotches.

Charger, Sgraffito bird, "1986", 12½" D

Pie Plate, Sgraffito Washington on horse back, "1993". 10½" D . . .$88.00

Five Stoneware Mugs, w/ various blue slip decor., 4" to 5" H $60.50

Pie Plate, Sgraffito tulips, "1985", 10½" D $88.00

Three Sm. Plates, Sgraffito, "1981" and "1985" (two), 5¾" to 7" D .$66.00

Fifteen Pieces, Thirteen by Breininger, two are mini. stoneware marked "CNC" $247.50

Charger, Sgraffito couple, "1977", 16" D $192.50

A-OH Jan. 1996   Garth's Auction

A-OH May 1996   Garth's Auction

Regulator Wall Clock, walnut case w/ ebonized trim & gilded detail on moldings of face & door, "Ansonia Clock Co." w/ pendulum & key, 31" H $495.00

Arts & Crafts Era Desk, oak w/ old finish, 18" x 38", 30½" H $220.00

Victorian Shelf Clock, walnut case w/ old finish, brass works w/ separate alarm movement, "The E. Ingraham & Co." orig. reverse painted glass, w/ pendulum & key, 21½" H $192.50

Soapstone Carving, oriental woman, filled age crack & repr., 11½" H$82.50

Table Lamp, cast metal base & shade frame w/ caramel & white slag glass panels, 21½" H $330.00

Doll, china head, blue paperweight eyes & open mouth w/ teeth, white kid body w/ china hands, brown wig, mkd. "1235 Germany PH DEP", made by "Alt, Beck & Gottschalck", hands have some damage, 22" H $220.00

Doll, china head, blue paperweight eyes & open mouth w/ teeth, white kid body & china hands, blond wig, head mkd. "Made in Germany 1123½ P10", made by "Alt, Beck & Gottschalck", 21" H $330.00

Meissen Dish, blue & white w/ reticulated rim, crossed swords mark, 11⅝" L $104.50

Tin Candle Sconce, removable candle arm w/ crimped pan, center reflector loose, 12" H $660.00

Architectural 2 Part Mirror, mahogany w/ reeded pilasters, Eglomise glass scene w/ ruins, trees and ship is worn and flaked, applied leaf ornament minor damage, 27¼" H, 14" W $220.00

Bowback Windsor Armchair, old mellow ref., repr. break in one arm, breaks in bow & back of arm rail, 34½" H $110.00

Country Hepplewhite Stand, birch w/ old worn finish, age crack in top, replm. brass pull, 14¾" x 15⅛", 26" H $275.00

Mercury Glass Wig Stand, made in 2 pcs., ball has been reattached, 10¼" H $330.00

A-OH June 1996   Garth's Auction

Country Pie Safe, yellow pine w/ old worn blue paint over gr., mortised const. w/ edge beading, 12 punched tin panels all w/ compass star & circle designs, several end panels have rust damage, frame is loose & one back foot ended out, 19" x 39", 54¾" H .$660.00

Blue & White Sponge Spatter Pitcher, sm. rim flake, 9" H .$330.00

Blue & White Sponge Spatter Cooler, w/ lid, mkd. "5", has bung hole but no spigot, chip on one handle, 14¾" H overall $154.00

Blue & White Sponge Pitcher, barrel shaped w/ stripes, hairlines, 8⅝" H $302.50

Blue & White Sponge Cooler, w/ lid, mkd. "8", nickel plated spigot, minor chips on inside flange of lid, 18" H overall $341.00

A-OH June 1996   Garth's Auction

Chippendale blanket chest, PA, walnut w/ old worn ref., dovetailed case, two dovetailed overlapping drawers & applied moldings, feet repl., hardware & lock removed, poplar secondary wood, 49¾" W, 24" D, 27" H .$715.00

A-OH June 1996   Garth's Auction

Chippendale Slant Front Desk, PA, walnut w/ old finish, dovetailed case & drawers, fitted interior w/ center door, old reprs., repl. brasses, poplar & chestnut secondary woods, 39¾" W, 22½" D, 47" H $2,200.00

Three English Pewter Plates, "Hale & Sons" touch, minor dents, 8½" D $247.50

Pewter Teapot, "Boardman" eagle touch, minor damage & dents, 7⅜" H $302.50

Pewter Lamp, "R. Gleason" touch, burning fluid burner w/ snuffer caps slightly oversize, 5½" H plus burner $385.00

Pewter Water Pitcher, w/ hinged lid, "Boardman", lion touch, battered, 8¼" H $247.50

Pewter Plate, "Frederick Bassett, New York" touch marks, wear, pitting & knife scratches, 8½" D $165.00

Pewter Jar, 4¾" H $99.00

Pewter Plate, "Gershom Jones, Providence" touch marks, wear, knife scratches and a 1" crack along edge of booge, 9⅛" D $357.50

English Pewter Teapot, pear shaped, "Townsend & Compton" touch, top of handle resoldered & finial wafer damaged, 7" H $412.50

Am. Pewter Plate, touch mark has "F.B." in rectangle, worn & pitted w/ some battering & sm. rim splits, 8¼" D $110.00

Pewter Syrup Pitcher, w/ hinged lid, "Hall & Catton" touch, 6⅛" H .$660.00

English Pewter Soup Plate, "T.C." touch, wear, knife scratches and rim split, 8⅛" D $110.00

A-OH June 1996   Garth's Auction

Southern Pie Safe, ref. walnut, w/ two dovetailed drawers & double doors, six orig. punched tins w/ boldly executed pot of flowers detail, tins have light rust & one has old pieced corner repr., pine secondary wood, 51¼" W, 74¾" H $3,300.00

Stoneware Preserving Jar, mkd. "Scheuter Bros. Yonkers, NY. 2", flower in cobalt blue quill work, sm. chips & rim hairline, 11½" H $115.50

Two Stoneware Canning Jars, stenciled cobalt blue mkd. "A.P. Donaghho, Parkersburg, W.Va.", lip chips, 9½" H $143.00

Ovoid Stoneware Cooler, impressed mkd. "Gate City Stoneware Cooler, Patented 9", floral design in greyish blue quill work, repl. wooden lid, chips & hairline at spigot, 14½" H $220

Ovoid Stoneware Canning Jar, stenciled cobalt blue mkd. "T.F. Reppert, Greensboro, PA" 9½" H $93.50

Ovoid Stoneware Jar, w/ impressed mkd. "Burger & Lang Rochester, NY." , flower & "2" in cobalt blue quill work, sm. chips 11¼" H $258.50

Stoneware Barrel Shaped Jar, blue stenciled mkd. "The J. Weller Company Acme Pickles, Cincinnati, Ohio", repl. wooden lid, wear & chips, 13" H $143.00

Ovoid Stoneware Jar, w/ applied shoulder handles, cobalt blue stenciled & freehand mkd. "R.W. Williams New Geneva, PA. 5", hairlines, 15½" H $165.00

Ovoid Stoneware Jar, w/ cobalt blue stenciled mkd. "A.P. Donaghho, Parkersburg, W. Va. 3", sm. chips, 13½" H $143.00

A-OH May 1996   Garth's Auction

Slant Front Desk, ash or oak w/ worn finish, three dovetailed drawers, one fake drawer, hinged lid & fitted interior w/ ten drawers & door, two ivory escutcheons are old replacements, age cracks in ends, 47¼" W, 23" D, 46¾" H $495.00

Ovoid Stoneware Jar, mkd. "Hall & Thomas, Springfield, O. 2", cobalt blue brushed flower., sm. chips, 11" H $522.50

Stoneware Crock, w/ cobalt blue quill work mkd. "Ed Berry, Brit-, O.", sm. chips, 10¼" H $275.00

Ovoid Stoneware Jar, w/ cobalt blue quill work label w/ floral design on reverse, "H. Loundes Maker Petersburg, Va. A.D. 1841", 12¼" H $1,732.50

Ovoid Stoneware Jar, cobalt blue brushed floral decor. on both sides, w/ incised "4", sm. chips & hairlines, 14¼" H $467.50

A-OH May 1996   Garth's Auction

Empire Chest of Drawers, refin. cherry, w/ dovetailed drawers & paneled ends, finish has wear & stains, 43" W, top is 21" x 44", 44¾" H . .$522.50

Ironstone Chamber Set, four piece, blue sponged border & Blue Willow transfer: bowl & pitcher; chamber pot & tumbler or brush holder, 16½" D, 11¾" H $148.50

Spool Cabinet, refin. walnut, worn eglomise panel labels & orig. pulls, "Clarks Ont, Spool Cotton", stains, 21¾" W, 15" D, 7¼" H $220.00

Clear Blown Canister, w/ applied rings, domed lid has high finial, chip on inner lid flange & top of finial has been ground, 17½" H $27.50

Clear Blown Canister, w/ applied rings, w/ domed lid w/ finial, sm. chips, 11⅝" H $115.50

A-OH May 1996   Garth's Auction

Wall Cupboard, two piece, cherry & poplar w/ old cherry finish, 45" W, 80" H $1,540.00

Ovoid Stoneware Pitcher, w/ cobalt blue stenciled mkd. "Jas Benjamin, Wholesale Stoneware, Cincinnati, O", chip on lip, 11" H $357.50

Butter Crock, stoneware, w/ cobalt blue brushed floral decor. on two sides, edge chips, 13" D, 6" H $385.00

Stoneware Jar, w/ cobalt blue stenciled mkd. "John Conley Mfr. & Dealer in Stoneware, White Cottage, Post Office, O", 11½" H $126.50

Ovoid Stoneware Jar, w/ cobalt blue stenciled & freehand decor. mkd. "From R.J. Smyth, Grocery, Wheeling, W.Va", stains, 8" 19¾" H . . .$1,980.00

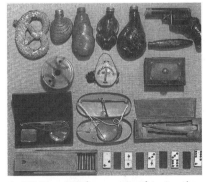

A-OH May 1996   Garth's Auction

Row 1, Left to Right

Pretzel Shaped Bottle, porcelain w/ br. glaze & white applied "salt", 5¾" L $110.00

Figural Glass Bottles, two, w/ worn paint & metal screw caps, potato in brown, 5½" L, and clam in gold, 3¾" L $55.00

Figural Glass Bottles, two, amber w/ metal screw caps, oyster w/ traces of paint, 6" L & dressed bird, 4⅝" L $187.00

Figural Glass Bottles, two, amber, revolver w/ screw cap, "Pat applied for", 7½" L, & cigar, 5¼" L . . .$209.00

Row 2

Drum Shaped Ink, stoneware, top has designs in cobalt blue slip, 3⅝" L $495.00

Miniature Canteen, stoneware, blue & white w/ red painted cross, "Utica Commandery, Rochester Sept 4, 1900", orig. cord w/ tassels, 2¾" L . .$440.00

Sm. Tin Spice Box, w/ tooled brass star medallions, four part interior w/ sm. grater, some damage, 4½" L $71.50

Row 3

Brass Balance Scales, two portable, one in leatherized case, the other in tôle case w/ very worn reddish br. paint w/ blk. transfer of eagle$187.00

Straight Razor, w/ horn handle w/ worn gilt mkd. "Original Pipe Razor", in a case whittled from one piece of wood, 8" L $49.50

Row 4, Left to Right

Dominoes, box w/ twenty eight ivory & ebony dominoes, box has damage, 7" L $385.00

A-OH May 1996   Garth's Auction

Ladderback Side Chairs, (1 of 2) old blk. repaint w/ yellow striping, replaced seats, 34¾" H $143.00
Empire Stand, cherry w/ old worn refin., w/ dovetailed drawer & one board top (w/ poorly reprd. break), some edge damage, 20⅜" x 24", 29" H $220.00
Stoneware Butter Crock, w/ brushed cobalt blue floral decor. on both sides, mismatched lid, 8½" D $550.00
Ovoid Stoneware Churn, w/ cobalt blue quill work flower & "5", hairlines & sm. chips, 16½" H $137.50

A-OH May 1996   Garth's Auction

Hepplewhite Style Chest, refin. cherry w/ inlay, dovetailed drawers, wood, 36" W, 37½" H $852.50
Pewter Candlesticks, w/ reeded detail, 10⅝" H, pair $385.00
Pewter, two pieces, Flagg & Homan (unsigned) teapot, 8⅜" H, & Eng. "half pint" tankard w/ engraved pub label "Black Lion", 4⅝" H $165.00
English Box, mahogany veneer w/ banded inlay, int. has lift out two section dovetailed tray, lock & diamond escutcheon missing, 11" L . . .$192.50

A-OH May 1996   Garth's Auction

Sawbuck Table, poplar w/ old cream colored repaint, two board bread board top, one leg has wooden brace fastened w/ square nails, 26" x 39", 29" H $440.00
Ovoid Stoneware Jar, w/ cobalt blue stenciled & freehand mkd. "G.A. & J.E. McCarthey Maysville, Ky 2", 12¼" H $1,072.50
Wash Board, yellowware insert w/ br. sponging in wooden frame, yellowware has some wear, 12½"x 24" . . .$495.00
Dovetailed Table Top Desk, refin. pine w/ age cracks & repl. hinge, 15" L $38.50
Stoneware Jar, w/ cobalt blue brushed floral design, 11" H .$385.00
Ovoid Stoneware Jar, w/ cobalt blue stenciled mkd. "Fred Kapfer Gen. Store. Clarington, O. 2", 11¾" H $385.00
Wrt. Iron Toaster, w/ twisted handle & wooden grip, 12" W, & 22" w/handle $110.00
Ovoid Stoneware Jar, w/ cobalt blue stenciled mkd. "Manufactured by S. Hutchison & Sons. Matamoras, Ohio 3", bottom drilled & chips on handle, 14" H $495.00
Ovoid Stoneware Jar, w/ cobalt blue stenciled mkd. "George Davenport, Dealer in Dry Goods &c. (etc.) Matamoras, Ohio, 4", dk. spots (stains) & sm. lip chips, 15" H $467.50
Hay Fork, mini. or child size, all wood, traces of red paint & stamped star designs, 35" L $467.50

A-OH May 1996   Garth's Auction

Sheraton Stand, refin. cherry, three dovetailed drawers w/ edge beading & two board top, reprs., drawer fronts replaced, 21½" x 21", 29" H . .$412.50
PA Side Chairs, (1 of 6) w/ worn orig. br. paint w/ yellow & blk. striping & polychrome floral decor., 17" seat, 33¼" H $495.00
Stoneware Milk Bowl, pouring spout w/ "1" in circle & four cobalt blue flowers around rim, 11½" D, 4½" H $577.50
Stoneware Jar, w/ cobalt blue stenciled decor. mkd. "Hamilton & Jones, Star Pottery 3" w/ roses, 14" H $660.00

A-OH May 1996   Garth's Auction

Candlestand, refin. cherry & maple, age cracks, 17½" D, 26" H . . .$137.50
Windsor Side Chair, dk. br. repaint, front edge of seat probably reshaped, 35½" H $104.50
Stoneware Bowl, w/ molded ribbed exterior & cobalt blue decor., chips & hairline, 10¾" D, 5½" H $143.00
Ovoid Stoneware Jug, w/ cobalt blue brushed flower & #2, 13¾" H $346.50

A-OH May 1996   Garth's Auction

Stoneware Crock, w/ flared sides, mkd. "A. & W. Boughner 4", cobalt blue brushed decor., chips on lip & one handle, faint crow's foot on bottom, 12⅜" H $1,485.00

A-OH May 1996   Garth's Auction

Carved Wooden Scoop, w/ duck butter print on end of handle, 9" L $302.50

Butterprint, round w/ whittled inserted handle & well detailed stylized flower & foliage, 3½" D $115.50

Chocolate Molds, two, tin, mother rabbit w/ umbrella, "Dresden", 7¼" H & circus elephant, 4¼" H, both are two part hinged molds $357.50

Burl Butter Paddle, ash w/ figure in bowl, 8½" L $302.50

Two Paddles, w/ old fin. & figured wood, one w/ cracked handle, 8" L $66.00

Cast Iron Frog, traces of old blk. paint, 5" L $82.50

Butterprint, w/ natural growth handle, rectangular tulip design w/ stars, 8½" L $148.50

Cookie Cutters, three, tin, hand, bear (handle missing), & bear w/ handle, some resoldering $49.50

Sm. Burl Dipper, w/ tab handle w/ scrubbed interior, 4" L $352.00

Butter Paddle, curly maple, old worn finish., 9" L $170.50

PA. Ger. Book, religious verse, printed in Phila. in 1818, pen & ink & watercolor fraktur bookplate in red & blk., "Esther Schultz...1834", leather binding, 4½" x 6⅞" $275.00

Watercolor Drawings, two mini. pen & ink, certificate of merit fraktur bird in red & blk. on dk. laid fin. paper & map of "Kentucky", in blk. & gr. (taken from an 1859 book), gilt frames . . . $132.00

Ice Cream Molds, four, pewter, cardinal 4"; squirrel "CC", 3½"; heart w/ cupid 3" & child riding rabbit, "E & Co., NY", 5½" L $660.00

Pewter Ladles, two, one w/ turned wooden handle, other w/ twisted baleen handle, 13½" L $55.00

Pewter Stuffing Spoon, w/ bright cut floral designs on handles, anchor mark & "DEP", 14" L $110.00

A-OH May 1996   Garth's Auction

Victorian Bed, refin. walnut w/ burl veneer, orig. side rails, full size, 83" H $880.00

Victorian Desk, two piece, fall front, walnut w/ old finish, one dovetailed drawer, paneled lid & pigeon hole interior w/ stenciled mkd. "A.O. Huffman, Springfield, O.", interior has been altered, 35"W, 23½"D, 55"H . . $605.00

Folding Highchair/stroller, hardwood w/cane seat, 24"H plus handle $302.50

A-OH June 1996   Garth's Auction

Country Stand, pine & hardwood w/ orig. red graining, birdcage w/ turned posts & revolving one board top w/ cut corners, 23" x 23¾", 31" H . . . $880.00

Brass Bedwarmer, w/ punched design on lid & turned chestnut handle, 42" L $275.00

Redware Pie Plate, w/ coggled rim, yellow slip decor., wear & old chips, 12¼" D $302.50

Redware Dish, yellow slip decor., wear & chips, 8" D

A-PA Nov. 1995   Pook & Pook, Inc.

Corner Cupboard, PA, 2-pc. flame grain decor., 71" H, approx. 46" W $4,250.00

Flow Blue Service, 8 pcs. by Doulton in Madras patt., 2 open vegetable dishes, covered vegetable dish, meat platter, 8 each of dinner plates, bowls, butter plates, cupts & saucers, ca. 1891 . . . . $1,300.00

Chippendale Tall Case Clock, Chester Co. PA, walnut, w/ 8-day works, white painted face, ogee feet, ca. 1780, 96" H $4,500.00

Stoneware Jug, blue decor., stamped "From C.W. Hubbard & Co. Manchester, N.H." 12" H $175.00

Stoneware Crock, blue decor. & applied handles, 15" H $225.00

A-OH May 1996   Garth's Auction

Stoneware

Ovoid Jar, w/ flared & tooled lip, cobalt blue brushed flower w/ "2", wear & sm. flakes on bottom edge, 11½" H $275.00

Pitcher, cobalt blue brushed initials w/ decor., wear, chips & short hairline, 11" H $412.50

A-OH May 1996   Garth's Auction

Stoneware Ovoid Jar, mkd. "Havens", cobalt blue brushed designs, and "2", sm. flake on one handle, 11½" H $605.00

A-OH May 1996   Garth's Auction

Stoneware Ovoid Jug, w/ strap handle, mkd. "S. Hart Fulton", cobalt blue brushed design, minor flake on lip & some short hairlines, 14" H . .$302.50

A-OH May 1996   Garth's Auction

Oil On Canvas, landscape w/ autumn foliage signed "E.R. Sitzman '33", 24" H, 32" W $440.00

Roll Top Desk, oak w/ orig. carved pulls, fitted interior, 42" W, 31¾" D, 50" H $1,650.00

Hall Tree, oak w/ lift lid seat & beveled mirror, orig. hooks damaged & incomplete, 36" W, 83" H $880.00

G.W.T.W. Lamp, w/ enameled opaque white glass w/ floral decor. on a deep burnt orange ground, gilded brass fittings w/ orig. burner intact, 26¼" H, plus chimney $330.00

Banquet Lamp, base in guilded cast iron w/ brass & bronze finish., filler cap mkd. "B & H" (Bradley & Hubbard), electrified & drilled, clear frosted globe w/ enameled flowers in purple, white, yellow & gr., bottom flange of globe chipped, 24¾" H $247.50

Brass Balance Scale, on mahogany base, "C.W.S. Walkers, Manchester" w/ incomplete set of weights, 22" L, 22" H $192.50

Brass Tea Kettle, w/ dovetailed copper bottom & old soldered repair, 9¾" H, plus swivel handle $82.50

Brass Oil Can, mkd. "10 QT", 16½" H $104.50

A-OH May 1996   Garth's Auction

Eastlake Victorian Bookcase, ref. walnut, 30"W, 13½"D, 61½"H .$715.00

Eastlake Victorian Commode, ref. cherry, paneled door & one dovetailed drawer, minor edge damage, 18" x 36", 28½" H $302.50

Banquet Lamp, blk. ceramic base, brass stem & cased font that shades from light to deep pink, electrified (but not drilled), 33" H overall $192.50

Decanter, cobalt cut to clear w/ cut panels, minor stain, 11¾" H . .$60.50

Hanging Lamp, cranberry hobnail font & shade w/ brass frame & clear cut prisms, electrified, 40" H$1,375.00

Banquet Lamp, brass base w/ Corinthian column & cranberry font, electrified, no shade, 33" H . .$412.50

Flow-Blue Dinnerware, fortyeight piece set, "Oxford" by "Johnson Bros." incomplete service for eight plus three serving dishes & similar teapot w/ metal strainer by "Buffalo Pottery", Argyle pattern $1,210.00

Cylinder Music Box, rosewood veneer case w/ floral inlay, 16¾" H . .$467.50

"Mira" Music Box, regina type in mahogany case, w/ thirty four disks, 21" W $2,420.00

Cylinder Music Box, in rosewood veneer case w/ floral inlay, 14" H .$495.00

A-OH June 1996   Garth's Auction

Left to Right

Lollipop Butter Print, stylized floral design, old worn patina, 7¾"L $247.50

Round Butter Print, stylized pineapple, 1 pc. w/turned handle, worn patina w/ age cracks, 4½" x 4¾" . .$93.50

Butter Paddle, w/ carved butter print on handle, one side has fruit, the reverse has star flower, worn soft finish, 11¾" L $797.50

Round Butter Print, cow, turned inserted handle, scrubbed patina w/ minor age cracks, 4" D $137.50

Round Butter Print, w/ deep cased sides, star flower, one piece w/ turned handle, 5" D $412.50

Lollipop Butter Print, primitive cow or goat, worn patina, 9¼"L . .$181.50

Wrt. Iron Pipe Tongs, simple tooling, 16½" L $220.00

Round Butter Print, primitive tulip, one piece turned handle, age cracks, 5" D $110.00

Lollipop Butter Print, heart & sunburst design, worn patina, age cracks in carving, 6¾" L $214.50

Two Round Butter Prints, both have one piece turned handles & worn scrubbed surface w/ age cracks, flower 4½" D, strawberries 3¼" D . . .$121.00

Blue & White Stoneware Soap Dish, lion head, sm. chips, 4½" D $49.50

Blue & White Stoneware Soap Dish, roses, 5" D $71.50

Blue & White Stoneware Soap Dish, flowers, dk. blue rim, sm. flakes, 5" D $38.50

Blue & White Stoneware Marble, wear, 1½" D $82.50

Blue & White Sponge Soap Dish, minor damage, 3½" x 4¾" $60.50

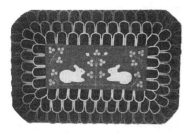

A-MA Aug. 1996   Rafael Osona

Figural Applique Penny Rug, 19th C. w/ trapunto white rabbits & gr. clover on red worsted panel, enframed by three rows of oval "pennies" w/ yellow, red & gr. borders, 24⅝" x 37⅝" $650.00

A-OH Mar. 1996   Garth's Auction

Hooked Rag Rug, blue bird on branch w/ reds, greys, brown & black, 26" x 40". $247.50
Hooked Rag Rug, reds, greys, brown, green etc. signed " E.W. 1984", 26" x 36" $357.50

A-MA Oct. 1995   Skinner, Inc.

Low Post Bed, N. Eng., 1830-40, orig. red & black graining, gilt accents, feet repr., ht. loss, 46½" H, 53" W, 79" D $862.50

A-MA Aug. 1996   Robert C. Eldred Co., Inc.

Lift-Top Blanket Box, maple & curly maple w/ dovetail construction, molded top, interior till, 27¼" H, 41½" L, 21½" D $1,100.00

A-OH Mar. 1996   Garth's Auction

Hooked Yarn Rug, in shades of blues, green, brown, white etc., some wear, fading, w/ light stains, 40" x 49". $506.00

A-MA Aug. 1996   Robert C. Eldred Co., Inc.

Split-Banister-Back Armchair, maple w/ rush seat, one ear missing in back $825.00

A-MA Aug. 1996   Robert C. Eldred Co., Inc.

Brass & Copper Fire Dept. Side Lamp, mid-19th C., Worcester, MA, w/ clear engraved lenses, 8½" H .$715.00
Silver Plated Fireman's Horn, w/ engraved decor., ca. 1860, 19½" H $632.50

A-MA Aug. 1996   Robert C. Eldred Co., Inc.

Silver Chatelaine, w/ ivory & silver notepad, sm. purse, pillbox, pen knife & bird-form pin $357.50

A-OH Nov. 1995   Garth's Auction

Left to Right

Stoneware Pitcher, w/ applied strap handle, cobalt blue brushed floral design, old chips, 7⅜" H $495.00

Minature Stoneware Pitcher, W/ Applied Strap Handle, cobalt blue brushed inscription "EVE" w/ stylized floral design & polka dots on front & handle, small chips, 5" H $797.50

Miniature Blanket Chest, cherry w/ old finish & ebonized trim, dove tailed case& drawers, poplar secondary wood, one drawer & lid have lock w/ key, other drawer has underside spring catch, minor edge repair to drawers & case has pieced repairs at lock & one hinge, 15" W, 7⅝ D, 11½ " H $1320.00

Ovoid Stoneware Jug, w/ applied strap handle, impressed label "J. Seymour, Troy" & incised bird, both highlighted in cobalt blue slip, minor small chips, 15¾" H $1705.00

A-MA Mar. 1996   Skinner, Inc.

Shaker Armed Rocking Chairs, two, maple, Enfield, CT., C. 1820-30, sm. chair w/ old surface, reprs, other imperf., 41″ H and 45½″ H .$1,035.00

A-MA June 1996   Skinner, Inc.

Arrow-Back Windsor Side Chairs, assembled set of six, dark brown painted, N. Eng., 1820-30, br. paint w/ gold & gr. striping, old repaint, minor imperf., ...$977.50

A-Wash. DC Apr. 1996   Wechler's

Windsor Bamboo-Turned Chairs, painted & decor., assembled set, N. Eng., ca. 1810, five side chairs & one armchair w/ seven spindles, ea. w/ later overall yellow paint w/ gr. & red floral & leafage decor. w/ blk. highlights, some loss to paint ..$1,265.00

A-MA Oct. 1995   Skinner, Inc.

Tavern Table, maple, MA, late 18th c., old red surface, minor imperf. $1955.00

A-MA June 1996   Skinner, Inc.

Arrow Back Windsor Side Chairs, set of four, graining painted & stenciled, N.Y. State, 1820-35, red & blk. graining w/ old yellow & gr. painted embellishments, old surface, minor imperf., 31¾″ H $920.00

A-MA June 1996   Skinner, Inc.

Q.A. Maple & Pine Table, N. Eng., 18th C., ref., imperf., 28″ H, 48½″ W, 28½″ D $2,990.00

A-MA Jan. 1996   Skinner, Inc.

Federal Painted Dressing Glass, MA or NH, ca. 1810, cream w/ red & gray, minor imperfections, 19¼″H, 17¾″ W, 10″ D $1,092.50

One-Drawer Dressing Table, ylw. paint, ca. 1830, imperfections, 29¾″ H, 31½″ W, 17¾″ D $1,265.00

A-MA June 1996   Skinner, Inc.

Dressing Stand, grain painted & stencil decor., Maine, C. 1820, old red & blk. graining w/ stenciled floral & fruit decor., yellow striping throughout, early surface, minor imperf., 33¾″ H, 29¼″ W, 15⅛″ D $460.00

A-VA Sept. 1995 Ken Farmer Auctions

Tavern Table, paint decor., red over mustard, N Eng., ca. 1790, 29½″ H, 35¼″ W, 29½″ D $2,200.00

A-MA Aug. 1996   Skinner, Inc.

Nightstand, bird's eye maple, ca. 1820s, w/ drawer, ref. 27¾"H $920.00

A-MA Aug. 1996   Skinner, Inc.

Federal Mahogany Card Table, w/ inlay, ca. 1790, imper. 29½" H, 36" W $4,025.00

A-MA Aug. 1996   Skinner, Inc.

Pine Cupboard, N. Eng., 1st qtr. 18th C., old refinish, minor imperf., 73¼" H, 38" W, 17" D $2,645.00

A-MA Aug. 1996   Skinner, Inc.

Carved Wood Sewing Box, Am., 19th C., w/ spool rack, minor imperf., 14" H $258.75

A-MA June 1996   Skinner, Inc.

Coin Silver Tea & Coffee Set, two of four-piece, John B. Jones Jr., Boston, C. 1816-37, coffeepot, teapot, creamer & covered sugar, monogrammed, very minor dents, scratches, coffeepot 9" H, 79 troy oz. $1,840.00

Coin Silver Tea Set, three of four-piece, Garrett Eoff, N.Y. City, C. 1789-1845, teapot, covered sugar, creamer & wastebowl, monogram, minor dents, teapot 9" H, 70 troy oz. $1,725.00

Coin Silver Oval Footed Serving Bowl, Jones, Ball & Co., Boston, C. 1852-54, engraved, very minor dents, 8" L, 11 troy oz. $632.50

Coin Silver Tea Set, one of three-piece, William Gale & Son, N.Y. City, C. 1850-66, teapot, creamer & covered sugar, very minor dents, teapot 8½" H, 54 troy oz. $1,610.00

Coin Silver Long-Handled Serving Fork, late 18th / early 19th C., w/ two "WS" touchmarks, 18" L, 4 troy oz. $1,092.50

A-MA Mar. 1996   Skinner, Inc.

Eagle w/ Shield, carved & painted, Am. 20th C., w/ banner "Live and Let Live", paint wear & loss, 25" H, 73" L $2,300.00

Copper Banneret Weather Vane, "North Wind", attrib. to J.W. Fiske, N.Y., late 19th C., mounted on Gothic fretwork base, fine verdigris surface, minor imperf., 60" H, 36" L $13,800.00

Capitol, carved & painted, 19th C., decor. w/ grape clusters & leaves, sm. losses & imperf., 14½" H . .$1,610.00

Wooden Tobacconist's Figure, carved & painted, ca. 1865, Pierre G, Gaspari, Baltimore, brass plaque stamped "P.G. Gaspari," some losses & wear, 48" H $29,900.00

Gilt Gesso Carved Eagle, N. Eng., late 18th / early 19th C., imperf., 34" H, 27½" W $55,200.00

Copper Weather Vane, 19th C., verdigris surface, repr. bullet holes, minor dents, 29½" L $5,750.00

A-KS Mar. 1996   Woody Auction

Navajo Pitched Basket, w/ Ute beading, basket is solidly beaded including bottom, horse hair braided handles, 11" Diam., 14" H . . .$400.00

A-MA Aug. 1996   Skinner, Inc.

Spice Cabinet, butternut, Am., 19th C.
ref., 14″ H, 20″ W, 10¼″ D . . .$977.50

A-MA Aug. 1996   Skinner, Inc.

Wall Box, w/ red stain, late 18th / early
19th C., imperfections, 15¼″H .$632.50

A-MA Aug. 1996   Skinner, Inc.

Wall Box, Am., 19th C., w/ dark reddish stain, 19¾″ H $747.50

A-MA Aug. 1996   Skinner, Inc.

Carved & Painted Carousel Horse,
Am., early 20th C., w/ paint losses, 60″
H $10,350.00

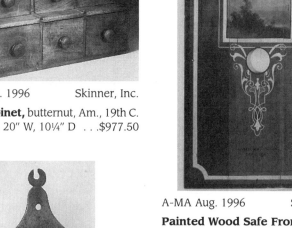

A-MA Aug. 1996   Skinner, Inc.

Painted Wood Safe Front, Am., pat.
date Dec. 1, 1863, minor imperf., 40½
x 24¼″ $488.75

A-NH Aug. 1996   Northeast Auctions

**Q.A. Southern Walnut Sugar Chest
on Frame,** w/ drake feet, 25″ H, 24″
W $20,000.00

A-MA Aug. 1996   Skinner, Inc.

**Coalbrookdale Style Cast Iron Gar-
den Furniture,** (2 of 5 pcs.), English,
late 19th C., imperfections .$5,750.00

A-MA Aug. 1996   Skinner, Inc.

Chair Table, pine & birch, N. Eng.,
early 19th C., w/ scrubbed top, minor
traces of orig. paint, repairs, 27½″ H,
Top 47½″ sq. $1,850.00

A-MA Aug. 1996   Skinner, Inc.

Step-Back Pine Cupboard, N. Eng.,
ca. 1830, w/ 3 shelved int., old red stain,
rest., 7½″ H, 55⅞″ W, 17″ D .$1,610.00

A-MA Aug. 1996   Skinner, Inc.

Federal   Chest   of   Drawers,
mahogany & mahogany veneer, N.
Eng., ca. 1820, old refinish, 42″ H, 38″
W, 20″ D $1,035.00

A-OH June 1996   Garth's Auction

Handcolored Lithograph by "Currier & Ives", "A New England Home", matted and framed, 19¼" H, 23¼" W $192.50
Chippendale Chest, cherry w/ old ref., dovetailed bracket feet, drawers have applied top edge molding, pine & poplar secondary wood, repl. brasses, minor age cracks, pieced repr. & feet are old replm., 39" W, 31¼" H $2,200.00
Pewter Candlesticks, pr., some wear, battering & pitting, 9¼" H . . .$165.00
Polychrome Imari Bowl, 12⅜" D, 5¾" H $440.00
Blue & White Canton Chop Plate, sm. rim flakes, 16¼" D $632.50

A-OH June 1996   Garth's Auction

Empire Chest of Drawers, Ref. cherry w/ curly & bird's eye maple drawer fronts & curly maple end panels, curly maple pulls, poplar secondary wood, 46" W, 20" D, 41½" H, plus top drawers, 46½" H overall $660.00
Blue & White Sponge Spatter Jug, w/ molded leaf detail, wire bail & wooden handle, "Mfg'd by F.H. Weeks Style XXX Pat. Pending, Akron, O." dk. blue, chips on spout, 5½" H . .$550.00
Blue & White Sponge Spatter Jug, white in pattern, 5½" H $770.00
Blue & White Sponge Spatter Jug, w/ advertising "Grandmother's Maple Syrup of 50 years ago"... patent apl'd for F.H. Weeks, Akron, O." Chips, hairline & wooden handle has deteriorated, 6½" H $467.50
Blue & White Sponge Spatter Jug, w/ molded detail & dk. blue color, bottom mkd. "Mfg'd by F.H. Weeks, Akron, O.", chips, wire bail & wooden handle is an old replm., 7¾" H $660.00

A-OH June 1996   Garth's Auction

Child Size Kitchen Cupboard, ref. pine, base has bin & four drawers, reprs. & some reconst. w/ repl. plywood top or shelf for base section, 32½" W, 14" D, 43" H $247.50
Child Size Treadle Sewing Machine, iron base mkd. "Ideal", & ref. oak top, 25" H, plus machine, 31" H, overall $1,485.00
Child Size Tea Set, 16 piece, red spatter mkd. "Staffordshire England": teapot (sm. chip on spout), 5¼" H; creamer (sm. hairline); sugar; waste bowl; six cups & saucers & six plates, 5½" D $357.50
Teddy Bear, worn red, white & blue mohair w/ straw stuffing, one eye, movable arms, 15" H $126.50
Teddy Bear, worn gold mohair w/ straw stuffing & bead eyes, articulated limbs, paw pads repr., 12" H .$247.50
Teddy Bear, worn gold mohair w/ straw stuffing & bead eyes, articulated limbs, 15" H $192.50
Sm. Size Spinning Wheel, w/ old blk. paint, impressed "N. Wolf T", distaff missing, 21½" H $220.00
Doll Size Ice Cream Set, 5 piece, w/ table & four chairs, white repaint, chairs are 16" H, table is 15" D, 10" H $137.50

◄ **Running Horse Weathervane,** good detail w/ copper body and cast zinc head, old patina and soldered repairs, modern wall mounting bracket, 44" L. $2,200.00
Graduated Set of Three Woven Splint Melon Rib Baskets, two smaller are ten ribs, larger is fourteen ribs, old patina, minor damage, bentwood handles, 6" D, 7" x 7½" and 8½" x 9½" $165.00
Blanket Chest, curly maple w/ old mellow refinishing w/ traces of old red, 42" W, 16½" D, 31" H $495.00
Brass Andirons, pr., iron rods have heat damage and one back foot is missing, 19" H $82.00
Eng. Pewter Charger, incomplete touch marks, rim stamped "A.G.", wear, scratches and splits in rim, 16¾" D. $341.00

A-KY Oct. 1995 Ken Farmer Auctions

Lift Top Blanket Chest, NH, green, vinegar style paint decor. over white pine, old pulls replaced, 35" H, 36" W, 19½" D $2,310.00

A-OH Nov. 1995   Garth's Auction

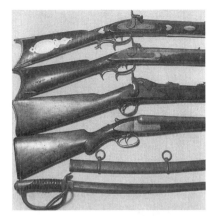

A-OH Oct. 1995   Garth's Auction

Half Stock Percussion Rifle, curly maple stock w/ twelve German silver inlays & brass hardware, German silver cap box, 36" octagon barrel is mkd. "Postley, Nelson & Co.", top flat of barrel engraved "C. K." $742.50

Ohio Percussion Long Rifle, signed "J. Legg", curly maple stock w/ old worn finish, 37½" barrel & brass hardware, lock has cast detail of a dog & bird, old repair at wrist & toe $632.50

Springfield 1873 Saddle Ring Carbine, has 1879 alts., very good condition & receiver probably reblued, 22" barrel w/ adjust. rear sight, S/N 145788 . . . .$880.00

Westley Richards Double Barrel Shotgun, receiver & trigger guard have fine engraved detail w/ scrollwork & dog, 32" damascus barrels are mkd. "W.R.", "J.P.C." & "AB", sm. dents, good bore, checkered walnut stock .$330.00

1860 Cavalry Officer's Saber, signed "C. Roby, U.S.", & "1864", brass hilt w/ worn leather & missing wire, pitting $385.00

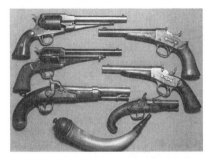

A-OH Oct. 1995   Garth's Auction

Remington .44 Caliber Revolver, percussion new model Army, very good condition w/ crisp signature on top flat of barrel, S/N 124304 $990.00

Remington Rolling Block Pistol, .50 caliber w/ inspector's stamp on grip, traces of case coloring on frame, 8" round barrel, wood has dents $935.00

Remington Single Action Revolver, model 1875, .44 caliber, metal surface reblued & has a sm. putty repr. in grip $880.00

Remington Navy Rolling Block Pistol, 7" barrel, metal has bright finish w/ anchor & "J.M.B.C." at breech. Frame is stamped "P.& F.C.W." $825.00

Johnson 1836 Pistol, converted to percussion, lock has signature, town & 1838, steel has bright finish & walnut stock is chipped beneath lock, 14" overall $330.00

Flintlock Pocket Pistol, 4" octagon to round barrel w/ simple scroll engraving, stock has raised carved leaf around tang & incised line detail around lock & sideplate, restoration, 8½" $220.00

Screw Tip Powder Horn, good color, w/ turned & carved end plug, 11½" L $275.00

A-OH Oct. 1995   Garth's Auction

Rare Henry Rifle, w/ martial marks, .44 caliber. 24" barrel w/ worn rebluing, barrel is also mkd. "C.G.C.", at breech end. brass frame mkd. "H.H.", walnut stock shows faint inspector's mk., good signature remaining, S/N 3237, butt plate is mkd. 3347 . . . .$17,050.00

Winchester High Wall Rifle, standard model, 32 - 40 caliber, very good condition, w/ case colors remaining on receiver, 30" octagon barrel, minor scratches on stock & spots of surface rust, S/N 54378 . . . .$1,320.00

Whitney 1841 U.S. Percussion Rifle, .54 caliber w/ a 33" barrel, lock has a boldly stamped signature w/ "U.S., N. Haven" & "1851", stock has inspector's stamps, very good condition $1,677.50

German Jaeger Rifle, flintlock converted to percussion, walnut stock is checkered & has a sliding wooden patchbox, brass hardware w/ deep engraving, one ramrod pipe is repl., 26" swamped barrel is fitted w/ an ornate rear sight, spur of hammer has been broken off $880.00

Flintlock Fowler, cherry fullstock w/ good color & checkering at the wrist, simple brass hardware & a diamond shape inlay behind breech, round barrel measures 40", age cracks & restoration, top jaw missing $330.00

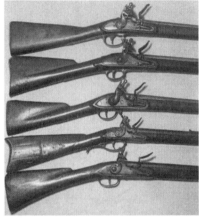

A-OH Oct. 1995   Garth's Auction

1816 Flintlock Musket, Harper's Ferry model, 42" barrel is secured w/ three bands, lock is stamped w/ eagle, "U.S.", signature and 1839, walnut stock shows faint inspectors markings, barrel has bold eagle head stamp and "1840", metal is light gray in color w/ areas of light pitting, short age crack at lock bolt area of stock $1,540.00

Brown Bess Flintlock Musket, third model, 39¼" barrel has bright finish w/ usual pitting around breech, stock shows good dk. patina w/ inspector's marks & three short cracks around lock, lock is stamped w/ a crown, "G.R." & "Tower", barrel & lock also have crown & arrow marks w/ initials "S.G." $990.00

1798 U.S. Contract Musket, Whitney second model, barrel measure 43" w/ areas of pitting, lock plate is stamped "U. States" & "New Haven" w/ eagle, walnut stock w/ orig. finish has carved initials "A.F." & "T.C." the letters "S.C." are stamped ahead of buttplate tang. 3½" sliver of wood has been prof. repl. beneath lock $1,540.00

Fullstock Flintlock Rifle, high quality workmanship w/ a 40½" barrel signed "J. Mason" ,cherry stock has a checkered wrist, silver wire inlay & engraved brass patchbox, restoration $1,760.00

Early Flintlock Musket, 43½" octagon to round barrel, stock has relief carved molding around lock, tang & sideplate, appears to be missing the buttplate $495.00

A-OH Oct. 1995   Garth's Auction

Row 1, Left to Right

Tin Petticoat Peg Lamps, pair, orig. br. japanning, 4" H, plus whale oil burners, minor scratches $165.00

Wrt. Iron Betty Lamp, hanger & pick are old, chain is repl., 4⅜" H . .$99.00

Redware Turk's Head, w/ swirled flutes & scalloped rim, amber & gr. w/ dk. br. sponging on exterior, wear & sm. chips, 9" D $165.00

Cast Iron Hanging Grease Lamp, w/ relief design of dog and flowers on edges of pan, 4" H, plus decor. hanger $93.50

Round Woven Splint Basket, thirty-three ribs, good age & color, minor break in rim, 8" D, 3¼" H, plus bentwood handle $115.50

Row 2, Left to Right

Two Pieces Redware, w/ ribbed strap handles, Ovoid jar w/ br. sponging, 6" H, and Ovoid jug w/ dk. br. shiny glaze, chips, 6½" H $247.50

Redware Shaving Cup w/ strap handle, brownish gr. mottled glaze, 5¾" H $286.00

Two Ovoid Redware Jars, one w/ ribbed strap handle, one is light amber, the other dk. both w/ br. splotches, minor chips, 6" & 6½" H $605.00

Wrt. Iron Hanging Grease Lamp, pan w/ single spout & ratchet arm to adjust cant., 5⅜" H, plus twisted hanger w/ crest $115.50

Row 3, Left to Right

Wooden Keg, w/ worn red paint & scratch carved initials & date "J.G. 1809", minor age cracks, 6¾" L $137.50

Tin Lard Lamp, on saucer base, old soldered repr., 7¼" H $99.00

Coffee Grinder, walnut base & cast iron top w/ cast floral design & mkd. "Strobridge Coffee Mill, Logan & Strobridge", corner chip on drawer, 8¼" H overall $110.00

Redware Birdhouse, w/ opaque cream colored glaze w/ yellow highlights, crazing, 7½" H $49.50

Wooden Canteen, stave const. w/ scratch carved initials, bung hole is damaged, 7" D $165.00

A-OH Oct. 1995   Garth's Auction

Row 1, Left to Right

Redware Plate & Jug, plate w/ pale amber slip & br. splotches, 8⅞" D, ovoid jug w/ strap handle, br. fleck glaze, 6¼" H, both have minor chips $330.00

Sheep w/ Santa Claus, German type sheep, Japanese type Santa Claus, wood, cloth, bisque & papier mâché, some wear & damage, 5¾"H overall $137.50

German Type Sheep, wood & papier mâché w/ woolly coat, neck ribbon w/ bell, wear, 5¼" H $137.50

Two Santas & Feather Tree, Santas mkd. "Made in Japan", cloth, bisque, papier mâché, etc., wear & some damage, 4½" H, tree w/ wooden base, 9½" H $148.50

Row 2

Wakeshan Basketry Piece, Am. Indian, finely woven Makah basket covered bottle in natural twined grass w/ birds, whale boats & whalers along w/ colored bands, wear, minor damage & sm. repr., 10¾" H $236.50

Coffee Grinder, dovetailed curly maple case w/ tin hopper & wrt. iron (steel) fittings, handle mkd. "A. Keine", dovetailed drawer has clear lacy pull, hopper old replm. & inside lip is damaged, 7" x 7" $385.00

Bentwood "Spice" Box, w/ seven interior canisters, all w/ tin edging & stenciled labels (eighth canister missing), mkd. "New York", 9" D .$247.50

A-PA Nov. 1995   Aston Auctioneers & Appraisers

Stoneware Jug, w/ brown tulip decor, mkd. L. Norton & Son $560.00

A-OH Oct. 1995   Garth's Auction

Oil On Canvas, primitive Hudson River Valley landscape, minor surface damage & repr., 15" H, 20" W, modern frame, 16" H, 21¼" W $385.00

Chippendale Bowfront Chest, refin. birch, bracket feet, four dovetailed drawers set in a beaded frame & molded edge top, orig. oval brasses, pine secondary wood, stains in top & crack in left front foot, 39" W, top is 21¾" x 40½", 36" H $4,070.00

Brass Candlesticks, two, early primitive, one w/ saucer base, the other w/ domed base, minor damage, 6¾", 8½" H $495.00

Ovoid Stoneware Churn, cobalt blue brushed primitive tree & w/ blue at handles, rim chips, 16" H $187.00

A-OH Oct. 1995   Garth's Auction

Jacquard Coverlet, one piece, single weave, floral medallion center w/ eagle corners, floral borders & edge mkd. "Henry Gabriel, Allentown", navy blue, gr. red, & natural white, overall wear, no fringe, 74" x 90" . . .$357.50

A-OH Oct. 1995   Garth's Auction

Tin Sconces, pair, minor resoldering, 12½" H $770.00

Blanket Chest, sm. painted, poplar w/ old red paint, bracket feet, dovetailed case & molded edge lid, unusual reworking w/ orig. lid reused as bottom board & w/ feet & lid that are old replm., some edge damage & left front foot is incomplete, 37½" W, 18¾" D, 22½" H $495.00

Weathervane, Running Horse, hollow copper body & cast zinc head, old dk. patina, 17" L $825.00

Ovoid Stoneware Cooler, mkd. "Harts, Fulton", cobalt blue quill work w/ name "D. Perry" & flourish, 12" H $247.50

Stoneware Jug, w/ pouring spout & ear handles w/ wire bale, long tailed bird in cobalt blue quill work, chips & hairlines, 9" H $495.00

A-OH Oct. 1995   Garth's Auction

Jacquard Coverlet, 2 pc. single weave, four rose medallions, vintage border & corners mkd. "Emanuel Ettinger Aronsburg, 1840", navy blue, teal blue, tomato red & natural white, some overall wear & stains, 73" x 86" $357.50

Top Hutch Table, poplar w/ old worn yellow repaint over gray, one board ends w/ cutout feet, mortised through seat & two board top, top is scrubbed & has minor age cracks, top has one orig. steel barn hinge, the other is missing, Ex Bonnie Rolands, 35½" x 72", 30" H $1,760.00

Dome Top Trunk, grain painted, pine w/ orig. red sponging on a yellow ground, wrt. iron end handles & lock, hasp is incomplete, has till w/ lid, age cracks in top, found in N. Eng., 27¾" L $137.50

Round Woven Baskets, two w/ lids, faded painted designs, yellow, natural & blue, 16" D, red, gr. & natural 13½" D, both have wear & damage $187.00

Vinegar Grained Box, walnut & poplar w/ worn orig. br. graining, wrt. iron lock, hasp is incomplete, 31"L .$275.00

A-OH Oct. 1995   Garth's Auction

Country Water Bench, pine w/ old red repaint, one board ends, cutout feet, paneled doors, head board back & open shelf, cast iron latches w/ porcelain knobs, one door has edge damage on top rail, 42" W, 16½" D, 51½" H $1,870.00

Snake Neck Decoy, w/ carved wing detail & old white and blk. paint, age cracks, 20th C folk art, 19" L .$104.50

Stoneware Milk Bowl, brushed cobalt blue "commas" at lip, edge chips, 9" D $115.50

Ovoid Stoneware Jug, incised tulip design is highlighted w/ cobalt blue slip, 15" H $935.00

Canada Goose, weathered block w/ age cracks & old worn working repaint, head has minor age cracks & glass eyes & may be an old replm., 23" L $275.00

A-OH Oct. 1995   Garth's Auction

Stepback Wall Cupboard, one piece, butternut & poplar w/ old red stain, drawers are replm. & side feet have damage, 42¼" W, 78" H . . .$1,100.00

Sponge Spatter Wash Bowl, blue & white w/ stripes, stains & sm. chips, 13¾" D $93.50

Stoneware Crock & Yellowware Jar, crock w/ blue stenciled mkd. "H.C. Ward, Stoneware Depot, Zanesville, O.", chips, 7¾" H & jar w/ white band & tan stripes, wear, crazing, stains & minor damage, 8¾" D, 6¾" H $286.00

Stoneware, 3 pieces, jug mkd. "J.W. Stearns Jr... Boston", 9¾" H,; preserving jar mkd. "C.H. Ketter... Ironton, O.", 9¾" H & jug w/ impressed swan in blue, 9¾" H, chips $495.00

Ovoid Stoneware Jar, cobalt blue stenciled & freehand mkd. "Jas Hamilton & Co., Greensboro, Pa. 10", prof. repr., 23½" H $330.00

A-OH May 1996   Garth's Auction

Stoneware Ovoid Jug, mkd. "Stetzenmeyer & Co. Rochester N.Y.", cobalt blue quill work, & "2", sm. flake on handle, 14½" H $935.00

A-OH Oct. 1995   Garth's Auction

Country Chest, refin. cherry, four dovetailed drawers, one drawer front has pieced reprs., repl. brasses, poplar secondary wood, 42¼" W, top is 19¾" x 44", 38½" H $880.00

Stoneware Batter Jug, bird on branch in cobalt blue quill work, mkd. "4", bale handle is repl. & tin lids are missing, surface flakes & chips on bottom edge, 9" H $550.00

Dovetailed Box, poplar w/ old reddish finish, wrt. iron lock & hasp w/ brass escutcheon, 14" L $115.50

Ohio Fraktur Bookplate, pen & ink & watercolor w/ pen flourishes & "Daniel Sehaey, Smithmille, Wayne County, Ohio Oct. 11th AD 1854. Written by JKCB", red, blk. & olive yellow, old beveled walnut frame, 8¾" H, 10¾" W $577.50

Stoneware Batter Jug, simple flower in cobalt blue slip, wire bale handle, old prof. repr., 8½" H $275.00

A-OH Oct. 1995   Garth's Auction

Opaque Watercolor on Paper, Civil War veteran wearing medal of honor, paper backed on stretched canvas, signed lower right "A.G. 1897", minor paper damage & a sm. tear, 20" H, 15¾" w/inlaid frame 22¾"H, 18½"W $110.00

Sheraton Table, curly maple w/ good old soft finish, turned legs and one board top and leaves, leaves & top have slight warp, minor age cracks & a little edge damage, 17" x 38" w/ 13¼" leaves, 28½" H $1,045.00

Redware Ovoid Jar, w/ applied shoulder handles & flared lip, dk. greenish amber glaze, minor edge chips, 10" H $275.00

Redware Ovoid Jar, w/ applied shoulder handles & flared lip, light greenish amber glaze, chips & hairlines in neck, 11½" H $165.00

Stoneware Crock, w/ applied handles, mkd. "White & Wood, Binghamton, N.Y. 4", bird on branch in cobalt blue quill work, hairline & sm. rim chips, 11¼" H 379.50

A-OH Oct. 1995   Garth's Auction

Empire Chest of Drawers, hardwood w/ orig. graining in imitation rosewood, three dovetailed drawers & two stepback drawers, repl. eagle brasses, 38" W, 17" D, 40" H $660.00

Figural Wig or Hat Stand, papier mâché & gesso, worn white, tan & brown paint, age cracks & wear, 13" H $632.50

Folk Art Box, walnut, cherry & curly maple w/ two sm. drawers & inlaid polka dots, attrib. to Brown County, Ohio, 20th C., 10½" L $110.00

Inlaid Box, figured veneer w/ mahogany cross banding & inlaid, fitted interior w/ dovetailed drawer, some edge & veneer damage, 11½" L $330.00

Stoneware Jug, mkd. "F. B. Norton & Co., Worcester, Mass", cobalt blue brushed leaf, hairline beside handle & lip chip, 11½" H $137.50

A-OH Sept. 1995   Garth's Auction

Row 1, Left to Right

Syrup, fiery opalescent w/ applied handle, 6" H $330.00

Two Syrups, opaque pressed glass, w/ applied handles, blue w/ single flower & pewter lid, 5½" H & pink quilted & patent labels, 6¼" H . . .$297.00

Rubina Glass Syrups, three, hobnail w/ pewter lid, some hobs are damaged, 6⅜" H; ribbed w/ brass lid has damage, 6⅜" H; deco example w/ resoldered metal handle, 7½" H $385.00

Hobnail Syrups, two w/ pewter lids & applied handles, amber & vaseline w/ opalescent highlights, lid is loose, 6¾" H $357.50

Glass Syrups, three blue patt. w/ pewter lids, two have applied handles, 7½" to 8" H $341.00

Row 2, Left to Right

Two Syrups, w/ applied handles & tin lids, amber thumbprint, some rust, 7" H, vaseline w/ white & red end of day pressed in a leaf patt. mold, 6½" H $302.50

Roseville Ewer, foxglove on a blue ground, mkd. "Roseville, USA. 4-6½", 6½" H $110.00

Roseville Vase, bulbous w/ shoulder handles, w/ a gr. fern fronds on a blue ground, paper label "Roseville Pottery", 7½" H $275.00

Roseville Ewer, ...$137.50

Pottery Jar, Br. glaze w/ applied amber busts of George Washington, attrib. to Peters & Reed, 5½" H $82.50

Row 3, Left to Right

Fulper Pottery Vase, metallic glaze shades from pale amber to gunmetal w/ greenish streaks, 7¾" H . .$269.50

Gouda Pottery Vase, polychrome geometric design on a blk. ground, underglaze blue label & paper label, 6⅝" H $82.50

Silver Plated Desk Set, w/ swivel candle holders & clear cut ink 6½" H $192.50

Rookwood Vase, w/ running gr., red & blue glaze, "1914" mark, 8¾" H $357.50

Cowan Pottery Vase, metallic light blue w/ dripping dk. iridescent gunmetal color, chips on foot, 7"H $198.00

A-OH July 1996   Garth's Auction

Weathervane, running horse figure, full bodied w/ good detail, copper w/ old dk. patina & traces of gilt, bullet holes in body, 28" L $1,100

Blanket Chest, walnut w/ old worn finish, dovetailed case & molded edge lid, till missing, lid edge damaged & age cracks, 45½" W, 14½" D, 19¾" H $770.00

Tin Semi-circular Candle Lantern, w/ hinged door, (old glass has edge damage), conical vent top is punched, 12" H, plus ring handle $275.00

Ash Burl Bowl, w/ carved rim handles, 17" D, 7" H $770.00

Tin Candle Lantern, w/ star pierced design on pyramidal top, worn dk. br. japanning, mkd. "Boston, Mass", some soldered repairs, 11½" H, plus ring handle $165.00

Paul Revere type Barn Lanterns, two (one pictured), punched tin, blk. repaint, 14" H and 15" H, plus ring handles $220.00

Inlaid Wooden Checkerboard, maple, cherry, walnut & rosewood, wear & age cracks, 17¼" x 17¼" $330.00

Punched Tin Footwarmer, in mortised wooden frame w/ turned corner posts, worn old dk. finish, punched circle & heart pattern, 8⅝"x9⅞", 6½" H .$220.00

A-OH May 1996   Garth's Auction

Crock, mkd. "W.T. Moore, Middleburg, Summit Co. Ohio", cobalt blue brushed flower & "3", 11¼" H $330.00

A-OH July 1996   Garth's Auction

PA Rag Carpet, Five rolls (2 pictured), stripes of browns, blues & greys w/ warp stripes of beige, yellow, white & blue, unused, 37" W, rolls are of different lengths: 31', 13'10", 14'1", 13'3", & 13'9" $935.00

Curly Maple Bed, w/ turned posts & crest rails, old varnish finish, 51½" W, rpl. walnut side rails are 72" L, 42" H $550.00

Stoneware Crock, w/ brushed cobalt blue flower & "4", rim chips, 11½" H $165.00

Woven Splint Goose Feather Basket, w/ handles & lid, 24" H .$357.50

Stoneware Crock, w/ applied shoulder handle, mkd. "Whites Utica N.Y. 3", backwards looking bird in cobalt blue quill work, crack through decor. & rim repair, 10½" H $110.00

A-OH July 1996   Garth's Auction

Chippendale Slant Front Desk, maple w/ some curl & old mellow ref., w/ dovetailed case, four dovetailed overlapping drawers & hinged lid w/ fitted interior that consists of seven dovetailed drawers & pigeon holes, pine secondary wood, repl. brasses, 36" W, 19¼" D, 40½" H, 30½" writing height $5,500.00

Pewter Lamp, ear handle, unmarked Am., soldered reprs. around collar, 5¾" H, plus mismatched burner w/ snuffer caps $137.50

Pewter Teapot, "Savage #6" touch, some battering, lid finial wafer missing & split in bottom, 6¾" H $110.00

Pewter Lamp, ear handle, unmarked Am., some corrosion & burner damage, 5¾" H, w/ snuffer caps .$137.50

Pewter Basin, unmarked, 9" D 2¼" H $220.00

A-OH May 1996   Garth's Auction

Empire Chest, refin. cherry, curly maple & bird's eye maple, paneled ends, sleigh front pilasters & four dovetailed drawers, drawers are solid curly maple, 42" W, 52" H . . .$605.00

Alabaster Pedestal, w/ gr. coloring, edge chips, 40" H $357.50

Victorian Candlesticks, pair, brass, w/ beehive detail, one w/ pushup also has dents, 10⅞" H $203.50

"Sterling" Silver Candelabra, pair w/ weighted bases, 8¼" H . . .$192.50

"Sterling" Silver Bowls, two reticulated w/ paw feet, one w/ basket handles, 10.3 troy oz. total, 5¾" & 7¾" L $126.50

Victorian Candlesticks, pair, brass, 20th C., 10⅝" H $110.00

Basket Epergne, silver plated, engraved initials w/ date "Sept. 24", bowl is a bit crooked, 14¾" H .$77.00

Brass Andirons, pair, 20th C., dents, 18" H $27.50

Copper Tea Kettle, handle mkd. "Thomas Bishop, Clyde Place, Glasgow", minor dents, 11" H . . .$137.50

A-OH Mar. 1996   Garth's Auction

Row 1, Left to Right
Handcolored Lithograph by "Currier & Ives" "Great Eastern" w/ Teacher presentation inscription in margin, stains, beveled frame w/ orig. red flame graining, 13" H, 17" W .$522.00
Needlework Panel, sculptured relief scene of parrot on branch w/ berries hooked in wool yarn on black velvet, faded, 20" H, 14" W $214.50
Handcolored Lithograph by "Currier & Ives" "Hiawatha's Wedding", minor stains, 15" H, 18" W . .$330.00

Row 2, Left to Right
Set of Four Country Bamboo Windsor Side Chairs, old refinish, 17½" seat, 34½" H $1,034.00
Tilt Top Candlestand, ref. cherry & curly maple, repaired cracks in base of column where legs join & replaced two board top, 15¾" X 22", 30" H .$302.50
Staffordshire Watch Hutch, two children asleep in a grape arbor, edge damage, 8¾" H $275.00

A-OH Mar. 1996   Garth's Auction

Highback Rocker, old black repaint, gold striping w/ foliage detail & basket of fruit, replaced seat, 42½" H $115.50
Rack for Utensils or Game, pine w/ old green repaint & seven wrought iron hooks, 25" L $440.00
Commode, refinished pine, porcelain knobs, one drawer has repair to overlap, 27" W, top is 14" X 28½"", 26¾" H $247.50
Pair of Hogscraper Candlesticks w/ Push Ups & Lip Hangers, push ups mkd. "Nicholson & Hoole", bases dented, 9⅛" H $440.00
Early Wrought Iron Camp Stove or Brazier w/ Wooden Handle, the type used in Revolutionary war. 8" H $440.00
Cast Iron Doorstop, full bodied Boston Bull, original paint, 8¾" H $275.00

A-OH Mar. 1996   Garth's Auction

Weathervane Figure, primitive silhouette of a rooster in sheet iron, old dark pitted surface, 14" H . . .$297.00
Sewn Yarn & Rag Rug, hooked on canvas, shades of red, blue, brown and green on a multicolored, olive and brown background, worn, 24" H, 42" W $148.50
Bowback Windsor Side Chair, refinished, 16" seat, 36¾" H $176.00
Dough Box, poplar w/ old refinish & red painted interior, stains from use, one board top, 17½" X 38¾", 26¼" H $330.00
Punched Tin Footwarmer in Mortised Wooden Frame w/ Turned Corner Posts, old black repaint, punched hearts & circles, new base has been added, with pan, 9" L . .$357.50
Woven Splint Basket, dark stain w/ reddish orange & blue, wear & damage, 19½" L $71.50
Woven Spint Buttocks Basket w/ Eye of God Design at Handles, seven rib, some damage, 15" X 16½", 6½" H, plus bentwood handle. $71.50

A-OH Mar. 1996   Garth's Auction
Advertising Sign, reverse painted eglomise glass w/ silver gold & nacre, scene also has horse drawn street car, lumber wagon & steam locomotive, orig. oak frame, 30½" H, 46½" W . .$1,100
English Sideboard, refinished oak, made from old wood, 63" W, 19 D, 36" H $440.00

Country Store Tin Canister, polychrome repaint w/ gilding & original portrait transfer, "Defiance Mills Baking Powder, J. Rhodes & Co. Pittsburgh Pa", bottom has damage & some repairs made before repaint, 24½" H $467.50
Country Store Tin Canister, original black paint w/ polychrome facade & stenciled decoration, "Dunhams Concentrated Coconut", 12" H . . . . .N/S
Country Store Tin Canister, black repaint w/ polychrome gilt & original portrait transfer, "Allen Kirkpatrick & Co. Pittsburgh Pa", rotating label on top, some repair & top hinge is loose, 16" H $192.50
Country Store Tin Canister w/ Beveled Mirror, worn original black paint w/ stenciled decor., "Curry & Metzgar, Pittsburgh Pa", rotating label on top, cylinder lid is loose, 19½" H $302.50
Country Store Tin Canister, original black paint w/ stenciled decor. and portrait transfer, "American Can Co PA" and "Thos C. Jenkins, Pittsburgh Pa", rotating label on top, 16" H, dents & some wear. $577.50

A-MA Oct. 1995   Skinner, Inc.

Painted and Gilt Dec. Tavern Sign, N. Eng., 1845, minor restor., 43" H, 44" W. $5750.00

A-MA Jan. 1996   Skinner, Inc.

Shaker

39-Three Shaker Oval Covered Boxes, pine & maple, brown stain, 1⅝" H, 2⅛" H, 2⅝" H $345.00

79-Two Oval Covered Boxes, 1 pine, 1 maple, 2⅛" H, 2½" H $402.50

83-Oval Carrier, N.H. pine, maple or birch w/ash handle, 4"H, 13¼"L, 9" D $805.00

75-Oval Box, Pine & maple or birch, yellow paint, 1¼" H, 33/16" L, 21/16" D . . .$5,175.00

11-Oval Box, N.H. pine & maple, orig. orange stain, 2⅛" H, 5⅛" L, 3¼" D $3737.50

54-Oval Box, pine & maple, old red painted surface, 2⅞" H, 11" L, 7¾" D $345.00

1-Oval Box, N.H., pine & maple, orig. paint, 4¼"H, 11⅛"L, 7¾"D $10,925.00

25-Oval Box, pine & maple, olive green paint, 4⅝" H, 11⅜" L, 8½" D $1,265.00

43-Oval Box, pine & birch, yellow stain, 2" H, 4½ L, 2¾" D $373.75

69-Oval Box, pine & maple, orig. green paint, 2⅜"H, 6"L, 3⅝"D $5462.50

15-Oval Box, pine & maple, orig. yel.-green paint, 4⅝" H, 11⅞" L, 8⅛" D $1,725.00

35-Oval Box, pine & maple, brn. stain, 5⅜" H, 13¼" L, 9" D $431.25

100-Oval Carrier, c. 1840-70, pine, maple & ash handle, orig. yellow paint, inscribed, 3½" H, 12⅞" L, 9⅜" D, overall ht. 7¾" $28,750.00

18-Oval Carrier, pine, maple & ash handle, yel. paint, inscribed, 3⅝" H, 11" L, 8" D, overall 7⅝" $862.50

92-Round Covered Box, maple sides, pine top & bottom, dk. red over blue-grn, 4¾ H, 10¼" D $517.50

109-Oval Carrier, pine & birch, reddish-brn stain, 2⅜" H, 6⅜" L, 4⅛" D $402.50

A-VA Sept. 1995 Ken Farmer Auctions

Paint Decorated Wardrobe, GA, ca. 1840, red over mustard, simulates raised panels, yellow pine, 71¼" H, 47" W, 19¾" D 2,200.00

A-VA Sept. 1995 Ken Farmer Auctions

Rocking Chair, signed Hunzinger, NY, dated 1876, walnut w/ bamboo turnings, fabric covered woven metal strips on back & seat $110.00

Rocking Chair, signed Hunzinger, NY, dated 1876, walnut, finial top, bamboo turnings, fabric covered woven metal strips on back & seat $110.00

A-OH June 1996   Garth's Auction

Q.A. Tavern Table, pine w/ old worn blk. paint, age cracks and edge damage, one leg is broken & glued, 27¼" H $1,100.00

Pair of Pewter Candlesticks, one has pushup, 9⅞" H $231.00

Pewter Charger, touch marks for Gershom, Jones, worn & pitted surface, 13½" D $445.50

Pewter Tall Pot, "J. Munson" touch, Yalesville, CT, minor dents & sm. nick in bottom edge, handle repainted blk. 11⅜" H $220.00

Pewter Charger, eagle touch & "Boston", Thomas Badger, wear, scratches & pitting, 15" D . . .$522.50

A-KY Oct. 1995 Ken Farmer Auctions

Blanket Chest, PA, orig. green sponged paint decor. w/ red oval in center of front, orig. hinges & till lid, untouched, 26" H, 54" W, 21½" D $2,475.00

A-OH Jan. 1996   Garth's Auction

Checkerboard, plywood w/ applied gallery edge, old varnish & black paint, some wear, 18½" x 30" $99.00
Country stand, chestnut & pine w/ old worn dark varnish, Lancaster Co., PA, 20¼" x 21¼", 29¾" H .$176.00
Bowback Windsor Armchair, black repaint, reprs. & replm., turnings don't match & age cracks, 31½" H $247.50
Tramp Art Box, worn reddish varnish, 11½" L $115.50
Tole Coffee Urn, very worn black paint w/ gold striping & floral decor. w/ city scene, 19¾" H $357.50

A-OH July 1996   Garth's Auction

Two Piece Corner Cupboard, curly maple & walnut w/ old worn finish, partially removed, w/ dovetailed drawers in base, minor edge damage, 47¼" W, 88¾" H $4,510.00
Ovoid Stoneware Churn, w/ applied shoulder handles, mkd. "H. Purdy 4" (Ohio), cobalt blue brushed flower, crazed surface, chips & hairlines, 17½" H $440.00

A-OH Jan. 1996   Garth's Auction

Mule Chest, pine w/ old dark ref., int. lined w/ 1875 Boston newspaper, pieced reprs. to feet & drawer fronts, 40" W, 18" D, 34¾" H $522.50
Redware Loaf Pan, w/ coggeled rim, yellow slip decor., minor wear, scratches & chips, 10¾" x 15¾", 3" H $1,430.00
Woven Splint Buttocks Basket, 16 ribs & old dark finish, minor damage, 12" x 12", 5½" H $55.00
Eng. Footstool, hardwood w/ old dark worn finish, 13⅜" L . . .$132.00
Stoneware Jug, cobalt blue slip floral decor., sm. lip flakes, 11¾" H .$165.00

A-OH July 1996   Garth's Auction

Row 1, Left to Right
Two Turned Wooden Jars by Pease, old varnish finish 6" H & bulbous w/ old soft patina, age crack, 5¼" H . .$220.00
Box w/ Lift Out Fitted Tray, curly maple & old varnish finish, good striped figure, 11½" L $467.50
Two Turned Wooden Jars by Pease, old soft patina 4⅝" H & footed w/ old varnish finish, 6½" H $220.00
Row 2, Left to Right
Wrt. Iron Hanging Lighting Device, w/ adjustable sawtooth ratchet & two candle sockets, 19½" $660.00
Minature Blanket Chest, cherry w/ dovetailed drawer, lid, escutcheon missing, 10¼" W, 8" D, 8" H $1,265.00

A-OH July 1996   Garth's Auction

Bench, ref. pine, cut out ends are mortised through top, 12½" x 35½", 14" H $275.00
Tin Two Tube Candle Mold, w/ ear handle, 15½" H $302.50
Candle Mold, w/ twenty-four pewter tubes in wooden frame, pine & poplar w/old patina, 6½" x 22½", 18" H $962.50
Hog Scraper Candlestick, w/ push up & lip hanger, 6¼" H $165.00
Hog Scraper Candlestick, w/ push up & lip hanger, push up is an old replm., 6½" H $110.00
Hog Scraper Candlestick, w/ push up & lip hanger, push up is mkd., 6¾" H $137.50
Hog Scraper Candlestick, w/ push up, lip hanger missing, push up is mkd., base is loose, 5¼" H $60.50
Wrt. Iron Lighting Stand, w/ four scrolled feet, candle socket & spring clip socket, 17¾" H $412.50
Tin Candle Mold, twenty-four tube, w/ ear handle, 10" H $302.50
Tin Candle Mold, eight tube, w/ ear handle, 10⅜" H $247.50

◄

Turned Wooden Jary by Pease, soft finish, age cracks, 6⅝" H $275.00
Octagonal Sailor Art Box, w/ geometric designs in sea shells, one side has heart & flower, the other has "A Present from Barbados", mahogany case w/ glass, some shells are loose, 9" $1,430.00
Row 3, Left to Right
Turned Wooden Jar by Pease, old varnish finish & wire bale w/ wooden handle, minor age crack in base, lid has glued repairs, 7½" H $550.00
Miniature blanket chest, pine w/ old mellow refinishing, two false drawers & detachable lid w/ wooden hinges, some edge damage, 12¼" L . .$440.00
Redware Pitcher, w/ strap handle, tooled band at shoulder & lid, br. sponging w/ deep orange color, chips, 6½" H $192.50

A-OH Mar. 1996   Garth's Auction

Oil On Canvas, rebacked on cardboard w/ old patches & touch up restoration, face, collar & bonnet have a coat of shiny varnish that is not on the rest of the surface, 30" H, 23" W, modern frame is 34½" H, 28" W . . .$550.00

Queen Anne Mirror, molded frame & mahogany veneer crest, pine secondary wood, old finish, replaced glass & veneer repair, 27½" H, 17¼" W $220.00

English Country Chippendale Chest, pine w/ old mellow refinishing, bracket feet, five dovetailed drawers & molded edge top, replaced brasses, feet have old repairs, 30" W, top is 18" x 31¼", 30¾" H $1870.00

Fanback Windsor Side Chair, old ref. seat repair & one back post is ended out, 17½" seat, 35½" H $313.00

A-MA Jan. 1996   Skinner, Inc.

Shaker Lift-Top Chest & Cupboard, ca. 1840, Canterbury, N.H., pine, brass hardware, old varnish finish, ends of chest are dovetailed front and back, single board bottom to entire piece, salmon wash on back, interior has red wash, exterior old refinish with varnish, 63⅝" H, 81" L overall, 56⅝" L chest, 23¼" D $4,600.00

A-OH Mar. 1996   Garth's Auction

One Piece Stepback Wall Cupboard, cherry w/ old refinish, old glass, 44¼" W, 80½" H $2750.00

Overshot Woven 2 Pc. Coverlet, med. blue & white optical patt., minor stains, no fringe, 68" x 96" $220.00

Pair of Cast Aluminum Horse Heads "J.E. Burke Co, Fond du Lac, Wis", traces of paint, 14½" L .$220.00

Cast Iron Windmill Weight, rooster w/ old white, red, green & yellow repaint, Elgin Wind Power & Pump Co, Elgin, Ilinois, 16" H $660.00

Child's Push Sleigh, red repaint w/ painted flowers, orig. upholstery, some age cracks & damage, 46" L .$467.50

A-OH Mar. 1996   Garth's Auction

Decorated Empire Chest of Drawers, pine w/ original red flame graining, wooden knobs old replacements, one scrolled end of crest broken & glued, 41½" W, 47" H overall. $660.00

Hepplewhite Wingback Armchair, 48" H $660.00

Two Kugels, w/ Brass Hangers, green 3½" D, and gold (silvering worn) 2⅝" D $82.50

Rose Medallion Chop Plate, 16¼" D $550.00

Large Silver Kugel, w/ Brass Fastener, 10" D $137.50

A-OH Mar. 1996   Garth's Auction

Pieced & Appliqued Rug w/ wool hexagons w/ contrasting embroidery, wear & red yarn edging replaced, 42" x 83" $110.00

Blanket Chest, pine w/ worn red graining w/ stamped design over yellow ground & black painted trim, dovetailed case & bracket feet w/ till, lid has repaired crack, replaced hinges, top is worn down to yellow ground color, 49¾" W,22¾" D, 24¼" H $275.00

Yellowware Flower Pot w/ Attached Saucer Base, Dalton Ohio, molded design w/ white & green glaze, very minor rim chip, 9⅞" H $137.50

Dalton Ohio Yellowware Flower Pot w/ Attached Saucer Base, molded design w/ white & green glaze, 5½" H $82.50

Burl Bowl, ash burl w/ worn surface, rim has edge wear & notch that has smoothly worn edges, old varnish, 16" D, 7½" H $770.00

A-VA Sept. 1995 Ken Farmer Auctions

Pie Safe, Scott Co., VA, ca. 1830-50, walnut, poplar secondary, punched eagle tines, one replaced foot, drawer sides replaced, 48½" H, 45" W, 17" D $660.0

A-MA Jan. 1996   Skinner, Inc.

Wood Box, pine, old gray-green paint over red, iron hinges & hooks, 30¾" H, 23¾" W, 16¼" D $3220.00

Cupboard, ca. 1870, pine, orig. bright yellow stain, replm. iron latch, 27½"H, 25½" W, 17⅜" D $1955.00

Work Chair, maple and pine, leather seat, seat ht. 27¾", 40¾" H .$1840.00

Foot Stool, pine, brown stain, 9½" H, 14¾" W, 8" D $747.50

A-OH July 1996   Garth's Auction

Carved Wooden Cookie Board, birch w/ old varnish finish, man on horse back w/ flag, reverse has rooster & hen, age cracks & a few worm holes., mkd. "F.E.", 9¾" H, 6" W $467.50

Burl Butter Paddle, w/ crook end, old varnish finish, 10" L $220.00

Two Curly Maple Utensils, dipper w/ crook handle & old varnish, age cracks in bowl & handle (pictured), 11¼" L & butter paddle w/ soft finish & bird head handle, chips on bowl (not pictured) $187.00

Herb Grinder, mortar & pestle w/ mortar that has table clamp, hardwood w/ old varnish finish, worm holes in mortar, 5¾" plus thumb screw$302.50

A-OH July 1996   Garth's Auction

One Pc. Step Back Wall Cupboard, pine w/ old mellow refin., some edge damage, 28¼" W, 81½" H . . .$2,860.00

Stoneware Jug, w/ strap handle, mkd. "Edmands & Co", polka dot bird on branch in cobalt blue quill work, hairlines, 11½" H $770.00

Stoneware Butter Crock, w/ lid & applied shoulder handles, cobalt blue brushed leaf designs w/ blue at handles, hairline & edge chips, mismatched lid, 12" D, 8" H $660.00

Stoneware Ovoid Jar, w/ cobalt blue brushed flowers w/ blue at handles, minor rim chip, 9¾" H $550.00

_____

 ◄

Wafer Iron, w/ round cast iron ends that have good eagle & shield design w/ "E. Pluribus Unum", wrt. iron handles, 27" L $467.50

Round Wooden Butter Print, deeply carved swan, old finish w/ varnish, edge damage, age cracks & small hole, 5½" D $137.50

Two Treen Utensils, w/ old patina, taster w/ long curved handle, 11" L & sm. butter paddle w/ birds head handle, 7¾" L $440.00

Two Treen Utensils, w/ old patina, spoon w/ elongated bowl, 11½" L & butter paddle w/ long handle, minor damage on side of bowl, 11½" L$99.00

A-OH July 1996   Garth's Auction

Bentwood & Woven Splint Cheese Sieve, 23" D $121.00

Painted Checkerboard, old worn red & blk., 15" x 25" $550.00

PA Dry Sink, poplar w/ old wrn orange grained repaint, hardware repl., 66" W, 19" D, 47½" H $2,585.00

Graduated Copper Pitchers, assembled set of nine, minor repr., 2¼" to 10" H $478.50

Rockingham Covered Jar, molded ribs, lid has chips & hairline, 8⅜" H $110.00

Brass Bed Warmer, w/ tooled bird & flowers on lid & turned wooden handle, repr. in bowl, 41" L $214.50

A-OH July 1996   Garth's Auction

English Gate Leg Table, oak w/ old dk. finish, old reprs., 16" x 45", 27¾" H $385.00

Dovetailed Copper Pots, assembled set of six, w/ ear handles, 8¾" H to 5½" H $605.00

Copper Pans, graduated set of six, w/ cast iron handles, 4¾" D to 2⅛" D $247.50

Dovetailed Copper, two pieces, cylindrical pot w/ lid & flared pot w/ pouring spout, mkd. "Thos Mills & Bros.,.Philada.", 8¼" D $220.00

Skimmer, w/ wrt. iron handle & large copper bowl, some old alterations & repr., 24½" D $104.50

A-PA Oct. 1995   Pook & Pook, Inc.

Oil on Canvas, English, tavern scene, late 18th c., 17" x 23" $850.00
Chippendale Slant Front Desk, Lancaster Co., PA, secret compartment, ca. 1780, 44¾" H, 38" W $8,000.00
Corner Cupboard, pine, ca. 1780, approx. 78½" H, 38" W $3,000.00
Theorem, watercolor on paper w/gilt frame, 19th c., 12¾" x 14" ...$450.00
Flemish Tapestray Fragment, depicting a king w/scepter on throne w/lady kneeling, surrounded by court figures & flowers, 17th c., 5'6" x 1'5¾" $550.00

A-PA Oct. 1995   Pook & Pook, Inc.

Chippendale Mahogany Mirror, w/carved crest, retaining old glass, ca. 1780, 38¾" H $375.00
George II Mahogany Mirror, w/gilt decor., approx. 60" H $6,000.00
Chippendale Mahogany Mirror, w/ gilded crest, ca. 1780, 33" H $1,300.00
Q.A. Mahogany Side Chairs, ca. 1770, pr., ...$3,750.00
Q.A. Mahogany Bachelor's Chest, w/pull out slide above 3 grad. drawers, ca. 1760, 30" H, 31¾" W ...$1,700.00
Georgian Mahogany Tea Caddy, together w/carved wooden candlestick (not shown) $225.00

A-PA Oct. 1995   Pook & Pook, Inc.

Georgian Mahogany Knife Boxes, w/inlaid rosettes, 15¼" H ..$1,500.00
Hepplewhite Sideboard, mahogany, w/line inlaid front, banded cuffs, ca. 1790, 56¼" W $3,750.00
Chinese Porcelain Nanking Dinner Service, (3 illus.), w/cobalt blue floral medallions & banding, comprising: platter w/liner, cider jug (damage), 4 veg. dishes (1 w/cover), 2 covered sauce tureens, 3 undertrays, deep dish, sm. plate, 12 plates w/chips, pr. of leaf dishes & creamer $2,000.00
Brass Sextant, w/sm. mahogany case w/inscription, London, 19th c. $375.00

A-OH July 1996   Garth's Auction

Watercolor on Paper, of two blk. chickens, paper has stains & short tear, 11½" H, 18" W $467.50
Ladderback Armchair Rocker, old ref. & repl. woven cane seat, rockers added & one arm repl. 38" H .$121.00
Country Washstand, walnut, partially stripped of old varnish, 26" W, 15½" D, 35¼" H $385.00
Wooden Birdcage, w/ wire bars, old gr. paint w/ br. glaze, clear blown water fountain, 10¼" x 15", 18" H ...$313.50
Brass Swift on Marble Base, acorn finial, 14¼" H $247.50

A-OH July 1996   Garth's Auction

Decorated Settle Bench, orig. grey paint w/ light grey seat, striping is blk. & dk. grey w/ stenciled & freehand flowers & fruit w/ angel wing crest designs, minor repr. on one arm, 80" L $2,090.00
Three Decoys: two Redhead drakes w/ wooden bodies & molded heads by Herters, working repaint, 16" L & Pintail Drake w/ glass eyes & orig. paint, 18" L $280.50
Round Woven Splint Basket, w/ twelve melon ribs, old patina, 9½" H plus bentwood handle $220.00
Oblong Bentwood Box, w/ laced seams, pine w/ worn old blue paint, edge damage, 14¾" L $247.50
Woven Splint Buttocks Basket, 20 ribs, old patina, some damage, 14" x 15", 9" H plus bentwood handle $66.00

A-OH July 1996   Garth's Auction

Cast Iron Garden Bench, mkd. on seat "Mfg by the Kramer Bros. Fdy Co. Cayton, O.", white repaint, 43" L $1,017.50
Cast Iron Garden Bench, good fern detail, reprs., white repaint, 58½" L $220.00

A-OH July 1996   Garth's Auction

Wall Cupboard, two piece, walnut w/ old ref., dovetailed cases w/ paneled doors set in beaded frames & two dovetailed drawers w/ cock beading, pine secondary wood, some edge damage, repl. hardware & lock missing from top drawer, 46" W base is 17½" x 47½", 80½" H $1,045.00
Dome Top Tôle Box, worn orig. dk. br. japanning w/ stylized floral decor. in red, white, yellow & gr., lid has oval brass bale handle, hasp is incomplete, 10" L $118.50
Dome Top Tôle Box, worn orig. dk. br. japanning w/ stylized floral decor., in red, white, gr. & yellow, some seams loose, 9¾" L $104.50
Dome Top Tôle Box, orig. dk. br. japanning w/ floral decor. in gr., red, blk. & white, some wear, 9" L .$88.00

A-OH July 1996   Garth's Auction

Wrt. Iron & Brass Utensil Set, w/ simple tooling on handles, 24¾" L $275.00
Long Handeled Wooden Dipper, old dk. finish, 45" L $247.50
Three Pieces of PA Woven Rag Carpet, w/ similar stripes in reds & olive gr., worn & damage, 2'11" x 10'2" x 6'3" and 2'11" x 4'6" $110.00
Bench, walnut w/ soft natural patina & water stains, curved front corners on seat, 13¾" x 63", 17¾" H $368.50
Sugar Bucket, all wooden stave constructed, w/ branded label "C. & A. Wilder, So Hingham, Mass", 9¾" H $247.50
Wrt. Iron Toaster, w/ scrolled detail, 17" L $275.00
Apothecary Case of Drawers, pine w/ worn ref. w/ stains, drawers have some reprs. both to faces & interiors, 19¾" W, 23⅔" H $1,155.00
Two Wrt. Iron Broilers, w/ shaped handles, square w/ removable drip pan 11" x 12" & round w/ rotary top 12" D, size plus handles $440.00
Doll Size Cradle, pine w/ old dk. red finish, 9½" x 19" $104.50

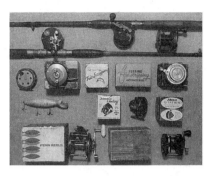

A-OH July 1996   Garth's Auction

Two Split Bamboo Rods, one w/ Ocean City reel, the other w/ Vomhofe reel, 73", 67" L $247.50
"Pennell Supra" Brass Reel, ca. 1890's $27.50
Five Fly Fishing Reels, four automatic, "Ocean City", "Oren-O-Matic", "Perrine Free Stripping", "H-I, Utica NY" & "Hovrocks Ibbotson", four have boxes $38.50
Wooden Muskie Lure, w/ worn orig. yellow & orange paint, 8" L . . .$27.50
Two Johnson Spinning Reels, closed face, in boxes $16.50
Two Reels, in boxes, "Hovrocks-Ibbotson" (Salt water No. 181) & "Penn" (410 Senator No. 113H) $27.50

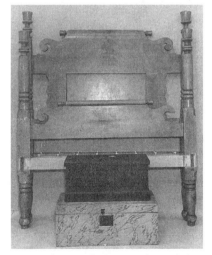

A-OH APR. 1996   Garth's Auction

Pennsylvania Grain Painted Rope Bed, poplar w/ orig. br. yellow graining on a white ground, 50" x 70½", 62¾" H, minor wear, footboard has age crack $770.00
Painted Box, pine w/ orig. gr. paint & blk. label "Bates & Co. 1860", 10¼" x 11½" x 23" $330.00
Decorated Box, pine w/ orig. blk. freehand marbling on white ground, inside of lid signed in pencil "Samuel Jameson", initials "AG" & "1823" are hidden in the painted design, wrt. iron lock w/ hasp, 10½" x 14" x 26¾" $1,430.00

A-OH June 1996   Garth's Auction

Country Kitchen Wall Cupboard, two piece, ref. pine w/ pullout bin, reconstr. w/ old alterations to both pieces, 48½"W, 18"D, 71½"H . .$385.00
Blue & White Sponge Spatter Stoneware Crock, brown Albany slip interior, sm. chips & hairline, 7¾" D, 7¼" H $110.00
Blue & White Sponge Spatter Pitcher, w/ blue flower, chip on base, 9" H $335.50
Blue & White Sponge Spatter Pitcher, w/ molded horizontal ribs, rim hairline at handle, 9" H . .$192.50
Spatterware Bowl $250.00

A-OH July 1996   Garth's Auction

Decorated Hanging Spice Box, pine w/ orig. salmon pink paint w/ striping in blk., yellow & red, polychrome floral decoration on lid, ends & front surface, w/ hinged lid & two nailed drawers w/ porcelain pulls, varnish is alligatored, poplar secondary wood, 13" W, 7½" D, 15½" H $19,250.00

A-OH July 1996   Garth's Auction

Homespun Linen Tablecloth, br. & natural, machine sewn hem & off center seam, 57½" x 74" $137.50
Set of Shelves, hardwood w/ old gr. paint, 24" W, 9" D, 28" H $522.50
Round Woven Splint Basket, attrib. to the Shakers, bentwood rim handles, break in bottom, 9" D, 5" H . .$302.50
Oblong Woven Splint Basket, attrib. to the Shakers, 6½" x 5¼", 3½" H plus bentwood handle $165.00
Three Pieces: round woven splint basket w/ bentwood rim handles, dk. patina w/ blue & yellow, 12" D; not pictured, woven cane cheese sieve basket, w/ damage, 7¼" D & a bentwood sieve w/ woven poplar splint, 12" D $93.50
Oblong Woven Splint Basket, attrib. to the Shakers, blue woven bands, some pencil scribbles, 4¼" H . .$93.50

A-OH July 1996   Garth's Auction

Early Miniature Slant Front Desk, maple w/ old mellow ref., dovetailed case, 3 dovetailed overlapping drawers, hinged lid & fitted interior w/ pigeon holes, lid has butterfly hinges, engraved brass hardware, pine secondary wood, reprs., edge damage & age cracks, 19" W, 13" D, 19½" H $1,430.00

Redware Pie Plate, w/ coggeled edge, three line yellow slip decor., old chips & hairline, 10" D $220.00

Chalk Cat, red, yellow & blk. decor. has wear, 9½" H $715.00

Three Small Pieces of Chalk, bird w/ yellow & blk., 4¼" H; pear bank in red, blk. & gr., 4" H & dog in gr., red & blk., 4¼" L $412.50

A-VA Aug. 1995 Ken Farmer Auctions

Westmoreland County, PA Fraktur, "Johannes Sell, 1823", green, red & blue tulips, exc., period red & yel. paint decor. frame, 15" H, 12½" W $3,850.00

A-PA Apr. 1996   Pook & Pook Inc.

Row 1
Taufshein, attrib. to Friederich Speyer, watercolor, dated 1784, 13" x 6" . .
. . . .$3,750.00
Taufshein, Franklin Co. PA, watercolor, dated 1800, 12½" x 15¼" . . . .
. . . .$2,250.00
Row 2
Taufshein, Johannes Bard, York Co., PA, hand drawn watercolor, sgn., 13" x 15¾" $6,000.00
Taufshein, Friederich Speyer, Lancaster Co., PA, watercolor/pen & ink, dated 1768 . . . .$6,000.00

A-OH Jan. 1996   Garth's Auction

Country Jelly Cupboard, ref. walnut, sm. pieced repr., MO, 40½" W, 17¾" D, 48½" H, 55½" at gallery $990.00
Tin Candle Lanterns, 2, w/ punched designs & 3 glass "windows" & hinged door, cracked glass, other minor damage, 12" & 10" H plus handle .$385.00
Tin Lantern, N.E. Glass Co., base dented, 11" H plus handle . . .$154.00
Tin Lanterns, 2, traces of blue paint, 13½" H plus handle $484.00
Tin Tube Candle Mold, w/ double ear handles, battered & several loose tubes, 11¾" H $126.50

A-OH July 1996   Garth's Auction

Row 1, Left to Right

Lehn Ware Covered Footed Jar, red, blue & pink paint w/ strawberries & foilage in red, gr., yellow & blk., wear but good color, 4¾" H $1,265.00

Lehn Ware Egg Cup, red & pink w/ tulips & foliage in pink, gr., yellow & blk., interior is yellow, some wear, 3" H $880.00

Lehn Ware Cup & Saucer, yellow w/ strawberries & foliage in red, gr., blue, white & yellow, pencil presentation inscription on bottom dated "1881", wear $2,530.00

Lehn Ware Dish, pink w/ flowers & foliage in gr., red, white & yellow, old worn paper label "Made by Joseph Lehn in his 93 year, March 3, 1888", wear, 2⅞" D $1,045.00

Lehn Ware Covered Jar, pink w/ polychrome flowers, strawberries on lid & striping in red, gr., & blk., wear, 4½" H $880.00

Lehn Ware Covered Footed Jar, pink & red & polychrome flowers, strawberries on lid & striping in red & gr., wear & foot is chipped, 4½" H $220.00

Row 2

Two Pieces: Chinese woven rice straw basket w/ double lids, minor damage, 3⅜" H, plus handle & a miniature turned wooden bucket w/ orig. yellow paint w/ blk. striping, wire bale & wooden handle, 2⅜" H . . .$165.00

Noah's Ark, w/ thirty-seven animals & two women, ark is wood w/ worn straw inlay, animals are carved wood w/ polychrome paint, some damage & missing limbs, several from another set, 8" L $330.00

Row 3

Two Pieces: poplar box w/ worn red sponging on a yellow ground, minor edge damage, 3½" D, 3½" H, & an oblong bentwood box w/ worn wallpaper covering, dk. blue w/ faded colors, age crack, 7½" L $357.50

Two Pottery Banks, w/ orig. red paint, apple 3" H, & jug (handle may have repr.), 4⅜" H, both have some wear $220.00

A-PA Oct. 1995   Pook & Pook, Inc.

Cigar Store Indian, w/polychrome decor., on br. base inscribed "7-20-4 R.G. Sullivan's", early 20th c., 48" H $9,000.00

Wooden Rooster, hand carved w/polychrome decor, early 19th c., 6¼" H, together w/ oval storage box $700.00

Soap Hollow, PA, sm. storage chest w/orig. red paint & blue trim, 19th c., 9" H., 12½" W. $1,900.00

Theorem, oil on velvet w/fruit, black & gilt painted frame, 19th c. $625.00

Dower Chest, PA German, decor. & dated 1803, 27½" D, 50" L $3,500.00

Weathervane, molded copper running stag., 19th c., 28" H, 30" L $1,300.00

Stoneware Jar, gray w/floral decor., 10½" H . . . . .N/S

Stoneware Jar, gray w/ blue floral decor., 10½" H $325.00

Stoneware Pitcher, gray w/extensive cobalt blue decor, 8" crack, ca. 1840, 16½" H $1,400.00

Stoneware Pitcher, gray w/ blue floral decor., 1 gal, 10¾" H $800.00

Redware Vase, w/mottled gr. & br. glaze by Jacob Medinger, 11" H . . .$800.00

Stoneware Crock, 6 gal. w/blue floral banding, ca. 1840, 8" H $600.00

Felt Parade Fire Hat, Phil., painted & decor., ca. 1850 . . . .$2,500.00

Redware Pie Plates, PA, 2 w/ylw. slip decor., early 19th c., 8¼" diam. . .$700.00

N.J. Watercolor on Paper, from song book, w/hand colored face, pin wheels & trailing vines, early 19th c., 7½" x 11¼" $500.00

A-OH July 1996   Garth's Auction

Row 1, Left to Right

Pottery Spout Lamp, buff clay w/ br. flecks, chips, 8" H $275.00

Redware Ovoid Jug, w/ strap handle, clear glaze w/ good deep org. color & dk. br. splotches, chips, 5¾" H $275.00

Redware Ovoid Jug, w/ strap handle & incised straight & wavy lines w/ brownish amber spotted glaze, 4⅞" H $165.00

Redware Toddy Plate, clear glaze w/ light amber color, 4⅞" D $165.00

Redware Toddy Plate, clear glaze w/ deep orange color & br. spatter, sm. edge chips, 6⅜" D $71.50

Row 2, Left to Right

Redware Ovoid Jug, w/ strap handle, greenish orange glaze w/ br. flecks, chips on base & handle, 8¼" H $165.00

Miniature Redware Ovoid Jugs, pr., w/ strap handles, br. flecked glaze, wear & chips, 2½" H, 4¼" H . $165.00

Redware Turks Head Food Mold, gr. glaze w/ amber & orange spots, hairline & edge wear, 10¾" D, 5" H $49.50

Miniature Pottery, two pieces, redware jar w/ applied handles, chips, 3⅛" H & buff clay jug w/ strap handle, reddish br. mottled glaze, 3" H . .$330.00

Redware Ovoid Jar, greenish glaze w/ orange spots, wear & sm. flakes, 8¼" H $220.00

A-OH Nov. 1995   Garth's Auction

Pewter Candlesticks w/ Mismatched Bobeche, similar pr., one has repaired break where stem meets base, unmarked, 8½" H. $55.00

Pewter Charger, faint crowned rose mark, wear, knife scratches, repaired split in rim along booge, 12⅛" D. $110.00

Pewter Tall Pot, "R. Dunham" touch, (Rufus Dunham, Westbrook, Maine), damage along bottom edge, hole base of spout and hinge is loose, 11¾" H. . .$55.00

Pewter Charger, wear and scratches w/ small splits in rim, unmarked, stamped and tooled initials in bottom 11⅞" D. $49.50

Pennsylvania Work Table, ref. walnut w/ inlay on drawers, two dovetailed overlapping drawers and removable three board top, pine secondary wood, orig. oval brasses, sides of drawer have been gnawed and large drawer has replaced bottom, 32¼" W, 52¾" L, 29" H. $2530.00

Ovoid Stoneware Jug w/ Strap Handle, impresed label "I.M. Mead, Mogadore, Ohio", 15¼" H $247.50

Cast Iron Coffee Grinder, "Enterprise Mfg. Co. Philadelphia", worn orig. red and black paint w/ decals, wooden base, 12½" H. $522.50

Stoneware Jug w/ Strap Handle, cobalt blue brushed floral design with "3", small flake on base, 15" H. $137.50

A-MA Oct. 1995   Skinner, Inc.

Silver Plated Lantern, Am., late 19th c., with acid etched blue-to-clear shade, presentation plaque reads, "Evening Record Prize Lantern, number of votes 115537, 1890", 11¼" H $977.50

A-MA Mar. 1996   Skinner, Inc.

Commode, Biedermeier, Fruitwood, Part-Ebonized & Parcel Gilt, early 19th C., 33¾" H, 40 L, 21½" D 3,737.50

A-OH Mar. 1996   Garth's Auction

Copper Weathervane Figure, running horse, very battered w/ bullet holes, incomplete, 32" L $192.50

Empire Two Part Mirror, gilded pilastered corner blocks, orig. reverse painting w/ two children, repl. mirror, gilt has wear & overpaint & reverse painting has some flaking, 34" H, 15½" W $247.50

Country Sheraton Chest, ref. walnut w/ inlaid curly maple escutcheons, paneled ends & four dovetailed drawers w/ beaded edges, secondary wood walnut, brasses & escutcheons are replaced, 39" W, top is 18½" x 40", 39½" H $660.00

Two Child Size Chairs, English Windsor w/ worn black paint, 12½" seat, 24" H, & American, Hitchcock type w/ partial old repaint & replaced cane seat, 13½" seat, 25¾" H $770.00

Seven Gaudy Ironstone Plates, w/ rose dec. in red, blue, green & black, lion & unicorn mark w/ "England", similar but marks differ, some wear & a few chips, 8⅞" D $192.50

Six Gaudy Ironstone Handleless Cups & Saucers, similar but not matching. $132.00

Pearlware Teapot, w/ red striping & strawberry dec. in red, green, yellow & black, impressed "Davenport", wear, small chips & hairlines, lid has old yellowed repair, 7¾" H $220.00

Two Gaudy Dutch Plates: urn, 9⅞" D, & dove, 8⅛" D, both are very worn w/ scratches & stains, larger has rim chips. $412.50

Two Cast Iron Doorstops w/ Old Polychrome, wear, basket of flowers, 9½" H & tulip, 8½" H $253.00

Four Cast Iron Doorstops, baskets & urns of flowers w/ old worn polychrome, one is marked "Hubley", 6¼" to 7¼" H $330.00

A-OH Mar. 1996   Garth's Auction

Sheraton Chest, refinished cherry w/ banded veneer around base, paneled ends, molded stiles & four dovetailed drawers w/ edge beading, orig. oval brasses, poplar secondary wood, 41¾" W, 44½" H $1,100.00

A-OH Mar. 1996   Garth's Auction

Pieced Quilt, flying geese bands in multi-colored prints & solids w/ red calico bars, minor stains, 78" x 88"$275.00

PA Work Table, walnut w/ old refinish, dovetailed drawers & removable four board poplar top, repairs, feet replaced, drawer overlaps restored & top replaced, brasses replaced, 35" x 66", 29½" H $990.00

Hanging Cupboard, pine w/ old olive green paint, dovetailed case, back edge of top has damage, 18¼" W, 9" D, 18½" H $412.50

Child's Sled, w/ All Wooden Construction & Steel Tipped Runners, top painted red w/ stenciled & freehand floral decoration in gold, black, maroon & white, 34" L $517.00

Three Staffordshire Handleless Cups & Saucers, dark blue transfer: two mkd. "Adams", third is unmarked, small edge chips $330.00

Staffordshire Sugar Bowl, w/ dark blue transfer & teapot w/ scene by "J. Hall & Sons", both have damage & repairs. $357.00

Staffordshire Platter, dark blue transfer "R. Hall's Select Views Church of St. Charles & Polytechnic School, Vienna, Germany", wear & scratches, 19" L $495.00

A-OH Mar. 1996   Garth's Auction

Empire Chest of Drawers, poplar w/ old alligatored red finish, gold stenciled designs on pilaster, brass pulls w/ clear ribbed glass inserts, added castors, 41" W, 49½" H $1,100.00

German Pewter Flagon, battered & lid has damage, 10⅝" H $82.50

Dome Top Hide Covered Box, w/ Worn Red & White Leather Trim, Brass Tacks & Brass Bale Handle, lined w/ 1823 newspaper & printed English label "W. Chapple Junr...", wear, 12" L $60.50

Pewter Teapot, "J.H. Palethorp, Philada", worn & battered w/ soldered repair, finial wafer incomplete, 9⅞" H $165.00

A-OH Mar. 1996   Garth's Auction

A-OH Mar. 1996   Garth's Auction

Chippendale Scroll Mirror, walnut w/ old finish, molded frame & applied composition eagle on crest, old repairs & replacements, mirror replaced, 29¼" H, 15¾" W $330.00

Framed Lace Collar & Cuffs, three dimensional vintage design piece in center, old gilt frame. $165.00

Hepplewhite Pembroke Table, mahogany w/ inlay & old finish, one dovetailed drawer, inlay consists of banding around feet & apron ends w/ diamonds on posts, attributed to New York State, minor inlay damage, 28¼" H $1,870.00

Wrought Iron Kettle Stand, w/ decor. cast iron grill top, 9½"x15" . . .$357.00

Oil on Wooden Panel, Dutch landscape w/ windmill, initialed in lower right, 20th ca., 19" H, 27" W, framed, 24¾" H, 32¾" W $165.00

Country Chippendale Tavern Table, maple & pine w/ old worn refinishing, square molded legs, mortised & pinned stretcher base & apron & one dovetailed drawer, two board breadboard top w/ some surface burns, top is loose, 26¼" x 35¾", 28" H . . .$522.50

Banister Back Armchair, old black repaint, 10" of each leg is ended out, one arm has repair where it meets back post & back posts have spliced repairs, old rush seat, 18½" seat, 46½" H $660.00

Sewerpipe Rabbit Bank, initialed "R.L" 10" L $385.00

Stoneware Jar w/ Applied Shoulder Handles & Lid, impressed label "John Burger, Rochester", feather wreath & 2" in cobalt blue quill work, 11" H$330.00

A-OH Mar. 1996   Garth's Auction

Two Handcolored Lithographs: "My Little White Kittens Taking the Cake" by Currier & Ives, C#4338, stains & tears in the margins & "Home & Friends' by "Kellogg", paper has darkened, both are framed, 15½" H, 19½" W & 12½" H, 16⅝" W $385.00
Country Table, hardwood & pine w/ red repaint on base, stretcher base & mortised apron, hree board top, wear, age cracks & edge damage, 24¼" x 44½", 28" H $660.00
Built in Cupboard, refinished pine, one dovetailed drawer & paneled door set in beaded frames, door lock missing, 19" W, 33¼" H, 15" D . . .$385.00
Stave Constructed Oil Can w/ Steel Bands, old red paint w/ black stenciled label "Kerosene Oil", brass spigot, paint has touch up repair, 13" H $159.00
Dovetailed Dough Box, poplar w/ worn yellow & green repaint, 30½" L $192.50

A-MA Aug. 1995   Skinner, Inc.

Left to Right
Austrian Faux Burl Wood Grained Automobile-Form Box, 20th c., w/ 2 hinged lids, 11" L $546.25
Fruit Wood Tea Caddy, 19th c., 5½" H $230.00
Late Georgian Apple-Shaped Tea Caddy, pear wood, early 19th c., foil lined int., 4½" H $1,495.00

A-OH Mar. 1996   Garth's Auction

Sampler, silk on linen homespun, vining border, stylized flowers & trees in pots, birds, squirrel, crowns, alphabets, verse & "Alice Stephenson Aged 8 years, born Sep 14, 1792", shades of green, brown, blue, white & gold, blue border colors have bled along bottom edge, framed, 19½" H, 19½" W $660.00
Pair of Handcolored English Engravings of American Scenes, published 1798, I. Stockdale, Piccadilly, "View of Mount Vernon" & "View on the Patowmac (sic) River", matted & framed, 11½" H, 13¼" W $330.00
Pair of Cast Iron Andirons, fancy scroll designs, one foot replaced, 14¼" H $71.50
Banister Back Armchair, hardwood w/ worn black repaint, repairs & replm. & feet are ended out, paper rush seat, 16½" seat, 45¾" H $495.00
Sewerpipe Squirrel, hand molded & tooled w/ green painted eyes, 11" H $181.50

A-MA Oct. 1995   Skinner, Inc.

Tiffany Desk Set w/ gilt bronze zodiac patt., each piece impressed "Tiffany Studios New York" & numbered $1,265.00
Tiffany Bronze & Favrile Glass Counterbalance Lamp, impressed "Tiffany Studios New York" 15½" H, shade 3¾" D $2,645.00

A-OH Mar. 1996   Garth's Auction

Country Sheraton Chest of Drawers, ref. cherry & walnut, turned legs, paneled ends, four dovetailed drawers w/ edge beading & rounded edge top, replaced brasses & locks removed, poplar secondary wood, minor repairs & top reattached, 39¼" W, top is 19" x 40½", 44" H $550.00

Two Handcolored Lithographs, by "N. Currier", "English Snipe", (presentation inscription title) & "Quails" both have minor stains, old beveled frames, 12⅜" H, 16½" W $308.00

Empire Sewing Rocker, curly maple w/ old finish, good detail, cane seat. $148.50

Applique Penny Rug w/ Tab Border, wool, felt & velvet in dark colors on a white flannel ground, minor wear & stains, 41" x 17½" plus tab fringe. $165.00

Large Stuffed Rabbit by Steiff, articulated head, arms & feet have platinum mohair, legs are plush, body is white cotton, glass eyes &"Steiff" ear botton, pink embroidered nose is replaced, mohair has wear as does old blue dress. (dress is not orig.) 31" H $522.50

Santa Claus, red satin suit w/ white mohair trim, black composition boots & white flannel hands, face is molded fabric w/ painted detail & white beard, used in Hudson's store display, Detroit, ca: 1915, minor wear, 27½" H $357.50

Goose Pull Toy by Steiff, white & black mohair w/ leather beak & glass eyes, steel frame w/ wooden wheels, "Steiff" button on underside, worn, red leather surface on head (above beak) is old replacement & eyes are reattached or replaced, 21" L $275.00

Green Feather Christmas Tree, orig. base w/ stenciled roping in red & green on a white ground base marked "Made in Germany", wear & damage, 46" H $247.50

A-OH Mar. 1996   Garth's Auction

European Two Piece Cupboard, pine w/ natural finish, paneled construction w/ good architechural details, three drawers, wire nail construction, 52" W, cornice is 28½" x 57", 80½" H $715.00

Jacquard Two Piece Single Weave Coverlet, floral medallions in red, navy blue, olive gold & natural white, corners dated 1855, 70" x 88" $225.00

All Wooden Toddler Walker, w/ Chicken Heads, worn polychrome, "Rock-A-Tot", 30" L $115.50

Stoneware Churn, w/ Wooden & Cast Iron Frame, "Red Wing", wood has old red, chips on lid, iron has patent date '94, 45½" H $247.50

A-OH Mar. 1996   Garth's Auction

Handcolored Lithograph, by "Kellogg & Bulkeley", "Our Pony", stains, curly maple beveled frame w/ old alligatored varnish finish, 16¼" H, 12" W . .$99.00

Handcolored Lithograph, by Currier & Ives, "The Little Drummer Boy, Rub-A-Dub-Dub", stains & paper creases, modern frame, 18" H, 15" W .$115.50

Handcolored Lithograph, (unmark.), "Uncle Tom & Little Eva", minor stains, framed, 15" H, 10⅞" W $71.50

Country Empire Chest of Drawers, ref. cherry & curly maple, paneled ends, 52½" H overall. $825.00

Set of 4 Sabre Leg Side Chairs w/ Caned Seats, ref. curly maple, minor damage, 17½" seat, 32" H $418.00

A-OH Mar. 1996   Garth's Auction

Row 1

Handmade Wooden Model of the "Delta Queen", polychrome, 12½" L & small box w/ twenty seven tiny ivory dominoes, 1½" L $357.50

Miniature Tole Dome Top Deed Box, old black repaint w/ gold striping, 3 " L, & wrought iron toaster w/ label "Found in Phila. in the 1950's by Sally Hall", 15" W, 18½" L . . .$154.00

Gaudy Welch Ironstone Toddy, w/ floral decoration, impressed "J. Harl White", 5½" D $192.50

Staffordshire Seated Dogs, pr., red & white, not an exact pair, 5" H .$231.00

Redware Turk's Head Mold, w/ swirled flutes & black sponging, 7¾" D $44.00

Row 2

Cast Iron Toy Ladder Wagon, w/ two horses, two firemen & two ladders, old worn polychrome has some rust, 15½" L $121.00

11 Tiny Wooden Wagons, most w/ horses along w/ people & other small wooden toys, orig polychrome, wear & damage, many parts loose. . . .$170.50

Cast Iron Toy Fire Pumper, old polychrome has wear, 13" L $159.50

Row 3

Cast Iron Bank, sharecropper w/ "Give Me A Penny", polychrome w/ light rust, 5⅝" H $71.50

Folky Wooden Sewing Caddy w/ drawer, wire nail construction, green, yellow & black paint w/ red crochetted pincushion, 12" H $38.50

Thirteen Piece Porcelain Child's Tea Set, marked "Germany", polychrome transfer scenes of "Jumbo Plays Tennis"; teapot, 6¼" H; sugar (finial broken); creamer; six plates & four cups & saucers, chips. . .$247.50

Seven Piece Doll Size Cottage Furniture Bedroom Suite, orig. pinkish grey paint w/ red striping & polychrome floral designs: bed, 22" L; dresser w/ mirror, 17" H; commode; chair; table; rocker & towel rack. . . .$522.50

Three Pieces: cherry patent model of a washing machine w/ orig. paper label, varnish finish w/ red & black, 9¼" L, plus crank; folding wooden doll chair, cloth seat is very worn, 11½" H & a wooden noggin pitcher, 7" H . .$385.00

A-OH Mar. 1996   Garth's Auction

Wooden Shaker Seed Sower, in old red, 120" L $71.50

Carved Wooden Indian Princess, gold over polychrome, weathered w/ age cracks, 61" H plus loose three feather headdress. $1,430.00

Relief Carved Plaque of Bob Hope, orig. polychrome, by Henry Walgreen, Sugar Grove, Illinois, (unsigned), 16" H, 12" W $71.50

Wood & Wire Birdcage, in old blue, worn, wires are rusted, bottom is missing, 11" x 12½", 16" H $126.50

Two Wooden Frames, w/ louvered fans & pierced spandrels, old red repaint, bottom of frames are open, 59¼" H, 35¾" W $715.00

Papier Mache Clown Box, (lid separates at waist), orig. polychrome, worn & damaged, base is restored, 19" H $66.00

Large Wood & Wire Birdcage, w/ three domes, old green paint, 16¼" x 31¾", 33½" H $275.00

Cast Iron Windmill Weight, letter "W" made by Athouse Wheeler Co., Waupun, Wisconsin, 16¾" L .$302.50

Cast Iron Gypsy Kettle, w/ relief design of bears, "Camp-Fire Club, Keep The Faith Tho I Go Empty", 11" D, 8½" H w/ wire bail handle. $495.00

Martin House, in weathered white & blue paint, from Maine, plywood construction, 27" H $247.50

Jacquard 2 Pc. Single Weave Coverlet, "Mfg. by Henry Oberly, Wornelsdorf, PA", navy blue sage green, deep red and natural white, some minor stains and wear w/ fringe loss in a few spots. 76" W, 94" L. $400.00

Staffordshire Platter, dk. blue Eng. hunting scene w/ two men w/ long rifle and two dogs, impresed "Clews", small edge flakes and minor scratches, 16¾" L. $825.00

Early PA Work Table, walnut w/ old worn finish, one dovetailed overlapping drawer and two board removable top w/ molded edge, pine secondary wood, 32" W, 49½" L, 29½" H. $20,900.00

Decorated Leather Fire Bucket, early repaint is olive green w/ tan rim and black and white letter "No. 15, Academy 1817", handle is an old replacement, 13" H. $330.00

Decorated Leather Fire Bucket, w/ wrought iron rim, worn red repaint w/ gold letters, "Little Giant", 12¼" H. $220.00

Painted Tin Scull, Am., 1920 c., w/ painted wood and compo. articulated rowers, imperfections, scull 40" L. $4025.00

Decorated Leather Fire Buckets, pr., impressed label on bottom "C.M. Domett Maker", worn old yellow paint w/ red rim and white and brown banners w/ black letters "Citizens Fire Society 1825, J. Armory Jr.", one has "No. 1", the other "No 2", leather handles are worn and one is broken at ring, 13¾" H. $1,760.00

Oblong burl bowl, ash burl w/ good dense figure and old worn patina that shades from light to dark at rim, 11" W, 18¾" L, 5½" H. $3,135.00

PA Decorated Blanket Chest, pine and poplar w/ original brown sponged paint w/ black feet, red moldings, dovetailed case, bracket feet and till w/ lid and secret compartment with two drawers, wrought iron strap hinges and bear traplock w/ escutcheon, 51¼" W, 24" D, 23½" H. $19,250.00

A-OH Jan. 1996   Garth's Auction

Bennington Name Plate, Rockingham glaze w/ one white letter "F", 7⅜"
L $247.50
Bennington Name Plate, Rockingham glaze, chip on one end, 8¼" L .$247.50
Primitive Clay Head, Rockingham glaze, 3½" L $60.50

Opera Glasses/Binoculars, in gilded brass and nacre, "Le Maire, Paris", w/ case, 4" . . . . .N/S
Sewerpipe Plaque, dog head on diamond back w/ "H.R.", edge chips, 8¼" L $203.50
Miniature on Ivory, young woman on red chair, minor edge wear, case has broken hinge, 3¼" H $385.00
Miniature on Ivory, young man w/ blue tie, gilded case has lock of hair on back, 2½" L $275.00
Oval Minature on Paper, woman reputed to be Maria Louisa, signed, some damage, 3¾" $82.50
Sewerpipe Fish, unglazed reddish clay w/ old patina, back has incised signature "B.___", small edge chips, 10¾" L $165.00
Glazed Silver, eagle w/ sword pin, 3¼"L, double bar trade cross excavated in St. Louis-1979, trade cross from Carondelet site, Vernon County Missouri, mkd. "L.C.". $522.50
Nine Pieces of Silver, sugar tongs w/ incomplete Eng. hallmarks, seven coin silver spoons by various makers and a silver plated spoon, dents in bowls. $27.50

A-OH Jan. 1996   Garth's Auction

Articulated Wooden Figure, worn paper litho covering, one foot incomplete, attrib. to Charles M. Crandall Co., 9" H . . . . .N/S
Pencil Box, w/ swivel lid, carved from one piece of pine w/ old red, 10½"
L $165.00
Three Tin Nutmeg Graters, one is labeled. $495.00
Three Tin Nutmeg Graters, two stationary, one w/ table clamp and three sizes of grater inserts. $137.50
Cookie Board, figure w/ goatee, old patina, 4¾" W, 10⅞" H $110.00

Jumping Jack Toy, turned wood w/ old patina and red and blue, one leg has damage, 14½" L $165.00
Shooting Gallery figure, cast steel, steam ship, edge damage and pits, 9¾" L $49.50
Wrought Iron Spatula, good detail, 14¾" L $60.50
Two Round Wooden Butter Prints, w/ one piece turned handles, sheaf and pineapple, old worn patina, sheaf has glued cracks, 3⅛" H, 4½" D . . .$143.00
Two Round Wooden Butter Prints, sheaf w/ one piece turned handle, edge damage and age cracks, 4½" D and single flower w/ screw in handle. $231.00
Shooting Gallery Figure, cast steel, donkey, 6½" H $192.50
Wooden Candle Holder, w/ tin socket and crimped pan, 21" L . . .$209.00
Brass Tobacco Box, w/ three compartments, one w/ miniature clay pipe, the other with flint and steel, 5" L $192.50
Door Knocker, wrought iron w/ heart and scrolled detail, 8" L $357.50

A-OH Mar. 1996   Garth's Auction

Decanter Set w/ Case, made from stack of four leather bound books, two clear pressed decanters & five small tumblers all w/ gilt trim, one stopper is broken off in neck, 8¼" L . .$165.00
2 Tole Tea Caddies, worn orig. black paint w/ gilded dec., larger has two compartments, 4⅜" & 5¾" H . .$302.50
Tole Oval Bowl, w/ scalloped rim & wrought handles, old red repaint w/ stenciled gilded dec., bottom has rust damage, 11" L $143.00
Miniature Empire Stand, curly maple & figured veneer w/ old varnish finish, applied half turnings on posts, two dovetailed drawers & cherry top, bottom on top drawer signed "M. Ilger 1840, Nov. the 30 CWI", edge of top top has filled nail holes & was possibly upholstered at one time, 9" x 8½", 11¼" H $1,980.00
Miniature Decorated Box, pine w/ orig. polychrome floral dec. w/ yellow, blue, white, gold & green on a red ground, marked "Germany", 4⅝" L $385.00
Miniature Empire Footstool, mahogany flame veneer w/applied molding & cut out feet, bottom branded "P. Torrey", some edge damage & wear, old cushion is removable & has faded mauve floral design, 5¼" L $148.50
Miniature Chest of Drawers, pine w/ orig. red flame graining, square corner posts w/ whittled feet, paneled ends & two drawers, square nail construction, back inscribed in pencil "Agnes M. Criste Bureau", one back leg replaced, nail pulls, some wear, 8⅛" W, 6¼" D, 7¼" H $357.50
Two Carved Wooden Chickens, hen & rooster, old patina w/ red painted detail & bead eyes, 6½" H . . .$385.00
Box, w/ Exotic Figured Wood Veneer W/ Edge Inlay, brass buckles hold top, metal lined, 6¼" H $159.50
2 Carved & Painted Birds on Branch Bases: cardinal is initialed & dated "C.A. 1938", 5¾" H, swallow has tail damage, 6¼" H, both have chips on beaks $132.00
Marquetry Inlay Jewelry Box w/ lift out tray & mirror on inside of lid, some wear, 10¾" L $115.50

A-OH Mar. 1996   Garth's Auction

Row 1
Heart Shaped Tin Cheese Mold, w/ Sieve Holes, some old resoldering, 4½" L $247.50
Carved Wooden Shoe, w/ Old Black Repaint, some edge damage, 9½" L $137.50
Springerle Rolling Pin, w/ Twenty-Four Squares, 17¾" L $137.50
Round Pewter Food Mold, removable top has relief design of fruit & vegetables, base missing, 6½" D . .$82.50

Row 2
Redware Pie Plate w/ Coggeled Rim, yellow slip design, chips & wear, 9¼" D $247.50
Two Tin Lanterns: "Dietz Scout" w/ original globe, 7½" H & folding candle lantern w/ mica glazing & worn brown japanning, A Minors Patent lamp type but has scratched name, "J.E. Keller, East Machias, Maine 1867, 7½" H . .$132.00
Redware Loaf Pan w/ Coggeled Rim, three line yellow slip decor., very worn w/ chips front & back, 11¾" L $126.50
Blown Glass Hour Glass in Wooden Frame, 7" H $495.00
Redware Pie Plate w/ Coggeled Rim, three line yellow slip decoration, wear & chips, 9½" D $247.50
Redware Pie Plate w/ Coggeled Rim, three line yellow slip decor., wear & chips, 10¼" D $330.00

Row 3
Two Pieces of Lighting: wrought iron candle holder w/ spring clip, feet & hanger, 7⅝" H, & tin lamp on cast iron foot, whale oil burner, bl. & gr. repaint, 8¾" H $385.00
Two Pieces of Primitive Woodenware w/ Chip Carving, salt box, repair & renailing, 10½" H & mortar & pestle, 6" H $82.50
Redware Pie Plate w/ Coggeled Rim, yellow slip decor., rim chips, 11¼" D $88.00
Wrought Iron Rush Light Holder, w/ Twisted Detail & Turned Wooden Base, 9½" H $121.00

A-OH Mar. 1996   Garth's Auction

Sheraton Style Two Piece Secretary, cherry w/ old finish, made up from old parts & using old wood, 28" W, 19" D, 69" H $1,430.00
Pastel on Heavy Paper, portrait of child, minor edge damage & water spots, old gilt frame, 27½" H, 21¾" W $302.50
Miniature Sheraton Chest of Drawers, cherry w/ old refinishing, dovetailed drawers, underside of top drawer signed "Made in 1830", top drawer missing lock, filled age crack in top poplar secondary wood, pulls mismatched, 21¾" W, 31¾" H . .$1,705.00
Painted Knife Box, pine w/ orig. red & black graining, divider w/ handle is signed, edge wear, 8¼" x 13¼" $275.00
Stoneware Jug, impressed, "E. & L.P. Norton, Bennington, Vt. 3", leaf design in cobalt blue slip, stains & flakes on lip, 15½" H $220.00

A-IL Nov. 1995   James D. Julia, Inc.
Barber Chair, restored. . . .$1750.00

A-OH Jan. 1996   Garth's Auction

Eng. Engravings, pr., black & white, N. Am. scenes, pub. by William Lane, ca. 1789, stains, tears & fold lines, matted & framed, 16" H, 23" W $275.00

Map of the World, handcolored, engraved, pub. in 1782, fold lines & edge tears, modern frame, 15½" H, 21⅜" W $291.50
Windsor Side Chairs, w/ rabbit ear backs, (2 of 4), decor. half spindle back, worn old red & black graining w/ white striping & faint ghost stenciled decor., N. Eng., 33½" H $330.00
Country Table, MO, cherry, w/ old finish, 27" x 30¼", 30" H $412.50
Dovetailed Book Box, walnut w/ old varnish & marbelized paper, minor age cracks & edge damage, 12½"L $330.00
Book Box, poplar w/ old black paint & red design, wear, 12" L . . .$357.50
Decoys, two, w/ old working repaint, 16½" L & 15¼" L $187.00
Canada Goose, mid 20th c., Chesapeake Bay area w/ org. paint, minor wear, 23½" L $192.50

A-MA Oct. 1995   Skinner, Inc.

Carved and Painted Cigar Store Figure of Indian Squaw, Am., late 19th c., old repaint, minor repairs, 43" H not including base. $14950.00

A-OH Jan. 1996   Garth's Auction

Printed Cotton Handkerchief, blue & white, "The Love of Truth, Mark the Boy", good color, framed, 12¾" x 12¾" $357.50
Country Hepplewhite Stand, walnut w/ old worn ref., repl. 3 board top, 19½" x 19½", 27½" H $247.50
Bowback Windsor Armchair, old mellow ref., left end of bow from last spindle to arm is old repl., 39" H $990.00
Cast Iron Cat Door Stop, orig. white paint, 10¾" L $209.00
Stoneware Crock, w/ applied handles, cobalt blue brush floral decor., minor bubbling and flakes, 8¾" H $330.00

A-PA Oct. 1995   Pook & Pook, Inc.

Chippendale Block Front Secretary Bookcase, MA, cherry w/bonnet top, ca. 1760, 98" H, 39" W $25,000.00
Chippendale Block Front Chest of Drawers, MA, mahogany, retains most orig. brasses, ca. 1765, 31¼" H x 30¾" H $32,500.00
Chippendale Mirror, PA., mahogany, retains orig. label of John Elliot, 51" H, 26½" W $5,000.00

A-PA Oct. 1995   Pook & Pook, Inc.

Still Life, w/fruit, mahogany frame, late 19th c. $325.00
Soap Hollow Chest of Drawers, w/scrolled backsplash, orig. flame grained paint decor., initialed L.L., ca. 1885, 49¾" H, 38" W $3,200.00
Redware Pie Plates, PA, w/slip decor., early 19th c., each 8¼" D. .$700.00
Painting, PA, on velvet, sgn. D.Y. Ellinger, ca. 1860 ....$2,250.0

A-PA Oct. 1995   Pook & Pook, Inc.

Hepplewhite Cherry Bow Front Shaving Stand, w/line inlaid drawers, ca. 1790 ....$950.00
Chippendale Chest of Drawers, PA, w/orig. brasses, ca. 1770, 66¼" H, 41" W
..........................$6,000.00
Q.A. Tall Case Clock, PA, by John Miller, Germantown, 30 hr. works, ca. 1760, 90" H $5,750.00

A-PA Apr. 1996   Pook & Pook, Inc.

Whirligig, carved figure of soldier, 19th C., orig. polychrome decor., 19½" H $3,100.00
Apothecary Chest, pine, mid 19th C., orig. gr. paint w/ yellow stenciling, 24" H, 29" W, 8½" D $1,900.00
Weathervane, molded copper, weathered, VT, 18" H, 31 " L $2,700.00
Plate, Jacob Medinger, PA, w/ sgraffito decor., gr. & bl., 8" D ...$1,000.00
Fraktur, Am. attributed to Johannes Spangenberg, watercolor, late 18th C., minor damage, 5¾" x 6" ...$5,000.00
Whirligig, carved figure of acrobat, orig. red & gr. polychrome decor., 13" H $2,100.00

A-PA Nov. 1995   Pook & Pook, Inc.

Copper Horse Weathervane, full bodied w/ zink head, retaining much orig. gilding, late 19th C., 18½" x 24" . $1,250.00
Q.A. Miniature Blanket Chest, PA., walnut w/ lift lid, dovetailed case, 18th C., 12½" H, 23½" L $1,400.00
Copper Horse Weathervane, retaining much of its orig. gilding & fine patina, 18" x 27", late 19th C. ...$700.00
Blanket Chest, walnut, PA, Lancaster Co., inlaid front, 20½" H, 51" L .$900.00

A-OH Jan. 1996   Garth's Auction

Country Chippendale Linen Press, 2 pc., pine w/ old reddish brown flame graining, 49½" W, 75¼" H . . .$2,750.00

Woven Splint Buttocks Baskets, set of 4, 24 to 30 ribs w/ old brown patina & distinctive handle detail, minor wear & damage, 6" x 7" thru 11½" x 13" $990.00

Cast Iron Windmill Weight, w/ raised letters, "Fairbury, NE", bull w/ old red & white repaint over silver, 18" H added wood base $990.00

A-OH Mar 1996   Garth's Auction

Table, poplar, cherry & maple w/ worn red stain, w/ dovetailed drawer. Rounded curly maple front, two board top has cracks & edge wear, 28¾" H .$330.00

Banister Back Side Chair, worn dark varnish stain, pieced repair, old worn splint seat, 37½" H $110.00

Three Sponge Spatter Bowls w/ Simple Molded Panels, blue & brown sponging on a greyish ground, wear & crow's foot in two larger bowls, 6⅜", 8⅜" & 9½" D . . .$181.50

A-OH Nov. 1995   Garth's Auction

European Hanging Bowfront Corner Cupboard, pine w/ old white repaint with blue trim, insect damage and old repair, door crooked, 30½" W at cornice, 43½ H. $770.00

Homespun Tablecloth, gold and white check, hand hemmed, 40" W, 68" L. $220.00

Framed End Panel From A Pennsylvania Blanket Chest, pine w/ orig. blue paint, white panel w/ red border and basket of flowers in red, blue, black, complete end w/ dovetails hidden by frame, 20¾" H, 21¼" W. $880.00

Ovoid Stoneware Jug, stains and minor chips, 16" H. $1,265.00

Ovoid stoneware Jar or Small Churn, w/ applied shoulder handles, imp. label "E. & L.P. Norton, Bennington, VT. 3", decor. in cobalt blue slip, chips on base and lip, 14½ H. $577.50

A-PA Apr. 1996   Pook & Pook, Inc.

Fraktur Bookplate, PA, Bucks Co., hand colored w/hearts & tulips, inscribed Elisabeth Teaubn 1818, 6½" x 3¾" $3,250.00

Redware Jar, Jacob Medinger, PA, w/ sgraffito decor., 20th C., 9" H $4,500.00

Stoneware Jar, late 18th/early 19th C., w/ incised blue decor., 4½"H . .NS

Christian Weber Box, (attributed), PA, w/ painted decor., dated 1848, 6¾" H, 10" W, 5¾" D $20,000.00

A-PA Apr. 1996   Pook & Pook, Inc.

Q.A. Candlestand, walnut, PA., ca. 1770, w/ tilt top & bird cage support, repr. to top, 26½" H, 17½" D$1,300.00

Candlestand, walnut, PA., ca. 1800, w/bl. marble top above bird cage support, 27¾" H, top 21" D $2,400.00

Candlestand, PA. Sellersville, ca. 1800, 27½" H, top 19½" D .$2,250.00

Nantucket Baskets, nest of three, finely woven, minor damages . .$1,800.00

A-OH Mar. 1996   Garth's Auction

Hanging Jigsaw Work Box, w/ worn old green paint, square nail construction, 19¾" H $550.00

House Blessing PA German Fraktur, pen & ink w/ watercolor, "Haus Segen", w/ text in heart surrounded by flowers & birds, dated 1859, stains & minor insect damage, old beveled frame, 16" H, 20" W $495.00

Windsor Side Chairs Youth Size, (1 of 4), worn old refinish, some wear, scarring. $572.00

Grained School Master's or Clerk Desk, pine & poplar w/ old worn greyish yellow graining on a white ground, one dovetailed drawer, w/ pigeon hole interior, drawer has pieced repair & lock is missing, 33" W, 22½" D, 36¼" H plus crest. $742.50

Victorian Shaving Mirror, poplar w/ old dark brown finish, some wear, 25¾" H $242.00

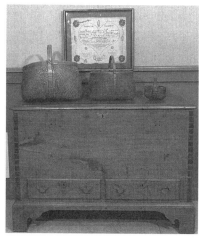

A-OH Mar. 1996   Garth's Auction

PA German Fraktur by Frederick Krebs, recording 1809 birth in Northampton, some damage, 12½" H, 15½" W $550.00

A-OH Mar. 1996   Garth's Auction

Hepplewhite Chest, cherry w/ old refinish, banded inlay on front apron & top edge, dovetailed drawers, pine secondary wood, wear, 43¼" W, 43½" H $1,430.00

Cut Silhouette, Probably Edouart, w/ orig. labels front & back read: "The Bishop of Bristol, Dr. Grey, Cheltenham, 30th June 1829", framed, 12" H, 7¾" W $220.00

Carved Eagle, pine w/ old worn finish & gilt, one glass eye replaced, glued repairs, 13½" H $275.00

Shaving Mirror, ref. mahogany veneer on pine, w/ dovetailed drawer, veneer repairs, 15½" H $115.50

A-MA Mar. 1996   Skinner, Inc.

Vanity Set, Foster & Bailey 14 pcs., 19th C., light blue enamel & silver $805.00

 PA Chippendale Walnut Chest, refinished walnut, drawers w/ original brasses, wrought iron strap hinges & till, feet have old repair poplar secondary wood, 44½"W, 22" D, 30¾" H . . .$990.00

Splint Buttocks Basket, traces of old green, some damage & holes, 10" H $214.50

Splint Buttocks Basket, wear & damage with holes in bottom, 7½" H $203.50

Small Woven Splint Buttocks Basket, some damage, 3½" H . . .$104.50

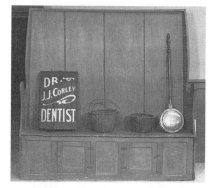

A-OH Mar. 1996   Garth's Auction

Fireside Settle Bench w/ High Curved Back, pine w/ old mellow refinish, one "arm" has old nailed split, 69" W, 68" H $3,190.00

Curved Tin Sign w/ Wooden Frame, silver & black w/ sanded ground, some wear, 23¾" H, 16" W $247.50

Two Woven Splint Baskets w/ Old Dark Patina, damage, 12" D, 8" H & 11" D, 6½" H $60.50

Brass Bedwarmer, w/ engraved lid & turned wooden handle, traces of old graining,$40¾" L $258.50

A-PA Dec. 1995 Horst Auction Center

Spatter Plate, red & blue variegated, mkd., Adams Rose patt., 9¼" dia.$190.00

Spatter Plate, red & gr. Adams Rose flower, mkd., 8¼" dia. $210.00

Ironstone Pekin, mkd. "Booth's Silicon China, England, Pekin" w/floral decor., rim damage, 18¼" x 14⅝" $25.00

Milk Pitcher, Adams Rose-type decor., 8¹⁄₁₆" H $280.00

Plate, Adams Rose patt., minor glaze nicks, 8¾" dia. $190.00

Masonic Punched Tin Pie Safe, walnut case, iron butt hinges & brass catch, 42¾"W, 18"D, 44½"H .$1,450.00

A-IL Apr. 1996 Olivers

Occupational Shaving Mugs, *Row 1, Left to Right*

Fanny Booth 1857, w/floral decor., spider crack in bottom 95.00

W.L. Davis, w/floral decor ..$275.00

Row 2, Left to Right

Fireman's Mug, Wilmette Fire Company No. 1 ....$230.00

Barber's Mug, R.T. Davidson$225.00

Blacksmith's Mug, (crack) .$110.00

Row 3, Left to Right

Barber's Mug, S.M. Stone w/horse head decor $230.00

Barber's Mug, w/golden pheasant decor $65.00

Hanging Cupboard, w/glazed door & drawer, dk. mustard paint w/striping, 21¼" H $700.00

A-OH APR. 1996 Garth's Auction

Decorated Side Chairs, set of six, orig. gr. paint w/ yellow striping & gold stenciled floral dec., plank seats, minor wear, 33¾" H $3,630.00

A-PA May 1996 Pook & Pook Inc.

MA. Federal Cherry Bowfront Chest of Drawers, ca. 1785, w/ D-shaped maple inlaid top, orig. brasses, 35¾" H, 37¾" W $3,800.00

Mahogany Side Chairs, pair, NY Federal, ca. 1790, ...$650.00

Alfred Jansson Portrait, 20th C., oil on canvas, 4-masted ship on high seas, relined, 31¼" x 47" $500.00

Canton Export Porcelain Sugar Bowl, covered, early 19th C., 5" H., together w/ a similar oval blue & white serving dish, 11" W $375.00

Canton Porcelain Salad Bowl, cut corner, early 19th C., w/ rain and cloud border, 4½" H, 10¼" W $850.00

A-MA Oct. 1995 Skinner, Inc.

Child's Bed, Rosewood Grained, ME, 2nd qtr. 19th c., orig. surface, imperfs., 41" H, 32¼" W, 72" D $632.50

A-OH May 1996 Garth's Auction

Ovoid Jar, mkd. "L. Marsilliot", w/ cobalt blue highlights, polka dots & "2", small rim chips, 10" H $880.00

A-PA May 1996 Pook & Pook Inc.

PA. Lift Lid Bench Table, ca. 1800, retaining orig. red washed surface, 27½" H, 51" W $2,700.00

Running Horse Weathervane, molded copper & iron, early 20th C., w/ old white overpaint, some damage, 19¼" H, 28" W $850.00

Horse & Sulky Weathervane, molded copper & zinc, ca. 1940, attrib. to Fiske, damage to horse ear, 17½" H, 32½" W $700.00

Folk Art Wooden Rooster, carved, 19th½0th C., mounted on a giltwood pedestal, 42" H $600.00

Barber Pole, turned wooden & polychrome, 44" H $500.00

Theorem by David Ellinger, (Am., 20th C.,), oil on velvet w/ basket of fruit, 13¾" x 17" $500.00

Carved Decoys, two, wooden, early 20th C., one of a canvasback duck & the other a goose $200.00

Umbrella Trade Sign, painted sheet iron, late 19th C., w/ red body & goose head handle, 37¼" W ....N/S

Folk Art Wooden Whirligig, wooden, early 20th C., red painted Indian in canoe w/ paddles, damages, 17½" H $150.00

Eaglet, carved wooden paint decor., 11½" H $400.00

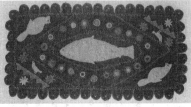

A-OH APR. 1996 Garth's Auction

Applique Rug, all wool w/ circles in white, red, yellow, gr. & blue on a blk. ground, wear, moth damage & old repairs, 22" x 43" $1,925.00

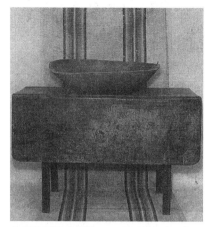

A-OH APR. 1996   Garth's Auction

Pennsylvania Rag Carpet, ivory w/ colorful stripes in red, purple, yellow-green, white & lavender, 70" x 75", binding on one end replaced, some wear & damage. $165.00

Drop Leaf Swing Leg Table, maple w/ curl in top & worn old red paint, 13¾" x 45¼ " w/ 15¼" leaves, 28¼" H $990.00

Rectangular Wooden Bowl, poplar w/ traces of old red, & carved hand holds ends & later eye hook added to rim for hanging, 19¾" x 28", 5½" to 7¼" H $467.50

A-OH APR. 1996   Garth's Auction

Pennsylvania Folded Valentine Fraktur, pencil, crayon, pen & ink on ledger paper w/ cut out birds & hearts, yellow, orange & blue, some damage, 12" x 12" $1,760.00

Decorated Oval Bentwood Box, hardwood & pine w/ orig. crewel like floral decoration in blk., blue, white & pink, dated "1808", rim is damaged, 22½" L $4,510.00

Decorated Pennsylvania High Chair, orig. salmon paint w/ white & blk. striping & polychrome floral decoration, wear, 36" H $715.00

Dovetailed Knife Box, w/ cut out handle in center divider, mahogany w/ chestnut bottom board, old finish, 14" L $412.50

A-OH APR. 1996   Garth's Auction

Rhode Island Queen Anne Tea Table, pine w/ old dk br. finish retains orig. red graining, 22" x 33¼", 26½" H $4,125.00

Burl Bowl, w/ protruding rim handles, ash, old worn soft patina, 14½" D, 5" H $2,310

Wrought Steel Candlestick, w/ spiral pushup, lip hanger & wooden base, top spiral is stamped "LM-LN", 7¼" H $357.50

Stoneware Crock, w/ applied handles, cobalt blue date & flourish "1876", stains & hairline, 14¾" H $192.50

A-OH APR. 1996   Garth's Auction

Stave Tub, w/ wooden bands, w/ laced seams & cut out handles, w/ traces of paint, 6¾" D, 4¼" H, plus handles $495.00

Reddish Purple Spatterware Plate, w/ thistle in red & gr., sm. edge flakes, 8¼" D $330.00

Rockingham Tobacco Jar, molded vintage, sm. chips, 7½" H . . .$220.00

Rockingham Paneled Pitcher, w/ mask spout, br. & gr., kiln adhesion chips on bottom, 9" H $192.50

Blue Spatterware Platter, Adam's Rose in red, gr. & blk., wear, stains & sm. edge chips, 13¾" L $495.00

Pease Jar, old soft finish, minor age cracks, 8½" D, 8¼" H $797.50

A-OH APR. 1996   Garth's Auction

Sheraton Server, birch & bird's eye maple w/ old mellow finish, four dovetailed drawers, replaced brasses, 36¼" H overall $825.00

Double Student Lamp, brass frame w/ gr. cased shades, some soldered repair & electrified, 22" H . . .$770.00

A-OH APR. 1996   Garth's Auction

Moravian Side Chair, attrib. to Zoar, pine w/ old worn mustard paint over red, age cracks in seat, 17¼" seat, 33" H $82.50

Brown & White Linen, homespun, hand hemmed w/ 4" strip added to on end, 20" x 39" $71.50

Nesting Set of Eight, bentwood measures w/ sheet iron fittings, 9¾" D to 1⅝" D $605.00

Andirons Wrought Iron, w/ penny feet & scrolled finials, tooled, 12½" H $165.00

A-PA May 1996   Pook & Pook, Inc.

PA. Maple Wagon Seat, ca. 1800, retaining old blk. painted surface w/ rush seat, 33½" W $275.00
Q.A. Chest of Drawers, PA., ca. 1770, w/ 4 lipped drawers above straight bracket feet, retains orig. old surface, 37½" H, 36" W $3,000.00
Stoneware Crock, 4-gal., 19th C., incised "Evan R. Jones, Pittston, Pa" w/ blue floral decor., 11½" H, together w/ a 2-gal. example by White, Utica w/ blue floral decor. $375.00
Stoneware Ovoid Jar, 3-gal., 19th C., w/ applied handles & cobalt floral decor., lg. chip to rim, 13½" H $250.00
Stoneware Crock, 2-gal., 19th C., incised "Edmands & Co.", w/ cobalt bird & branch decor., 9½" H . . . .N/S
Stoneware Jar, early 19th C., attrib. to Commerau Pottery, Corlear's Hook, NY, w/ incised cobalt floral decor., old chip, 13" H . . . . .N/S
Stoneware Crock, 6-gal., 19th C., incised "S. Hart, Fulton", w/ blue decor. dog carrying basket, restored . . .N/S
Stoneware Jar, PA., 3-gal., 19th C., sgn. "D.P. Shenfelder Reading, Pa", w/ blue floral decor., cracks, 14" H $275.00

A-OH APR. 1996   Garth's Auction

Hooked Rag & Yarn Rug, all wool, three masted ship w/ Am. flag, blk., several shades of blue, yellow & white w/ red, white & blue flag, minor wear, 40" x 59" $1,155.00

A-OH APR. 1996   Garth's Auction

A-OH APR. 1996   Garth's Auction

Hepplewhite Drop Leaf Table, walnut w/ orig. surface, banded inlay & swing legs that support leaves, hinges reset & one leaf has old shallow chip at rule joint, pine secondary wood, 29¾" H $1,100.00
Pennsylvania Chippendale Bible Box, walnut w/ old finish, dovetailed case & bracket feet, poplar secondary wood, orig. lock w/ brass bird head escutcheon, hinges replaced, 14¼" D, 22¾" L, 8½" H $907.50
Pintail Drake, orig. paint & glass eyes, 19" L $357.50
Burl Bowl, ref. ash w/ good figure, old putty repairs to bottom, 17" D, 6" H $770.00
Burl Bowl, ash w/ soft scrubbed finish w/ stains, minor age cracks & small plugged holes, 17" D, 6" H $660.00

A-OH APR. 1996   Garth's Auction

Hooked Yarn "Waldoboro" Type Rug, yellow, red, gr. magenta, orange, purple & blk. on a br. ground, "1910" sewn in blk. thread to back, 21" H, 37" W, mounted on linen covered foam core board $1,430.00

A-OH APR. 1996   Garth's Auction

Pennsylvania Woven Rag Carpet, stripes of olive & blue w/ narrow orange bands, 40' approx. . . .$440.00
Pennsylvania Decorated Blanket Chest, pine w/ orig. br. "vinegar" graining on a yellow ground w/ br. & gr. trim, lock & key, cast butt hinges are marked "W.H. Carr, Phila"., dovetailed case, minor edge wear, hinge rail of lid prof. restored & age crack in lid, 49" W, 23" D, 27½" H $1,430.00
Decorated Dome Top Box, pine w/ worn orig. landscape paintings, polychrome houses & trees on a white ground, wire hinges & homemade lock & escutcheon, wear & edge damage, 15¾" L $1,017.50

A-OH APR. 1996   Garth's Auction

Decorated Dressing Table, maple & other hardwood w/ orig. red & blk. graining w/ blk. & yellow striping, 28" W, 20" D, 31" H, plus top drawers, 44¾" H overall $1,870.00

Hooked Rag Rug, horse & cart w/ boy driver, blk., grey, blue, beige & br. on a grey ground, red & purple in details, br. crocheted yarn binding, 17" x 33¾" $412.50

A-OH   Jan. 1996 Garth's Auction
Top to Bottom
Kentucky Rifle, curly maple full stock attrib. to Samuel Baum, Penn., percussion lock marked "Rashmore & Son", incised carving w/ brass patch box and silver inlays, 54" L $2310.00

Indian Trade Gun and an Engraved Powder Horn, walnut full stock w/ engraved brass barrel and flint lock marked "Ketland Adams", 40" L, horn has scene and "F.S. Johnson, 1818", 11" L $742.00
German Dress Sword, w/ gilded hilt and trim from scabbard, engraved blade is nicked, 36" L $121.00
Rapier, w/ wrought steel basket hilt and sharkskin grip, point broken off, 41" L $60.50
Sword and Walking Stick, sword cane, 35" L, stick w/ silver head eng. "J.H. '85", 35" L $165.00
Burled Walking Stick, several knobs have carved heads or animals, horn handle, 34" L $302.50
Double Barreled Pistol, walnut stock w/ silver inlaid shield and percussion lock, ball storage in butt, 7³/₄" L $247.50
Three Pipes, stoneware w/ hand and "Helping tobacco", small flakes, two white clay pipes, one w/ ship, other with early steam ship and train. $27.50
Two German Porcelain Pipes . . . .
. . . .$16.50

A-MA Jan. 1996   Skinner, Inc.
37-Shaker Oval Boxes, two, 19th c., stained, minor staining & scratches, 2⅝" H, 7¼" L; & 3⅞" H, 10¼" L $488.75
23-Shaker Three-Finger Oval Box, 19th c., minor staining, 4⅜" H, 8⅞" L $1,035/00
31-Shaker Three Finger Oval Box, 19th c., staining, minor cracks & losses, 4¼" H, 11½ L $258.75
46-Three Shaker Wood Pounce Sanders, (1 of 3), 19th c., staining, 3 - 3½" H $230.00
27-Shaker Red Stained Three Finger Oval Carrier, 19th c., minor cracks & loss to finish $747.50
30-Shaker Yellow Painted Three Finger Oval Carrier, 19th c., minor break lower edge, 4¼" H, 11½ L $8,625.00
33-Shaker Yellow Painted Three-Finger Oval Carrier, 19th c., even wear, cracks, 6½" H, 11" L $2,990.00

A-OH June 1996   Garth's Auction

Handcolored Lithograph by "Currier & Ives", "Terrific Combat Between the 'Monitor' 2 gun and 'Merrimac' 10 guns", light stains, new curly maple frame, 14⅜" H, 18½" W $550.00
Handcolored Lithograph by "Currier & Ives", "A Fast Team Taking a Smash", new curly maple frame, 14" H, 19" W $275.00
Sheraton Bowfront Chest, ref. cherry w/ curly maple veneer facade, paneled ends & four dovetailed drawers, reprs., 37¾" W, top is 22½" x 40", 40¾" H $1,595.00
Mocha Pitcher, w/ applied leaf handle, pale yellow band w/ running "dots" in blue, white & dk. br., blue band & dk. br. stripes, stains & old prof. repr., 7" H $192.50

A-IL Apr. 1996 Olivers

Row 1, Left to Right

Hanging Pine Grater, w/pierced tin $130.00

Stoneware Jug, mkd. Norton & Fenton, East Bennington, VT., 11½″ H .$130.00

Stoneware Jug, half gal. w/floral decor., chips, 8½″ H $210.00

Stoneware Bird Feeder, w/blue decor. on handles & knot on top $140.00

Stoneware Crock, 2 gal. w/cover & blue pecking fowl $400.00

Treenware Carved Urn Shaped Jar, w/dark finish, 11½″ H $180.00

Row 2, Left to Right

Yellowware Pottery Rolling Pin, w/wood handle $210.00

Brick Soap Dish, IL factory .$130.00

Yellowware, 4 pcs., butter box, 2 sm. bowls & bottle (see row 3) . .$110.00

Row 3, Left to Right

Stoneware Crock, 2 gal., w/blue floral decor., mkd. N.A. White & Son, Utica, NY, 13½″ H $135.00

Stoneware Open Crock, w/handles & blue decor., 11″ H $210.00

Stoneware Jug, w/blue floral scroll, mkd. J. & E. Norton, Bennington, VT, 11¼″ H $180.00

Stoneware Crock, 2 gal. w/eagle & scroll decor., mkd. J.C. Waelde, North Bay, NY, 9″ H $550.00

Row 4, Left to Right

Stoneware Spitton, w/blue sponge decor $130.00

Yellowware Chamber Pot, .$90.00

Yellowware Milk Pitcher, .$130.00

Yellowware Mug, w/white band around top $115.00

Stoneware Hanging Salt Box, cracked, lid missing $20.00

Row 5, Left to Right

Windsor Fanback Arm Chair, PA, w/dark finish, 42″ H $5,000.00

Stoneware Crock, w/blue decor. of bird on branch, 17″ H $375.00

Stoneware Butter Churn, 4 gal., w/blue floral decor., orig. cover & agitator, 17″ H $340.00

A-IL Apr. 1996 Olivers

Pine Open Cupboard, painted red & gr., 71″ H, 39½″ W $1,550.00

Row 1, Left to Right

Nantucket Basket, round w/articulated handle, 10″ diam. $850.00

Nantucket Basket, oval w/articulated handle, 9″ L, 5¾″ W $500.00

Nantucket Basket, oval w/articulated handle, 13″ L, 9″ W $650.00

Nantucket Basket, oval, w/articulated handle, 8″ L, 4″ W $750.00

Row 2

Nantucket Basket, oval w/articulated handle, 10¼″ L, 6½″ W . . .$550.00

Sweet Grass Baskets (2), 11″ & 5″ diam. $70.00

Row 3

Indian Splint Baskets (3), 1 w/handle, (1 on Row 2) $105.00

Hanging Wall Box, painted red & blk., 13″ L $160.00

Row 4

Indian Splint Basket, w/handle & blue/blk. inserts $120.00

Indian Melon Basket, w/handle . . . $180.00

Row 5

Cheese Basket & Lg. Handled Basket, ...$65.00

Stoneware Jug, w/br. glaze, wire & wood handle w/tin lid $225.00

A-PA May 1996 Pook & Pook, Inc.

Yellow Pine Blanket Chest, southern, early 19th C., w/ lift lid, center drop, straight bracket feet & blue paint, 25″ H, 50″ W, 19″ D $650.00

Maine Grain Painted Washstand, ca. 1810, w/ yellow pinstriping on a rosewood decor. surface, 38″ H . . .$800.00

Fold Art Rocking Horse, w/ stuffed wool body & horsehair mane, on a red frame, 34″ H $950.00

Watchmaker's Trade Sign, carved wood, late 19th C., w/ gold rim, 23½″ dia. $600.00

Tax Assessor's Sign, carved wood, early 20th C., 33″ W $650.00

Stoneware Crock, 3-gal., 19th C., w/ cobalt bird on branch & applied handles, 10″ H $325.00

Stoneware Ovoid Jug, 2-gal., 19th C., "Cowden & Wilcox Harrisburg, Pa.", w/ cobalt floral decor., minor chips/ cracks, 14″ H, together w/ smaller example by Havana, NY, crack/old repair, 12½″ H $400.00

Stoneware Jug, 2-gal., w/ blue decor., 19th C., incised "Haxtun Ottman & Co., Fort ____, NY", 15″ H, together w/ Cowden & Wilcox, Harrisburg 2-gal. stoneware jug w/ blue decor. leaf, chip to handle, 15″ H $225.00

A-OH May 1996 Garth's Auction

Stoneware Ovoid Jar, cobalt blue stencils & freehand mkd. "Hamilton & Jones, Greensboro, Pa 2", interior lime deposits, hairline in base, 10½″ H $1,595.00

A-OH Mar. 1996 Garth's Auction

Two Knives: kitchen knife w/ handle carved "C.J. 1905" w/ foliage, 15½" L & one w/ carved curly maple handle (crack) & mismatched, 14" L . . $77.00

Pair of Cast Iron Gate Weights, w/ pulley tops & grape design w/ flat backs, one pulley pin repl., 9" L $330.00

Brass Telescope, extends to 24" w/ iron chart scribe w/ line. $49.50

Pair of Cut Overlay Mercury Tie Backs, cobalt cut to clear, silver gilt fittings & screw backs, 2" D . . . $154.00

Two Pieces: wrought steel food chopper w/ dec. scroll blade & wooden handle, 6" W, & an all wooden pastry wheel w/ floral designs. $236.50

Horn Whetstone Sheath, eng. "Benjamin Light, June 26, 1839" w/ dec. branded design, minor age cracks, w/ whetstone, 8½" L $154.00

Small Powder Horn, w/ decorative carved tip, wooden plug & eng. inscription "Powder, David Crist. Nov 26, 1828, Warren County, Ohio", 7½" L $577.50

White Clay Heart Shaped Paperweight, w/ brown metallic glaze, incised "Mary Etta Wright, Lisbon, Ohio, Col. Co. Feb 19, 1904:, 3½" H $121.00

Beaded Bag, w/ Eagle & "A.H.W. to C.D___, Anna N. Whitemore '36", multicolored on white ground w/ gold, white satin binding, drawstring is in tatters, w/ minor bead loss in fringe, 8" x 8" plus fringe. $412.50

Small Beaded Bag, w/ Flowers, "A. Whitmore 1832", white, maroon, green, red, blue & gold, minor bead loss & wear, 3½" x 3½" $104.50

Needlework Bag w/ Beaded Fringe, design is similar to above w/ "Anna Whitmore, 1832", reds, brown, etc. on a two tone blue ground, green fringe & green silk ruffle trim, wear & floss is missing, 5" x 6¾" $220.00

Four Cast Iron Porringers: "Clark's Patent"; "Kerrick"; "Bellevue": "T.Clark" & "Kenrick half Pint", largest has worn white enamel int., rest have pitting w/ some solder in bottom of one, 4½" x 6¼" D $247.50

Pewter Porringer, w/ Cast Old English Handle, 3⅞" D $148.50

A-PA Apr. 1996 Pook & Pook Inc.

Pine Bench, PA, 19th C., partial orig. red painted surface, 35" H, 75" L 2,400.00

Carved Wooden Zouave Civil War Infantry Soldier, 19th C., poor cond., paint of later date, 36" H . . . $3,900.00

Stoneware Jar, 4 gal., F.L. Norton & Co., Worchester, MA, 11" H . . $375.00

Rooster Weathervane, copper hollow form, 19th C., retaining traces of orig. br. & gilt paint, 30½" H$1,700.00

Staved Porridge Container, Norwegian w/ polychrome decor., dated 1835, 13" H, 10¼" D $1,300.00

Horse Weathervane, molded copper w/ cast iron head, bullet holes, 15½" H, 31½" L $900.00

Pine Box, w/ polychrome decor., dated 1828, w/ initials "S.D." int. till, 8½" H, 13¼" L $450.00

A-OH July 1996 Garth's Auction

Dome Top Box, mahogany veneer w/ inlay & orig. finish, orig. oval brass handle & lock, some edge damage & inlay damage, pine secondary wood, 12" L $2,970.00

Decorated Oblong Bentwood Band Box, w/ laced seams, pine w/ orig. blue paint, polychrome floral designs & full figure of man raising glass on lid, red, white, blk. & yellow, wear & edge damage, edge of lid band is incomplete, 16¼" L $935.00

Decorated Box, pine w/ orig. br. flame graining w/ striping in imitation of inlay, minor wear, interior edge break on hinge rail, 18" L . . . $550.00

A-OH Jan. 1996 Garth's Auction

Left to Right, Top to Bottom

Kugel, deep red, brass hanger, 4" D $412.50

Kugel, deep red, brass hanger, 4" D $385.00

Kugel, med. red, brass hanger, 3⅞" D $247.50

Kugel, cobalt bunch of grapes, brass hanger, 6½" L $495.00

Two Kugels, bunch of grapes, cobalt, 4¼" L and gr., worn silvering, brass hangers $95.00

Kugel, bunch of grapes, amber, worn silvering, brass hanger, 5½" L $192.50

Three Kugels, mauve, worn, 3" D, gr. tear drop, 2¼" and deep pink, 2½" D, brass hangers. $247.50

Two Kugels, both cobalt blue, one slightly darker, 3¼" D, brass hangers. $165.00

Two Kugels, med. gr., 2⅝" D, and lt. gr., 4" D, wear, brass hangers. . $60.50

Four Santas, w/ bisque faces and felt or flannel coats $110.00

Fourteen Christmas Ornaments, nine glass lt. bulbs incl. lrg. socket Santa, 5¼" H and Japanese lanterns, five birds w/ bright colors, to tin clips and two have tails. $192.50

Three Kugels, gold, 4¾" D, silver, 5" D, and mauve, 4¾" D, brass hangers. $165.00

Four Kugels, gold, 4¾" D, gold, 2¾" D, lt. gr., 3¾" D and yel. gr., 2¾" D, all have wear, brass hangers. $71.50

A-VA Sept. 1995 Ken Farmer Auctions

Bride's Box, early 19th C., polychrome paint decor., 19" H, 11½" W, 5½" D $1,155.00

A-OH Mar. 1996   Garth's Auction

Row 1

Miniature Shaving Mirror, pine w/ rosewood graining, ebonized posts & gilded decoration, one drawer has ivory pull, mirror is worn, 6" H $247.50

Two Decorated Treen Inkwells by "S. Silliman, Chester, Conn." (One is labeled), worn brown flame graining w/ gold stencling, glass inserts, 3⅜" & 3¾" D $275.00

Miniature Decorated Dome Top Box, pine w/ orig. blue paint w/ floral dec. in red, white, black & yellow, one staple hinge is broken, 4¼" L .$165.00

Yellowware Pig Bank, w/ Blue & Brown Sponging, chips, 6" L .$220.00

Three PA folk Art Carvings, initialed "C.S." (Carl Snavely, 20th c. carver): rooster, 4" H; distlefink in polychrome, 4⅜" H, & gooney bird, 4¾" H .$522.50

Row 2

Chalk Santa Claus, worn surface w/ traces of paint that are mostly mottled brown, 7½" H $60.50

Small Wooden Swift, base missing, 6⅝" H $27.50

Treen Plate, w/ orig. orangish red paint w/blk. & yellow, 7"x7½"$357.50

Child's purse, embossed tin w/ worn lithograph of cats in blue, gold, red & black, 5" L $302.50

Shenandoah Redware Pitcher, white slip w/ clear glaze & running green & brown, minor hairline in bottom, 6" H $990.00

Row 3

European Redware Pitcher, two tone orange & tan slip w/ wavy lines in red slip, wear & edge chips, 9" H $165.00

Dovetailed Coffee Grinder, poplar w/ old finish, pewter hopper & wrought iron crank, 8½" H . .$165.00

Nantucket Basket, turned wooden bottom, woven cane & splint w/ bentwood swivel handle, worn old varnish finish, 10" D, 5½" H, plus handle. . . . .
. . . .$880.00

Cast Iron Doorstop, cockatoo w/ old polychrome repaint, good color, 8⅛" H $220.00

Pottery Figural Jug, buff clay w/ white glaze, blue, brown, yellow & green detail, edge chips, 8¾" H $159.50

A-OH Mar. 1996   Garth's Auction

Pieced & Appliqued Baby Quilt, pink & blue w/ animals in white, yellow, pink & green w/ embroidered detail (& embroidered letters), 33½" x 51½". $38.50

Wrought Iron Utensil Rack, w/ scrolled detail & five hooks, 24" W, 18" H $440.00

Writing Armchair, Ohio, old red w/ traces of gold stenciling on crest, bulbous & bamboo turnings, scrolled arm, plank seat, half arrowback & wide writing arm, splits in seat where writing arm attaches, 17¾" seat, 38" H . . $825.00

Small Blanket Chest, ref. poplar, dovetailed case, applied base & lid edge moldings, w/ lid, feet replaced, some puttied edge repair, 37½" W, 16" D, 21" H $330.00

Tin Candle Screen, w/ Adjustable Shield, 25½" H $247.50

Balance Scales, wrought iron frame, worn gilded trim, two brass pans on chains, lever that lifts pans is labeled "Degrave, Short & Fanner, London", 19¾" H $275.00

Two Stoneware Jugs, w/ applied decorative detail, Albany slip, wire bail & wooden handle (dark brown), 8½" H. Double spout w/ decorative handle & applied foliage type decoration (reddish brown), chips on one spout, 9½" H $451.00

Tin Dutch Oven, w/spit, 19" L . . . . . .
. . . .$346.50

Jan. 1996   Skinner, Inc.

Stove, cast iron, wooden knob, 16⅜" H, 28¾" L, 12" W $460.00

Stove, cast iron, wooden knob, cracked on left side, 17½" H, 33" L, 12¾" W $805.00

A-OH Mar. 1996   Garth's Auction

Pieced Quilt, flying geese grid in pink & blue on white ground, machine & hand sewn, hand quilted, stained in white areas, 80" x 91" $121.00

Hanging Spice Box, w/ Eight Drawers, beech w/ traces of green & stenciled label "Home Furnishing Co. 4th St", 16¾" H $192.50

Open Floor Standing Shelves, pine or poplar w/ old worn brown repaint, cut out feet, some age but not 19th c. 41" W, 42¾" H, 10" D $550.00

Country Corner Chair, old black repaint, turned legs, posts & stretchers w/ shaped arms & simple crest, repairs to arms, paper rush seat, 17½" seat, 30" H $165.00

Banister Back Armchair w/ Added Rockers, old black repaint, old repairs & replacements, replaced rush seat, 42¼" H $522.50

Stoneware Jug, impressed label "E. & L.P. Norton, Bennington, VT", floral design in cobalt blue slip, surface flake at dec.12" H $220.00

Stoneware Pig Bank w/ Metallic Brown Albany Slip, 13" L $247.50

Ovoid Stoneware Jar, impressed label "Clark & Fox, Athens", flourish design w/ polka dots in cobalt blue slip, cracked, 13¼" H $181.50

German Stoneware Pitcher, English inscription in cobalt blue, 8¾" H .N/S

Ovoid Stoneware Jar w/ Applied Shoulder Handles, running daubs of blue at shoulder, chips & hairlines, 12¾" H $159.50

A-PA Nov. 1995   Aston Auctioneers
& Appraisers

Pictorial Fraktur, watercolor & ink w/ rooster, distelfink & floral motifs .
. . . .$440.00

A-PA Nov. 1995   Aston Auctioneers & Appraisers

Baby Carriage, Victorian, horse drawn $2,300.00

A-PA Nov. 1995   Aston Auctioneers & Appraisers

Furniture Crest, w/ roosting bird & moon face, hand carved $875.00
Glazed Redware Mug, wheel-thrown w/ applied handle, mold chips on rim $45.00
Glazed Redware Apple Bank, polished w/ paint decor $390.00

A-PA Nov. 1995   Aston Auctioneers & Appraisers

Wooden-Cased Candlemold, w/ 18 pewter tubes & wick spools $1,650.00
Tallow Candles, 6 unused . .$290.00

A-PA Nov. 1995   Aston Auctioneers & Appraisers

Three-Legged Stool, w/ folk carved distelfink & pinwheel designs $250.00

A-PA Nov. 1995   Aston Auctioneers & Appraisers

Tape Loom, walnut w/ unusual cut-out handle $380.00

A-PA Nov. 1995   Aston Auctioneers & Appraisers

Redware Bird Whistle, molded & wheel-thrown w/ clear lead glaze . . .
. . . .$930.00

A-PA Nov. 1995   Aston Auctioneers & Appraisers

Circus Wagon Crest, highly-carved eagle w/ lioness & dolphins (1 missing) $650.00

A-PA Nov. 1995   Aston Auctioneers & Appraisers

Redware-Tubed Candlemold, mid 19th C., 24 tubes in bootjack-end wooden frame w/ fitted wooden cover $1,900.00

A-PA Nov. 1995   Aston Auctioneers & Appraisers

Row 1, Left to Right
Lard Lamp Fill Can, tin, PA, German $85.00
Role Toddy Warmer, red, w/ turned wooden handle & rosette knob top $180.00
Wooden Candle Dipper, w/ wire wick holders $260.00
Row 2, Left to Right
Wooden Cheese Press, w/ lightly-carved floral design $160.00
Wooden Swizzle Stick, utilitarian-form $85.00
Doughnut Box, mustard yellow, small size, sgn $700.00

A-OH Jan. 1996   Garth's Auction

Pieced Quilt, sawtooth designs in multi-colored prints & white, colors faded w/ overall wear, binding machine sewn, rest hand sewn, 80" x 86" $412.50
Paper Collage, pen & white ink on black paper, drawn by E.W. Merrill, Concord, NH, framed 16½" x 26¾" W $165.00
Windsor Bench, old worn black re-paint, 20th c., 63" L, 43¾" H .$1,430.00
Brass Sauce Pans, set of 5, w/ wrought iron handles 8½" to 5¾" D, 1 has decor. end on handle . . .$330.00

A-OH May 1996   Garth's Auction

Ovoid Stoneware Jar, mkd. "T.F. Field, Utica", cobalt blue highlighting label & decor., Field discontinued pottery operation in 1830, sm. flakes on lip & old repr. to right of label at stone, 10½" H $4,290.00

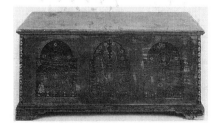

A-PA May 1996   Pook & Pook, Inc.

PA. Lancaster Co. Dower Chest, w/ lift lid opening to fraktur by Bauman, dated 1801, w/ tulips & birds, case w/ 3 dk. blue panels & stenciled star & tulip decor. on light blue background, 23½" H, 51½" W $4,000.00

A-OH July 1996   Garth's Auction

Row 1, Left to Right
Half Buttocks Basket, woven splint w/ old dk. patina, eleven ribs, 7" W $247.50
Burl Bowl, old worn varnish finish, wear & age cracks, 2¼" H 192.50
Sm. Woven Splint Buttocks Basket, old br. patina, 3" H, minor damage $302.50
Miniature Woven Splint Buttocks Basket, old patina, 2" H $632.50
Tiny Woven Splint Basket, some age, eye of God at handle, 1⅛" H plus handle $115.50
Sm. Woven Splint Buttocks Basket, 3⅝" H plus handle $192.50
Row 2, Left to Right
Woven Splint Buttocks Basket, two tone w/ dk. varnish finish, minor damage, 4½" H plus handle $192.50
Burl Bowl, w/ turned ring at base, old inletted repr. in bottom & puttied repr. inside, soft finish, 8" D, 3½" H $302.50
Sm. Woven Splint Basket, traces of red & green, 3½" H plus wooden handle $137.50
Rectangular Woven Splint Basket, dk. worn finish, some damages, 4½" H plus handle $104.50

A-PA May 1996   Pook & Pook, Inc.

NY Federal Mahogany Veneered Work Table, ca. 1830, base w/ acanthus carved frieze, downturned legs ending in animal paw feet, 27½" x 23" W $1,600.00

A-OH Mar. 1996   Garth's Auction

Country Empire Couch, maple w/ curly maple legs, posts & arms, old finish has wear, 71" L $1,430.00

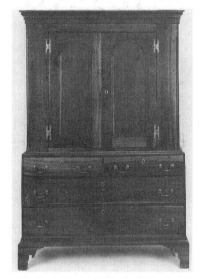

A-PA May 1996   Pook & Pook, Inc.

NJ Federal Cherry Linen Press, ca 1790 w/ dental molded cornice, fluted quarter columns, 76½" H, 52½" W, 19⅞" D $7,200.00

A-OH July 1996   Garth's Auction

Settle Bench, that folds open into a bed, pine w/ old worn finish & traces of paint, paneled constr. 68 ¾" L .$522.50
Canada Goose, old worn working repaint, 24½" L $258.50
Stoneware Jug, impressed mkd. "Wilson, Fairbanks & Co, 43 & 45 Hanover St. Boston 5", compote of flowers in cobalt blue quill work, badly cracked $220.00

A-OH Mar. 1996   Garth's Auction

Chest of Drawers, birch, cherry & pine w/ old nut brown varnish finish, dovetailed drawers w/ early dovetailing, feet have repairs, replaced brasses, pine secondary wood, 35¼" W, 38¼" H $1,760
Rockingham Seated Dog, w/ free standing front legs, 10¼" H . .$440.00
Dovetailed Knife Box, mahogany w/ old finish, scrolled divider, 15¼" L $357.50
Stoneware Ovoid Jug, tooled lines & impressed mark "Boston", grey salt glaze w/ amber pebbled highlights, old chips, 10" H $93.50
Stoneware Jug, mkd. "E.S. Taft & Company, Keene, N.H.", bird on branch in cobalt blue quill work, stains, wear & flaking w/ chips on lip, 11¼" H$143.00

A-OH Mar. 1996   Garth's Auction

Tramp Art Shield Mirror Frame w/ Applied Eagle & Star, old varnish finish w/ some edge damage, 14" H, 13½" W $440.00
Fanback Windsor Armchair, old worn nut brown finish, feet ended out & arm rail has break at one spindle w/ pieced repair, age cracks in seat, 41¾" H $1,430.00
Early Candlestand, hard & soft woods w/ old refinishing, damage, stains & age cracks, 13" D, 24½" H $247.50
Round Woven Splint Basket w/ Bentwood Rim Handles, 11½" x 12", 4½" H $104.50
Punched Tin Revere Type Candle Lantern, 13¼" H $203.50

A-OH Mar. 1996   Garth's Auction

Pair of Handcolored Lithographs by "Currier & Ives", "George Washington" & "Martha Washington", stains, framed, 18½" H, 14½" W $330.00
Black & White Lithograph by "Currier & Ives", "President Lincoln at Home", full margins are soiled, matted & unframed, 19¾" H, 16" W .$165.00
Hepplewhite Bowfront Chest, refinished mahogany w/ flame veneer facade, drawers w/ applied edge beading & oval brasses, cross banded veneer w/ edge inlay around top edge & banding around base, age cracks in sides, feet are old replacements, minor pieced repair, pine & poplar secondary wood, 41" W, top is 22½" x 42", 37" H $1,870.00

A-OH Mar. 1996   Garth's Auction

Pair of Oil on Canvas Paintings, primitive portraits of two children w/ birds, one signed "M. Tenducci", early to mid 20th ca., some crazing & touch up repair, 24½" H, 19" W, framed, 27¼" H, 21¾" W $770.00

Country Architectural Mirror, pine frame w/ old dark red finish, reeded pilasters & molded cornice, orig. reverse glass painting of house w/ yellow & white walls & red roof has some flaking but good color, old glass, 22¾" H, 13½" W $385.00
Pair of Fanback Windsor Side Chairs, old refinishing, splayed base w/ bulbous turned legs & "H" stretcher, saddle seat, one has repaired split in seat, the other has skillfully repaired break in crest, 17¼" seat, 34¾" H . . . $1265.00 . . . .
Country Stand, refinished pine, splayed base w/ turned legs, one nailed drawer & rounded corner top, one end of top ended out, 18½" x 18¾", 29" H $385.00
Stoneware Jug w/ Strap Handle, impressed label "E & L.P. Norton, Bennington, VT", floral decoration in cobalt blue quill work, cracked & lip chips, 10¾" H $220.00

A-MA June 1996   Skinner, Inc.

Federal Mahogany Stand, Middle Atlantic States, 1815-25, w/ orig. casters, old pulls, old ref., imperf., 49½" H, 21½" W, 15½" D $920.00

A-OH July 1996   Garth's Auction

Country Chippendale Table, cherry w/ old finish, one dovetailed overlapping drawer & two board breadboard top, top has old reprs. & age cracks, 25¾" x 37¾", 27" H $990.00
Stoneware Pitcher, w/ strap handle, tooled lines & brushed cobalt blue floral decor., chips on base, handle & spout, 10⅝" H $880.00
Hanging Paint Cupboard, decor., pine w/ old worn dk. gr. repaint w/ compass star in diamond in blk. & red on door panel, dovetailed case, 14½" W, 18" H $385.00
Lantern, tin w/ brass dome & clear blown globe, removable font w/ whale oil burner, some rust damage, 13½" H plus ring handle $357.50

A-OH Mar. 1996   Garth's Auction

Table, poplar, cherry & maple w/ worn red stain, dovetailed drawer & rounded curly maple front, 2 board top has cracks, & edge wear, 28¾" H .$330.00
Banister Back Side Chair, worn dark varnish stain, pieced repair, old worn splint seat, 37½" H $110.00
Sponge Spatter Bowls, 3 pcs., simple molded panels, blue & brown on greyish ground, wear & crow's foot in two larger bowls, 6⅜", 8⅜" & 9½"D .$181.50

A-OH July 1996   Garth's Auction

Row 1, Left to Right

Two Ironstone Carpet Balls, w/ design spatter decor., one red & one blue, 3" D $308.00
Two Fish Decoys, attrib. to Oscar Peterson, orig. paint, glass eyes Brook Trout, 7" L & Pike, 8" . . . .
Fish Decoy, Wood & tin w/ orig. red, yellow & white paint, 6" L $77.00
Three Ironstone Carpet Balls, blue & white plaid, gr. & white plaid & white, white one has some surface chips, 3" D $297.00

Row 2, Left to Right

Pottery, two miniature pieces w/ strap handles, ovoid jug, gr. glaze, handle glued, 4½" H & yellowware w/ gr. sponging, wear & sm. flakes on rim, 3¾" H $165.00
Pottery Pig Bank, two-tone br. marbleized glaze, chips at coin slot, 4⅛" L $27.50
Three Toy Santa Claus Figures, composition, cloth, fiber etc w/ bisque faces, "Japan", some wear & damage, 5½" H .137.50
Wooden Nesting Blocks, set of six, w/ colorful lithography on paper covering w/ children, birds, animals & alphabets, two largest have corner damage, four have had corners reinforced w/ glue, 3¼" x 3¼" x 3½" $110.00

Row 3, Left to Right

Porcelain Boar Hat Pin Holder, polychrome & blk., damage, 6" L . . .$77.00
Pottery Pig Bank, blk. & white paint, 6" L $126.50
Pottery Pig Bank, br. glaze w/ four yellow spots, 6" L $115.50
Pottery Pig Bank, two-tone br. & blue marbleized galze, sm. flakes & short hairlines, 6½" L $71.50

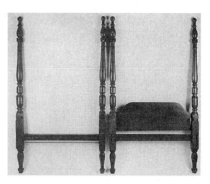

A-MA Jan. 1996   Skinner, Inc.

Tall Post Bed, tiger maple, N. Eng., early 19th c., old ref., 82" H, 48½" W, 79¼" D $2,415.00

A-OH APR. 1996   Garth's Auction

Pennsylvania Blanket Chest, poplar w/ orig. br. graining w/ six white tombstone reserves w/ tulips in green, red, yellow & blk., stars on ends, dovetailed case, till w/ lid, wear, particularly on lid, 43¾" W, 18¾" D, 22½" H $1,430.00

A-PA May 1996   Pook & Pook Inc.

Mass. Sheraton Mahogany Work Table, ca. 1790, w/ sandwich glass knobs & delicate tiger maple legs, 27¾" H, 19¾" W $1,700.00

A-OH   Jan. 1996 Garth's Auction

Theorem on Velvet, 20th c. Penn. folk artist, student of David Ellinger, all have orig sponge painted frames, Colorful Cornucopia w/ Fruit and Bird, sgn. "Wm. Rank", 27½" H, 37¼" W $495.00

A-OH July 1996   Garth's Auction

Sawtooth Trammel, all wooden, 32¾" H $137.50
Wrt. Iron Hanging Grease Lamp, w/ round pan & twisted arm, long twisted hanger, 21" L overall . .$99.00
Splint Cheese Sieve, round bent-wood, splint has some damage, 23" D $66.00
Tin Hanging Lamp, w/ traces of old green paint, wire hanger, 10" L overall $77.00
Lighting Trammel, all wooden, worn dk. patina, bottom ratchet stop is repl., one end has split, 25" L $275.00
Bench, pine w/ layers of worn old repaint, cut out ends are mortised through top, one end has repr. cracks, 12¾" x 62", 18½" H $467.50
Tin Candle Mold, twelve tube w/ large ear handle, 10⅞" H $99.00
Vegetable Washing Basket, all wooden, 19½" x 20", 10½" H .$357.50
Tin Candle Mold, eight tube w/ ear handle, 10⅝" H $110.00
Candle Mold, w/ sixty-three tin tubes (one is missing) in wooden frame, pine & poplar w/ old worn patina, one foot is repl., 8½" x 29", 17" H . . .$1,650.00

A-OH July 1996   Garth's Auction

Two Handcolored Lithographs by "N. Currier", "Isabella", stains, fading & some damage, 14" H, 12" W, curly maple veneer frame, 18" H, 16" W & "Emma", stains & damage, back of print is covered w/ old calling cards, 16" H, 12" W, beveled frame, 18¾" H, 14¾" W $77.00
Empire Chest, ref. cherry, paneled ends, turned & rope carved pilasters & dovetailed drawers, sm. pieced reprs., to back edge of lid, 41" W, 43" H .$495.00
Cast Iron Doorstop, full bodied Boston Bulldog, worn orig. blk. & white paint, 9½" H $55.00
Cast Iron Doorstop, full bodied Boston bulldog, worn orig. blk & white paint, 10¼" H $220.00
Cast Iron Doorstop, full bodied Airesdale, black & brown repaint, 8½" H $220.00

A-VA Sept. 1995 Ken Farmer Auctions

Decorated Bed, mid. 19th C., PA, black sponging over ochre, 65" H, 77" L 53" W $9,625.00

A-OH July 1996   Garth's Auction

Row 1, Left to Right

Pewter Creamer, w/ ear handle, unmarked Am., 4⅝" H $275.00
Pewter Plate, eagle touch w/ "J.E." (Jacob Eggleston, Middletown, CT), 7⅞" D $715.00
Three Lamps, two are pewter w/ ear handles, one is clear glass peg lamp w/ pewter collar, 2⅞" H, plus single spout burner w/ snuffer cap, 2½" H, plus whale oil burner (threads are stripped) & 4⅝" H, plus burning fluid rabbit ear burner w/ snuffer caps $247.50
Pewter Plate, "J. Martine, Fayt N.C.", minor wear & scratches, 9" D $962.50
Pewter Basin, unmarked, wear & scratches, 6⅝" D $137.50
Pewter Sugar Bowl, beaded trim & lid has reeding plus acorn finial, unmarked, some battering, 4¾" D, 4⅝" H $110.00
Pewter Plate, sm. eagle touch, Thomas Danforth Ill., minor wear & scratches, 6⅛" D $550.00
Pewter Plate, eagle touch w/ "J.E." (Jacob Eggleston, Middletown, CT) 7⅞" D $1,210.00
Pewter Creamer, w/ ear handle, wear & soldered repr., loose, unmarked, Am., 4½" H $110.00

Row 2

Two Butter Prints, semi-circular wooden w/ inserted handles, worn patina, eagle & pineapple, 7" $880.00
Two Butter Prints, semi-circular wooden w/ inserted handles, worn patina, heart & flowers, some damage, 7" $440.00

Row 3

Two Butter Prints, semi-circular wooden w/ inserted handles, sun-burst floral designs, one has edge damage, 7" $330.00
Two Butter Prints, semi-circular wooden w/ inserted handles, floral, 7" $550.00

A-OH June 1996   Garth's Auction

Jacquard One Piece Coverlet, single weave, four rose medallions, vintage border & corners, mkd. "Manufactured expressly for ___ 1858" & eagle w/ "Chesterfield, Ohio, 1858", navy blue & natural white, minor stains, 70" x 90" $495.00

Checkerboard, pine w/ worn cream & tan paint, three boards w/ applied edge, applied end dividers are cracked at nails, 19½" x 25¾" $247.50

Curly Maple Drop Leaf Table, ref., apron has added interior braces & one board top has age crack, 21" x 41¾" w/ 14½" leaves, 29" H $632.50

Old Sleepy Eye Pitcher, blue & white, minor stains & sm. flake on handle, 8⅞" H $357.50

Old Sleepy Eye Pitcher, blue & white, stains, chip on spout & short rim hairline, 8" H $247.50

Old Sleepy Eye Milk Pitcher, blue & white, stains, hairline at spout & sm. flake on base, 6½" H $247.50

Old Sleepy Eye Pitcher, blue & white, minor stains & crazing w/ sm. bruise at spout, 5¼" H $324.50

Old Sleepy Eye Creamer, blue & white, minor edge wear & pinpoints, 4" H $330.00

Blue & White Spongeware Pitcher, two rim hairlines & sm. chip on base, 8⅞" H $192.50

Blue & White Spongeware Pitcher, barrel shaped, spout is chipped, 9⅞" H $170.50

A-OH June 1996   Garth's Auction

Allen & Wheelock Drop Breech Rimfire Rifle, barrel is octagon to round w/ a br. finish & measures 26", 1" chip w/ repr. at wrist & hairline, serial no. 176 . . . .$275.00

A-OH June 1996   Garth's Auction

Jacquard Two Piece Coverlet, double weave, in navy blue & white, corners dated "1853", minor wear & stains, top edge is turned & stitched, 76" x 85" $275.00

Rope Bed, ref. curly maple, w/ trumpet finials, 54" W, repl. steel side rails, 76"L, 57½" H $1,100.00

Rocking Horse, wood w/ old worn dapple grey paint & red rockers, saddle w/ stirrups, incomplete harness & traces of mane & tail, 42½" L $440.00

Pull Toy, donkey w/ stuffed brownish amber velvet body, glass eyes & blk. mohair tail & mane, wooden base w/ tin wheels, 13" L $302.50

A-IL Apr. 1996   Olivers

Wm. & Mary Tavern Table, w/ orig. blk. over red paint, top ref., 25½" H, 30" L, 18" W $1,400.00

Round Treeware Box, w/ dark gr. paint, 6¼" H, 7" Diam. $1,400.00

Splint Holder, iron & wood w/sq. full base, 18" H $450.00

A-OH June 1996   Garth's Auction

Pieced Quilt, star design in red calico & white, minor stains, 70"x71" $412.50

Sheraton Dressing Table, ref. cherry, w/ bird's eye maple veneer drawer front, one dovetailed drawer, poplar secondary wood, one corner of drawer has veneer repr. & top has putty filled gouge, 34" H $467.50

Blue & White Sponge Spatter Bowl & Pitcher, w/ blue stripes, color & width of stripes varies, 14½" D, 12" H $330.00

Blue & White Sponge Spatter Pitcher, 9" H $302.50

Blue & White Sponge Spatter Pitcher, chip on table ring, 8¾" H . .$467.50

A-OH June 1996   Garth's Auction

Long Flint Rifle, PA, hunting pouch & horn, rifle is engraved, "S.B.", on top of barrel & has carving characteristic of the maker Samuel Baum, Columbia Co., PA, curly maple stock w/ incised carving around cheek piece, behind tang & on either side of ramrod entry pipe, brass hardware includes pieced and engraved patchbox, silver barrel pin escutcheons, restor. breaks at wrist & around lock are well done, 60", leather pouch has a D shaped flap & restor. handle, horn is 8½" L . .$6,050

A-OH Jan. 1996   Garth's Auction

Federal Two Part Mirror, ref. mahogany, orig. reverse glass painting of yellow house has wear, flaking & some touch up repr., 21½" H, 13¼ W $220.00

Watercolors on Paper, pr., minor stains, framed, 9¾"H x 7¾"W .$143.00

Chippendale Candlestand, NH, ref. birch w/ some curl in top, 16¼" x 17", 28¼" H $990.00

Q.A. Side Chair, hard & soft woods w/ old mellow refinishing & replm. rush seat, 40½" H $1,100.00

Copper Tea Kettle, dovetailed, w/ cast brass handle & goose neck spout, 10½" H $121.00

A-OH July 1996   Garth's Auction

Row 1, Left to Right

Chickens, pr., wood & tin w/ composition, orig. polychrome paint has wear but good color, 7¾" H $825.00

Stave Constructed Tub, w/ edge carving & cut out hearts, old red & gr. repaint, 9¼" D $495.00

Schimmel Type Carved Wooden Eagle, w/ orig. white, red, yellow, blk. & gr. paint, minor wear & chip on base, 6⅜" H $3,520.00

Chalk Seated Dog, white w/ blk., red, & yellow paint, 5¾" H . .$110.00

A-OH Mar. 1996   Garth's Auction

Staffordshire

Row 1

Two Plates (L & R), dark blue transfer "R. Hall's Picturesque Scenery, Fulham Church, Middlesex", minor wear, 8½" D $253.00

Soup Plate, light blue transfer of English village w/ church, minor wear & small edge flakes, 10" D $165.00

3 Pcs, dark blue transfer: creamer w/ chip on spout, 3⅞" H; sauce tureen, "Italian Scenery, Terni", small chips, 6½" H & creamer w/ English country house, chips & hairline, 5⅛"H $671.00

Row 2

Plate, medium dark blue transfer, "Thornton Castle, Staffordshire", impressed "Enoch Wood", minor wear, 10⅛" D $148.50

Open Vegetable, dark blue transfer "Rode Hall, Cheshire", stains & chips, 12" L $330.00

Invalid Feeder, dark blue transfer still life of flowers, old professional repair, 3" H $220.00

Two Plates, (1 illus.) dark blue transfer still life w/ fruit & flowers, minor wear & scratches, 8⅞" D, 10" D $241.50

Row 2, Left to Right

Box w/ Sliding Lid, poplar w/ old reddish br. stain, divided interior has three sections, 5" x 9" $247.50

Cast Iron Eagle, w/ traces of old worn polychrome paint, tip of one wing has minor old damage, wooden base, 16½" wing span $385.00

Two Tôle Children's Mugs, worn orig. paint & stenciled design: "My Girl" on yellow ground & "My Boy" on red ground, 2¾" D $110.00

Two Pieces of Child Size Tôle, w/ worn orig. red paint w/ stenciled design: cup w/ "For a Child", 2¾" D & pail w/ flower, wire bale handle, 2¼" D $55.00

Oval Bentwood Shaker Box, old worn gr. paint, steel tacks, 10½" L ... $1,045.00

Oval Bentwood Shaker Box, similar to above, old worn gr. paint, steel tacks, damage to lid & base at fingers, 6⅞" L $60.50

A-OH June 1996   Garth's Auction

Two Piece Wall Cupboard, ref. butternut, two dovetailed drawers, poplar secondary wood, 46½" W, shelf is 84" H $2,530.00

Stonewae Jug, w/ applied handle, impressed mkd. "West Troy Pottery", bird in cobalt blue quill work, stains, chip on lip and hairline in handle, 12" H $352.00

Woven Splint Basket, 7¼" H, bentwood handle, minor damage . .$93.50

Stoneware Jug, w/ applied handle, impressed mkd. "Wm. E. Warner, West Troy", cobalt blue flower & label highlighted in blue, hairline in base of handle, 10½" H $132.00

A-OH July 1996   Garth's Auction

Decorated PA Blanket Chest, pine & poplar w/ orig. br. & blue vinegar graining w/ reserves on front, sides & lid, w/ name & date in red & blk., "Johan Witmer 1799", moldings & feet are blk., dovetailed case w/ bear trap lock & wrt. iron strap hinges till w/ lid & secret compartment w/ two dovetailed drawers, minor wear & edge damage, paint wear is primarily on lid, 51¼" W, 23" D, 27" H $22,000.00

A-MA Aug. 1996   Robert C. Eldred
Co., Inc.

Double Melon Basket, painted red, 10" diam. $330.00
Double Melon Basket, painted blue, 11½" diam. $330.00
Rockingham Pitcher, w/ hound handle & vintage decor., 11" H . .$132.00
Brown & White Staffordshire Platter, "Delhi" patt., 19½" L $275.00
Tavern Table, in pine w/ breadboard ends, orig. red paint, top 30" x 48", 30" H $522.50
Am. Chippendale Brass Andirons, pair, w/ two matching fire tools, ball & spire finials, 22" H, 20" L $770.00

A-MA Aug. 1996   Robert C. Eldred
Co., Inc.

Carved Wood Tackle Shop Sign, "Live Bait", in the form of a sturgeon, old paint, 48" L $852.50

A-MA Aug. 1996   Robert C. Eldred
Co., Inc.

Rare Early High Wheeler Bicycle, leather seat, paint worn, pedals missing, 60" H $770.00

A-MA Aug. 1996   Robert C. Eldred
Co., Inc.

Chinese Carved Teakwood Stands, w/ bamboo style turnings, largest 20" H $825.00

A-MA Aug. 1996   Robert C. Eldred
Co., Inc.

Left to Right
Brass Andirons, baluster turned, 18" H, pair $220.00
Eng. Brass Footman, 12½" H $495.00
Brass Steeple-top Andirons, 15" H, pair $412.50

A-MA Aug. 1996   Robert C. Eldred
Co., Inc.

Pine Blanket Chest, w/ lift-top & one drawer, bootjack ends, snipe hinges, 44" W, 35" H $302.50
Wicker Sewing Basket, two-handled, 7" H $104.50
Oval Wooden Hatbox, w/ floral decor., 22" L, 9" H $440.00
Cast Iron Doorstop, "Highland Light Cape Cod" w/ lighthouse & 2 houses, orig. paint, 8" H $770.00

A-MA Aug. 1996   Robert C. Eldred
Co., Inc.

Left to Right
Staffordshire Figures, hunter & wife w/ game birds, 15¼" H $467.50
Staffordshire Figure, "Going to Market", 12½" H $121.00
Hepplewhite Drop-Leaf Table, cherry, 36" L, 28½" H $440.00
Brass Ball & Spire Andirons, 19" H $412.50
Staffordshire Figure, "The Harvesters", by Joseph Unwin, 15½"H $368.50

A-MA Aug. 1996   Robert C. Eldred
Co., Inc.

Tavern Table, w/ one-drawer, pine & maple w/ breadboard top, 37½" x 22½", 27" H $605.00
Fanback Windsor Side Chair, old finish, 36½" H $1,485.00

A-MA Aug. 1996   Robert C. Eldred
Co., Inc.

Salem Rocker, w/ orig. grain-painted decor. $220.00
Q.A. Drop-Leaf Table, cherry, 20th C., red finish, 43" L., 28½" H .$715.00

A-OH June 1996   Garth's Auction

English Gothic Hanging Alms Box, oak w/ old br. grained repaint, wear & one scalloped bracket is incomplete, 10¾" W, 16" H $139.50

Candlestand, ref. cherry, one board top, two feet have repr. breaks, 14⅝" x 15" $522.50

Bowback Windsor Armchair, old ref., minor age cracks in seat, 39½" H $660.00

Rainbow Spatter Bowl & Pitcher, red, and gr., both pieces are cracked, foot has been off pitcher & reattached, 12" D, 10½" H $313.50

Punched Tin Foot Warmer, hardwood frame w/ punched diamonds & sm. punched date "1800" on door, 6" x 8" x 9" $225.50

A-OH June 1996   Garth's Auction

Jacquard Two Piece Coverlet, single weave, floral medallions, w/ bird & tree borders, corners have eagles w/ "F. Yearous, Loudonville, Ohio 1850", navy, teal, red & white, minor edge & fringe wear, 71" x 85" $550.00

Jacquard Two Piece Coverlet, single weave, star medallions w/ chanticleer borders & corners mkd. "J. Heeter, Scipio township, Seneca County, Ohio" (unlisted), navy blue & white, one area of border has moth damage in blue wool, minor fringe loss, 64" x 90" $495.00

A-OH June 1996   Garth's Auction

Jacquard Two Piece Coverlet, single weave, floral medallions w/ stars, bird border & corners mkd. "William Fasig, Richland County, Ohio 1846", navy blue & white, seams resewn & end turned & stitched, minor fringe loss, 66" x 88" . .$660.00

Jacquard Two Piece Coverlet, single weave, floral medallions, vintage border & corners mkd. "W. in Mt Vernon, Knox County, Ohio by Jacob & Michael Ardner 1852", navy blue & white, 70" x 79" $577.50

A-OH June 1996   Garth's Auction

Jacquard One Piece Coverlet, single weave, central floral medallion w/ eagles in the spandrels & rose border, edges mkd. "Philip Allabach", red & white, minor stains & soiling, 72" x 79" $330.00

Jacquard One Piece Coverlet, single weave, floral w/ corners mkd. "Made by R. Peter in Heidelberg for ___AD 1843", red & white, minor overall wear, applied fringe, 68" x 79" $330.00

A-OH June 1996   Garth's Auction

Pieced Quilt, calico & other prints, solid red & goldenrod, applique vining floral borders in red & gr. calico, wear, fading & stains, one pink calico triangle has bleached spot, 70" x 85" . .$330.00

Applique Quilt, flowers & eagle in teal & yellow calico w/ solid red, minor stains, red backing, 80" x 94" $550.00

A-OH June 1996   Garth's Auction

Row 1, Left to Right

"Butter" Crock, w/ lid, white & blue sponging, hairlines & sm. chips, 5¾" D $55.00

Small Crocks, (1 of 2), blue & white spongeware, 5" D, 2¾" H $44.00

Spongeware Bowl, (1 of 2), blue & white, crazing & hairline, 7¼" D, 2⅜" H & aMatch Holder , 2⅞" H . . .$49.50

Dishes, (1 of 3), blue & white spongeware dishes, minor crazing, 3¼", 4¼" & 4½" D . . . . .NS

Small Size Bean Pot, blue & white spongeware, 4⅝" H $412.50

Row 2, Left to Right

Blue & White "Butter" Crock, w/ lid, molded fruit, wire handle missing, minor edge chips & crazing, 7" D . . .$137.50

Blue & White "Salt" Crock, molded eagles, firing chip in back of crest, hairline & sm. chip, no lid, 5⅞" D .$55.00

Blue & White "Butter" Crock, spongeware, w/ "Village Farm Dairy" on back, dk. blue labels, hairlines, 5¾" D $165.00

Blue & White "Salt" Crock, w/ lid, molded "Salt" and swallows, 6" D $495.00

1 of 2 blue & white "Butter Crocks, spongeware, 5¾" D & smaller w/ blue stipe, 4⅜" D, both have hairlines & larger one is pictured $247.50

Row 3, Left to Right

Blue & White Spongeware Bowl, straight sided w/ rim spout & wire bail w/ wooden handle, rim chips, 6¾" D $330.00

Crock w/ Grey Salt Glaze, w/ impressed designs highlighted in blue, rim chip, 6¾" D $247.50

Blue & White "Salt" Crock, w/ pinwheels, repl. wooden lid, hairline & sm. flakes, 6" D $49.50

Blue & White Spongeware "Butter" Crock, w/ molded pinwheels, lid & wire bail w/ wooden handle, chip on bottom edge, 5¾" D $137.50

Blue & White Spongeware "Butter" Crock, w/ molded pinwheels, lid & wire bail w/ wooden handle, 7½" D $220.00

A-MA Aug. 1996   Robert C. Eldred
Co., Inc.

Sheraton Two-Drawer Stand, mahogany w/ cookie corners, top 18½" x 20", 27¾" H $1,155.00

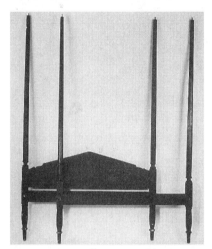

A-MA June 1996   Skinner, Inc.

Gr. Painted Tall Post Bed, N. Eng., C. 1810, octagonal tapering posts, block feet, peaked molded headboard, reprs., 83" H, 50¾" W, 68½" L $3,105.00

A-MA Aug. 1996   Robert C. Eldred
Co., Inc.

French Provincial Tall Case Clock, by Cherden, pine case, enamelled brass dial, 89" H $770.00

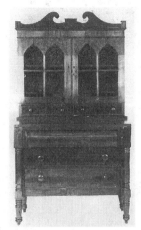

A-MA Aug. 1996   Robert C. Eldred
Co., Inc.

Sheraton Secretary, two pcs., mahogany veneers, 74" H, 40" W $880.00

A-MA Aug. 1996   Robert C. Eldred
Co., Inc.

Eastlake Armchair, walnut w/ inlaid lyre-form crest & figural carved arms, 19th C., ...$550.00

A-MA Aug. 1996   Robert C. Eldred
Co., Inc.

French Bucket Bench, in pine w/ shaped sides, 59½" H, 43¼" W, 16" D $660.00

A-MA Aug. 1996   Robert C. Eldred
Co., Inc.

Sheraton Two Drawer Work Table, maple & tiger maple veneers, top 13" x 24", 28" H $495.00

A-MA Aug. 1996   Robert C. Eldred
Co., Inc.

French Armoire, walnut w/ paneled sides, 82½" H, 56½" W, 23½" D $3,410.00

A-MA Aug. 1996   Robert C. Eldred
Co., Inc.

Hepplewhite Corner Washstand, Eng., mahogany w/ banded inlay, ivory pulls, 50" H $440.00

A-OH June 1996   Garth's Auction

Country Two Piece Wall Cupboard, ref. butternut, w/ two dovetailed drawers, one drawer is an old (non-dovetailed) replm., some edge damage & repr., old lamp burn at pie shelf, 47¾" W, 88¼" H $1,870.00
Blue & White Sponge Spatter Pitcher, barrel shaped, sm. edge flakes, 7½" H $165.00
Blue & White Sponge Spatter Plates, two similar w/ molded scroll rims, 8½" D $187.00
Blue & White Sponge Spatter Teapot, chips on table ring & prof. repr., 7" H $825.00
Blue & White Sponge Spatter Pitcher, very minor glaze flakes, 6¾" H $412.50

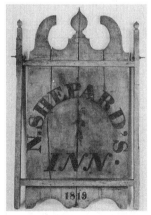

A-MA June 1996   Skinner, Inc.

Tavern Sign, painted wood, N. Eng., late 18th C. w/ pewter gray paint & blk. lettering on the two-sided sign reading "N. Shepard's Inn", old paint, imperf., 67" H, 42" L $4,312.50

A-OH June 1996   Garth's Auction

Country Two-Piece Corner Cupboard, pine w/ old mellow ref., feet missing, orig. wrt. iron rat tail hinges, some edge damage & repr., 45" W, 84¼" H $1,760.00
Ovoid Stoneware Jar, w/ floral lip & applied shoulder handles, mkd. "S.S. Perry, Troy", cobalt blue brushed decor., sm. chip on base, 11" H $82.50
Ovoid Stoneware Jug, w/strap handle, cobalt blue brushed designs w/ chevron stripes on handle, 15" H $55.00

A-OH June 1996   Garth's Auction

Hepplewhite Chest, walnut w/ inlay & old soft finish, dovetailed drawers w/ applied edge beading, inlaid escutcheons, repl. brasses, pine secondary wood, age crack in top, 41" W, 39¼" H $2,090.00
Staffordshire Seated Dogs, red & white w/ polychrome, one is cracked, 13" H $495.00
Tea Caddy, mahogany w/ light wood inlay & brass feet, some edge damage, 8" L $55.00
Ironstone Platter, bluish black floral transfer, 18⅞" L $104.50

A-OH June 1996   Garth's Auction

Wall Cupboard, two piece, walnut w/ old worn ref., poplar secondary wood, cast iron thumb latches, two board panels in doors, one bottom door has separation between panels, 44¾" W, 83¾" H $1,650.00
Brass Student Lamp, gr. ribbed cased shade has chips on top rim, chimney ring is mkd. "Manhattan Brass Co.", electrified, some damage, 20½" H $330.00
Blue & White Spongeware Bowl, w/ molded ribs, crazing in bottom does not show on exterior, 11¼" D, 4¼" H $77.00
Brass Student Lamp, opaque white shade, damage & soldered repr., electrified but needs rewired, 24½" H $220.00
Toy Dog, grey & white plush w/ glass eyes, tubular steel frame w/ red paint & rubber wheels, wooden foot rests, mkd. "Northern Ireland", 24" H . . . . .
. . . .$165.00

A-OH May 1996   Garth's Auction

Ovoid Jar, cobalt blue stenciled & freehand mkd. "T.F. Reppert Manufacturer, Best Blue Stoneware, Greensboro, Pa 2", hairline in base, 10" H $330.00

A-PA Nov. 1995   Aston Auctioneers
& Appraisers

Pedestal-Form Double Butter Print, w/ chip carved eagle & rose . .
. . . .$600.00

A-PA Nov. 1995   Aston Auctioneers
& Appraisers

Peaseware Spice Containers, assembled set of 8, 1 w/ damaged finial $1,800.00

A-PA Nov. 1995   Aston Auctioneers
& Appraisers

Amish Gift Dolls,
w/ cotton batting, repairs . . .$170.00

A-PA Nov. 1995   Aston Auctioneers
& Appraisers

Miniature Box w/ slide top, Fresian-style carving, dated 1779 . . . .$875.00

A-PA Nov. 1995   Aston Auctioneers
& Appraisers

Scherenschnitte, PA, scissor cutting w/ watercolor & ink decor .$1,250.00

A-PA Nov. 1995   Aston Auctioneers
& Appraisers

Faceless Full-Bodied Whirligig, Amish, family of four $2,900.00

A-PA Nov. 1995   Aston Auctioneers
& Appraisers

Left to Right
Bentwood Trinket Box, w/ freehand painted tulips & designs, laced joining
. . . .$300.00
Bride's Box, w/ painted figures of seated smoking man, woman & faint German script $460.00
Bentwood Ribbon Box, w/ freehand painted tulips, laced joining . .$210.00

A-PA Nov. 1995   Aston Auctioneers
& Appraisers

Left to Right
Folk Art Erotica, man in barrel . . . .
$70.00
Folk Art Erotica, man in coffin w/ verse $160.00

A-PA Nov. 1995   Aston Auctioneers
& Appraisers

Left to Right

Burl Scoop, miniature, small chip . .
$150.00

Burl Ladle, w/ hairline age crack & repair, swan handle $400.00

Footed Burl Bowl, ...$700.00

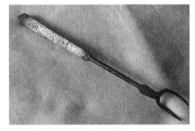

A-PA Nov. 1995   Aston Auctioneers
& Appraisers

Two-Tined Flash Fork, w/ hooked terminus, lightly inscribed . . .$220.00

A-PA Nov. 1995   Aston Auctioneers
& Appraisers

Elephant Pull-Toy, carved from single block of wood, damages $860.00

A-PA Nov. 1995   Aston Auctioneers
& Appraisers

Two-Fingered Oval Spice Box, w/ natural finish $280.00
Shaker Yarn or String Holder, maple w/ removable slotted top . . . .
$500.00
Round Box, w/ painted & stenciled decor $280.00

A-OH APR. 1996   Garth's Auction

Row 1, Left to Right

Clear Blown Lamp, pewter collar & burning fluid burner w/ snuffer caps, 8⅛" H, plus burner $412.50

Clear Blown Pittsburgh Canister, w/ applied blue rings & finial, finial has chip & top has been ground flat, 12¼" H $660.00

Clear Flint Lamp, w/ heart & thumbprint font, pewter collar w/ cylindrical brass strainer in font & burning fluid burner w/ snuffer caps, minor flakes on base, 8⅝" H, plus burner $275.00

Row 2, Left to Right

Small Clear Blown Lace Maker's Lamp, w/ hollow tear drop stem, 6¼" H $275.00

Clear Blown Mug, w/ opalescent looping & clear applied handle, 6¼" H $104.50

Deep Sapphire Blue Soda Water Bottle, w/ molded label "This bottle to be returned, C. Lewis Bottler, Cleveland". Iron pontil & applied lip, 7⅜" H $467.50

A-OH APR. 1996   Garth's Auction

Pennsylvania Chippendale Blanket Chest, refin. walnut, 52¼" W, 22½" D, 28" H $1,650.00

A-OH APR. 1996   Garth's Auction

Pennsylvania Show Towels

Towel, linen homespun w/ cut & drawn work panel, stains, 13" x 59" . .$137.50

Towel or Runner, cotton homespun in diamond's bird's eye weave, 11" x 86" $38.50

Towel, linen homespun in white on white woven patt. w/ stylized star flowers, tulips & checkerboard band, stains, 16" x 53" $275.00

A-OH APR. 1996   Garth's Auction

Sea Captain's Box, rosewood w/ inlaid whale bone, ebony & exotic wood, w/ decor. is on four sides & lid. Fitted dovetailed tray in mahogany w/ mahogany & rosewood lids inlaid w/ whale bone & exotic wood, ivory knobs, minor repair to some inlay, 5" x 7" x 14" $1,650.00

A-MA Mar. 1996   Skinner, Inc.

Chippendale Polescreen, mahogany, w/ hinged shelf, N. Eng., late 18th C., old ref. w/ petit point floral panel, restored, 63½" H $2,070.00

A-MA June 1996   Skinner, Inc.

Weather Vane, copper horse & rider, attrib. to A.L. Jewell & Co., Waltham, MA., third quarter 19th C., surface w/ traces of gilt, imperf. incl. repr. bullet holes, 27" H $7,475.00

A-PA May 1996   Pook & Pook Inc.

Wrt. Iron 4-Pc. set, skimmer, ladle, fork & spatula, all w/ brass inlay . . .
. . . .$1,300.00

A-OH July 1996   Garth's Auction

Piece of Blue & White Homespun, unhemmed 41¾" x 55" $121.00
Hanging Shelves, worn olive gr. repaint, 31" H, 25 " W $330.00
Horse Pull Toy, wood & papier mâché w/ orig. dapple grey paint, fiber tail & tin wheels, wear, ears are missing & some damage, 9½" L, 10" H . .$302.50
Chalk Squirrels, pr., worn orig. red, blk. orange & gr. paint, both are hollow one has closed base w/ chip on bottom, 6½" H $330.00
Chalk Bird, perched on a spherical plinth, old dk. yellow paint w/ red & blk. 7⅞" H $165.00

A-MA Oct. 1995   Skinner, Inc.

Left to Right
53-Copper Horse Weathervane, Am., late 19th c., gilt verdigris surface, (repaired bullet holes), 37" L $1725.00
493A-Gilt Copper running Horse Weathervave, Am., 19th c., (imperfections), 37½" L $1265.00
56-Copper Running Horse Weathervane, attrib. to A.L. Jewell & Co., Waltham, Mass., (bullet holes), 26" L $2760.00
59-Copper running Horse Weathervane, Am., late 19th c., verdigris surface, (imperfections), 31¼" L $1380.00
55-Gilt Copper Running Horse Weathervane, Am., late 19th c., (regilt, tail detached), 42" L .$1610.00

A-OH July 1996   Garth's Auction

Wooden Butter Prints & Cookie Boards
Row 1, Left to Right
Oval Butter Print, w/ one piece handle, eagle, old greyish finish & minor age cracks, 4¼" x 4½" $715.00
Cookie Board, maple w/ well detailed carvings & cherry colored old finish, minor age cracks, 6⅛"x11¼" . .$797.50
Lollipop, w/ primitively carved design w/4 hearts, old patina, 9⅜" . .$275.00
Cookie Board, w/ chip carved letters, beech w/ worm holes & some edge damage, old patina, 4⅝" x 21"$192.50
Row 2, Left to Right
Round Butter Print, w/ one piece turned handle, cow w/ tree, old greyish finish, 4⅝" D $357.50
Three Round Butter Prints, w/ turned inserted handles & similar stylized carvings of sheaf & pomegranate, old patina, 4½" $467.50
Row 3, Left to Right
Two Round Butter Prints, w/ one piece turned handles, cow 3¾" D & star flower, 4½" D $220.00
Two Round Butter Prints, w/ one piece turned handles, stylized tulip, 3¾" D & floral, 3⅞" D $412.00
Two Round Butter Prints, w/ inserted handles, tulip & star flower, old patina, 4½" D $330.00
Two Round Butter Prints, w/ one piece chunky handles, pinwheel w/ simple second design carved on handle, 4½" D & tulip, 4" D, both have old patina w/ age cracks & old damage $198.00

A-OH May 1996   Garth's Auction

Stoneware Crock, Brown Albany slip w/ sgraffito mkd. "W.J. & E.G. Sc-Springfield, Summit County, Ohio", hairlines in base, 9¾" H $935.00

A-OH July 1996   Garth's Auction

PA Rag Carpet, roll, shades of blue, lavender, blk., white etc., unused, 36" x 46' (approx.) $495.00
Blanket Chest, ref. walnut w/ till, poplar secondary wood, hinge strip of lid restored, 43¾" W, 20¼" D, 24¾" H $412.50
Wooden Barn Lantern, cherry w/ old dk. patina, pinned construction, old glass in three sides, glass missing from door, top has age crack & slight warp, 11¾" H, plus wire bale .$346.50
Stoneware Bowl w/ Lid, br. glaze, molded serrated diamond designs & zigzag rims, attrib. to Ohio, wear & chips & exterior flakes, 16" D, 11¼" H (overall) $440.00
Wooden Barn Lantern, ash & other hardwoods w/ old dk. patina, mortised & pinned const., old glass in three sides, door has solid wooden panel, tin chamberstick w/ push-up inside, 10¾" H $478.50

A-MA Jan. 1996   Skinner, Inc.

Copper Weathervanes
Gilt Rooster, Am., 19th c., traces of red paint, 22" H $2,530.00
Gilt Rooster, Am., 19th c., traces of dk red paint, 21" H $1,725.00
Arrow, copper, zinc & iron, 19th c., 24½" H, 35½" L $3,220.00
Running Horse, Am., early 20th c., 22" H, 42" L $1,955.00

Jan. 1996   Skinner, Inc.

Shaker

39-Three Oval Covered Boxes, pine & maple, brown stain, 1⅝" H, 2⅛" H, 2⅝" H $345.00

79-Two Oval Covered Boxes, 1 pine, 1 maple, 2⅛" H, 2½" H .$402.50

83-Oval Carrier, N.H. pine, maple or birch w/ash handle, 4"H, 13¼"L, 9" D $805.00

75-Oval Box, Pine & maple or birch, yellow paint, 1¼" H, 33/16" L, 21/16" D $5,175.00

11-Oval Box, N.H. pine & maple, orig. orange stain, 2⅛" H, 5⅛" L, 3¼" D . . . $3737.50

54-Oval Box, pine & maple, old red painted surface, 2⅞" H, 11" L, 7¾" D $345.00

1-Oval Box, N.H., pine & maple, orig. paint, 4¼"H, 11⅛"L, 7¾"D .$10,925.00

25-Oval Box, pine & maple, olive green paint, 4⅝" H, 11⅜" L, 8½" D $1,265.00

43-Oval Box, pine & birch, yellow stain, 2" H, 4½ L, 2¾" D $373.75

69-Oval Box, pine & maple, orig. green paint, 2⅜"H, 6"L, 3⅝"D $5462.50

15-Oval Box, pine & maple, orig. yel.-green paint, 4⅝" H, 11⅞" L, 8⅛" D $1,725.00

35-Oval Box, pine & maple, brn. stain, 5⅜" H, 13¼" L, 9" D . . .$431.25

100-Oval Carrier, c. 1840-70, pine, maple & ash handle, orig. yellow paint, inscribed, 3½" H, 12⅞" L, 9⅜" D, overall ht. 7¾" $28,750.00

18-Oval Carrier, pine, maple & ash handle, yel. paint, inscribed, 3⅝" H, 11" L, 8" D, overall 7⅝" $862.50

92-Round Covered Box, maple sides, pine top & bottom, dk. red over blue-grn, 4¾ H, 10¼" D $517.50

109-Oval Carrier, pine & birch, reddish-brn stain, 2⅜" H, 6⅜" L, 4⅛" D $402.50

A-MA Mar. 1996 Skinner, Inc.

Watch Hutch, cherry, N. Eng., early 19th C., w/ vestiges of blk. paint, dovetail const., 11" H $4,025.00

Jan. 1996   Skinner, Inc.

Shaker

7-Pail, pine staves and bottom, orig. ochre-brn paint, 9¼" H, 12" D $1,380.00

50-Firkin, pine staves and bottom, orig. blue paint, 11"H, 12⅞" D $1,610.00

23-Pail, pine staves and bottom, orig. chrome yel. paint, int. white, 5⅜" H, 7" D $1,035.00

3-Pail, pine staves and bottom, orig. ochre-orig. paint, 7¼"H, 10"D $1,380.00

104-Lidded Pail, wooden w/ heavy wire bail, wooden handle, 7⅝" H, 9¾" D $230.00

A-OH Mar. 1996   Garth's Auction

Corner Cupboard, 2 pc., PA., pine & poplar cleaned down to yellow color w/ brown stain highlights, dovetailed drawers w/ orig. hardware, one glass cracked, another scratched, 65¼" W, 85" H $2,200

Rocking Horse, old white & black repaint w/replaced black yarn mane & tail, red vinyl saddle, worn painting on foot rest, 46" L $302.50

A-OH July 1996   Garth's Auction

Chippendale Slant Front Desk, ref. walnut, w/ dovetailed case, fitted interior, feet repl., door is rehinged & pieced reprs., repl. brasses, pine & poplar secondary wood, 40" W, 21" D, 42¼" H $1,320.00

Pewter Plate, Eagle touch "S. Kilbourn, Baltimore", 7¾" D $385.00

Pewter Teapot, unmarked Am. 8" H $110.00

Pewter Plate, "Love" touch, some wear, 7⅞" D $192.50

Pewter Shallow Bowl, Lion touch for Thomas Danforth II, Middletown, CT, wear, pitting and scratches, 13¼" D $357.50

A-OH July 1996   Garth's Auction

Step Back Two Piece Bookcase, cherry w/ old ref., cornice restored, 56" W, 91" H $3,850.00

A-OH Aug. 1996   Garth's Auction

Jacquard Two Piece Single Weave Coverlet, mkd. "Emanuel Etteinger, Aronsburg 1840". Navy blue, teal blue, red & natural, minor stains, 72" x 88" $550.00
Settle Bench w/ baby guard w/ orig. dark paint & touch up striping & floral decor., 45' L $715.00
Stoneware Jug mkd. "L. Minier 2", w/ cobalt blue flower $165.00
Stoneware Jug mkd. "P Fisher" & adv. label in blue quill work, 11¼" H $253.00
Ovoid Stoneware Jug w/ cobalt blue freehand & stenciled decor. "Williams and Reppert, Greensboro, PA 2". Chips on lip, 13½" H $660.00

A-OH Aug. 1996   Garth's Auction

Q.A. Highboy, refinished maple, mismatched top, repairs, 69" H $1,100.00
Leather Fire Bucket w/ old black paint & faded gold letters, 12" H $467.50
Pewter Food Dome Top mkd. James Dixon & Sons, Sheffield" $110.00

A-OH Aug. 1996   Garth's Auction

Federal Chest of Drawers, mahogany & mahogany veneer w/ old finish, 53¼" H $3,410.00
Empire Clock, mahogany veneer w/ ebonized pilasters & paper label "Patent Clocks invented by Eli Terry", w/ weights & pendulum, 31" H $522.50

A-OH Aug. 1996   Garth's Auction

Hepplewhite Candlestand, pine & maple, ref., w/ replaced top, 29¼" H $275.00
Shaker Ladderback Armchair Rocker w/ shawl bar, orig. finish w/ traces of Mt. Lebanon label, #7, repl. tape seat, 41" H $660.00
Shaker Swift, worn orig. yellow varnish w/ minor crack in clamp, 15" H $220.00
Shaker Tin Pieces, sugar bowl w/ lid and creamer w/ hinged lid, not a set $165.00
Tin Lantern w/ clear blown globe w/ removable font & whale oil burner, parts mismatched $214.50

A-OH Jan. 1996   Garth's Auction

Country Sheraton Chest of Drawers, cherry w/ old ref., pieced reprs. & edge damage, replm. brasses, extra hole in 1 drawer front, 38" W, 21½" D, 44⅜" H $770.00

Hide Covered Box, for storing military accouterments, decor. leather trim & brass studs, wear, 7½" X 10½" $330.00

Oval Burl Bowl, w/ cutout end handles, edge wear & one handle restored, Am. Indian, 14" x 20", 7" H .$2,090.00

Cast Iron Door Stop or Garden Figure, old white repaint, 10½" H $187.00

A-OH Nov. 1995   Garth's Auction

Left Side

Ink & Watercolor on Paper Map, "Drawn by J.A. Ruggles, A map of Garratt Van Wagoner's Farm Containing Two hundred and Forty Two Acres". Colorful w/ four houses, trees, etc., stains, framed, 18¾" H, 24½" W. $605.00

Early Brass Candlesticks, pr., detail & size vary slightly, 10½" H & 9¾" H. $247.50

Mah-jong Set in Mahogany Case w/ Patong Fittings, four drawers of ivory/bone and bamboo playing pieces, fifth drawer is missing, case marked "China". . . . . .N/S

Country Stand, ref. curly maple, one dovetailed drawer and two board top, poplar secondary wood, lock and escutcheon missing and top is an old replacement, 18½" W, 20" L, 29" H. $385.00

Redware Umbrella Stand, molded tree bark with ivy, worn original brown and white paint with red paint interior $110.00

Right Side

Round Cookie Board, inlay in center of back , hanging hole in handle, poplar with old dark patina with wear on cutting surface, 16¾" D. plus handle .$165.00

Ironstone Mocha Pitcher, leaf handle, blue bands and black stripes w/ earthworm design in black, white and blue, wear, hairlines, stains and rim chips, 7⅝" H. $357.50

Ironstone Mocha Mug, blue bands, black stripes and seaweed design, "Pint, G.R." mark, 5" H. $192.50

Country Stand, walnut w/ old finish, two dovetailed drawers and one board top, poplar secondary wood, orig. brass pulls, 16" W, 18¾" L, 28¾ " H. $412.00

Ovoid Stoneware Jug, impressed label "L. Norton & Sons, Bennington, Vt. 2", faint blue floral brushwork, minor crazing, short hairlines and small chips, 13½ H. $55.00

A-VA Aug. 1995 Ken Farmer Auctions

Pie Safe, Wythe County, VA, ca. 1825, cherry w/ poplar secondary, old ref., 49" H, 52" W, 18" D $3,850.00

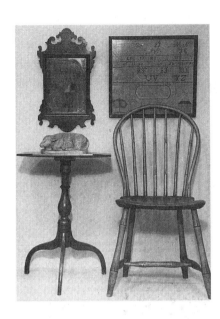

Row 1

Chippendale Scroll Mirror, walnut w/ old finish, orig. mirror glass, worn silvering, old replm. break in top crest, 22½" H $236.50

Sampler, silk on linen homespun, alphabets, stylized tree, house flowers and "Philomela E. Flint, aged 12 yrs. 1830". Faded shades of green, brown, blue & yellow w/ white & black. Stains & repairs, 17½" H, 19½" W $236.50

Hepplewhite Stand, cherry & birch w/ old mellow refinishing, top stained, 14½" x 19½" $660.00

Bowback Bamboo Windsor, old refinishing, saddle seat, partial label, 37¼" H $209.00

Stoneware Sleeping Sheep, grey salt glaze w/ brown highlights, base broken & glued & 1 broken off ear, 10" L $307.50

Painted Cast Iron Fire Mark, Fire Assoc. of Phil., ca. 1860-70, minor paint loss, rust, 11¾" H . . . . .N/S

Painted Cast Iron Fire Mark, Assoc. Firemen's Insurance Co. of Baltimore, MD., ca. 1847-99, minor paint loss, 11¾" H $316.25

Painted Cast Iron Fire Mark, Am., 19th C., "Valiant Hose No. 2," minor paint loss, rust, 10⅝" H $402.50

Painted Cast Iron Fire Mark, Am., 19th C., "UF" w/ spread eagle, minor paint loss, 11" L $287.50

Left to Right, Row 1

Tin Container, curved to carry close to body, hinged lid and brass heart w/ primitive eng. "H. Reinhold 1845", hinge is damaged, dents, found in Penn., 6½" H $165.00

Hogscraper Candlestick, w/ push up and brass ring, worn black paint over red, ring has damage and soldered repr. . . . . .6¾" H

. . . .$165.00

Hogscraper Candlestick, w/ push up, painted blk., 7½" H $93.50

Tin Tinder Box, w/ old blk. paint over red, int. has flint and steel. $220.00

Chip Carved Tea Caddy, cherry w/ old finish, ivory inlaid diamond excutcheon, small feet, age cracks in bottom, 6½" L $110.00

Wrought Iron Candlesticks, w/ spiral push ups and worn wooden bases, smaller is stamped "L.N.", 6¾" H, 8½" H. $275.00

Left to Right, Row 2

French Brass Lamp, single spout burner is marked "F.T. Brevete", wick advance knob is missing, 11"H $16.50

Tin Lantern, w/ bulbous glass globe, ex Roger Bacon, top has worn black paint, base has rust, no font or burner, 8½" H plus ring handle. $181.50

Wrought Iron Rush Light Holder, 10" H $302.50

Brass Telescope, five sections w/ lens cap.

Brass Telescope, four sections w/ worn brown leather, gilded name "Chas. Blackburn" and lens cap, one lens has minor flake.

Wrought Iron Rush Light Holder, wooden base, 10½" H $275.00

Brass Gimbal Lamp, 10½" H 137.50

A-MA Aug. 1996   Robert C. Eldred Co., Inc.

Four-Piece Wooden Toy Train Set, w/ orig. handpainted decor., minor wear, overall length 35" $770.00

A-MA Aug. 1996   Robert C. Eldred Co., Inc.

Chippewa Beaded Cloth Bandolier Bag, w/ colorful flowers on white ground, 45" L $3,300.00
Beaded Cloth Bag, Am., decor. w/ eagle, two songbirds flanking frog, all on brown/black ground, scrolled flowers throughout, 16½" L $715.00

A-MA Aug. 1996   Robert C. Eldred Co., Inc.

Beaded Bags
American Indian, w/ floral design on blue velvet, red border & beaded fringe, 4¾" x 5½" $66.00
American Indian, w/ floral design on brown velvet, outer pocket has red border w/ beaded fringe, 5½" sq. . . .$77.00
American Indian Bag, w/ floral design, 4" x 3¾" .$77.00

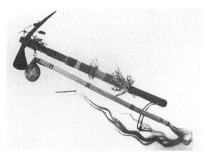

A-MA Aug. 1996   Robert C. Eldred Co., Inc.

North Am. Iron Trade Axe, w/ multi-colored beadwork handle & rawhide embellishments, 20" L $357.00
Stone War Club, North Am. Indian Hide-Bound Swingint w/ blue & turquoise beadwork shaft & horsehair tassel, 21½" L $247.50

A-OH Aug. 1996   Garth's Auctions

Victorian Cylinder Two Piece Secretary, walnut & walnut burl w/ old finish, fitted interior of pigeon holes & pull out writing shelf, top has adjustable shelves, 38" W, 85½" H $1,760.00

A-OH Nov. 1995   Garth's Auction

Left to Right

Stoneware Flower Pot, greyish pink glaze w/ brushed cobalt blue tulip, drainage hole in bottom, 8" H $220.00

Redware Shallow Bowl, w/ Coggled Rim, three line yellow slip decoration, wear & edge chips, 13½" D, 2⅝" H . . $825.00

Ohio Sewerpipe Lion on Rectangular Base, old brown paint over red & other colors, minor old chips, 10⅜" L $385.00

Q.A. Tavern Table, hard & soft wood w/ old dark finish, edge damage, top has old repairs & has been reattached & is loose, top edge of apron has been chewed by an animal, 25½" W, 43½" L, 24½" H $1,430.00

Dovetailed Copper Tea Kettle, w/ Gooseneck Spout, Swivel Handle & Brass Lid Finial, spout has old reattachment repair, handle has indistinct maker's mark that appears to be "J.H._T", 6¾" H, plus handle, .$522.50

A-PA Nov. 1995   Pook & Pook Inc.

New England Federal Style Mirror, gilded scrolled crest & fan inlaid plinth, 47" H $750.00

Staffordshire Seated Whippets, pr., late 19th C., 12½" H $750.00

Canton Punch Bowl, rain & cloud border, ca. 1870, 11¾" dia. .$1,800.00

Q.A. Lowboy, Delaware Valley, walnu, shell carved knees ending in trifid feet, ca. 1770, 33" H, 35" W, 19¾" . $7,250.00

Phil. Brass Lemon Top Andirons, late 18th C., 24½" H $3,000.00

A-PA Nov. 1995   Pook & Pook Inc.

Left to right

Am. oil portrait, by Erastus Salisbury Field, early 19th C., 33¾"x27½" $1,600.00

Delft Canisters, pr., blue floral glazed decor., damage to one, early 19th C., 10½" H $150.00

Federal Cellerette, southern walnut & yellow pine w/ 16 square bottle comp., on lower base, ca. 1790, 35½" H, 18" W, 18" D $3,500.00

Spice Chest, George I, oak w/ 11 drawer int., all above a single long drawer, 30½" H $2,500.00

A-MA Jan. 1996   Skinner, Inc.

Shaker Side Chairs, pair, N.H., ca. 1840, maple, old brn. stain, cane seats, replm. tilters, 40¾" H, 18¾" W, 13⅜" D $8,625.00

Sewing Desk, ca. 1840, pine w/ fruitwood pulls, salmon paint, sliding work surface repr., 36" H, 26" W, 18" D $8,625.00

A-PA Apr. 1996   Pook & Pook, Inc.

Pine Articulated Artist Model, 19th C., 20½" H $700.00

Tole Sugar Bowl, PA, early 19th C., 3½" H $300.00

Lehnware Storage Box, PA, late 19th C., decor., 7⅛" H, 10¼" W, 6" D $1,400.00

Child's Bow Back Windsor Side Chair, early 19th C., 28" H . .$650.00

Taufshein, PA, watercolor, dated 1819, 7½" x 12" $9,500.00

Earthenware Pie Plate, 19th C., gr. & bl. slip, rim chips, 11½" D $5,500.00

Toleware Document Box, PA, w/orig. red & yellow decor. . . . .N/S

Pine Box, w/polychrome decor., early 19th C., w/ painted houses & trees, 3" H, 4" W $425.00

N.E. Basswood Storage Box, 19th C., w/polychrome decor., 4" H, 12" W, 10" D $2,100.00

A-PA Nov. 1995   Pook & Pook, Inc.

Plates, blue Fitzhugh, 3 of 5 plates pictured, 9¾" dia., w/ 11 bowls w/ chips, 9¾" dia., 19th C. $650.00

Burl Veneer Highboy, Wm. & Mary, 61" H, 34" W $4,250.00

Oval Porcelain Platter, blue Fitzhugh Chinese export, 19th C., 21½ L $700.00

A-PA Apr. 1996   Pook & Pook, Inc.

Nuremberg alms dish, brass, 17th C., 16¼" dia. w/ another example $1,600.00

Earthenware Loaf Dish, w/white slip decor., 4½" H, 27" L $425.00

Chippendale High Chest, PA, walnut, w/repr. to feet, 63" H, 42" W, 20¾" D $3,250.00

Andirons, NY Federal, brass, ca. 1790, 19" H $400.00

A-MA June 1996   Skinner, Inc.

Carved Mahogany Veneer Sofa, North Shore, MA., 1830-50, upholstered in old stamped velvet, minor imperf., 36" H, 77" L $1,265.00

A-PA Apr. 1996   Pook & Pook, Inc.

Row 1

Taufshein, Frederich Spyer, Lancaster Co., hand colored, dated 1802, sgn., 13½" x 16½" $1,900.00

Fraktur, Daniel Schumacher, Albany Twn., Berks Co., PA, dated 1777, sgn., 7½" x 12" $9,000.00

Row 2

Vorschrift House Blessing, ink & watercolor, early 19th C., 7½" x 12" $2,500.00

Taufshein, Frederich Speyer, Lancaster, PA, watercolor/printed, ca. 1795, 13" x 16" $1,900.00

A-PA Sept. 1996   Aston Auctioneers & Appraisers

Folk Art Box, PA, carved w/ applied doves & acorns $935.00

A-OH Mar. 1996   Garth's Auction

Tall Case Clock, cherry w/ old dark finish, brass gears in wooden plates w/ painted wooden face, base old replm. & is removable, small repairs, old restoration, finials old but replms., repl. weights & pendulum, 92½" H $1,760.00

A-OH May 1996   Garth's Auction

PA. Rag Carpet, three strips, w/ similar red & gr. stripes on beige ground, soiling, 3' x 16' $82.50

Horse Weathervane, sheet metal w/ blacksmith riveted constr., tail damaged, probably early 20th C., blk. repaint, 30" L $137.50

Decorated Blanket Chest, pine w/ orig. br. graining, dovetailed, interior has till w/ lid & four drawers, lock repl. in till, 38" W, 18¼" D, 21½" H $715.00

Game Box, curly poplar w/ old fin., worn blk. & red paint, checkerboard on ext. & int. has backgammon board w/ ivory dice, wear & edge damage, 15" L $253.00

A-MA Jan. 1996   Skinner, Inc.

J.M Young Chairs, 3, w/ 2 matching, signed Jordan Marsh, Boston, 1 w/ J.M. Young paper label, orig. finish, 38" H .747.50

A-OH May 1996   Garth's Auction

Row 1, Left to Right

Redware Creamer, w/ strap handle, cream colored slip w/ br., edge wear & minor flakes, 3½" H $198.00

Stoneware Conical Ink, mkd. "Vitreous Bottles. Boss Brothers, Middlebury", lip repair, 2⅝" H $137.50

Mini. Stoneware Figure, blue & white, begging dog, chips & hairlines, 1⅞" H $33.00

White Clay Spool, w/ br. glaze & sgraffito inscription "Thomas S. Campbell, Lisbon, Ohio. Aug. 2, 1904, Good Luck", 2" D, 2" L $55.00

Pottery Pig Bank, two tone marbelized br., tan & blk. glaze on cream, edge chips, 4" L $27.50

Cast Iron Bank, mosque M-1175, traces of gold paint, 3½" H . . .$55.00

Cast Iron Bank, laughing pig, M-640, orig. blk., white & pink paint w/ some pitting & minor wear, 5⅜" L .$220.00

Row 2, Left to Right

Five Mini. Hats, orig. boxes, three are flocked plastic, two are felt, cardboard boxes w/ printed labels $330.00

Row 3, Left to Right

Yellowware Mug, white band w/ medium blue stripes & darker blue seaweed decor., stains & sm. chips, 3¾" H $220.00

Sewerpipe Duck, felt glued to bottom, 5½" L $126.50

Sewer Brick, hollow interior has mkd. "The United States Food Co., Mfgrs. U.S. Poultry Food Tonic, Pleasant City, Ohio", chips, 8" L $93.50

Pottery Puzzle Mug, w/ gr. glaze, bottom has incised mkd. "G.E. Ohio", prof. repr. 3½" H $99.00

◄

A-PA Sept. 1996   Aston Auctioneers & Appraisers

Game Board, PA German "Fik Muhl" $2,970.00

A-OH May 1996   Garth's Auction

Sheraton Chest, cherry w/ old worn refin. w/ inlay of stringing drawers & top edge & figured walnut panel on stiles, poplar secondary wood, 39¾" W, top is 20½" x 40½", 41½" H $1,375.00

Staffordshire Plate, dk. blue transfer "Hollywell Cottage, Cavan, Riley", mkd. "Riley", minor wear w/ slight stains & crows foot hairline, 10" D . . .$121.00

Staffordshire Tureen, dk. blue transfer, molded lion head scroll handles & lid has molded leaves w/ fruit finial, sm. edge chips w/ larger shallow flake on underside of lid at notch for ladle, floral border transfer on ladle matches tureen, 12" D, plus handles, 11¼" H $2,420.00

Staffordshire Plate, dk. blue transfer oriental scene "Marine-", mkd. "Jackson", rim hairline, 10½" D . . .$132.00

A-OH May 1996   Garth's Auction

Two Eng. Chromolithographs, horses, pub. in 1870 & 1876, one on right has minor damage, similar frames, 25" H, 29" W, & 24¼" H, 29" W . .$352.00

Decorated Settle Bench, worn, orig. br. paint w/ yellow, white striping & polychrome floral decor., 72½" L $495.00

A-OH May 1996   Garth Auctions

Stoneware

Row 1, Left to Right

Canning Jar, w/ cobalt blue stenciled mkd. "J. & H. - St. Clairsville, Ohio", sm. flakes on lip, 8" H $302.50

Crock, w/ cobalt blue stenciled mkd. "H.C. Ward Stoneware Depot, Zanesville, O." , 7¾" H $302.50

Canning Jar, w/ cobalt blue stenciled mkd. "J. Carnes & Bro. Bridgeport, O.", sm. flakes, 8" H $660.00

Row 2, Left to Right

Canning Jar, w/ cobalt blue stenciled mkd., "L.B. Potts, Captina, O.", 9¾" H $385.00

Canning Jar, w/ cobalt blue stenciled mkd., "From C.H. Dankwerth, Clarington, Ohio", chips & sm. flakes, 10" H $247.50

Canning Jar, w/ cobalt blue stenciled mkd., "Watson Boothover, Craysville, Ohio", chips on lip, 6⅛" H . . .$797.50

Canning Jar, w/ cobalt blue stenciled mkd., "Geo. H. Muth, Dealer in Poultry and Staple and Fancy Groceries, Belleair, Ohio", lip chips, 9⅞" H .$687.50

Row 3, Left to Right

Crock, w/ cobalt blue stenciled mkd., "Jacob Rohmer, Dealer in Dry Goods, Groceries, Clarington, Ohio, 2", 10¼" D, 7¾" H $935.00

Crock, w/ cobalt blue stenciled mkd., "John Hyer Dry Goods &c. (etc.) Hannibal Ohio 2", 9¾" D, 7¾" H $1,100.00

Crock, w/ cobalt blue stenciled mkd., "F.M. Amos, Antioch, Ohio 2", 9¾" D, 8" H $385.00

A-MA Mar. 1996   Skinner

Maple Tavern Table, N. Eng., late 18th C., repl. top, other imperf., 26" H, 52" W, 34¼" D $920.00

A-MA June 1996   Skinner

Whale Bone & Ivory Swift, 19th C., on turned wood base, w/ ivory feet, reprs to ribs, 18½" H $1,840.00

A-MA Aug. 1996   Robert C. Eldred Co., Inc.

Hepplewhite Bowfront Chest, cherry w/ inlaid edge, cockbeaded drawer fronts, 35" H, 41" W, 22" D . .$3,080.00

A-MA Aug. 1996   Robert C. Eldred Co., Inc.

Mechanical   Writing   Table, mahogany veneers w/two drawers, elaborately inlaid marquetry top w/classical decor. on vase flanked by a wolf & stork, adjustable for height, angle & distance from user, top 34" x 26", 36" H $412.00

A-OH Sept. 1995   Garth's Auction

Tiffany Favrile Glass Vase, peacock feather in gold & olive w/ violet blue highlights, engraved "L. C. T. K13", minor wear & sm. broken surface blister, 8¼" H $1,210.00

Tiffany Favrile Glass Vase, flower form, gold w/ blue highlights, engraved "L.C.T. W9695", interior of bowl has two broken surface blisters, 11" H $1,540.00

Tiffany Favrile Glass Compote, diamond quilted design in bowl, gold w/ blue & violet highlights, engraved "L.C.T. N9239", pinpoint edge flakes, 7⅞" D, 2¼" H $440.00

Tiffany Favrile Glass Perfume, w/ gilded atomizer, blue, engraved "L.C.T. 7086", wear & scratches, 9½" H, overall $495.00

Art Glass Vase, w/ opaque swirls of red & opalescent bluish white, gold enameled flowers & mkd. "Sevres", 7¾" H $38.50

A-MA Mar. 1996   Skinner

Tall Case Clock, federal mahogany, MA., late 18th C., movement by John Carmichael, Greenock, Scotland, imperf., 93¾" H $4,140.00

A-OH Oct. 1995   Garth's Auction

Watercolor Theorem on Paper, basket of roses & other flowers in red, blue gr., & yellow, minor stains, beveled frame w/old alligatored finish, 14¾" H, 17¼" W $550.00

Fraktur w/ Stylized Tulips, pen & ink & watercolor on paper, shades of blue, yellow, blk. & faded red, "Maria Cetch 1848", stains & fold lines, 10¾" H, 9¾" W $495.00

Country Stand, refin. poplar & walnut, tripod base w/ one board top, 18½" x 18¾" x 27" H $137.50

Arrowback Sewing Rocker, sm. decor., orig. gr. paint w/ blk. striping & floral decor. , 31" H $82.50

Chalk Ewe & Lamb, orig. red, yellow & black paint, repr. cracks, 8¾" L $522.50

A-MA June 1996   Skinner

Stoneware Jug, w/ incised & cobalt decor., Am., early 19th C., minor chips, cracks, glaze wear, 15" H . .$1,265.00

Stoneware Jug, w/ incised decor., Am. early 19th C., decor. w/ flower, cracks, chips, glaze wear, 15¼" H $230.00

Stoneware Jug, w/ incised & cobalt decor., Boston, early 19th C., mkd. twice "Boston", chips, minor cracks, glaze wear, 13" H $2,415.00

Stoneware Jug, w/ incised & cobalt decor., Am., early 19th C., minor chips, cracks, glaze wear, 16" H . .$4,410.00

A-OH Oct. 1995   Garth's Auction

Q.A. to Chippendale Chest of Drawers, curly maple w/ old finish, bracket feet, four overlapping drawers w/ wide early dovetailing & thumb molded top, brasses repl., bracket feet have damage & one side bracket is repl., poplar secondary wood, 36" W, top is 16½" x 38, 37" H $2,420.00

Stoneware Pitcher, tooled lip & shoulder & applied strap handle, cobalt blue brushed floral designs, 10¾"H .$495.00

Reverse Painting on Glass, oval portrait of "Washington", white border is flaked & blue sky has touch up repr., framed under glass in mahogany veneer frame, 12¼" H, 10¼" W $220.00

Stoneware Crock, mkd. "F.B. Norton Sons, Worcester, Mass", bird on branch in cobalt blue quill work, surface glaze flakes, 7¼" H $385.00

Stoneware Jug, w/ applied handle, mkd. "Wm. E. Warner, West Troy 2", chicken on table and "2" in cobalt blue quill work, prof. reprd. area in chicken tail, 13½" H $605.00

A-MA June 1996   Skinner

Windsor Commode Chair, grain painted & stencil decor., CT., early 19th C., w/ yellow & sienna graining sim. tiger maple, seat fittings, minor imperf., 46½" H $1,725.00

A-OH Sept. 1995   Garth's Auction

All pieces are polychrome enamel on copper unless otherwise noted.

Troubador, artist signed, gilt frame w/ worn burgundy velvet, 8" H, 5" W $440.00

Oval Portrait, of young girl in picture book hat, 5¾" H, 3¾" W $330.00

Mini. Folding Triptych, one panel has sm. edge flake, Ormolu frame, 3⅞" H, 6" W $330.00

Brass Pen Holder, w/ enameled insert w/ couple in garden, 6⅜" x 4⅛" $330.00

Mini. Portrait, on ivory, artist signed, brass frame, 6⅜" H, 5⅛" W . .$302.50

Profile Portrait, of young woman "Lauretta", gilt brass frame, 7⅜" H, 4⅜" W $440.00

Round Profile Portrait, of young woman w/ jeweled cap, gilded artist mark, gilded brass architectural frame, 5¼" H, 3½" W $385.00

Oval Portrait, of regal gentleman, green background, gilded brass frame w/ burgundy velvet, 4⅝" H, 3¼" W $247.50

Russian Enamel Box, w/ birds on lid, marked, 4" D, 2" H $412.50

Portrait, young woman in plumed hat, minor scratches in enamel on face, gilded brass frame has worn velvet insert, 8¼" H, 5½" W $440.00

Small Clock, w/ enameled oval face, some damage, 5½" H $165.00

Oval Portrait, regal young woman w/ elaborate gold jewelry & head gear, gilded brass frame, 10⅛"H, 7½"W .$522.50

Oval Miniature, on ivory, young woman in pastel colors, artist signed, gilded brass frame, easel back missing, backing marked "Mme de Montesson", 4½" H $165.00

Mosaic Frame, w/ easel back & gilded brass fittings, beveled glass has chips & a few tiny pieces of glass are missing, blue & white in floral design, 4½" H, 3½" W $148.50

Oval Miniature, on ivory, portrait of "R. Wagner", artist signed, gilded brass frame w/ burgundy velvet, 7⅛" H, 5¾" W $357.50

A-OH Aug. 1996   Garth's Auctions

Row 1, Left to Right

Redware Pie Plate, yellow slip w/ green glaze & sgraffito peacock & rim inscription "I am not a shame that Peacock is my name. Made in Stahl's Pottery, Sept. 20, 1934", wear & edge chips, 10¼" D $115.50

Punched Tin Foot Warmer, in martised hardwood frame, old red stain $180.50

Miniature Blanket Chest, ref. poplar, dovetailed case & till, 13½" L $181.50

Redware Chamberstick, w/ brown glaze, mkd. I.S. Stahl, Dec. 6, 1938, rim flakes, 7" D $27.50

Miniature Tin Two Tube Candle Mold, w/ petticoat base, 5" H $357.50

Punched Tin Foot Warmer, old dark finish w/ punched circle & heart design $137.50

Row 2

Ovid Stoneware Jar, w/ applied handles, mkd. "S Purdy Portage Co., Ohio", w/ cobalt blue decor., chips & hairline, 10" H $357.50

Candle Mold, w/ twenty four tin tubes in pine frame, orig. red paint & gold stenciled label "J. Walker, Livonia, NY.", 7¾" x 13", 11" H $1,595.00

Ovid Stoneware Jug, mkd. "A. States" (Adam States) w/ cobalt blue decor., 10¾" H $467.50

A-OH Aug. 1996   Garth's Auctions

Bedwarmer, copper w/ simple floral engraving on lid, 45½" L $214.50

European Churn, w/ oak staves & brass bands, 39" H, plus lid & dasher, ...$302.50

Two Pieces: Kraug Cutter, bird's eye maple back board, 39" L, Sausage Grinder, w/ replacements, 14" L . . .$192.50

Hooked Rag Rug, w/ geometric floral design on grey-olive ground, 32" x 42" $170.50

Wooden Vegetable Washing Cage, w/ dowel rod spindles repl., 23½" D $302.50

Primitive Corn Cutter, on turned legs, old dark finish, 35½" x 41", 28" H $99.00

Ovid Stoneware Jar, mkd. "I.M. Mead, Portage Co., Ohio #3" w/ cobalt decor., 12" H $137.50

Stoneware Jar, w/ lid, mkd. "J.F. Norton & Co., Worcester, Mass. #1½ w/ cobalt blue decor., chips, 10½" H . .$165.00

Tin Seventy Tube Candle Mold, w/ ear handles, 10½" H $165.00

Ovid Stoneware Jar, w/ cobalt blue brushed floral design, 13½" H $220.00

A-MA Aug. 1996   Robert C. Eldred Co., Inc.

Hunting Horn, 18th C., w/ allover engraved decor. of animals, soldiers, shields, a mermaid, etc., sgn. Wm. Wait 1792 . . . .$522.50

◄

Western Saddle, w/ intricate tooling & conchos, ca. 1930, size 16 . . . .$440.00

►

A-OH Aug. 1996   Garth's Auctions

Gothic Revival Hall Tree, refin. walnut w/ cast iron pan for umbrellas, one drawer, 35"W, 91" H . .$605.00

A-MA Aug. 1996   Robert C. Eldred Co., Inc.

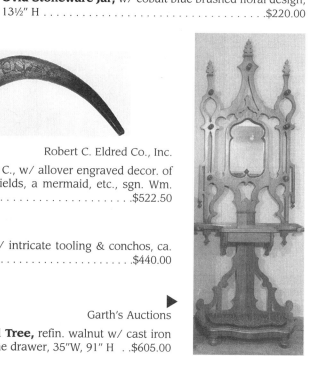

A-MA Aug. 1996   Robert C. Eldred Co., Inc.

Patchwork Quilt, red & white Hawaiian breadfruit patt., ca. 1900, 70" x 17" $880.00

A-MA Aug. 1996   Robert C. Eldred Co., Inc.

Pieced Quilt, in multi-color sunburst patt., white ground, 113"x114" $440.00

A-PA Sept. 1996   Aston Auctioneers & Appraisers

Quilt, Berks County PA, mid 19th C., red, gold & green on natural background $880.00

A-MA June 1996   Skinner, Inc.

Dome Top Trunk, paint decor., lined w/ southeastern MA., newspaper dated 1814, minor imperf., 11" H, 21¾" W, 12½" D $1,495.00

A-MA Aug. 1996   Robert C. Eldred Co., Inc.

Cupboard, in pine w/ two glazed domed doors, base restored, 53" H, 39½" W, 17" D $467.50

A-MA Aug. 1996   Robert C. Eldred Co., Inc.

Rabbit-Ear Windsor Armchair, w/ orig. grain-painted & stenciled decor. $247.50

Sheraton Pembroke Table, in cherry w/ one drawer, top 32" x 16" plus drop leaves, 29" H $440.00

A-MA Aug. 1996   Robert C. Eldred Co., Inc.

Dome-Top Cabinet, in pine w/ orig. grained decor., stamped on back "J.N. Perkins Maker", 43" H, 27" W . .$550.00

A-MA Aug. 1996   Robert C. Eldred Co., Inc.

Tri-Footed Candlestand, 18th C., in mahogany w/ padded snake feet, top 14" x 14½", 27½" H $357.50
Bamboo Windsor Armchair, $247.50
Candlestand, in mahogany w/ vase-turned pedestal & snake feet, oval top 18½" x 11½", 28" H $880.00

A-MA Aug. 1996   Robert C. Eldred Co., Inc.

Two Rush Seat Chairs, w/ eagle & stencil decor. $247.50
Hepplewhite Tavern Table, maple w/ 2-board top, ref., top 25½" x 34", 26½" H $357.50
Pair of Hessian Andirons, in old paint, 20" H $330.00

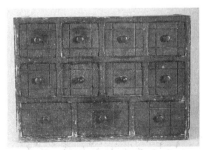

A-MA June 1996   Skinner, Inc.

11 Drawer Pine Spice Chest, red painted, last quarter 19th C., chamfered case, imperf., 17¼" H, 25" W, 10¼" D $805.00

A-OH Aug. 1996   Garth's Auctions

Framed Shaker Canned Goods Labels, for Butter Beans
& Fresh Tomatoes, Mt. Lebanon, NY, 15" x 20" $302.50
Shaker Wood Box, pine w/ old mellow finish, one over-
lapping drawer w/ bin-like top, wear from kindling, from
Canterbury, NH, reprs., 37½" W $880.00
Shaker Bentwood Box, w/ dark bluish gr. paint, wire bail
& wooden handle, minor damage, 9½" D $522.50
Shaker Tin Side Spout Tea Pot, 8½" H $765.00
Shaker Oval Bentwood Carrier, w/ four fingers, 11"
H $275.00

A-OH Aug. 1996   Garth's Auctions

Two-Piece Server, European, figured olive wood veneer w/
inlay, marble inset & leaded beveled glass, early 20th C.,
reprs. to marble, 53¾" W, 82½" H $825.00
Goblet, blown w/ green tint, hollow stem & copper wheel
engraved hunt scene, 11¾" H $192.50
Waterford Clear Cut Decanter, w/ silver trefoil top & stopper, silver has Sheffield hallmarks, ca. 1912, 10" H .$330.00
Banquet Lamp, peachflow cased w/ cast iron base & brass
connector & collar, 18" H $247.50

▶

A-OH Sept. 1995   Garth's Auctions

Country Store Lantern, brass font w/ embossed designs,
wire frame and tin shade, old electrification, needs rewired,
with chimney, 35½" H $275.00
Child Size Desk, poplar w/ old red paint, one bboard ends
w/ decor. cutout high feet, one nailed drawer, lift lid w/ simple fitted interior & gallery. Pieced repair before paint
applied, age cracks and minor damage. 22¾" W, 16" D, 30¾"
H $550.00
Decorated Sheraton Armchair, Hitchcock type w/ worn
orig. red & black graining, yellow striping & stenciled & free-
hand fruit & flower decor., old rush seat in taters, 34¼"
H $385.00
Cast Iron Tea Kettle, w/ wrought handle, brass finial, 8"
H $247.50
Woven Splint Buttocks Basket, 30 ribs, some age & slight
patina, 4¾" H $93.50

A-OH Aug. 1996 Garth's Auction

Row 1, left to right

Tin Grater in pine box w/ sliding lid & drawer, wire nail construction, 9⅝" L $93.50

Two Tin Nutmeg Graters, one marked "bread", the other marked "nutmeg" $115.50

Three Nutmeg Graters, two tin, one w/ advertising label, cast iron, tin & wooden handles $225.50

Painted Pine Box w/ old red, black edge striping & date 1729, 13" L $71.50

Tin Tinder Box w/ candle socket on lid, interior holds flint, steel & damper, 4½" diam. $368.50

Tin & Brass Lamp w/ filler hold cap & side lever to raise wick, 4½" diam...........................$170.50

Three Primitive Tin & Wood Grater, 1 w/ drawer, wire nail const. $451.00

Two Pieces: Wooden five section spice box w/ lid 7¾" H (ea. section screws together); tin grater w/ drawer 9¾" L $533.50

Row 2

Tin Twenty Five Tube Candle Mold w/ ear handles, 11¾" H $181.50

Tin Eight Tube Candle Mold w/ curved foot & ear handle, 11" H $401.50

Tin Sixteen Tube Candle Mold w/ ear handles & solder repair, 11" H $121.00

Tin Twenty Four Tube Candle Mold w/ ear handles, 10¾" H $104.50

A-OH Aug. 1996 Garth's Auctions

Shaker Wrt. Iron, shovel & tongs, Canterbury, NH, 17½" & 22" L $495.00

Shaker Tin Scoop, 10¼" L & Dipper, 15" L $71.50

Shaker Brushes, w/ turned handles, two w/ maple, one w/ cherry $220.00

Treenware, shaker, glove stretcher & two darners $220.00

Treenware, shaker, clothes hanger & rectangular scoop made from one piece of wood, reprs. $220.00

A-OH Aug. 1996 Garth's Auctions

Oil On Canvas, primeval forest landscape w/ modern frame, 11" W, 24" H $105.50

Set of Four Handcolored Engravings, Westpoint, Dartmouth, Amherst & Hartford, CT., stains, gilt frames, 7¾" x 10¼" $104.50

Golden Oak Era Side Chairs, set of four, refin., laminated backs, 37" H $154.00

Victorian Dresser, w/ ash & curly ash veneers, fruit pulls, marble insert top & adjustable mirror, 39" W, 68¼" H overall $330.00

A-OH Mar. 1996   Garth's Auction

Oil on Academy Board, fisherman & boats at low tide w/ sunset, initialed "R. H." and dated "1876", 1½" tear in top margin, 13¼" H, 13⅝" W .$165.00

Country Stand, poplar w/ worn old brown flame graining, nailed drawer w/ square one board top cut corners, 28¾" H $330.00

Bowback Windsor Armchair, old refinish w/ dark brown stain, considerable repairs, feet ended out, age cracks in seat and one arm is broken and reinforced, 39¼" H $357.50

Case of 20 Drawers that originally held watch repair equipment from "Green Bros., New York", oak w/ orig. finish, 14¾" $412.50

Roseville Imperial I Vase, brown & green w/ vintage design, unsigned, 10" H $126.50

A-OH Mar. 1996   Garth's Auction

Flag w/ Thirty-Eight Stars, silk screened paint on gauze, wear, stains and small hole, ca: 1885, framed, 32¾" x 49" $467.50

Hitchcock Type Sheraton Chairs, (1 of 8), two arms & six sides, old black & red grained repaint w/ gold & orange striping & floral decoration, rush seats, repairs, 18" seat, 31¾" H $1,980.00

Federal Stand, mahogany & figured veneer, old refinish, two dovetailed drawers w/ top drawer fitted for writing tools. Drop leaf top, pine secondary wood, 29¼" H $1045.00

Armchair, (1 of 8), old red & black grained repaint w/ yellow striping & gold stenciled masonic device on crest, wear, 33¼" H $1,760.00

Milk Glass Bowl by Libbey, molded maize pattern w/ green enameled leaves, edge chips, 9" D, 3¾" H, sold w/ the book Libbey Glass since 1818 by Carl U. Foster. $49.50

A-OH Mar. 1996   Garth's Auction

Pieced Quilt, zigzag bars in red, grey w/ white diamonds in bluish purple print, Chintz back w/ flowers in brown, green & white on lilac ground, 78" x 106" $165.00

Pennsylvania Show Towel, cotton homespun w/ silk & wool embroidery w/ decor. birds, flowers & "Ann Hess 1841", wear, repairs & minor stains, 17½" x 67" $159.50

Hutch Table, refinished hardwood & pine, mortised and pinned construction, top has repairs, 53" x 60", 27½" H $770.00

Stoneware Preserving Jar, cobalt blue stenciled, "A. Conrad, New Geneva, Fayette Co. Pa", hairline, 9½" H .. $99.00

Cast Iron Tea Kettle, lid mkd. "Patented July 14, 1869, E. Ripleys", wrought iron handle, 7½" H ..$82.50

Two Pieces of Wrought Iron, toaster w/ swivel rack for one slice of bread, 14½" L & single fire dog w/ snake head finial, 18½" L $60.50

Sheet Metal Lantern w/ Old Black Repaint, glass in four sides and bottom with hinged doors in both ends, 25" H $247.50

A-OH Mar. 1996   Garth's Auction

Empire Chest of Drawers, refinished hardwood w/ mahogany & bird's eye maple veneer facade. Dovetailed drawers, repairs, 45½" W, 20¼" D, 43" H .. $797.50

Victorian Kitchen Shelf Clock, ref. walnut w/ Eastlake carving, paper label on back "Acheron, Wm. L. Gilbert Clock Co. Winsted, Conn.", w/ key & pendulum, 19½" H $165.00

Lamp, fiery opalescent base & clear font w/ mercury band, brass connector, collar and burner, chips on base, 9¼" H plus burner. $77.00

Art Deco Newel Post Cap w/ Lighted Frosted Glass Base & Gilded Cast Metal Figure of Scantily Attired Young Woman, marked "Fabrication Francaise", repairs, rewired, 18½"H $275.00

Blue & White "Dedham Pottery" Plate w/ Rabbit Border & Craquelle Glaze, chips, 11⅞" D $137.50

A-MA Aug. 1996   Robert C. Eldred Co., Inc.

Turned Wood Butter Churn, from a single piece of walnut, sgn. LR, 19" H $495.00